THE NEW BOOK OF KNOWLEDGE ANNUAL

1980

HIGHLIGHTING EVENTS OF 1979

THE NEW BOOK OF KNOWLEDGE ANNUAL

THE YOUNG PEOPLE'S BOOK OF THE YEAR

GROLIER
INCORPORATED
DANBURY, CONN.

ISBN 0-7172-0611-4
The Library of Congress Catalog Card Number: 79-26807

EXECUTIVE EDITOR   **FERN L. MAMBERG**
ART AND PRODUCTION DIRECTOR   **FRANKLIN N. SAYLES**

EDITORIAL STAFF

EDITORS   **LEO SCHNEIDER**
PATRICIA ELLSWORTH
WAYNE JONES

EDITORIAL ASSISTANT   **PAMELA CARLEY PETERSEN**

COPY EDITOR   **ELAINE P. SEDITO**

INDEXERS   **JILL SCHULER**
SUSAN DEROMEDI

PROOFREADER   **ALEXIS TSAKONAS**

STAFF ASSISTANT   **MARILYN BULLOCK**

ART AND PRODUCTION STAFF

ANNUAL ART DIRECTOR   **MICHÈLE A. McLEAN**

PRODUCTION EDITOR   **SANDRA B. TAYLOR**

PICTURE RESEARCHER   **DIANE T. GRACE**

• • • • •

MANUFACTURING DEPARTMENT

DIRECTOR   **DALE E. BOWMAN**

SENIOR PRODUCTION MANAGER   **WESLEY J. WARREN**

PRE-PRESS SERVICES   **ELIZABETH CHASE**

• • • • •

YOUNG PEOPLE'S PUBLICATIONS DEPARTMENT

EDITOR IN CHIEF   **WILLIAM E. SHAPIRO**

• • • • •

GROLIER INCORPORATED

SENIOR VICE-PRESIDENT, PUBLISHING   **HOWARD B. GRAHAM**
VICE-PRESIDENT AND EDITORIAL DIRECTOR   **WALLACE S. MURRAY**

5

CONTENTS

7

CONTRIBUTORS

ASIMOV, Isaac
Associate Professor of Biochemistry, Boston University School of Medicine; author, *Breakthroughs in Science; Science Past, Science Future; Great Ideas of Science; Asimov's Guide to Science*
THE UNENDING WAR WITH THE INSECTS

BLANCHARD, Wendie R.
Managing Editor, *Creative Crafts* magazine
A DECADE OF CRAFTS

CAPEN, Peter D.
Author and Photographer, Terra Mar Productions; Fellow, the Explorers Club
NATURE'S LIVING LIGHTS

CRONKITE, Walter
CBS News Correspondent
THE YEAR IN REVIEW

DOMOFF, Daniel J.
Consulting Editor, Educational Developmental Laboratories, McGraw-Hill Book Company
MESSAGES FROM THE PAST

FRENCH, Bevan M.
Discipline Scientist, Planetary Materials, National Aeronautics and Space Administration; author, *The Moon Book; Mars: The Viking Discoveries; What's New on the Moon?*
PROBING THE PLANETS
SPACE BRIEFS

GLEASON, Judith
Author, *Orisha: The Gods of Yorubaland*
AFRICAN LITERATURE

GOLDBERG, Hy
Co-ordinator of sports information, NBC Sports
SPORTS, 1979
THE PAN AMERICAN GAMES

GOLDSMITH, Harry
Former patent counsel
EINSTEIN—AN INVENTOR

GRIMM, Michele and Tom
Writers and photographers; authors, *What Is a Seal?; The Basic Book of Photography; Hitchhiker's Handbook; My Brown Bag; Twisters; Florida; All About 35 mm Photography; The Manners Book*
REID RONDELL: A TEENAGE STUNT MAN
SCULPTURES IN THE SAND

HAHN, Charless
Stamp Editor, *Chicago Sun-Times*
STAMP COLLECTING

HENSON, Jim
Creator of the Muppets
THE MARVELOUS MUPPETS

JANKOWSKI, James Paul
University of Colorado at Boulder
PALESTINE

KULL, David J.
Senior Associate Editor, *Medical Laboratory Observer* magazine
THE I.Q. ZOO
HELPING-HAND MONKEYS

KURTZ, Henry I.
Author, *Captain John Smith; John and Sebastian Cabot*
LITTLE TOY SOLDIERS
SOUSA MARCHES ON
BLACK TUESDAY

MALCOLMSON, Anne
Author, *Yankee Doodle's Cousins; Mr. Stormalong* (collaboration)
CHARLIE BURNETT & THE SPRING FLOOD

8

MASSE, Laurie J.
1979 Member, The Rhode Island State Model
Legislature
STUDENT LAWMAKERS

MISHLER, Clifford
Publisher, *Numismatics News; World Coin
News; Coins Magazine*
COIN COLLECTING

MITCHELL, Denise
Girl Scouts of the U.S.A.
GIRL SCOUTS AND GIRL GUIDES

MORRISON, Louise D.
The Harpeth Hall School, Nashville, Tennessee
WHAT DO YOU SEE IN THIS PICTURE?

NEAL, Avon
Author, *Scarecrows; Molas, Folk Art of the
Cuna Indians*
GUARDIANS OF THE FIELDS

PERKINS, Carol
Author, *The Sound of Boomerangs*
AUSTRALIAN ABORIGINES

PRICE, Harvey
Chief Scout Executive, Boy Scouts of America
BOY SCOUTS

SCHLEICHER, Robert
Author, *Model Car Racing: Tabletop & Radio
Control*
AUTOMOBILE MODELS

SHAW, Arnold
Author, *The Rock Revolution; 52nd St.: The
Street of Jazz; The Rockin' 50's*
THE MUSIC SCENE

SKODNICK, Ruth
Statistician
INDEPENDENT NATIONS OF THE WORLD

SQUIRES, Dick
Author, *The Other Racquet Sports; The Com-
plete Book of Platform Tennis*
RACKET SPORTS

STEWART, Patrick
Assistant Professor of Art History, Williams
College
GEORGIA O'KEEFFE

STORIN, Diane
Sponsoring Editor, *Gateways to Science*
LIVING UNDERGROUND
NUCLEAR ENERGY: GOOD OR BAD?

TESAR, Jenny
Sponsoring Editor, *Gateways to Science*
TERRIFIC TONGUES
CHARLESTON: HARBOR OF HISTORY

TUCKER, Ken
Music Critic, *Los Angeles Herald Examiner*
COUNTRY AND WESTERN MUSIC

TYPOND, Don
Editor, *Model Airplane News*
AIRPLANE MODELS

UNGAR, Sanford J.
Managing Editor, *Foreign Policy* magazine
FEDERAL BUREAU OF INVESTIGATION

VICTOR, John
President, Program Design, Inc.
ROLLER COASTERS—SCARE MACHINES

WHITE, Jo Ann
Professional dog breeder and handler
THE NEW BREEDS

9

THE WORLD IN 1979

Demonstrators in Iran march with posters of Ayatollah Ruhollah Khomeini. In 1979, Khomeini's supporters toppled the Iranian Government and set the country on a new course—governed by the religious laws of Islam.

THE YEAR IN REVIEW

by WALTER CRONKITE

Sharp contrasts marked the events of 1979. Revolution threatened the stability of the oil-rich Persian Gulf region, and fighting continued in Southeast Asia. Around the world, people struggled with rising prices and tight supplies of oil. But at the same time, the world took important steps toward peace.

Events in the Middle East were colored by the growing importance of religion—Islam—as a political force. In Iran, revolutionaries led by Ayatollah Ruhollah Khomeini, a Muslim religious leader, deposed Shah Mohammed Reza Pahlavi. They set up a republic based on ancient Islamic law. In the fall, when the Shah entered the United States for medical treatment, a group of Iranian students stormed the U.S. embassy in Teheran and held the Americans there hostage. With Khomeini's support, they demanded the return of the Shah, whom they wanted to put on trial. The result was an international crisis that remained unresolved at year's end.

Fighting also erupted in Afghanistan, which borders Iran. Muslim guerrillas there opposed the government's close ties to the Soviet Union. Their opposition mounted after President Noor Mohammed Taraki was ousted by Hafizullah Amin in September, 1979. Then, late in December, Amin was deposed and executed in a coup supported by the Soviet Union. Thousands of Soviet troops moved into Afghanistan to halt the guerrilla war—an action that brought condemnation from many countries.

While events in the Persian Gulf region caused concern around the world, violence took perhaps its greatest toll in the Communist countries of Indochina. Early in 1979, Vietnamese troops and Cambodian rebels overthrew the Cambodian Government. China, which had supported that government, invaded Vietnam but withdrew within a month. Guerrilla fighting continued in Cambodia throughout the year, however. It created thousands of refugees, who added to the already staggering numbers of people who have fled Indochina in recent years.

But despite the violence that marked many areas of the world in 1979, there were signs of increased co-operation among nations. A peace treaty between Israel and Egypt, signed in March, ended more than 30 years of hostility between those two countries. The treaty was the result of negotiations begun late in 1978 at the invitation of U.S. President Jimmy Carter. Under its terms, Israel began the gradual return of the Sinai peninsula to Egypt. But other Arab nations were sharp in their criticism of the treaty and began a diplomatic and economic boycott of Egypt.

There were also major developments in relations between Western and Communist countries. The United States and the Soviet Union concluded an important round of arms-control talks, SALT II, and in June signed a treaty limiting some types

12

of nuclear weapons. But U.S.-Soviet relations were strained later in 1979 by the discovery that Soviet troops were stationed in Cuba, and by Soviet actions in Afghanistan. Because of this, the SALT treaty faced stiff opposition in the U.S. Senate, and by year's end had not been approved. Early in January, 1980, Carter asked the Senate to defer action on the treaty.

China continued its policy of increased contact with non-Communist countries. Teng Hsiao-ping, China's first deputy premier, visited the United States early in 1979, marking the start of diplomatic relations between the two countries. And in the fall, Premier Hua Kuo-feng traveled to Europe. As 1979 began, more freedom of expression was allowed in China than had been permitted in many years. But by the end of the year, China's leaders had drawn back some of this freedom, and several outspoken dissidents were put on trial.

In Africa, several governments that had been considered repressive fell during the year. Three dictators—Idi Amin of Uganda, Bokassa I of the Central African Empire, and Macie Nguema Biyogo of Equatorial Guinea—were deposed. Also in Africa, Zimbabwe Rhodesia seemed close to ending its long civil war. Guerrilla and government leaders agreed on a cease-fire and a new constitution in December, with elections set for 1980.

While the outlook for peace and human rights seemed to be brightening in these areas, one persistent problem—inflation— crossed international boundaries. Many people found that they had to make changes in their way of life to keep pace with rising prices. Not surprisingly, economic issues were the focus of election campaigns in several countries. In Britain, Conservative Party leader Margaret Thatcher campaigned on promises to cut taxes and reduce government spending. She won in general elections in May. In Canada, Joe Clark, the Progressive Conservative leader, was also elected in May on promises to reduce taxes and government spending. But in the final weeks of the year, Clark's government was defeated on a budget proposal that would have raised taxes on gasoline.

Rising prices were also a concern in the United States, where the cost of oil and gasoline was a big factor in inflation. That cost soared during 1979—OPEC, an organization of countries that export oil, raised prices 24 percent in June. And some OPEC countries upped prices still higher in December. Meanwhile, events in Iran and distribution problems triggered a summer shortage of gasoline in the United States. The shortage underlined the importance of conserving oil and of finding substitutes for it. One possible substitute for oil—nuclear energy— seemed to receive a serious setback. In March, a nuclear power plant on Three Mile Island in Pennsylvania broke down and released radiation into the air. The accident forced many people to look more closely at the design and operating procedures of nuclear power plants.

As the 1970's drew to a close, the possibility of a worldwide energy shortage continued to haunt the world. But there was hope that, with understanding and co-operation among nations, progress toward a solution to this and other problems would come in the decade of the 1980's.

JANUARY

7 Vietnamese soldiers and Cambodian rebels captured the Cambodian capital of Pnompenh. Premier Pol Pot was overthrown and a new government was formed. The victory had the approval of the Soviet Union but was condemned by China, the United States, and many other nations.

11 The U.S. Surgeon General released a massive report on the health dangers of tobacco. The report offered "overwhelming proof" that cigarette smoking causes lung cancer, heart disease, and other illnesses.

16 The Iranian crisis that had begun in 1978 moved quickly to a climax. Shah Mohammed Reza Pahlavi, the ruler of Iran for 37 years, could no longer control the country because of rising opposition. He left Iran for what was expected to be permanent exile. Ayatollah Ruhollah Khomeini, the religious leader who headed the opposition to the Shah, prepared to return to Iran. He had been in exile for almost 15 years. Khomeini promised to establish an Islamic government.

22 Edward R. Schreyer, leader of Manitoba's New Democratic Party, became Canada's 22nd governor-general. He succeeded Jules Léger, who had held that office since 1974.

Nelson A. Rockefeller, former governor of New York, died.

14

Another report on the dangers of smoking was released. This teenager collected 4,500 cigarette butts and made that message into a piece of art. The skull and crossbones means "dangerous."

25 Pope John Paul II became the first pope to visit Mexico. The primary purpose of his six-day visit was to open and address the Third Conference of Latin-American Bishops. In his messages to the group, he appeared to avoid siding either with conservatives who disapprove of social involvement or with liberals who believe in greater activism by the Catholic Church.

26 Nelson A. Rockefeller died of a heart attack at the age of 70. He was governor of New York for 15 years and U.S. vice-president under Gerald Ford.

28 Teng Hsiao-ping (Deng Xiaoping), the senior deputy premier of China, arrived in the United States for a nine-day tour. It was the first official visit to the United States by a top Chinese communist leader. His trip was a result of the establishment of diplomatic relations between the two nations, which had occurred on January 1.

31 Army Colonel Benjedid Chadli was named president of Algeria by the governing National Liberation Front. He succeeded Houari Boumédienne, who had died in December, 1978. Chadli pledged to continue Boumédienne's socialist policies.

FEBRUARY

1 Ayatollah Ruhollah Khomeini returned to Iran. Khomeini, the leader of Iran's Muslims, was the symbol of the revolution that ousted Shah Mohammed Reza Pahlavi. (Later in the month, Khomeini named Mehdi Bazargan to head a provisional government. Bazargan began forming a cabinet designed to govern Iran until an Islamic republic could be established in the country.)

14 U.S. President Jimmy Carter arrived in Mexico for discussions with Mexico's President José López Portillo. Talks centered on issues of common interest to the two nations. A major issue was

Soviet students demonstrate against China's invasion of Vietnam. The sign reads, "Hands off Vietnam."

This series of photographs shows several stages in the total eclipse of the sun that was visible across much of Canada and parts of the northern United States.

the possible sale of natural gas to the United States. Huge deposits of petroleum and natural gas have been discovered in the southeastern part of Mexico. These are being rapidly developed, and Mexico soon will be one of the world's most important oil producers.

17 Chinese troops invaded Vietnam. According to China, the attack was in response to Vietnam's "incursions into Chinese territory." It was also a retaliation for Vietnam's invasion of Cambodia in January. China indicated that its invasion of Vietnam was temporary, and that it "did not want a single inch of Vietnamese territory." (On March 15, China announced that it had completed the withdrawal of its soldiers from Vietnam.)

22 St. Lucia, an island in the Caribbean, became independent. The island had been under British rule since 1802.

26 A total solar eclipse was visible across much of Canada and parts of the northern United States. Such an eclipse occurs when the moon passes between Earth and the sun, thereby blocking the sun's light. The eclipse gave scientists a chance to study solar storms and other features of the sun's outer atmosphere. Scientists believe that the next total solar eclipse in North America will occur in the year 2017.

12 Luis Herrera Campíns was inaugurated as president of Venezuela. He replaced Carlos Andrés Pérez, who had held the office since 1974. Herrera was an unexpected winner in the election, which had been held in December, 1978.

13 In Grenada, Prime Minister Eric Gairy was overthrown in a coup. Gairy had led the island to independence from Britain in 1974. Maurice Bishop, the leader of the coup, became the new prime minister.

15 General João Baptista Figueiredo was inaugurated as president of Brazil. He replaced General Ernesto Geisel, who had held the office since 1974. Figueiredo is the fifth army officer to rule Brazil since a military coup in 1964.

26 A peace treaty was signed by the leaders of Israel and Egypt. This formally ended the state of war that had existed between the two countries since 1948, when Israel was founded. The treaty was signed at the White House in Washington, D.C. It was witnessed by U.S. President Jimmy Carter, who had played a major role in the negotiations that led to the treaty. The treaty called for Israeli withdrawal from the Sinai peninsula, the establishment of normal relations between the two nations, and the exchange of ambassadors. Negotiations between Israel and Egypt on the issue of Palestinian self-rule on the West Bank and in the Gaza Strip would begin later in 1979. The treaty is the first peace treaty between Israel and an Arab country. (Most Arabs opposed the treaty, and on March 31, 18 Arab countries agreed to end all economic and diplomatic relations with Egypt.)

From the preamble to the Egyptian-Israeli treaty—in Arabic, Hebrew, and English.

'To bring to an end the state of war'

Emmett Kelly, the world-famous circus clown, died.

28 The worst nuclear accident in U.S. history occurred at the nuclear-powered electric plant on Three Mile Island near Harrisburg, Pennsylvania. A major breakdown in the cooling system of one of the nuclear reactors released above-normal levels of radiation into the air. Pregnant women and young children were advised to leave the area until the radiation levels fell. (On April 9, it was announced that the crisis was over.)

28 Emmett Kelly died at the age of 80. The American circus clown was best known for his character Weary Willie, a sad hobo who dressed in ragged clothes and an old battered hat.

APRIL

4 Zulfikar Ali Bhutto, prime minister of Pakistan from 1971 to 1977, was hanged. Bhutto had been overthrown by the Pakistani Army in 1977 and was later convicted of plotting to murder a political opponent. Appeals by international leaders to spare his life were rejected by the Pakistani Government, headed by Mohammed Zia ul-Haq. In cities throughout the country, supporters of Bhutto demonstrated against the government, and hundreds were arrested.

11 An armed force of Tanzanian soldiers and Ugandan exiles captured Kampala, the capital of Uganda, and set up a provisional government. The new government replaced that of Idi Amin, who had ruled Uganda for eight years. It is believed that hundreds of thousands of Ugandans were killed during Amin's harsh regime. The conflict between Tanzania and Uganda had begun in late 1978, when Ugandan forces invaded Tanzania. Amin soon withdrew his army. But in March, 1979, Tanzania retaliated, invading Uganda and slowly driving Amin's forces back. Amin fled Uganda and was reportedly in hiding in the Middle East.

Idi Amin, dictator of Uganda for eight years, was deposed.

Jackson, Mississippi, was especially hard hit by spring floods.

21 Voters in Rhodesia (now Zimbabwe) elected representatives to the nation's first black-dominated parliament. Bishop Abel T. Muzorewa's party won 51 of the 100 seats in the new parliament. Muzorewa thus was elected Rhodesia's first black prime minister, replacing Ian D. Smith, prime minister for almost fifteen years.

29 Jaime Roldós Aguilera was elected president of Ecuador. He received almost 69 percent of the vote, in what was the first election to be held since 1968.

30 Spring floods in central North America left thousands of people homeless and caused billions of dollars worth of damage. Particularly hard hit was Jackson, Mississippi, where the Pearl River crested at a record height of 25 feet (7.6 meters) above flood stage. Tornadoes also caused much damage. One of history's most destructive tornadoes had swept through Wichita Falls, Texas, on April 10. It killed 44 people and injured almost 700.

MAY

3 In parliamentary elections in Britain, the Conservative Party, headed by Margaret Thatcher, won the most seats. Thatcher thus became the first woman to be elected prime minister of a major European nation. She replaces James Callaghan, leader of the Labor Party and prime minister since 1976.

16 A. Philip Randolph died at the age of 90. The black labor leader was a founder of the U.S. civil rights movement.

22 In parliamentary elections in Canada, the Progressive Conservative Party, headed by Joseph Clark, won the most seats. Thirty-nine-year-old Clark thus became the youngest person to be elected prime minister of Canada. He replaces Pierre Elliott Trudeau, the leader of the Liberal Party and prime minister for eleven years.

25 The worst accident in U.S. aviation history occurred when an American Airlines DC-10 jet crashed shortly after taking off from Chicago's O'Hare International Airport. The crash was apparently caused by defects in the structure that held one of the

Egyptian and Israeli soldiers stand by as Israel begins its withdrawal from the Sinai peninsula.

Mary Pickford, star of silent films, died. Here she
is shown in one of her earlier roles, as Pollyanna.

engines to the wing. All 273 people aboard the plane, plus 3
people on the ground, were killed. On May 29, after defective
engine mountings were found on other DC-10's, the U.S. Federal Aviation Administration ordered the grounding of all such
planes. (The ban was lifted on July 13, with the order that the
planes be carefully inspected at regular intervals.)

25 Following the terms set forth in a peace treaty signed on March
26, Israel began returning the Sinai peninsula to Egypt. It will
withdraw completely within three years. Israel had occupied the
Sinai in 1967, during a war between Israel and the Arab nations.

28 A treaty was signed making Greece the tenth member of the
European Economic Community, effective January 1, 1981. The
organization, commonly called the Common Market, was established in 1958 to eliminate trade barriers among member nations, which are Belgium, Britain, Denmark, France, Ireland,
Italy, Luxembourg, the Netherlands, and West Germany.

29 Mary Pickford died at the age of 86. The Canadian-born star of
silent films was known as "America's sweetheart."

JUNE

1 The nation of Rhodesia officially became Zimbabwe Rhodesia. A black government headed by Prime Minister Abel T. Muzorewa was installed, and a new Constitution came into force. The transition ended more than 88 years of white rule. (On August 26, it was announced that "Rhodesia" would be dropped from the name, and the country would be known as Zimbabwe.)

2 Pope John Paul II arrived in his native Poland for a nine-day visit. It was the first visit by a pope to a Communist country. In sermons and speeches made before millions of cheering Poles, the Pope urged them to remain strong in their faith and to see that children have an opportunity to learn about their religion. (Ninety percent of Poland's 35,000,000 citizens are Catholic.)

3 A blowout in an underwater oil well off the coast of Mexico produced the biggest oil spill in history. (In time, 30,000 barrels a day of oil and natural gas flowed from the well. An oil slick nearly 1,000 miles [1,600 kilometers] wide gradually formed and moved north through the Gulf of Mexico. The oil polluted Mexican and U.S. beaches, and threatened coastal wildlife preserves and fishing and shrimping industries.)

Pope John Paul II addresses a cheering crowd in Poland.

24

John Wayne, who died in June, was best known for his cowboy roles.

4 John Vorster resigned as president of South Africa after he was accused of covering up a government scandal. Vorster became prime minister in 1966 and president in 1978.

6 Jack Haley died at the age of 79. The American comedian was best known for his role as the Tin Woodman in the movie *The Wizard of Oz.*

11 John Wayne died at the age of 72. The American actor, whose career spanned 50 years, was best known for the roles he played in western movies.

18 At a meeting in Vienna, U.S. President Jimmy Carter and Soviet Union President Leonid I. Brezhnev signed a strategic-arms treaty (SALT II). The treaty sets limits on the number of long-range bombers and missiles each country may have. Before taking effect, the treaty must be approved by the U.S. Senate.

JULY

7 The United States and China signed a trade agreement that gives China "most-favored-nation" status. Such status means that tariffs imposed on Chinese goods entering the United States will be lowered from about 34 percent to about 5.7 percent of the goods' value. In addition, U.S. companies will be allowed to set up business offices in China. The agreement is expected to increase trade between the two countries.

9 Cornelia Otis Skinner died at the age of 78. The American actress and author, famous in the 1930's and 1940's, was noted for her sharp sense of humor.

10 Arthur Fiedler died at the age of 84. The conductor of the Boston Pops Orchestra for 50 years, he was one of the world's best-known and most popular musical figures.

11 The U.S. space station Skylab plunged into Earth's atmosphere and broke up into many pieces. The debris from the 77-ton station fell into the Indian Ocean and onto Australia. No injuries were reported. Sent into orbit in 1973, Skylab had been expected to remain aloft until about 1983. Increased sunspot activity, however, caused a slight increase in the diameter of Earth's atmosphere. This, in turn, increased the atmosphere's drag on Skylab and pulled it toward Earth.

Arthur Fiedler, the world-famous conductor, died.

26

Patricia Roberts Harris was named to a new post in the U.S. Cabinet—Secretary of Health, Education and Welfare.

12 The Gilbert Islands became the independent republic of Kiribati. The islands, located in the Pacific Ocean northeast of Australia, had been ruled by Britain since 1892.

15 Morarji R. Desai resigned as prime minister of India. He had been in office since March, 1977. (On July 28, India's president named Charan Singh prime minister. But Singh resigned on August 20 when it became apparent that he would not receive Parliament's approval.)

16 Ahmed Hassan al-Bakr resigned as president of Iraq. Bakr, who came to power as a result of a coup in 1968, named General Saddam Hussein as his successor.

31 By the end of the month President Carter had announced a number of changes in his Cabinet. **Secretary of Transportation:** Neil E. Goldschmidt, succeeding Brock Adams. **Secretary of Health, Education and Welfare:** Patricia Roberts Harris, succeeding Joseph A. Califano, Jr. **Secretary of Housing and Urban Development:** Moon Landrieu, succeeding Patricia Roberts Harris. **Secretary of Energy:** Charles W. Duncan, Jr., succeeding James R. Schlesinger. **Secretary of the Treasury:** G. William Miller, succeeding W. Michael Blumenthal. **Attorney General:** Benjamin R. Civiletti, succeeding Griffin B. Bell.

AUGUST

16 John G. Diefenbaker, prime minister of Canada from 1957 to 1963, died at the age of 83. A Progressive Conservative, he was elected to the Canadian House of Commons in 1940 and served there continuously until his death.

19 Soviet cosmonauts Vladimir Lyakhov and Valery Ryumin returned to Earth in their Soyuz 34 spacecraft. They had spent a record 175 days in space, performing a series of tests and experiments aboard the Salyut 6 space station.

27 Earl Mountbatten of Burma, 79, one of Britain's greatest heroes of World War II, was killed when his fishing boat was blown up. The incident took place off the northwestern coast of Ireland. (On August 30, two men were charged with the assassination. Both were members of the Irish Republican Army, an anti-British guerrilla group that said it was responsible for the explosion.)

28 It was announced that scientists had apparently discovered the existence of the gluon—a subatomic particle that holds all matter together. The existence of the particle had been predicted in the 1960's. Only recently, however, was equipment developed

Lord Mountbatten, shown here with Prince Charles, was assassinated by the Irish Republican Army.

28

Hurricane David left more than 100,000 people homeless in the Dominican Republic.

that could be used to detect the particle. The gluon's function is to hold together the tiny particles called quarks in the nucleus of an atom. Quarks make up the larger nuclear particles known as protons and neutrons.

29 It was announced that the *Monitor,* one of the world's first ironclad ships, would not be raised from its "graveyard" in the Atlantic. The ship, which fought a famous battle with the Confederate warship *Merrimack* during the American Civil War, sank in 1862. In 1973, the rusted hulk of the ship was discovered in the waters off Cape Hatteras, North Carolina. Efforts were made to raise the ship, but recently its remains were described as too fragile to be moved. Some parts of the ship, however, may be brought up and preserved.

31 After causing extensive damage on Martinique, Dominica, and Guadeloupe, Hurricane David struck the Dominican Republic. The storm, one of the worst of this century, devastated the Dominican Republic, killing more than 1,000 people and leaving at least 100,000 homeless. (The storm then turned north. It moved along the coast of the United States, from Florida to New England, where its high winds and heavy rains also caused much damage.)

31 Donald F. McHenry was named United States Ambassador to the United Nations, succeeding Andrew Young, who had resigned on August 15.

SEPTEMBER

2 Twelve Britishers began a three-year trip around the world. The group, led by Sir Ranulph Twisleton-Wykeham-Fiennes, plans to make the first longitudinal circumnavigation of the globe—that is, they will circle the world via the North and South poles. They left London by ship. They will use Land-Rovers to cross Europe and Africa, take a ship to Antarctica, use snowmobiles to cross the Antarctic ice, then go by ship to Alaska. They will travel in motorized rubber rafts up Alaskan rivers and through the Northwest Passage, use skis and snowmobiles over the Arctic icecap, and then take a ship on the last leg of the 52,000-mile (84,000-kilometer) voyage.

7 Robert Alexander Kennedy Runcie, Bishop of St. Albans (England), was named the 102nd Archbishop of Canterbury. He is to take office on January 26, 1980, succeeding Archbishop Donald Coggan. The Archbishop is the spiritual leader of the worldwide Church of England (sometimes called the Anglican Church).

9 The sixth summit meeting of nonaligned nations ended in Havana, Cuba. The group, founded in 1961, now has 95 members. Its purpose is to steer a course that is independent of either the United States or the Soviet Union. However, Cuban President Fidel Castro, chairman of the group until 1981, made a major effort to move the group's political views closer to those of the Soviet Union.

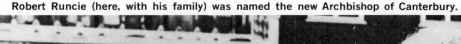
Robert Runcie (here, with his family) was named the new Archbishop of Canterbury.

30

At the summit meeting of nonaligned nations, Cuban President Fidel Castro tried to move the group politically closer to the Soviet Union.

12 Hurricane Frederic hit the central Gulf Coast, causing widespread destruction in Mississippi, Alabama, and Florida. It was the most costly storm ever to hit the United States. Losses were estimated at more than $900,000,000.

13 Venda became the third of South Africa's black homelands to be given independence. South Africa's 320,000 Vendas were made citizens of this homeland and thus had to give up their citizenship in South Africa. Almost all foreign nations view the homeland plan as South Africa's way of maintaining apartheid (separation of the races) and refuse to recognize the homelands as independent nations.

16 Hafizullah Amin became president of Afghanistan. He replaced Noor Mohammad Taraki, who had come to power as a result of a coup in April, 1978.

18 The 34th regular session of the United Nations General Assembly opened at U.N. headquarters in New York City. Salim Ahmed Salim of Tanzania was elected to serve as assembly president for one year.

27 The U.S. Congress approved the establishment of a new Cabinet department—the Department of Education. And the Department of Health, Education and Welfare, which was responsible for most of the programs that will be transferred to the new department, was renamed the Department of Health and Human Services. (On October 30, Shirley Mount Hufstedler was named Secretary of Education.)

OCTOBER

7 Pope John Paul II ended a seven-day tour of the United States that included stops in Boston, New York, Philadelphia, Des Moines, Chicago, and Washington, D.C. He spoke on human rights before the United Nations General Assembly and became the first pope to visit an American president at the White House.

9 Thorbjörn Fälldin, leader of the Center Party, was named premier in a three-party coalition government in Sweden. The parties had won a one-seat majority in parliament in the September 16 elections. Fälldin replaces Ola Ullsten, who had been premier since 1978.

12 In his first trip to the United States in nineteen years, Cuban President Fidel Castro addressed the United Nations General Assembly in New York. He called on the wealthy nations of the world to share their riches with the poorer nations.

15 El Salvador's President, Carlos Humberto Romero, was overthrown in a military coup. Romero, who had come to power in 1977, had faced increasing leftist opposition to his government. The leaders of the coup promised to hold democratic elections.

Park Chung Hee, leader of South Korea for 18 years, was assassinated in October.

16 Bulent Ecevit resigned as premier of Turkey after his party lost its majority in parliament. Ecevit, who had come to power in 1978, was replaced by Suleyman Demirel.

26 South Korean President Park Chung Hee, who had come to power in a coup in 1961, was assassinated by the head of the Korean Central Intelligence Agency. The killing appeared to be part of an attempted coup that failed.

27 St. Vincent and the Grenadines became an independent country. The islands had been ruled by Britain since the 1700's.

27 The James Bay hydroelectric project in Quebec, Canada, was inaugurated. This is the largest hydroelectric plant in North America and the largest underground hydro plant in the world.

THE 1979 NOBEL PRIZES

Chemistry: Herbert C. Brown of the United States and George Wittig of West Germany, for developing substances that make it easier to carry out certain chemical reactions. The substances are important in the mass manufacturing of drugs and industrial chemicals.

Economics: Sir Arthur Lewis, a West Indian and British subject working in the United States, and Theodore W. Schultz of the United States, for their work on the economic problems of poor and developing nations.

Literature: Odysseus Elytis of Greece, for his poetry, "which, against the background of Greek tradition, depicts with sensuous strength and intellectual clearsightedness modern man's struggle for freedom and creativeness."

Peace: Mother Teresa of Calcutta, an Albanian-born nun working in India, for her work on behalf of children and the poor. Mother Teresa's order, the Society of the Missionaries of Charity, which she began in Calcutta's slums in 1950, now has branches in more than 25 countries, including the United States.

Physics: Steven Weinberg and Sheldon L. Glashow of the United States and Abdus Salam, a Pakistani working in Britain and Italy, for their work on a theory called the Weinberg-Salam Theory of Weak Interactions. This theory says that two of the basic forces in nature—electromagnetism and weak interaction—seem to be parts of the same phenomenon.

Physiology or Medicine: Allan McLeod Cormack of the United States and Godfrey Newbold Hounsfield of Britain, for developing a computerized X-ray technique. Known as *c*omputerized *a*xial *t*omography, or the CAT scan, this technique gives doctors a clear cross-sectional view of a patient's body.

NOVEMBER

1 Army troops led by Colonel Alberto Natusch Busch staged a coup in Bolivia. They ousted President Walter Guevara Arze, who had been in office since August 6. Natusch installed himself as president, but opposition to his rule forced his resignation. On November 16, Lydia Gueiler Tejada, president of the Senate, became interim president. She was Bolivia's first woman president.

1 Mamie Eisenhower, the widow of former U.S. President Dwight D. Eisenhower, died at the age of 82.

4 Iranian students seized the U.S. Embassy in Teheran and held some 90 people hostage. The students, supported by Iran's leader, Ayatollah Ruhollah Khomeini, said they would not release the hostages until Iran's former ruler, Shah Mohammed Reza Pahlavi, was returned to Iran for trial. The Shah, who had been living in Mexico, had entered the United States in October for medical treatment. (By November 20, about 50 Americans remained hostage in the embassy. Non-Americans and some American blacks and women had been freed.)

Al Capp, creator of the Dogpatch cartoon characters, died.

34

The sacred Grand Mosque in Mecca (shown here with Muslim worshipers) was seized by extremists.

5 Al Capp died at the age of 70. The American cartoonist won fame as the creator of Li'l Abner, Daisy Mae, Mammy Yokum, and the other characters who lived in Dogpatch.

11 A 106-car train derailed in Mississauga, a suburb of Toronto, Canada. A tank car filled with chlorine gas ruptured and tons of the deadly gas slowly leaked into the atmosphere. Other tank cars, filled with propane gas, exploded. No one was injured or killed, but more than 250,000 people were evacuated. (By November 14, most residents had returned to their homes.)

15 Israel returned more of the Sinai peninsula, including Mt. Sinai, to Egypt. The transfer took place ahead of the schedule for Israeli withdrawal from the Sinai, which had begun in May. (On November 25, Israel returned its major Sinai oil field to Egypt.)

16 President Jimmy Carter named Philip M. Klutznick as secretary of commerce, to succeed Juanita M. Kreps. Kreps had resigned on November 1.

20 A group of Muslim extremists seized the Grand Mosque in Mecca, Saudi Arabia. The mosque is the most sacred place in the Muslim world. Only after receiving permission from religious scholars did Saudi troops move into the mosque to take control of the building.

22 Pakistani demonstrators, acting on rumors that the United States was involved in the seizure of the Grand Mosque in Mecca, attacked the U.S. Embassy in Islamabad. Two Americans and two Pakistanis in the embassy, and two of the demonstrators, were killed.

DECEMBER

2 The Democratic Alliance, a rightist group led by Francisco Sá Carneiro, won a narrow majority in elections in Portugal. The voting seemed to indicate a change in direction for Portugal, which has followed socialist policies in recent years. (Carneiro took office as premier in January, 1980.)

4 The United Nations Security Council demanded that Iran release the Americans being held hostage at the U.S. embassy in Teheran. The resolution reflected wide support for the U.S. position in the crisis. (Later in the month, the International Court of Justice also condemned the holding of the hostages. And on December 31, the Security Council voted to give Iran one week to release the hostages or face possible economic sanctions. On the same day, U.N. Secretary General Kurt Waldheim flew to Iran to try to negotiate a solution.)

5 John Lynch, prime minister of Ireland since 1977, announced his resignation. (On December 7, Ireland's ruling Fianna Fail party chose Charles J. Haughey to succeed Lynch.)

6 Choi Kyu Hah, acting president of South Korea since the assasination of President Park Chung Hee in October, was chosen to complete the five remaining years of Park's term of office.

9 Roman Catholic Archbishop Fulton J. Sheen died at the age of 84. His books, radio programs, and television shows had made him one of the best-known and most widely heard religious figures of the past 50 years.

Christmas cards from hundreds of thousands of people all over the United States were delivered to the hostages at the U.S. embassy in Teheran.

In Afghanistan, Soviet troops helped bring a new government to power, and then moved in force against a rebellion of anti-Communist Muslim guerrillas (shown here).

13 Canada's Progressive Conservative government, led by Prime Minister Joe Clark, was defeated in a vote of confidence on its budget proposals. As a result, the House of Commons was dissolved and elections were set for February, 1980. Clark's government, which had taken office in June, was one of the shortest-lived in Canadian history.

13 The Supreme Court of Canada ruled that laws and regulations in Manitoba and Quebec must be issued in both English and French. The ruling struck down an 1890 Manitoba law, which had made English the province's official language, and a 1977 Quebec charter, which had adopted French. The court said that under Canada's constitution both provinces are bilingual.

21 In Zimbabwe Rhodesia, government and guerrilla leaders agreed to a cease-fire, ending seven years of civil war. As part of the agreement, parliamentary elections will be held in 1980.

24 Three American clergymen and the Archbishop of Algiers held Christmas services at the U.S. embassy in Teheran for the Americans being held hostage there.

27 Hafizullah Amin, president of Afghanistan since September, 1979, was ousted and killed. The new president, Babrak Karmal, came to power with the support of Soviet forces. Soviet troops moved into Afghanistan in force in the wake of the coup to halt a Muslim guerrilla rebellion that had plagued the Afghanistan Government throughout much of the year. The Soviet action caused grave concern in many countries around the world.

30 Richard Rodgers, the American composer who wrote some of this century's most popular songs, died at the age of 77. Among the musical comedies for which he wrote the music are *Oklahoma, South Pacific, The King and I,* and *The Sound of Music.*

Posters criticizing the Chinese Government made headlines around the world.

CHINA—AFTER LONG ISOLATION

Late in 1978, hundreds of posters began to appear on a brick wall in Peking. The posters criticized the Chinese Government, praised free speech, and called for social change. This would have been commonplace in many countries. But because it was happening in China, it made page-one headlines in newspapers around the world.

Such events were surprising because China had for many years been a closed society, in which only thoughts approved by the country's Communist leaders could be openly expressed. China had also been isolated from the other countries of the world.

But by the late 1970's, China had begun to trade and establish relations with non-Communist countries. There also appeared to be changes in the way of life of China's 975,000,000 people. Many people who heard about the posters thought they might be a sign of a new China, in which freedom of speech would prevail. But by the end of 1979, such freedom seemed less sure.

▶ YEARS OF ISOLATION

The Communists came to power in mainland China in 1949, after a long civil war. Their opponents in the war, the Nationalists, fled to the nearby island of Taiwan. Both groups claimed to be the legal government of all China. The Nationalists kept ties with Western countries, particularly the United States. In time, Taiwan became a leader in the industrial development of Asia.

The situation was very different on the mainland. Under their leader Mao Tse-tung, the Communists imposed strict controls on daily life and tried to eliminate foreign influence. These measures were necessary, they said, to restore order after the civil war and to bring about social change.

Privately-owned farms were organized into state-owned communes in which many farmers shared the work. The government also took over private business and industry. But mainland China remained basically agricultural. It lacked many of the tools and techniques necessary for large-scale industrial development. And because it remained cut off from the rest of the world, it did not get these things through trade. For a while, the Communists received aid from the Soviet Union, but over the years political disagreements put an end to this.

Isolation and repression reached a peak in the late 1960's, during a period called the Cultural Revolution. All forms of art that did not reflect Mao's version of Communism were banned. Everything foreign was strongly condemned. Anyone who expressed a "wrong" opinion might be jailed or sent to the countryside to be "re-educated."

Universities were shut for several years, and students were sent to the country to learn field work. When the universities reopened, students were picked without the traditional entrance exams. Courses of study were shortened, and the quality of education suffered.

Daily life was even more strictly controlled by the government. Little recreation was allowed. People were expected to spend their free time attending lectures on Communism. No dancing was allowed, and no "Western" luxuries or colorful clothes were permitted.

China's leaders later said that these measures were brought about largely by a group of extremists led by Mao's wife, Chiang Ching. Although their programs continued to affect Chinese life, the extremists lost their influence in the government after 1969.

China's relations with other countries started to change in the 1970's, as Canada and other non-Communist countries began to recognize the mainland government as the legal government of all China. In 1971, mainland China was given the seat in the United Nations formerly held by the Nationalists. In 1972, Richard Nixon became the first U.S. president to visit China. At the time of Mao Tse-tung's death in 1976, China's long period of isolation seemed to be ending.

▶ TWO NEW LEADERS

The leaders who took over the government after Mao's death were Hua Kuo-feng and Teng Hsiao-ping. Hua became China's premier and, later, chairman of the Communist Party. Teng held the title of first deputy premier. But Teng seemed to wield more power than his title indicated. Teng had been known as a Communist revolutionary in the 1930's. In the early years of Communist rule, he had taken the position that China should develop through trade with other countries. Because of his views, he had been stripped of his government posts and publicly mocked during the Cultural Revolution. He had been allowed back into the government about two years before Mao's death.

One of the first signs of change after the new leaders came to power was the arrest of Chiang Ching and her three closest associates. Government-approved wall posters went up all over China, denouncing this group as the "gang of four" and blaming them for most of China's problems.

The new leaders then began a crash program aimed at modernizing the country by the year 2000. A plan announced in 1978 set goals in four areas—agriculture, industry, defense, and science and technology. This was a truly monumental task. China lagged so far behind in agricultural tech-

As China's relations with non-Communist nations improved, more Western goods entered the country.

39

nology, for example, that 75 percent of its workers were needed on farms. In the United States, where machines do much of the farm labor, about 5 percent of the work force is employed in agriculture.

To meet its new goals, China began to seek equipment and knowledge from non-Communist countries. These countries welcomed trade with China because it would provide a new market for their products. China signed letters of agreement promising to purchase many things from many countries—steel-making equipment from Japan, for example. Special arrangements were made with several U.S. companies. One U.S. textile firm sent materials and machinery to China, and finished goods were made by Chinese workers. And a U.S. hotel chain was chosen to build and run a string of hotels in major Chinese cities.

Then, late in 1978, China and the United States agreed to establish diplomatic relations, starting on January 1, 1979. In recognizing the Communist government, the United States ended diplomatic relations with the Nationalists on Taiwan. It did so with the promise of the Communists not to invade Taiwan. And the United States continued to trade with and sell arms to Taiwan.

The new relations with non-Communist countries seemed to be accompanied by an easing of the restrictions on daily life in China. The most visible signs of this were the Peking wall posters. For years, only the Chinese Government had put up such posters, telling people what the government wanted them to know. But suddenly hundreds of posters began to appear, placed by anyone who cared to hang one up. One poster even called on the government to add a fifth goal—democracy—to its modernization plan. Soon people began to gather to discuss such things as free speech and democracy. And the brick wall in Peking became known as Democracy Wall.

▶EVENTS OF 1979

China's contact with non-Communist countries continued to increase in 1979. Early in the year, Teng made a trip to the United States. In October, Hua became the first Communist Chinese head of state to travel to Western Europe. And throughout the year, trade delegations, government officials, and private individuals traveled back and forth between China and many other countries of the world.

Western arts began to return to China. In March, the Boston Symphony Orchestra played to audiences in Shanghai and Peking.

English is now being taught in Chinese schools.

THE PINYIN SYSTEM

For many years, Chinese words were reproduced in English according to a system known as the Wade-Giles system. In the 1950's, the Chinese Government developed a new system of writing Chinese in Roman characters that came closer to the actual sound of spoken Chinese. This system, called the Pinyin system, was adopted by the United Nations and the United States Government in 1979. Here are some examples of familiar names and places:

Wade-Giles	**Pinyin**
Mao Tse-tung	Mao Zedong
Teng Hsiao-ping	Deng Xiaoping
Hua Kuo-feng	Hua Guofeng
Chiang Ching	Jiang Qing
Peking	Beijing
Szechwan	Sichuan

For the first time in many years, China opened its doors to hundreds of foreign travelers.

A production of Shakespeare's *Much Ado About Nothing* was put on in Shanghai, and a Peking ballet company announced plans to stage *Swan Lake*. Later in the year, a group of paintings and sculpture that had no political message was approved for exhibition in a Peking museum. Such art had previously been banned.

There were other signs of change. One was the return of stricter standards in some Chinese schools. And many students were sent overseas to college.

But, despite these trends, by April the Chinese Government had begun to pull back from its course of rapid change.

Some Chinese leaders began to think that the modernization plans were too ambitious. As a result, China did not place orders for many of the major items it had promised to purchase. Instead, it made smaller purchases and concentrated on modernizing agriculture, utilities, and transportation rather than heavy industry.

Free speech and dissent seemed to suddenly go out of favor. Police began to tear down many of the Peking wall posters, and a number of people who had criticized the government were arrested. An article in the People's Daily, the party newspaper, reflected the position on dissent: "Only socialism can save China. . . . If anyone advocates going against the Communist Party, they are guilty of counter-revolution." Then, in December, posters were banned from Democracy Wall.

Not all criticism was outlawed. There were still a few rallies and demonstrations. But rather than freedom of expression, government reforms in 1979 focused on China's legal system. A new legal code—featuring open, rather than secret, trials—was promised by 1980.

The hundreds of foreign visitors who traveled to China during the year brought back varying reports of life there. Some reported great progress. Many agreed that China still faced great problems—in feeding and finding work for its huge population as well as in modernizing the country. Because foreigners are not allowed to travel freely in China, there was no way of knowing if the recent changes had improved life for the country people, who form the vast majority of China's population. It was also impossible to tell what further changes might be coming. Controls had been relaxed before and then tightened again. And China was still a country ruled by the decree of the Communist Party, whose leaders could cancel any plan or policy almost overnight.

BRITAIN AND CANADA: TIME FOR A CHANGE

"We want once again to restore for Britain the standing and prestige we used to have, and we want to restore a prosperous society for our people. It's time for a change."

With this call, Margaret Thatcher led the Conservative Party to victory in Britain's 1979 elections. She thus became the country's first woman prime minister—and the first woman to be elected prime minister of a major European nation. Thatcher succeeded James Callaghan, the Labour Party leader, who had served for three years.

The role of government in the lives of British citizens was the central issue of the campaign. Over many years, the British Government had been providing more and more services to the people. These included housing, medical care, education, and aid to people who were retired or out of work. To keep services running smoothly and to keep the economy stable, the government had also taken control of some industries and regulated others.

But in recent years, the cost of providing these services had helped make Britain's tax rates among the highest in the world. People at the top income levels payed 80 percent of what they earned in taxes. And the government's role in business did not prevent prices from rising sharply. Unemployment also rose, and strikes and labor disputes became common.

Long strikes that disrupted necessary services helped in the defeat of Britain's Labour Party.

Other problems stemmed from the gradual breaking up of the last pieces of the British Empire after World War II. Many people felt that Britain had lost its status as a major world power. In addition, the country had received large numbers of immigrants from its former colonies. They swelled the ranks of those looking for jobs, and racial tensions developed.

The Labour Party came to power in 1974 hoping that its strong ties to labor unions would end strikes and help the economy recover. Labour moved Britain into the Common Market. And it trimmed the rate of rising prices from 30 percent a year in 1975 to about 10 percent in 1978. But strikes continued, and recovery seemed slow.

Thatcher proposed that the country's economy would rally if individuals had a freer hand in business. She urged a smaller role for government in industry and social welfare. Tax cuts, she said, would encourage people to earn money and therefore help the economy. She also favored stricter controls on immigration and labor unions.

Callaghan argued that the Labour Party had started Britain toward recovery and should be allowed to continue. And he warned that social services and jobs might be lost if the Conservatives carried out their plans to cut government spending.

In the election of May 3, the Conservatives won a healthy majority in the House of Commons—339 seats to Labour's 268. The remaining 38 seats were held by various small parties. Under the British system of government, the leader of the party that commands a majority in Parliament becomes prime minister.

One of Thatcher's first actions was to cut income taxes. Along with this went cuts in unemployment payments and in aid to local governments and industries. Some restrictions on business were relaxed. And the Thatcher government began working on ways to slow immigration. Thatcher appeared to be keeping her election promises. But it was too early to tell if her programs would result in the economic growth and stability that Britain so badly needed.

Canadians, too, voted for change in 1979. Less than three weeks after the British vote, Canada's Progressive Conservative (PC) Party defeated the Liberal Party in general elections. And 39-year-old Joe Clark, the PC leader, became prime minister. He succeeded Pierre Elliot Trudeau, who had served for eleven years. But by year's end, Clark's government had fallen, and Canadians were preparing for new elections.

The spring campaign had focused on unity and the economy. In recent years, Canada has been faced with disputes between the federal government and the provincial governments. The most dramatic dispute involves Quebec, which is largely French-speaking and has its own distinct culture. The Quebec government wants its province to separate from English-speaking Canada. But there are also disputes with the western provinces—particularly Alberta. Alberta is enjoying the income from its vast oil reserves and wants less control from the federal government. In the Atlantic Provinces, Newfoundland was involved in a long-standing dispute over whether it or the federal government would control offshore oil deposits.

Trudeau had made national unity a theme of his years in office. He took the position that there could be no Canada without a strong federal government. Clark offered what he called a "fresh face on federalism." He said that the Liberals' firm stand had contributed to disunity. And he suggested that the federal government work more closely with provincial governments.

The PC's also attacked the Liberals' economic policies. While Canada has continued to be generally prosperous, prices were rising at an annual rate of more than 9 percent during the first part of 1979. Unemployment was also up. Clark proposed tax cuts to stimulate the economy. Along with these, he pledged cuts in government spending. He also opposed direct government involvement in industry. The Liberals, while supporting some tax cuts, countered that the economy was basically healthy.

The two party leaders presented a sharp contrast in personality as well as in their stands on the issues. Trudeau, who comes from Quebec and has a mixed Scots-French

After eleven years in office, Canada's Liberal leader, Pierre Elliott Trudeau, was defeated.

background, was known for his sophistication and wit. His time in office became known as the Trudeau Era. Clark, a native of Alberta, presented a youthful, rural image.

In the voting on May 22, Quebec and other French-speaking districts turned out for the Liberals—and Trudeau. The PC's carried Ontario and the western provinces. The final results were Progressive Conservative Party, 136 seats; Liberal Party, 114; New Democratic Party, 26; Social Credit Party, 6. While the Liberals won a greater share of the total popular vote, the PC's won more seats in Parliament, giving Clark the prime minister's job. But the PC's did not win a majority, so they needed support from other parties to stay in power.

In his first months in office, Clark set spending ceilings on government departments. Newfoundland was given control of the oil and other mineral resources off its shores.

Opposition to some of these measures began to mount in the fall. In December, Clark presented a budget that called for increased taxes on gasoline and other items. A confidence vote was brought on the issue of the budget, and the Clark government was defeated. New elections were set for February 18, 1980. Trudeau had planned to step down as Liberal Party leader, but he said he would stay on to run.

ARE WE RUNNING OUT OF GAS?

Was 1979 the year you spent your summer vacation close to home instead of traveling to the mountains or the shore? Did you spend mornings waiting on line at the gas station instead of going to the beach?

Many Americans did. In the United States and many other countries, gasoline was in short supply. People changed travel plans, formed car pools, and lined up at filling stations to get what gas they could. And as filling-station lines lengthened, tempers flared. People blamed the oil companies, the oil-exporting countries, the federal government, and even filling-station owners for causing the shortage.

▶ WHY THE PUMPS RAN DRY

The 1979 shortage was brought on by a special set of circumstances. But the underlying cause was a simple fact: The world is running out of oil.

Crude oil is refined to make gasoline, diesel fuel, heating oil, the heavy oil used by in-

dustry, and a long list of other products ranging from plastics to fertilizers. Oil in some form is used for nearly everything from growing tomatoes to generating electricity for homes and industries.

Oil was once cheap and plentiful. Now many experts think that known supplies of oil will be used up in about twenty years. Production has already begun to drop off in many places. For example, U.S. oil production has fallen by about 10 percent over the past ten years.

With more cars, homes, and factories using oil each year, the United States has had to depend more and more on oil from other countries. And events in those countries helped trigger those long gas lines.

Late in 1978, a revolution halted oil production in Iran, a Middle Eastern country that supplied about 10 percent of the oil used worldwide. U.S. motorists didn't feel the pinch at first because suppliers, certain that production would resume, dipped into

44

reserves to fill the gap. But Iran's new government decided to limit production. Iran did begin to export oil again, in March, 1979. But then other members of the Organization of Petroleum Exporting Countries (OPEC) cut their production, keeping the supply short. With their reserves running low, U.S. suppliers began sending less gas to filling stations. The stations closed some pumps and limited their selling hours, and lines began to form.

There was another aspect to the oil shortage—price. Many oil-exporting countries began to tack surcharges onto their oil prices. And in late June OPEC raised its average price for crude oil by 24 percent. Motorists who waited hours to get to a gas pump found they had to pay $1 for a gallon of gas—and sometimes more.

As the shortage began to be felt, many people panicked and rushed to fill up tanks that were more than half full, adding to the lines at filling stations. Truckers, protesting the shortage and the price increases, went on strike. As a result, shipments of farm produce rotted with no way to get to market. And people began to wonder if there would be enough heating oil for the winter.

▶ **COPING WITH THE SHORTAGE**

Several steps were taken to restore order at filling stations. Most states set minimums for gasoline purchases, to keep people from topping off their tanks. Many adopted odd-even rationing. In this system, cars with even-numbered license plates can buy gas on even-numbered days, and those with odd-numbered plates can buy gas on odd-numbered days.

The federal government set guidelines for temperatures inside buildings, so that less oil would be used for heating and cooling. And because cars use less gas at lower speeds, speed limits of 55 miles (90 kilometers) per hour were enforced on most of the country's highways.

These measures helped, but they did not deal with the underlying cause of the shortage. At the end of June, the leaders of Britain, Canada, France, Italy, Japan, the United States, and West Germany met in Tokyo to seek solutions to the problem. With the exception of Canada, all these

countries depend heavily on imported oil. They agreed to limit their imports for five years. They hoped this would lessen the effects of sudden shortages and price increases, and perhaps help the world's supply of oil last a bit longer.

How could imports be limited? In the United States, there were several proposals. One was decontrol of oil prices.

Since 1973, the U.S. Government has set limits on the price of oil produced in the United States and on the price of gasoline sold at pumps. It was thought that lifting the controls would have two effects. First, because gasoline would cost more, people would use less. Second, because U.S. oil companies would get a better price for their oil, they would be encouraged to drill more new wells and increase production. But many people said decontrol would only bring bigger profits to the oil companies, most of which had huge profits in 1979. In December, Congress passed new taxes on oil profits.

Attention was also focused on alternate sources of energy. Perhaps more coal, nuclear power, or even solar energy could be used to generate electricity. Some gas stations had already begun to sell a mixture of gasoline and alcohol called gasohol. Perhaps other types of fuels—made by liquifying coal or crushing oil-bearing rock called oil shale—could be produced.

There were problems with each of these energy sources. The United States has vast reserves of coal, but mining it often scars the land or is dangerous. And burning coal pollutes the air. Many people are worried about the safety of nuclear power. Solar plants that can provide a great deal of energy have not yet been developed. Fuels from coal and oil shale are generally more expensive to produce than gasoline. And all the proposals would take time to have an effect on the amount of oil used in the country.

Meanwhile, the only answer seemed to be to conserve oil. The shortage had eased by year's end, and Congress gave the president power to ration gas in emergencies. But when Iranian students took over the U.S. embassy in Teheran, U.S. imports from Iran were halted. And in December, OPEC countries raised prices again.

45

NICARAGUA'S CIVIL WAR

A long and destructive civil war in Nicaragua resulted in a new government in 1979.

Nicaragua, the largest country in Central America, has had a stormy history since its independence from Spain in 1821. The United States has had a strong influence there since the early 1900's. In 1912, U.S. Marines occupied Nicaragua to put down a revolt and protect American interests. They stayed there almost continuously until 1933. In an attempt to establish stability, the Marines organized the Nicaraguan National Guard. Anastasio Somoza, an American-trained general, became the National Guard's director.

The U.S. intervention was opposed by a Nicaraguan general named Augusto César Sandino. He and his followers began a guerrilla war against the American forces. In 1934, after the Marines had left, Sandino was assassinated on orders from Somoza.

In 1937, Somoza became president after an election in which he had been the only candidate. That was the beginning of more than 40 years of rule by the Somoza family. During that time Nicaragua saw very little economic progress. The people were poor, and abuses of human rights were common. By contrast, the Somoza family amassed a vast fortune.

The Sandinista National Liberation Front was founded in the early 1960's and was named for the slain rebel, Sandino. Its goal was to overthrow the Somoza government. At first, the Sandinistas' attacks on government forces resulted in only small skirmishes. But in time, guerrilla activity increased. And so did retaliation by the government. By 1978, the struggle had turned into a civil war. There were strikes. Entire cities and towns were devastated. Thousands of people died. There were no public services, no medical care, and little food.

By that time, too, the general resentment against President Anastasio Somoza Debayle had grown very strong. Many businessmen allied themselves with the Sandinistas because of the government's corruption. Other Central American countries began giving the guerrillas assistance. And while the United States did not support the Sandinistas, it did denounce the government's violation of human rights and cut off most military and economic aid to Nicaragua. By June, 1979, it was apparent that the Somoza government could no longer control the country.

On July 17, 1979, President Somoza resigned and went into exile. A five-member Sandinista junta took temporary control of the country. The junta vowed to bring peace to Nicaragua. Many wondered, however, if the new leaders could really offer the people a better government. Many of the Sandinistas are young Nicaraguans who support democratic principals. But some of the Sandinista leaders are Marxist Communists who have been trained in Cuba. It was too early to tell if Nicaragua would align itself with the Communists or would become a more democratic country.

The five Sandinista leaders promised to bring peace to Nicaragua.

46

INDOCHINA—STILL NO PEACE

Thousands of people died, tens of thousands were homeless, and millions faced starvation in Indochina during 1979. Their suffering was caused by fresh outbreaks of conflict in what was once one of the richest rice-growing regions in Southeast Asia. War has drained the countries of Cambodia, Vietnam, and Laos since they won their independence from France in the 1950's.

▶ **CAMBODIA**

Cambodia's toll of human suffering was already high when the year began. In 1975 the Khmer Rouge, a Communist regime, had taken power. Thousands of people were forced to leave Cambodia's cities and work in the countryside. Families were separated, and education and technology were all but eliminated. Those who opposed the regime were shot. It was estimated that between 500,000 and 1,500,000 people died as a result of the Khmer Rouge actions.

The stage was set for Vietnam to enter the picture. Vietnam and Cambodia have long been rivals. Each was, at different times, the center of a large empire that controlled the Indochinese Peninsula. Their ancient rivalry had been frozen by French colonization and, later, by U.S. intervention. The freeze ended when Communist regimes took power in both countries after the Vietnam War. Vietnam then became allied with the Soviet Union; the Khmer Rouge government, with China.

During 1978, Cambodia and Vietnam had each staged raids across their common border. In the closing days of the year, a force of Vietnamese troops and Cambodian rebels invaded Cambodia. They captured Pnompenh, the capital, on January 7, 1979.

A new government took power with the support of the Vietnamese. The government was supported by the Soviet Union and its allies. But China, the United States, and many other countries were sharply critical of the victory. The countries that opposed the new government said that no matter what the Khmer Rouge had done, Vietnam did not have the right to invade Cambodia. Moreover, the ancient hatred between Cambodians and Vietnamese was so deep that the Cambodian people seemed hardly better off under their new rulers. In September, the United Nations voted to seat the representatives of the Khmer Rouge rather than the representatives of the Vietnamese-backed government.

In the meantime, Vietnamese forces secured their hold over most of Cambodia's cities. But the Khmer Rouge fought back with guerrilla tactics and held large sections of the countryside.

The fighting sent tens of thousands of Cambodians pouring over the country's western border to Thailand, a U.S. ally. The Thais were already overburdened with refugees from elsewhere in Indochina. They feared that the new influx might bring the war to their country. During the summer monsoon rains, they sent 45,000 Cambodians back across the border at gunpoint.

Within Cambodia, an estimated 2,250,000 people faced starvation. The conflict had prevented rice and other foods from being grown and harvested. International relief agencies began an effort to supply food, but the rival Cambodian factions hindered their attempts. In October, some supplies arrived by air. But the Vietnamese-backed government refused to allow food and medicine to be brought in by truck from Thailand.

By fall, the monsoon rains had ended. Vietnamese troops began a new offensive to secure the countryside. Thailand changed its policy and accepted thousands of Cambodians who fled the fighting. But malnutrition and disease followed the refugees, and deaths reached tragic proportions.

▶ **CHINA AND VIETNAM**

Relations between China and Vietnam have been marked by suspicion and conflict for thousands of years. Although China supported the Vietnamese Communists during the Vietnam war, their relations have since gone downhill. Vietnam has said that China is trying to expand into Indochina. China has said that Vietnam is trying to set up a federation of states that would further Soviet interests in the area. China has also

Villagers were forced to flee their homes when China invaded Vietnam in February.

been angered by Vietnam's treatment of its 1,000,000 Chinese residents.

China's response to the Cambodian conflict was to invade Vietnam on February 17, 1979. The Soviet Union immediately threatened to come to the aid of its ally, although it took no action. Most of the world's other nations expressed concern over China's act.

The Chinese forces advanced about 10 miles (16 kilometers) into Vietnam. They took three or four important towns and disrupted utilities and services. Then, early in March, the Chinese withdrew. They said they had accomplished their goal of punishing the Vietnamese for their actions in Cambodia. Vietnam said it had driven the Chinese off.

Because Vietnam did not withdraw from Cambodia as the Chinese had demanded, the Chinese invasion was widely seen as unsuccessful. China was reported to be supplying the Khmer Rouge, and the risk of further fighting between the Vietnamese and Chinese seemed to remain.

▶ LAOS

Vietnam has supported the Laotian Communist government since it came to power in 1975. During much of this time, Laos kept a low profile in the disputes between Vietnam and its neighbors. But in 1979, the ties between the two countries seemed to grow stronger. Laos supported Vietnam against Cambodia. And the Laotian Government disclosed that 30,000 Vietnamese troops were stationed in Laos.

The Laotian Communist organization, the Pathet Lao, has faced stiff resistance from various groups within the country. It has resorted to large-scale imprisonments. And as many as 250,000 people have fled the country since 1975.

Resistance has been strongest among the Meo, who live in northern Laos. Thousands of these people have left the country, but others have stayed on to fight a guerrilla war against the government. Because of resistance, the Pathet Lao has had little control over northern and western parts of Laos near the border with China. But in 1979, the Vietnamese troops in Laos began to secure these areas.

▶ TRYING TO STEM A FLOOD TIDE

The flow of Indochinese refugees, a rising tide during 1978, reached flood proportions during 1979. At the start of the year, 200,000 refugees were in camps in non-Communist countries around the South China Sea, awaiting permanent homes. By mid-July, the number had reached 325,000. And new arrivals were pouring in at a rate of more than 20,000 a month.

Although Vietnam denied that it was forcing its Chinese residents to leave, ethnic Chinese from Vietnam accounted for much of the staggering increase. The Chinese living in Vietnam had traditionally been shop-owners and business people. The government had banned private trade and had taken over businesses. The Chinese, who now had no way to earn a living in this increasingly hostile land, were permitted to leave if they paid a stiff departure tax.

Food shortages, a failing economy, and government restrictions forced many Vietnamese to leave as well. Unemployment was high. Vietnam was in desperate need of food. And the government had sent thousands of people to "re-education" centers in remote jungle areas. It denied that the centers were concentration camps.

Those who left the country faced almost incredible risks and hardships. Most of them set out in small boats that were unsafe for ocean travel. If they managed to reach a friendly shore and enter a camp, they found crowded, often filthy conditions. Disease and death were commonplace. To help cut the toll of deaths, naval vessels from the United States and other Western countries were ordered in July to actively search for refugee boats.

But the countries that received the refugees into temporary camps were overburdened. Hong Kong, Thailand, Singapore, Indonesia, the Philippines, and Macao were heavily strained. Malaysia began to put its refugees into boats and send them back out to sea.

On July 22, a U.N. conference seeking solutions to the problem met in Geneva. Many nations offered to admit more of the refugees and to contribute money to help resettle them. Canada, for example, said it would take 50,000 by the end of 1979. The United States, which had admitted 230,000 Indochinese refugees since 1975, raised its annual quota to 168,000. Japan pledged money for resettlement. And Malaysia said it would again admit refugees on a temporary basis if other nations would help set up large processing centers to deal with the flow.

Vietnam agreed to let U.S. officials into the country to process visas, and it agreed to limit the number of people leaving each month. The numbers of new arrivals at the temporary camps seemed to drop off after the U.N. conference. But the flight of the "boat people" did not end, and some countries were still reported to be turning them away.

Some people saw the conflicts in Indochina as signs of a great rift between the two major powers of the Communist World, China and the Soviet Union. But whatever the cause, without peace and stability an end to the vast human suffering of Indochina seemed unlikely.

Refugees in Malaysia erected a monument in memory of the Vietnamese who died while trying to flee.

49

MONEY TROUBLES

Were you born in 1967? In that year, your parents might have spent $50 for a week's groceries. Today they will have to spend $110 or more for the same items. This is because many countries have been experiencing a period of inflation.

During inflation, prices go up. Money is worth less because it will buy less. Inflation reached an annual rate of 13 percent in the United States in 1979, so that by the end of the year each dollar bought 13 percent less than it did in 1978. And inflation rates were much higher in many other countries.

In addition, there were signs that inflation would be joined by a second economic trouble—recession. In a recession, business does poorly. Sales are off, production slows, and people are out of work.

▶ WHAT'S BEHIND INFLATION?

Economists don't agree about the specific causes of the present inflation. But there seem to be two kinds of inflation at work.

Demand-pull inflation begins with a combination of too much money and too few goods. Governments control the supply of money by issuing more or less of it. Recently, the money supply has increased in most countries, so that people have more money to spend. The demand for goods is high.

Prices begin to go up when the supply of goods does not increase along with the demand for them. In recent years this has happened in two important areas—food and petroleum. More food is being produced, but the world's growing population places a greater burden on the supply each year. And the countries that export much of the world's petroleum have limited their production and have raised prices.

Cost-push inflation enters the picture when businesses raise prices to cover increases in their expenses. For example, the high price of oil has increased costs for many businesses. And as a result of inflation, workers have demanded higher wages. When higher wages are passed along in the form of higher prices, the result is a wage-price spiral, with wages and prices pushing each other higher and higher.

As prices rose over the past few years, many individuals and businesses—and governments—borrowed money so that they could continue to live and operate as usual. But there are limits to the amount that any individual or business can borrow. And the interest charged on loans also rose, making it more expensive to borrow money.

For many people, the only way to deal with inflation was to buy less. They put off major purchases such as cars, canceled vacation trips, and did without a lot of extras.

Many businesses found that demand for their products and services had decreased. This raised fears of a recession. By late 1979, some economists were saying that the United States was already experiencing a mild recession.

▶ WHAT'S BEING DONE?

The U.S. Government has tried to slow inflation in several ways. Late in 1978, it set guidelines for wage and price increases that it hoped would keep either from rising more than 7 percent. But the guidelines were voluntary, and many businesses did not follow them.

The government also tried to slow inflation by limiting the money supply. It did this by raising the rate of interest charged by the Federal Reserve Bank. The Fed, as it is called, is the central bank of the United States. It lends money to commercial banks. These banks in turn charged higher interest on their loans to businesses and individuals. The government reasoned that if people found it hard to borrow, they would buy fewer goods. The hope was that this would slow the demand-pull inflation.

But many people feared that the government's actions would reduce demand too much and bring on a serious recession. Some wanted the government to fight the mild recession that seemed already to be developing. One way of doing this would be to reduce taxes, so that people would have more money to spend. This would stimulate production and create jobs—but it would also increase inflation.

It is very difficult to fight inflation and re-

Fight inflation by shopping wisely. Buying summer sporting goods in the winter will save money.

cession at the same time; what helps one seems to make the other worse. So far the United States has focused on inflation. And, despite disagreement about what is causing the problems and how to solve them, many economists do agree that an easy solution is not in sight. People may simply have to get used to getting less for their money.

▶ STRETCHING YOUR MONEY

Careful planning and wise shopping can help make the most of money during a time of inflation. Here are some ways to make your money go further.

• Plan on paper. Make a list of the things you know you will need to buy during the next few months, or perhaps the next year. How much will they cost you? If it looks like you won't be able to afford everything on the list, decide which items are most important and cross the others off.

• Make another list when you go shopping. This time, include just the things you plan to buy that day. With the list, you are less likely to be sidetracked by an attractive store display—and buy a model car, for example, when what you needed was a shirt.

• Buy things that will last. Look for things that are well made, so they will not wear out quickly. And try to avoid buying clothes that will quickly go out of style or toys and records that will probably bore you in a month.

• Be a smart shopper. Always compare prices—every store doesn't charge the same price for the same item. And take advantage of special sales. You can save money by buying winter clothes and sports equipment in the spring, and hot-weather items like bathing suits in September. If you've made a long-range list of your needs, you'll know exactly which items to buy.

AFRICA—STEPS TOWARD PEACE

In 1979 a number of changes took place in Africa that gave rise to hopes for more democracy and more peace on that continent in the future. Real black majority rule seemed about to be achieved in Zimbabwe Rhodesia, where a small white minority had formerly held full control. Cruel tyrants were overthrown in Uganda, the Central African Empire, and Equatorial Guinea. And Nigeria and Ghana were both returned to civilian governments after periods of military rule.

▶ **ZIMBABWE RHODESIA**

In April, 1979, the first free elections open to both blacks and whites were held in this southern African country, which was for many years the British colony of Southern Rhodesia. In 1965, Rhodesia's white colonial government had declared the colony independent. But Britain, the United States, and other countries had opposed rule by the white minority (about 250,000 whites to about 6,500,000 blacks). And within Rhodesia, black groups had begun a civil war. As a result, the white government promised to move the country toward black majority rule. The 1979 election resulted in a new name for the country—Zimbabwe Rhodesia—and its first black government. The government was headed by Bishop Abel T. Muzorewa, as prime minister.

But Muzorewa's party was strongly challenged by two other black nationalist leaders, Joshua Nkomo and Robert Mugabe, who had not taken part in the elections. These men led two guerrilla armies, based outside Zimbabwe, that for seven years had been carrying on the small but brutal civil war. They had vowed to fight this war until blacks gained control of the country. For the first six years, they had fought against the white government. When Muzorewa's black government was installed, they went right on fighting—saying that Muzorewa's government was a pawn of the whites and had no real power. Nkomo and Mugabe, whose united forces are called the Patriotic Front, said that under the Muzorewa government's constitution Rhodesia's large black majority did not really rule. The constitution gave the whites 28 of the 100 seats in the legislature. It also gave the white minority veto power. And it left the army, police, courts, and civil service under the control of the whites for five years.

All the black-ruled nations in Africa—as well as the United States, Britain, and many other countries—agreed that true majority rule had not yet come to Zimbabwe. And it appeared that until it did, the fierce civil war would grow worse and might spread all over southern Africa. So Britain, which had once ruled the country, called a conference in

Zimbabwe Rhodesia held its first free elections open to both blacks and whites . . .

52

London in September. Muzorewa, Nkomo, and Mugabe attended. By December they had reached agreement on a cease-fire, a new constitution, and new elections.

In order for the country to pass from civil war to peaceful all-party elections, the Muzorewa government voted itself out of office. The country returned, temporarily, to the status of a British colony. A British governor, Lord Soames, was sent to administer the country until the elections could be held.

The Cease-Fire. To bring about the cease-fire, the Patriotic Front was asked to rally its troops at fifteen "assembly points" throughout the country. And Zimbabwe's armed forces had to submit to the authority of the British governor until after the elections. Foreign troops were asked to leave the country, but a Commonwealth monitoring force of 1,200 was approved to observe the cease-fire.

The New Constitution. The new constitution would remove the whites' veto power, reduce white-chosen seats in the legislature to 20, and loosen the whites' grip on the army, police, courts, and civil service. It also promised money (from a British–U.S. fund) to any whites whose lands were taken.

The New Elections. The new elections, which, it was hoped, would bring peace and true majority rule, were expected to take place in the spring of 1980. At that time, the country would become the independent nation of Zimbabwe.

▶**THREE TYRANTS OUSTED**

In 1979 three harsh dictatorships in Africa came to an end. In April, President Idi Amin of Uganda was overthrown by Ugandan exiles and Tanzanian soldiers. During his eight-year rule, it is believed that Amin had murdered hundreds of thousands of people. Two civilian presidents followed Amin in quick succession. The second president, Godfrey Binaisa, took office in June. At year's end, Binaisa was trying to restore normal life to a land still torn by disorder.

In August, tiny Equatorial Guinea's president, Macie Nguema Biyogo, was ousted after eleven years of rule. Biyogo had turned a rich country into an economic ruin. He was also said to have executed 50,000 of his people and driven half the population into

...resulting in the country's first black government, which was headed by Bishop Abel T. Muzorewa.

exile. Teodoro Obiang Nguema assumed the presidency, assisted by the Supreme Military Council.

The third tyrant to fall, in September, was the self-styled Emperor Bokassa of the Central African Empire. President since 1965, Bokassa had crowned himself Emperor in 1977. He often jailed and murdered his opponents, and it is believed that in 1979 he ordered the deaths of 100 schoolchildren who had refused to wear state uniforms. He was overthrown in a coup led by David Dacko, who then took office as president. Dacko restored the country's original name, the Central African Republic.

▶**OTHER CHANGES IN AFRICA**

The year 1979 was a time of change in several other African countries and regions.

Nigeria. Nigeria's first civilian president in over thirteen years, Shehu Shagari, took office in October, 1979. A Muslim from the north and a former businessman and finance minister, Shagari pledged to foster unity among the three main ethnic groups of Nigeria. A new constitution modeled on the Constitution of the United States went into effect. And a new two-house legislature, patterned on the Congress of the United States, was also established.

Ghana. In September, a new civilian government took office in Ghana. It was headed by President Hilla Limann, a former economist and diplomat. The shift to civilian government ended more than seven years of military rule.

Chad. Chad, which had been torn by war for fourteen years, saw the hope of peace in 1979 when nine rival groups agreed to form a government of national union. The accord, reached in August, named Goukouni Oueddei as the president. Free elections were promised within 18 months.

South Africa. In June, John Vorster resigned the ceremonial post of president that he had assumed in 1978. His resignation was prompted by the release of information alleging that he had helped cover up the use of public money for secret propaganda projects. He was succeeded as president by Marais Viljoen.

In 1979, South Africa made some improvements in its laws restricting the lives of blacks. Black trade unions were made legal for the first time. And Prime Minister Pieter Botha announced that companies could hire blacks for some jobs previously reserved for whites. He also promised to review the laws banning marriage between the races.

Talks about a cease-fire leading to free elections in Namibia, a territory claimed by South Africa, proceeded slowly. The United Nations has been urging South Africa to give independence to Namibia. But South Africa says it fears that Soviet-backed guerrillas in the territory would use terror tactics to swing any election their way.

Angola. Angola's president, Agostinho Neto—a poet, physician, and Marxist revolutionary—died in September. He was replaced by interim president José Eduardo dos Santos. Neto had come to power with the help of Cuban troops in 1975. And at his death the civil war, out of which his regime had emerged, was still going on. The rival guerrilla party, the National Union for the Total Independence of Angola (UNITA), controls the south. After Neto died, UNITA's leaders sought to end the civil war. They said the war had reached a stalemate and that many Angolans resented the presence in the country of an estimated 32,000 Cuban troops.

Algeria. Algeria's president, Houari Boumèdienne, who had served for thirteen years,

Three tyrants were ousted in 1979: President Idi Amin of Uganda . . .

died in December, 1978. In January, 1979, the ruling political party, the National Liberation Front (F.L.N.), chose Colonel Benjedid Chadli to replace him. Chadli, who was formally elected on February 7, promised to follow Boumèdienne's policies of economic progress and socialism.

Mauritania. President Mustapha Ould Salek of Mauritania resigned in June, less than a year after taking power. He was replaced by Lieutenant Colonel Mohammed Mahmoud Ould Luly.

Congo. Brigadier General Joachim Yombi Opango resigned as president in February and was replaced by Colonel Denis Sassou-Nguesso. Opango had been president since 1977.

Ethiopia's Ogaden War. Ethiopia's Ogaden province, a desert region in the country's southeast, remained the scene of a bitter war in 1979. The cause of the fighting is the wish of the region's mainly Somali population to be free of Ethiopia. Neighboring Somalia wanted to annex the region, but in 1978 Somalia withdrew from the war. Now the Ogaden's guerrillas are Ethiopia's chief opponents. About 20,000 in number, they have fought 60,000 Ethiopian troops, backed by 17,000 Cubans, to a standoff.

. . . Emperor Bokassa of the Central African Empire . . .

. . . and President Macie Nguema Biyogo of Equatorial Guinea.

55

IRAN—A CONFLICT OF CULTURES

Iran, one of the world's leading oil-producing countries, began 1979 in the midst of a revolution. In recent years, Iran had become one of the most rapidly developing nations in the Middle East. But within months, a new government had transformed Iran into a country governed by strict adherence to the ancient religious laws of Islam. And before the year's end, Iran was involved in a direct confrontation with the United States.

▶ IRAN UNDER THE SHAH

Iran, the Persia of ancient times, had been ruled since 1941 by Shah Mohammed Reza Pahlavi. He was deposed briefly in 1953 but was quickly returned to power with the backing of the United States. The Shah then began an ambitious modernization program aimed at making Iran an industrial nation along Western lines. Highways, factories, skyscrapers, housing projects, and luxury hotels were built at record pace.

Along with the boom in construction came improvements in education and medical care for Iran's people. There were other changes, too—television, movie theaters, and gambling casinos became common. Liquor, forbidden by Islamic religious law, was sold, and people were encouraged to wear Western-style clothes.

But modernization at this rapid pace brought problems. Iranians were making more money, but income was not evenly distributed. Many people still lived in poverty. In addition, the Shah's government was plagued with corruption and inefficiency, and little opposition to his policies was allowed. It was later charged that dissent had been suppressed with torture and other brutal tactics. The Shah's family was said to have drawn off huge sums from the nation's oil income for personal use.

Perhaps more important, however, was the reaction of the people to modernization

Ayatollah Ruhollah Khomeini became leader of Iran in 1979. He set up an Islamic republic that was based on the religious traditions of 1,300 years ago.

56

Shah Mohammed Reza Pahlavi, the leader of Iran for nearly 38 years, was forced out of office in 1979. He was accused of brutal tactics and of having used a vast amount of the country's monies for his personal use.

itself. The vast majority of Iranians are Shi'ite Muslims who take great pride in Iran's past. The Shi'ite sect was founded in the 7th century and became the official religion of Persia around 1500. Many Shi'ites felt that such things as liquor, gambling, and Western clothes violated traditional Iranian culture and the laws set forth in the Koran, the holy book of Islam. The Shah's policies, they felt, ran counter to values that were 1,300 years old.

The strongest opposition to the Shah came from two different sources—leftist groups, including the Iranian Communist Party, and Shi'ite religious leaders, who for centuries had been powerful in Iran. (Two ways in which Shi'ites differ from other Muslims are in their tradition of following individual religious leaders and in their deeper respect for martyrdom.) Moderate groups who sought a more democratic form of government also opposed the Shah.

These different groups came together behind Ayatollah Ruhollah Khomeini, a 78-year-old Shi'ite leader. Khomeini, long a foe of the Shah, had been arrested and exiled in 1964. From France, where he had sought political asylum, Khomeini called for a series of strikes and demonstrations in 1978. His calls were heeded, and riots and strikes shook Iran throughout the year.

The Shah responded by promising to end corruption, free political prisoners, and form a new, responsive government. But opposition continued, and the riots intensified. On January 16, 1979, the Shah left the country in the care of an appointed government. Khomeini announced that he would return to set up a regime that would restore the Islamic traditions of 1,300 years ago.

▶ THE ISLAMIC REPUBLIC

Within two weeks of Khomeini's return on February 1, the appointed government had resigned. A referendum held on April 1 asked voters to choose between the Shah's rule and an "Islamic republic." The vote was overwhelmingly for the republic.

In November, after the Shah had entered a U.S. hospital, Iranian students seized the U.S. embassy in Teheran—causing a crisis that lasted the rest of the year.

A civilian government was appointed to run the country while a constitution was drawn up. It was headed by Mehdi Bazargan, a moderate. But real power remained with Khomeini and with a group called the Revolutionary Council, whose members were mostly religious leaders. Neighborhood militias and courts, centered around local mosques, were formed to enforce the decrees of the regime.

Among the decrees were many that seemed strange to Western eyes. Women were required to wear the *chador,* a floor-length veil that left only their faces exposed. Liquor and gambling were banned, and soon music was forbidden as well. Most foreign reporters were expelled. And hundreds of people—many of them former supporters of the Shah—were executed.

While many Iranians approved of the new policies, there was some opposition. Many women, for example, did not want to give up the rights and freedoms that had come with modernization. Leftist groups and many members of Iran's educated middle class chafed at the new restrictions. Reli-

gious minorities—Jews, Armenian Christians, and others—feared discrimination. So did ethnic minorities. Among them were Arabs, particularly in the oil-producing region in the south; Azerbaijani Turks, in the northwest; and Baluchis, in the southeast. And the Kurds, a people who live in western Iran, demanded self-rule and rebelled. Iranian troops and Kurdish rebels fought sporadically throughout the year.

In early December, Iranians approved a new constitution. It provided for an all-powerful leader, and it was apparent that the position had been created for Khomeini. But many of the minorities had boycotted the polls, protesting the powerful role the constitution gave Khomeini.

▶ THE WORLD WATCHES IRAN
The policies of the new rulers caused concern outside Iran's borders, particularly in Western countries. The revolution had disrupted oil exports, and the new government decided to keep oil production at low levels. The role of foreign business in Iran was also cut back.

58

But to many people, the greatest cause for concern was the effect the Iranian revolution might have elsewhere in the Middle East. The Shah had been a strong supporter of the non-Communist countries and had maintained a powerful army, backed up by U.S. military equipment. Iran's position on the Persian Gulf had helped ensure the safe shipment of much of the oil exported by other Middle Eastern countries. The new regime rejected U.S. support, and the gulf seemed less secure. In addition, there was concern that Shi'ite unrest might spread to stable countries elsewhere in the Middle East, such as Saudi Arabia.

Resentment against the United States was strong in Iran because the United States had supported the Shah. This feeling reached a fever pitch in November, after the Shah, who had been living in Mexico, entered a New York hospital for treatment for cancer. On November 4, 500 Iranian students seized the U.S. embassy in Teheran, Iran's capital. They held about 90 people hostage there—including some 60 Americans and embassy employees from other countries. The students demanded that the Shah be returned to Iran to face trial and almost certain death.

The United States rejected the demand. Prime Minister Bazargan promised to negotiate with the students, but Khomeini praised their action, as did many other Iranians. Bazargan resigned, saying that it had become impossible for him to govern.

Feeling against Iran was running high in the United States. But the U.S. Government ruled out military action, reasoning that the hostages would be killed in retaliation. About 20 U.S. Navy vessels, including two aircraft carriers, were stationed in the Arabian Sea but were ordered to take no action. Instead, the United States began a series of economic and diplomatic moves it hoped would free the hostages.

Outside the United States, Iran was widely condemned for violating international law. (Under the conventions of diplomacy, embassies are never attacked.) Offers to negotiate for the hostages' release came from such different sources as the Vatican and the Palestine Liberation Organization. Khomeini rejected them. Non-American hostages were released, however. And on November 18, Khomeini freed American blacks and most of the women. He said this was to show respect for women and to express the belief that blacks were oppressed in the United States.

It was believed that fifty hostages remained within the embassy walls, and the students announced that they would be tried as spies. The United States appealed to the United Nations Security Council and to the International Court of Justice. Both organizations ordered the hostages' release. Iran ignored the orders. Khomeini continued to back the students' position—that the Shah's return was the sole condition for the hostages' release.

The Shah was reported to be well enough to travel at the end of November. But Mexico refused to allow him to return. Early in December, the Shah was flown to an Air Force base in Texas, where he stayed while efforts were made to find a permanent home outside the United States. Finally, on December 16, he flew to Panama.

But the Shah's move did not change matters for the hostages. And meanwhile, further division had grown out of Iran's constitutional vote early in December. Most of the Azerbaijanis had boycotted the polls. After the vote, they rioted and took over government buildings and radio and television stations in Tabriz, the capital of their province. Like the Kurds, they demanded more control over their affairs. And late in December, fighting broke out between minority groups living in Baluchistan, a province in the southeastern part of the country. There were also several border incidents with Iraq.

As December drew to a close, the Teheran embassy was flooded with hundreds of thousands of Christmas cards, sent to the hostages by well-wishers in the United States. U.S. clergymen were allowed to visit the hostages at Christmas. But there appeared to be no improvement in the standoff between Iran and the United States. On December 31, the U.N. Security Council ordered Iran to release the hostages within a week or face the possibility of a trade embargo. And U.N. Secretary General Kurt Waldheim flew to Iran to seek a solution.

SALT II—LIMITING NUCLEAR WEAPONS

In June of 1979, people on a Vienna street passed by a pastry shop and smiled at what was in the window. They saw two life-sized figures sitting at a chessboard. But the figures—which were likenesses of U.S. President Jimmy Carter and Leonid I. Brezhnev, the leader of the Soviet Union—were made of papier-mâché and candy. And their chess pieces were candy models of deadly attack missiles.

The display referred to an important U.S.-Soviet treaty signed by Carter and Brezhnev on June 18, 1979, in Vienna, Austria. The agreement grew out of a long round of talks called SALT II (*S*trategic *A*rms *L*imitation *T*alks). It was a promise by both nations to limit the numbers of long-range nuclear weapons they would have. However, any treaty must be ratified by the U.S. Senate before it can go into effect. And while many hailed this treaty as an important step on the road to peace, others weren't so sure.

▶ **THE SIGNIFICANCE OF THE TREATY**

For 35 years, the world has desired some safeguards against the possibility of nuclear war. In 1945, at the very end of World War II, the United States dropped atomic bombs on the Japanese cities of Hiroshima and Nagasaki. More than 100,000 people were killed. In time, about 100,000 more died from burns and radiation poisoning. These terrible numbers revealed to the world just how awesome nuclear weapons were. People realized that a full-scale nuclear war could wipe out all life on earth.

The United States and the Soviet Union had been allies during World War II. But as the war ended, the two great powers began to squabble with each other. In the early 1950's, it became obvious that the Soviet Union had also developed nuclear weapons. The United States and the Soviet Union never went to war with each other, but they had a lot of tough confrontations over the years. So the fear has always existed that the confrontations could erupt into a full-scale nuclear war.

For this reason, many people all over the world were happy in the late 1960's when the two countries sat down to discuss nuclear disarmament (getting rid of nuclear weapons). These discussions led in 1972 to the first SALT treaty, signed by President Richard Nixon and Soviet leader Brezhnev.

60

Since then, more treaty discussions have gone on, resulting in the SALT II agreement of June, 1979.

▶ THE DETAILS OF THE TREATY

What SALT II does is to limit the number of nuclear delivery systems each country may have. A nuclear delivery system is a method of delivering, or sending, a nuclear bomb to a target. A delivery system may be a long-range bomber, such as the U.S. B-52 and the Soviet "Bear." Or a delivery system may be a missile that is launched from land or from a submarine.

In the first step of the treaty, each nation agrees to limit its number of delivery systems to 2,400. In the second step, each nation agrees to cut back its total to 2,250 by 1981.

Many planes and missiles are able to carry more than one nuclear bomb. Under the 1981 limits, there are also restrictions on the number of nuclear bombs that each delivery system may carry.

The treaty would remain in effect until 1985. Until then, there would be further talks—SALT III.

▶ THE CONTROVERSY

Many people around the world think that the treaty is a necessary and important way to help preserve peace. But some in the United States fear that the SALT treaty gives too much advantage to the Soviet Union. They fear that the United States is being outplayed at the chessboard of world power.

In what way might the treaty give the Soviet Union an advantage? While the treaty allows each nation the same number of weapons, the weapons themselves are very difficult to compare. Some people say that certain Soviet missiles carry heavier and more destructive bombs than U.S. missiles do. Two sides may have the same number of weapons, but, they ask, are 100 pea shooters really equal to 100 shotguns?

Another argument that some Americans have against the SALT II treaty concerns the question of verification. As it applies to SALT II, verification means finding out if each side is carrying out the terms of the treaty. The critics of the SALT II treaty say that there is no completely sure way to monitor, or check on, whether the Soviets are really disarming.

A third problem concerns the Soviet TU-22M bomber, which the U.S. calls "Backfire." This bomber is not mentioned in the treaty because the Soviets say it is "medium-range," that is, it is not able to reach the United States. But the Backfire worries some people because it can certainly reach U.S. allies in Europe.

Because many U.S. senators held these views, the SALT II treaty still had not been ratified by the end of 1979. In addition, many senators were worried about the presence of 3,000 Soviet troops in Cuba. The Soviets said that these troops were only military advisers and not combat troops. But some senators said that they would not vote for the SALT II treaty until the Soviet troops left Cuba.

It was clear, though, that both President Carter and Soviet leader Brezhnev were counting on the treaty to be ratified.

Carter and Brezhnev after signing the SALT treaty.

NEWSMAKERS

A life of service to the "poorest of the poor" brought the Nobel peace prize to **Mother Teresa** of Calcutta in 1979. Born in 1910 in Skoplje, Albania (now in Yugoslavia), she became a Roman Catholic nun at age 18. She was assigned to a mission school in Calcutta, India, where she taught and eventually became principal. She was keenly aware of the poverty and suffering in Calcutta, one of the world's most crowded cities. In 1948 she received permission to leave her convent and work among the poor. Two years later, she founded the Missionaries of Charity. Today this order operates children's homes, medical stations, havens for the dying, and leper colonies around the world.

Two of China's most important leaders are **Hua Kuo-feng** *(left)* and **Teng Hsiao-ping** *(right).* **Hua** hold's China's two most powerful posts—premier and chairman of the Communist Party. He was born around 1920, but little is known of his early life. He became a vice-premier in 1975. Throughout his career, he held views midway between those of the radical and moderate Chinese Communists. This helped him emerge as Mao Tse-tung's successor in 1976. **Teng,** China's first deputy premier, is thought to have far greater influence than his title suggests. He is known as a moderate. Born in 1904, he studied in France and took part in China's civil war. He became a deputy premier in 1956 but was twice driven from power by China's radicals. Since his return to government in 1977, he has stressed a practical approach to economic growth and improved relations with non-Communist countries.

62

At 53, **Margaret Thatcher** became Britain's first woman prime minister. She is known for her determination, and she has said that her upbringing taught her that people must work hard to get ahead. Born Margaret Hilda Roberts, she was the daughter of a grocer in Grantham, a small town north of London. She earned a degree in chemistry at Oxford and, in 1951, married Denis Thatcher, a paint manufacturer. During the next few years she earned a law degree, raised twins, and was active in the Conservative Party. Her political career began to pick up when she was elected to Parliament in 1959. In 1970 she became minister of education under Prime Minister Edward Heath. In 1975 she challenged Heath for leadership of the Conservative Party and won, opening the way for her election as prime minister.

Charles Joseph (Joe) Clark took office as Canada's prime minister in June, 1979. At 39, he was Canada's youngest prime minister. The son of a newspaper publisher in the prairie town of High River, Alberta, he worked on his father's paper and headed his school's student council. He became active in the Progressive Conservative (PC) Party while attending the University of Alberta. In 1972 he was elected to Parliament. Four years later he won leadership of the PC Party and came to national attention. Clark's government lost a vote of confidence in December, 1979, just over six months after he had taken office. Clark and his wife, Maureen Anne McTeer, have one child, a daughter named Catherine.

THE ANIMAL WORLD

The creation of light by living organisms is called bioluminescence. These anglerfish have bulb-shaped "lights" attached to rods on their heads. The light attracts prey, like bait on a fishing line.

TERRIFIC TONGUES

A chameleon sits motionless on a branch. Only its bulging eyes move—in two different directions at once! When one eye sees an insect, the other eye swivels and soon also focuses on the unsuspecting victim. In less than a second, the chameleon judges the distance to the insect. Then, almost faster than your eye can see, it flicks its muscular tongue forward. The insect is caught on the sticky clublike tip and pulled into the chameleon's mouth.

Unlike the tongues of most animals, the chameleon's tongue is attached to the front of its mouth. When it shoots out of the mouth, the tongue expands and can actually reach prey that is more than a body's length away. The size of the prey depends on the size of the chameleon. Small chameleons catch mainly insects. Large chameleons feed on lizards, birds, and small mammals, as well as on insects.

Frogs and toads also have tongues that are attached to the front of the lower jaw and are loose at the back. They use their tongues in much the same way as the chameleon. But their tongues cannot be extended as far as the tongue of a chameleon. Frogs and toads feed mainly on insects, though some will eat almost anything that moves and is the right size.

▶AN EATING UTENSIL

Getting food and eating are the main functions of an animal's tongue. There are many different sizes and shapes of tongues in the animal world. Each is adapted for a certain type of food. Anteaters, like chameleons and frogs, eat insects. But they don't try to catch quick-moving flies and moths. Rather, they capture ants and termites that live in large nests. An anteater uses its sharp claws to tear open the nests. Then it

The chameleon flicks its sticky tongue forward and devours its victim.

66

Frogs use their tongues mainly to catch insects—but anything small that moves better be careful.

sticks its long snout into the opening. Its sticky, wormlike tongue moves in and out of the mouth, licking up insects by the hundreds. A giant anteater—whose tongue may be 2 feet (60 centimeters) long—eats as many as 30,000 ants and termites in a day to satisfy its great appetite.

The honey possum, a tiny mammal that lives in Australia, has a tongue that looks like a bristle brush. It uses its tongue to lap up nectar and pollen from flowers. When the tongue is retracted, ridges on the roof of the mouth scrape off the food.

Another animal that feeds on nectar is the honeybee. It has a tongue that is a hollow tube. When the bee finds a nice source of nectar, it sucks up the liquid much as you draw up soda through a drinking straw.

The hummingbird, another nectar feeder, has a long, slender tongue that is forked at the end. The bird curls its tongue inward, to form a tubelike structure, and drinks the nectar. The hummingbird often takes in tiny insects at the same time. Insects are an important source of protein for this tiny, colorful bird.

▶OTHER USES, TOO

Tongues are used for other activities besides getting food and eating. The gecko uses its tongue as a windshield wiper. This lizard has transparent eyelids. Unlike your eyelids, they do not move. The upper and lower lids are fused together, over the surface of the eye. This protects the eye from dust and other particles. If the covering be-

The honeybee's tongue works much like a straw.

The tongue of the hummingbird curls inward.

The gecko uses its tongue as a windshield wiper.

comes dirty, the gecko licks it clean with the tip of its tongue.

The okapi, a short-necked relative of the giraffe, can also stretch out its tongue far enough to lick dust from its eyes—and even from its ears. The giraffe may even lick the inside of its nostrils to remove insects and other foreign objects. Its tongue, which may be more than 20 inches (50 centimeters) long, is nearly black in color. It is thought that this dark coloring protects the tongue from being burned by the hot African sun.

Some animals use their tongues as a cooling device. Cats are good examples. A cat pants when its body temperature is too high. This increases the evaporation of water from the tongue and tissues lining the mouth. As the water evaporates, heat is removed from the body. In addition, the cat cools off by licking itself with saliva. If extremely hot, it licks every part of its body that can be reached by the tongue, to the point where it is dripping wet.

A cat does other things with its tongue, too. The surface of a cat's tongue is rough, like sandpaper. The cat makes use of this

This cat is grooming itself with its tongue.

The hedgehog uses its tongue to conceal its scent.

roughness as it grooms its fur—much as you use a comb to groom your hair. The cat uses its tongue to clean not only itself but also its children. It may also lick other animals and the human beings with whom it shares its home. Such licking is a sign of affection.

The hedgehog has a peculiar behavior called self-anointing. When a hedgehog comes upon an object that has a stimulating smell, it licks the object. Or, if the object is small enough, the hedgehog takes it into its mouth and chews it. (Stimulating objects may include flowers, soap, earthworms, rotten meat, books, and cigarette stubs.) As it licks or chews on the object, the hedgehog produces great amounts of saliva. It turns its head to the side and, using its tongue, tosses the foamy saliva over its spines. It does this three or four times before spitting out the object. The saliva dries on the spines. Scientists believe that the smell of the saliva conceals the hedgehog's true scent, thus protecting it from enemies that might otherwise find it.

The rattlesnake uses its forked tongue to detect the odor of prey. It flicks its tongue back and forth, picking up molecules of scent from the air. Then the rattlesnake draws its tongue into its mouth and places the tips to two small holes, or pits, called Jacobson's organs. These are located in the roof of the mouth. They have the same function as your nose. When the snake smells an approaching mouse or other animal, it prepares to strike. The sensory system also helps the snake track down an animal that it has bitten and that has crawled away to die. By continuously testing the air with its tongue, the snake can follow the trail of the victim.

Your tongue also has many uses. It helps you chew and swallow food. It tells you how the food tastes and whether it is hot or cold. And it does something that no animal tongue can do. It enables you to speak. Without your tongue, you would not be able to form many of the words that are part of your everyday speech. So you see, you too have a terrific tongue.

JENNY TESAR
Sponsoring Editor
Gateways to Science

69

THE NEW BREEDS

The Ibizan hound . . . the soft-coated wheaten terrier . . . the bichon frise . . . the akita . . . the bearded collie . . . the shih tzu . . . the Tibetan terrier. All these dogs have existed for centuries. But there is now something new about them. They have recently been recognized as true breeds by the prestigious American Kennel Club. Most of these breeds are still very rare. And since they are now eligible to earn the title "champion" at American dog shows, they draw attention wherever they go.

Ibizan Hound. The elegant and graceful Ibizan hound originated in the Balearic Islands, east of Spain. It is a strong and intelligent hunting dog. Noted for its speed and agility, it is able to jump very high into the air from a standstill. Ibizans are a mixture of white and red or white and gold, with amber eyes. Statues of dog gods from the tombs of the ancient Egyptians look much like today's Ibizan hounds.

Soft-Coated Wheaten Terrier. This medium-sized terrier is a native of Ireland. It gets its name from its light golden color and long, silky, slightly wavy coat. It was used to guard property, herd cattle, and hunt small game. Today it is an attractive and intelligent companion.

Bichon Frise. The bichon frise came from the island of Tenerife, the largest of the Canary Islands, off the northwestern coast of Africa. It is descended from an ancient breed of water spaniel. A small, white dog with a curly coat, the bichon frise resembles a white powder puff. It is hardy and fun-loving and makes a fine companion. In fact, its name means "curly lap dog." For centuries it was the pampered companion of the European nobility.

Akita. This large, powerful dog comes from Japan. It was bred for intelligence and courage and was used as a hunter and guard dog. The akita has a large curled tail, thick neck, and dense, straight coat. It can be any color, but it can have only small white markings. In Tokyo's main railroad station is a statue of an akita named Hachiko. For many years, the dog accompanied its master to the station each day and returned in the evening

Ibizan Hound

Soft-Coated Wheaten Terrier

Bichon Frise

to greet him. One day, its master did not come home. But Hachiko returned to the station every day to wait, until the dog died nine years later. Each year dog lovers pay tribute to Hachiko's devotion in a special ceremony.

Bearded Collie. The ancestors of the bearded collie are thought to have migrated into what is now Poland hundreds of years ago. The breed then spread across Europe, where it was used to herd sheep and cattle. The bearded collie looks like a lean old English sheepdog with a tail. Its thick, shaggy coat helps to protect it against rain and snow. It comes in many shades of gray, black, and brown and may have white markings.

Shih Tzu. The shih tzu is believed to have originated centuries ago in Tibet. These dogs were given to distinguished visitors from China and became pampered pets in the Chinese imperial court. The official description of the breed by the Peking Kennel Club said that the shih tzu should have a "lion head . . . , feather-duster tail . . . , pearly petal tongue, and movement like a goldfish." The shih tzu is sturdy for its small size and is a charming companion. Its long, luxuriant coat comes in a wide variety of colors. The hair on its head is often tied up in a little ponytail, giving it the look of an ancient Chinese mandarin.

Tibetan Terrier. The Tibetan terrier is a medium-sized breed with a long, shaggy coat that comes in many colors. It looks like a large lhasa apso or a small old English sheepdog. It is believed that this terrier was bred for centuries in the monasteries of Tibet, where it served as a watchdog and companion. Tibetan terriers were never sold, but they were sometimes given as prized gifts. The gift of a Tibetan terrier was believed to bring peace and prosperity to the person who received it.

And have you ever heard of an Australian cattle dog . . . an Australian kelpie . . . a border collie . . . a cavalier King Charles spaniel . . . a miniature bull terrier . . . a spinoni italiani? Keep your eyes open for them. They may very well be the next "new" breeds.

JO ANN WHITE
Professional dog breeder and handler

Akita

Bearded Collie

Shih Tzu

71

ADOPT A WILD HORSE

Manes and tails flying in the wind, a band of wild horses gallops across a sagebrush-covered plain. Riders follow in close pursuit, driving the band toward a makeshift corral. As the last horse streaks into the corral, the gate swings shut. The wild horses wheel, whinny, and mill about, unsure of what to expect from their captors.

That could be a scene from a Western movie. But perhaps a dozen wild horse roundups—with helicopters assisting the riders—were held in the United States in 1979. What happened to the horses? Many of them were adopted, for free, by families that wanted to give them good care. The horses found their new homes through the Adopt-A-Horse program run by the U.S. Bureau of Land Management (BLM).

▶ **HORSES WITH A HISTORY**

The horses of the West are not truly wild. They are feral, which means that their ancestors escaped from domestic life and returned to the wilderness. About 150 years ago, there were more than 1,000,000 of these horses. But as more settlers moved west, more and more horses were captured for use as saddle horses or killed because they competed with livestock for grazing land. After 1900, even greater numbers were slaughtered for pet food.

By 1971, so few wild horses were left that Congress passed the Wild Free-Roaming Horse and Burro Act. Under this law, horses and burros that live in the vast areas of government-owned range are not allowed to be killed or used for any moneymaking

72

purpose. The number of wild horses and burros has increased dramatically under the law's protection.

This has made problems for the BLM, which oversees much of the public range. The horses must share water and grass with other wildlife—and with livestock from ranches that lease grazing rights from the government. When too many animals graze an area of land, the grass is stripped or trampled. Pasture becomes desert.

The BLM is trying to prevent this by reducing the wild horse herds. And the Adopt-A-Horse program, begun in 1976, is one step the BLM has taken. About 9,000 horses and 3,000 burros have been placed since the program began.

Critics of the adoption program say that it favors ranchers and that wild horses should be free to roam the public ranges. They also feel that the roundups are often poorly conducted. The BLM answers that Adopt-A-Horse is a good way to preserve the land—and is good for the horses, too. The bureau says that it could reduce the herds by destroying some of the wild horses but so far has avoided doing so.

▶ **HOW TO ADOPT A WILD HORSE**

The first step in adopting a wild horse or burro is to send an application to the BLM's Adopt-A-Horse center in Denver, Colorado.

You must be able to provide good care, shelter, and pasture for the horse. You must be a U.S. resident. And if you are under legal age, a parent or guardian must sign the application.

Once the application is approved, a wild horse can be yours to train for riding, showing, or any personal use. You are its custodian. The BLM remains the legal owner for one year. During that time, the horse cannot be sold or rented out.

You don't have to pay for your horse, but it can still be expensive. To get the horse, you must travel to a distribution center in one of the ten western states where roundups are held. There is a small fee for a veterinarian's examination. And you will probably have to pay to have the horse shipped to your home.

It costs money to keep a horse, too—how much depends on the cost of hay and other necessities in the area where you live. It's a good idea to check with someone who has had experience with horses before you decide to adopt one yourself.

At first, you may need help in training and caring for the horse. Life on the range is hard, and these horses are thin and rough-coated. They have never seen a saddle or a bridle. But with enough good care and proper training, most of them can be turned into sleek and gentle companions.

This teenager adopted two wild horses, a mare and her baby.

73

THE I.Q. ZOO

Where can you see a raccoon play basketball, a parrot roller-skate, a rabbit play the piano, and a chicken play tic-tac-toe? If you think only in cartoons, you're wrong. At the I.Q. Zoo in Hot Springs, Arkansas, real animals perform these acts and do many other things that might surprise you. In fact, if you aren't careful, that chicken might even beat you in the game of X's and O's.

The animals at the I.Q. Zoo are special, but they're not really smarter than others of their kind. The thing that makes them different is the training they have had. They've been trained by an organization called Animal Behavior Enterprises, founded by Keller and Marian Breland, two psychologists, in 1947. The organization is made up of scientists and technicians who apply the science of behavior to understanding and controlling the behavior of animals. The organization has trained more then 8,000 animals, from cockroaches to whales. Many of these animals have performed throughout the world, at fairs, zoos, and on TV.

Animal Behavior Enterprises teaches the animals their acts using a method called be- havior modification. It is a method in which behavior can be controlled by using a system of rewards. No punishments are used.

The method is really very simple. Suppose you want to teach a duck to play a toy piano. You would begin by rewarding the animal immediately whenever it behaves the way you want. There are few things that ducks like better than food, so food should be the reward in this case. First feed the duck several times. Before each feeding, make a loud noise—a clap or whistle, for example, would be good.

Now put the duck near the piano. Each time it goes close to the piano, make the noise and give the reward. Soon the duck will learn that it can earn the food by going near the piano. After a while, don't give the reward unless the duck touches one of the keys. This is where the loud noise becomes important. It would be hard to give the food immediately after the duck touches the key. But you can make the noise immediately after. Thus, the duck touches the key; you make the noise; the duck "thinks" of the reward; then you give the reward. The duck

Using a method called behavior modification, you can teach a duck to play the piano...

74

will learn that it gets the food only after it touches the key. Using this method, you'll be able to teach the duck to play a simple tune on the piano.

This kind of training is not cruel, as some animal-training methods are. In fact, Animal Behavior Enterprise's methods are approved by the American Humane Association. And parents and teachers have been using similar behavior modification methods for years, even if they don't think of them in that way. You've probably gotten good grades for good work at school and some hugs and kisses for good behavior at home. They were really rewards for you.

How smart are the animals at I.Q. Zoo? That's a question scientists are still trying to answer. It depends a lot on what is meant by smart. The animals are good at learning to perform some amazing tasks in order to get rewards. But they learn only their set acts. And that is very different from the kind of thinking humans must do to solve complicated problems. But by understanding how animals learn, we may find out more about our own learning processes.

DAVID J. KULL
Senior Associate Editor
Medical Laboratory Observer magazine

This chicken might beat you playing tic-tac-toe.

. . . and a parrot to roller-skate. You can also see them at the I.Q. Zoo.

NATURE'S LIVING LIGHTS

Night settles over Palancar Reef in the Caribbean. A group of scuba divers puts on masks, fins, and tanks of compressed air. After checking their underwater lights, they walk up to the boat's railing and jump into the still, black water. The water explodes in a glistening froth of pale, greenish blue bubbles. Suddenly the divers pause and gaze in amazement at tiny specks of light twinkling brightly below the surface of the water. One of the divers waves his hand slowly through the water and the specks of light bounce off his fingertips like sparks of electricity. He waves his hand faster and a shower of sparks is given off. A fish swims past in the darkness, leaving a trail of light behind. The divers begin their descent. Kicking steadily downward, they are bathed in an eerie, green-blue glow, looking like creatures from a horror movie. Finally, they switch on their underwater lights to guide their way to the reef. And the luminescent glow and twinkling specks of light disappear in the powerful beams.

▶ **A FASCINATING OCCURRENCE**

What did the divers actually see? The water was filled with thousands of a certain kind of microscopic, one-celled protozoa. The movement of the divers through the water disturbed the protozoa, causing them to give off flashes of light. This creation of light by living organisms (both plants and animals) is one of nature's most fascinating occurrences. It is called bioluminescence.

Animals that give off light are found both on land and in the ocean. They include certain kinds of protozoans, crustaceans, sponges, corals, clams, jellyfish, snails, worms, and insects.

Among the insects are the fireflies and glowworms. Fireflies are not really flies at all; they are the adult stage of a kind of beetle. And most glowworms are the immature, or larval, stage of certain beetles.

While the more familiar bioluminescent animals—such as fireflies and glowworms—live on land, there is a much greater variety in the ocean. Most luminous fish spend their lives deep in the dark, underwater world of the sea.

There is only one luminous animal that has been found in fresh water—a kind of mollusk, called a limpet, that is found in New Zealand streams. It is a mystery to scientists why luminous organisms do not inhabit large bodies of fresh water. The depths of many lakes are as dark as the seas that are filled with bioluminescent life.

▶ **HOW IS LIVING LIGHT PRODUCED?**

How do animals produce their own light? This remained a mystery until the pioneering studies of French scientist Raphael Dubois in 1887. Dubois worked with luminous boring clams and discovered two key chemical compounds. He named these "luciferin," meaning "light bearer," and "luciferase," indicating that the chemical had the properties of an enzyme. Dubois believed that the luciferin combined with oxygen in the presence of luciferase to produce living light. It was not until years later that his theory was confirmed. Further studies revealed that all luciferins and luciferases are not the same. They vary with the animal or plant they come from.

▶ **WHY DO ANIMALS GLOW?**

Bioluminescent animals give off light in a number of ways and for a variety of reasons. Some use their luminescent organs mainly to hunt and lure prey. Others use their light to escape from their enemies. And still others light up to attract mates.

Hunting. Among the most interesting of the predators that hunt with light are the

There is a great variety of bioluminescent creatures in the ocean. These include the pinecone fish *(above)* and certain crustaceans and jellyfish *(below)*.

These fireflies put on a dazzling courtship display.

strange-looking female anglerfish of the deep sea. An angler is another word for a person who fishes. Appropriately named, the female anglerfish uses the same technique as a human fisher. Her light is a bulb-shaped lantern that is attached to a rod, which is hinged to a bone on the front of her head. The lantern works like bait on a fishing line, attracting small prey. The bulb dangles in front of the anglerfish's large mouth and long pointed teeth. Or she can swing it backwards, over her head.

Luminous hunters are also found on land. In New Zealand there is a glowworm that dwells on the ceilings of dark caverns, under bridges, and among ferns in deep ravines. This glowworm lives in a transparent, tubular home and has developed an ingenious method of capturing its prey. It secretes numerous sticky, threadlike fishing lines. Then it flashes on its lights and lures flying insects into the sticky threads. Once a victim has been trapped in the line, the glowworm simply reels it in and hungrily devours it. In New Zealand's famous Waitomo Caves, the glowworms light up the ceilings of the huge caverns so that they look like star-studded galaxies.

Defense. While some animals light up to capture food, others use their lights to avoid being eaten themselves. One of the loveliest of the glowworms is the railroad worm, which is found in Central and South America. This worm flashes its lights as a warning signal to ward off would-be attackers. It has eleven pairs of greenish light organs along the length of its body, and others that shine red on its head. When the railroad worm is disturbed, it flashes on all its lights at once, resembling a tiny toy train.

Squid rely on deception to protect themselves. They squirt out an inklike substance that clouds the water, confusing the enemy long enough to speed away. Some squid release a luminescent secretion, resulting in a glowing cloud of "liquid fire."

Mating. One of the most important uses of bioluminescence is to attract a mate. This is why the firefly gives off its flashing glow. A typical firefly mating ritual is performed by the common Tennessee firefly. After dark, the male and female emerge separately from the grass. To find each other, the male

Flashlight fish have compartments under each eye that are filled with bioluminescent bacteria.

flies low over the ground, giving off a single short flash at regular intervals. When he flashes close to the female, she flashes a short response. The male turns toward her and glows again. The female responds. This exchange of signals continues until the male reaches the female, and the two then mate.

The most dazzling courtship display is put on by the Malaysian firefly. The evening's performance begins in a large tree, such as a mangrove, with the last fading light of day. A single male flashes on his light. Here and there other males begin to follow suit. Soon the entire tree is full of twinkling lights. Then all the lights in one section suddenly start to flash on and off together, as if wired to a single switch. Others pick up the rhythm until nearly all the fireflies are flashing in perfect unison. Scientists think the purpose of this light display is to help the female fireflies easily find the males.

Other Uses. Among the most fascinating bioluminescent creatures are the little flashlight fish that live in the Red Sea, the Indian Ocean, and the Caribbean. On moonless nights they leave the dark caves and deep recesses of the coral reefs and swim up to shallower water, blinking the large light organs beneath their eyes as they move about. They give off the most intense light of any luminous animal. And their light organs serve many purposes—attracting prey, frightening enemies, and communicating with other flashlight fish. The light

organ also serves as a kind of headlight, to see what lies ahead in the darkness.

The flashlight fish, like certain other fish, does not produce its own light. Under each eye it has a crescent-shaped compartment. These compartments are filled with glowing bacteria. The fish provide a home and food for the bacteria, and the bacteria in turn give the fish its lights. Their relationship is so close that the bacteria cannot survive outside the fish's body.

Human beings have no bioluminescent organs. But people have used the luminescence produced by other creatures. During World War II, Japanese soldiers sprinkled a moistened powder on their hands that was made from the dried remains of tiny bioluminescent crustaceans. This made their hands glow with a light strong enough to read messages and maps by at night.

Many waters are teeming with glowing organisms. This strange spectacle was once referred to by mariners as "the burning of the sea." Today we would be able to reassure them that this was light created by protozoa such as those scuba divers encountered. But although we now know what it is, bioluminescence is a phenomenon that continues to fascinate people. And scientists are still probing into the complex secrets of nature's living lights.

PETER D. CAPEN
Author and Photographer
Terra Mar Productions

ANIMALS IN THE NEWS

The lights reflected in this kitten's eyes are the bright lights of Broadway. The kitten, a 5-month-old female named Jonesy, won a role in a new musical version of *I Remember Mama*, which opened in New York City in 1979. Jonesy played the part of a cat named Uncle Elizabeth. Most of her time on stage was spent in a box or in the arms of Dagmar, played by 7-year-old Tara Kennedy.

Saman, a 6-month-old elephant, is enjoying a snack at his new home—the world's only elephant orphanage. The refuge is in Sri Lanka (Ceylon). It is part of the government's effort to stop a decline in the country's number of wild elephants. Most of the orphans lose their parents through accidents. Saman will stay at the refuge until a permanent home is found —perhaps at a foreign zoo.

80

With the grace of an armored truck, an armadillo soars into the air in the slide and broad-jump event at the Brantley County Armadillo Olympics. The competition, held in May in Georgia, was believed to be the first of its kind. It sent armadillo athletes bumbling over hurdles, scooting along a footrace course, and paddling through a pond for the free-style swim. The contest was held to draw attention to these odd-looking mammals, which are unpopular with farmers and ranchers but are valuable in some kinds of scientific research.

Champion Oaktree's Irishtocrat, an Irish water spaniel from Canada, won the best-in-show award at the 1979 Westminster Kennel Club show in New York City. This show is the top event in the U.S. dog-show circuit. Irish water spaniels are quite rare in the United States. Dugan, as Irishtocrat is called by his friends, called attention to the curly-coated breed with his success.

81

A camera-shy coelacanth peers suspiciously at the photographer who snapped this rare picture. The coelacanth belongs to a group of fish that were ancestors of the first amphibians. It was thought to have died out 70,000,000 years ago. Then, in 1938, a live coelacanth was found. Since then, several have turned up in fishing nets, but most died. This fish, netted in the Indian Ocean, was shipped off to scientists after posing for the picture.

This ape has something to smile about. She's something new—a cross between a gibbon and a siamang, two species of Southeast Asian apes. Called a siabon, she was born in 1975 in an Atlanta, Georgia, zoo. During 1979, scientists completed an analysis of the siabon's chromosomes (materials in cells that carry inherited traits from parents to offspring). They wondered if new species might sometimes arise over a few generations through crossbreeding, rather than developing over thousands of years through many small changes. But the siabon is not likely to give rise to a new species. Like most such crosses, she is expected to be sterile (unable to reproduce).

Imagine that you are having breakfast in the kitchen of your sixth-floor apartment. Suddenly a huge, lizardlike head appears at the window. Science fiction? Of course—no creature six floors tall exists today. But in 1979, scientists in Utah found the remains of such a beast—a dinosaur of the genus *Brachiosaurus*. It was quickly dubbed Ultrasaurus, and it may have been the largest creature ever to have walked the earth. When it lived (more than 140,000,000 years ago), it stood about 60 feet (18 meters) tall and weighed about 80 tons. It is thought that Ultrasaurus ate leaves from the tops of trees. But scientists have many questions about the beast—how, for example, could it obtain enough food to fuel its huge bulk? And how could its heart pump blood up to its head? They hope to find some answers when Ultrasaurus' bones are completely unearthed and assembled.

Brontosaurus, an old friend to anyone who has studied dinosaurs, got a new look in 1979. A huge vegetarian who lived in swamps and ponds, *Brontosaurus* has usually been portrayed with a blunt, rounded head and broad teeth. After long study, many scientists became convinced that this portrait was the result of mismatched skulls. Researchers around 1900, anxious to unearth and identify new dinosaur species, had paired *Brontosaurus* skeletons with skulls of another dinosaur, *Camarasaurus*. The correct head, scientists now say, is longer and more tapered, with thin teeth suited to *Brontosaurus'* probable diet of tender water plants.

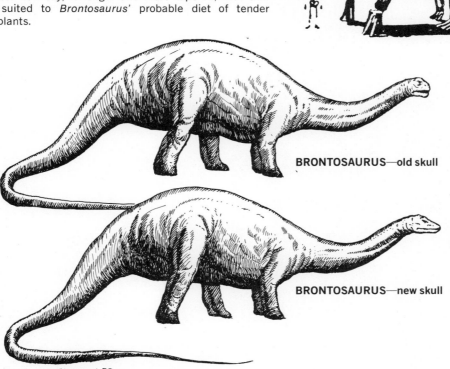

BRACHIOSAURUS

BRONTOSAURUS—old skull

BRONTOSAURUS—new skull

83

A NEW KIND OF FROG

Imagine living in a dense rain forest, far from supermarkets and other conveniences of modern civilization. You have to hunt for your food. What weapon would you use to catch and kill game animals?

The Emberá Choco, a group of Indians in western Colombia, live in such a place. Their choice of weapon is as effective as it is famous. They catch and kill birds, deer, jaguars, and other game by shooting darts from a long blowgun. The darts are deadly enough. But to make sure the prey is killed, each dart is tipped with poison. The Chocó get the poison from the skin of small frogs that live in the rain forest.

The Chocó have known about these frogs and their poisons for many generations. But for biologists, the frogs are a more recent discovery. The first such frogs studied and classified by biologists were given the names *Phyllobates aurotaenia* and *Phyllobates bicolor.*

In the early 1970's, two American scientists—Charles W. Myers of the American Museum of Natural History and John W. Daley of the National Institutes of Health—were in the rain forest where the Emberá Chocó live. They learned of a third frog that the natives were using as a source of poison. In February, 1973, they obtained a specimen. It was a frog unlike any ever before seen by scientists. In the following months they obtained nearly 400 additional specimens.

The frogs are land dwellers. They live on the ground, among tree roots and fallen leaves. They are quite small, averaging $1\frac{3}{4}$ inches (4.7 centimeters) in length. Some are a bright golden color; others are a pale metallic green.

Some of the frogs gathered by the scientists were killed so that their structure and chemistry could be studied. Others were kept in special cages. These frogs were fed a diet of crickets dusted with vitamin and calcium powder. The frogs do well in captivity—and even behave well. Only while feeding do they sometimes become aggressive.

The newly discovered frogs, called *Phyllobates terribilis,* are about as long as your thumb. Their color ranges from bright gold to green.

84

The Chocó catch game by shooting darts from a long blowgun. Each dart is tipped with a poison that comes from *terribilis* and other poisonous frogs in the area.

The Emberá Chocó, who protect their hands with leaves while catching the frogs, warned the biologists not to touch the frogs. The warning was good advice. The scientists soon learned how very, very poisonous these little creatures are.

The poison in the frog's skin secretions is a mixture of two substances: batrachotoxin and homobatrachotoxin. These are two of the most powerful poisons known. And there is no known antidote (medicine that would counteract the effects of the poison).

The frog is at least 20 times more poisonous, or toxic, than the two other poison-dart frogs. The average frog contains about 1,100 micrograms of poison—a mere fraction of an ounce, but enough to kill more than 20,000 mice! As a matter of fact, it is believed that the poison helps protect the frog from predators.

The scientists estimated that a lethal dose for a person would be 170 micrograms. But it may be even less, since large animals are usually more susceptible than small animals to poisons. If a person with a cut or open sore picked up one of the frogs, the toxin that entered the wound could easily be fatal.

The biologists wore rubber gloves, gog-gles, and disposable face masks when they worked with the frogs. They found that care must be taken even when disposing of these items. "At our camp, we unintentionally caused the death of a dog and a chicken that got into garbage containing such items," they wrote.

Myers and Daley decided that the frog belonged in the same genus (Phyllobates) as the other poison-dart frogs. This decision was based on the similar structure of the animals and on the fact that their poisons were identical. They named the species *terribilis,* which means terrible or frightful. Why this name? In the scientific paper that describes their discovery, Myers and Daley wrote: "The name describes the extraordinary toxicity of the frogs' skin secretions."

As it becomes easier to travel into tropical rain forests and other remote areas, biologists will discover other species. Some of the newly discovered species will closely resemble animals already known. And like the frog found in the Colombian rain forests, they will be placed in the same genus as their relatives. Others will be so different from known animals that they will form an entirely new genus, class, or even phylum.

85

HELPING-HAND MONKEYS

Little chores such as turning on lights and opening doors may not sound like monkey business—but they are. And the special monkeys who do these and similar jobs are not fooling around, either. They are helping human masters who cannot perform the tasks themselves.

These helping-hand monkeys are like the familiar seeing-eye dogs that use their vision and special training to aid blind people. But instead of their eyes, the monkeys use their hands and legs to assist people who have lost the use of their own limbs because of illness or accident. Of course, the monkeys must have special training too.

Psychologist Mary Joan Willard came up with the idea for the helping-hand monkeys when she was a student of psychologist B. F. Skinner. Dr. Skinner was one of the first scientists to work with a training method called behavior modification. Using that method, he found he could train many kinds of animals to perform many different tasks. Dr. Willard decided to try using the behavior modification method to teach monkeys to perform simple chores.

If you ever visit monkeys at the zoo, look closely at their hands. You may be surprised by how much theirs look like yours. In fact, humans and monkeys are both part of the same class of animals, called primates. All primates share one important trait—they can hold onto things with their hands. Thus, monkeys can use their hands to do many of the things that people do around the house. The trick is in teaching them what to do and when to do it. That's where Dr. Willard and behavior modification come in.

Dr. Willard chose capuchin monkeys for the first experiments. The capuchins are natives of Central and South America. They are between 1 and $1\frac{1}{2}$ feet (30 and 45 centimeters) tall, have tails about as long as their bodies, and can reach an age of 30 years. The capuchins are among the smartest of the monkeys, and they're very loyal to their owners. Because they're so small, they're easier to control than the larger primates. And the capuchins are already famous for serving humans in a special way—by doing tricks and collecting money for organ grinders.

Dr. Willard spent about a year using be-

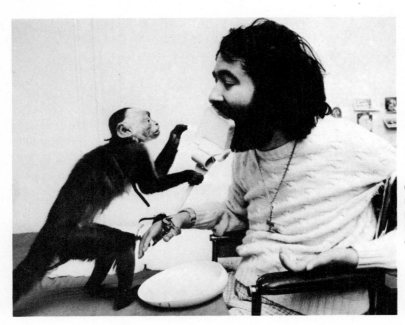

Crystal, one of the capuchin monkeys, did very well in the experiment. She learned to do simple things around the house and even help feed her master.

86

Tish, another capuchin monkey, helps her master adjust the window shade. But the experiment with Tish did not work out and was canceled after 3 months.

havior modification to train two capuchins as helpers. One of the monkeys, Crystal, has done pretty well. Her master had been paralyzed from the shoulders down in an accident about ten years earlier. After living with him for about six months, Crystal was able to follow his orders to turn lights on or off, open doors, fetch and return small items, and even put records on. Crystal also learned how to feed her master, but not very neatly.

Dr. Willard hopes to raise money in order to train more monkeys as helpers. Each animal costs about $350. And each needs a cage and special food dispenser. But even though the cost of one of the helping-hand monkeys is high, it is much less expensive than the cost of hiring human helpers.

The savings in money would not be the only benefit of the helping-hand monkeys. Perhaps more important, they would help their masters become less dependent on other people. Continually having to ask others for help with little things is difficult to do. It's much easier to give an order to a monkey. Not every paralyzed person would want to live with a monkey. But for those who do, the little capuchins may offer some very valuable assistance.

DAVID J. KULL
Senior Associate Editor
Medical Laboratory Observer magazine

"TALKING" WITH THE ANIMALS

American Sign Language is a "language" in which hand signs are used to communicate. It is no harder to learn than any other language. Hundreds of thousands of people, including many children, have learned it since it was invented to help the deaf communicate. What, then, is so special about an 8-year-old in San Francisco using the hand signs to talk with friends? This 8-year-old is a gorilla named Koko! And some scientists believe that she is the first animal ever to have a real conversation with humans.

Until recently, most people thought that only humans had the ability to use and understand language. Hardly anyone believed it was possible to talk with animals. But many scientists tried. And they usually tried with primates.

Primates include all animals that can stand on two feet and use their hands for grasping. That means apes, monkeys, baboons, chimpanzees, gorillas, and, of course, humans. Since humans and the subhuman primates are alike in some ways, perhaps they also share the gift of speech, some scientists thought.

The first attempts to teach subhuman primates to talk didn't work very well. After years of practice, the most talkative chimpanzee, a 6-year-old named Viki, was able to say only four words. They didn't sound much like human words, either, and Viki certainly didn't use them in real conversations. The researchers decided that subhuman primates would never learn to speak because they could not make the right sounds. Their voice boxes were not enough like humans' to form words.

Then two scientists who were watching a movie of Viki trying to talk made an important discovery. They noticed that whenever the chimp tried to say a word, she moved her hands in a certain way. Maybe Viki was trying to make signs for the words. That idea led to another. Even though chimpanzees could not speak, they still might be able to learn a language—sign language.

The two scientists, R. Allen and Beatrice Gardner, decided to test their idea using a chimp named Washoe. The Gardners taught Washoe word-signs taken from American Sign Language, called Ameslan for short. They showed her objects and guided her hands into the positions that stood for the words. It was slow work, but after about two years Washoe knew signs for 34 words.

Koko the gorilla is being told the story _The Three Little Kittens_. Koko is using the sign for "mad," referring to the mother cat in the story.

A chimp named Nim has been taught to communicate using word-signs. Left: Nim signs "red," in response to the teacher's signing "color?" Right: Nim is signing "eat."

After another year she was up to 85 words. And by the time she was 6 years old, after four years of study, she could use 132 signs.

But could Washoe really use language? Naming objects and carrying on a conversation are two very different things. Using language means putting words together in sentences to express an idea. If the language's rules of grammar are not followed, the words cannot make sense.

Take the words "hit," "you," and "ball." You can put them together in several ways. You might say, "You hit ball," or "Ball hit you." As any baseball player will tell you, the two sentences mean very different things. Even though you might know the meaning of each individual word, you won't understand the sentences unless you know the rules of grammar. In this case, you know that the thing that does the hitting comes first. The object that gets hit follows.

All languages, including Ameslan, have many rules like that. People who know the rules can talk about things that happened in the past or things that will happen in the future. They can even talk about imaginary things, things they've made up themselves.

Did Washoe understand and use any of Ameslan's rules of grammar? Or did she only understand the words? Sometimes Washoe did group words in ways that seemed to make sense. Some scientists thought these groups were real sentences. Others weren't so sure.

While other scientists were also trying to communicate with chimpanzees, psychologist Francine Patterson decided to try teaching sign language to another kind of primate—a gorilla named Koko.

Gorillas are big and often unfriendly. But Koko was not only very easy to get along with, she learned signs quickly. And Koko's use of Ameslan seems more like real conversation than Washoe's. Koko regularly uses nearly 400 signs. According to Patterson, Koko has used signs to talk about past events, and even to tell fibs. Telling tales isn't the nicest thing you can do with language. But since it takes imagination, it's one of the most difficult.

Sometimes Koko uses the signs to tell jokes.

"That red," Koko once signed while playing with a white towel.

"You know better, Koko," a human friend signed back. "What color is it?"

"Red, red, red," Koko insisted. Then she smiled and held up a speck of red fabric that had been stuck to the towel.

Koko now shares a specially designed trailer home with another gorilla, a young male named Michael. Patterson and other scientists are continuing their sign-language lessons. They are also trying to teach gorillas to "talk" using artificial voices operated by typewriter keyboards. And other researchers are working with other primates in various kinds of language experiments.

WORLD OF SCIENCE

This incredible picture of Jupiter was taken by a Voyager spacecraft in 1979. Two Jovian moons can be seen orbiting the planet. On the right is Europa, and on the left is Io, near the famous Red Spot.

PROBING THE PLANETS

When future histories are written, 1979 will go down as one of the great years of exploration. In a single year we took our first close looks at three planets—Jupiter, Venus, and Saturn—and more than half a dozen moons.

▶ **KING OF THE PLANETS**

In Roman mythology, Jupiter was the king of the gods. Today's Jupiter is the king of the planets. It is so huge that it would take 1,000 Earths to fill it up.

Jupiter is a cold, distant world whose atmosphere (like the sun's) is made up mainly of hydrogen and helium, two light gases that are the most abundant elements in the universe. Despite its great size, Jupiter spins quickly, rotating on its axis once every ten hours. Its great rotational forces pull its atmosphere into planet-wide bands of colored clouds parallel to the equator. Deep below the clouds is a huge core of compressed solid hydrogen so dense that it acts like a metal. Electric currents flowing through this core generate the intense magnetic field that makes Jupiter the noisiest radio transmitter in the solar system.

Jupiter is more than just the largest planet of our solar system. To space scientists, it is like a huge laboratory for studying how atmospheres circulate, how stars are born, what magnetism is, and perhaps even how life came into being. In 1979, scientists spent a great deal of time studying the planet. Two Voyager spacecraft streaked close by Jupiter on March 5 and July 9, after two-year journeys through space. Each brief flyby sent back to Earth vast streams of data, including almost 20,000 pictures. The pictures came in so fast that scientists

In the pictures taken by the Voyager cameras, Jupiter's Red Spot appears as a huge whirling storm. Around it are smaller white ovals about the size of Earth.

rarely had time to say more than "Oh, wow!" and "Look at that!"

Jupiter's atmosphere, which seems stable and permanent to Earth-bound eyes, becomes a living, changing thing in the Voyager pictures. Enormously powerful winds create saw-toothed waves of turbulence along the bands of clouds. Huge white plumes erupt from below the clouds and spread long trails around the planet. The famous oval Red Spot, observed from Earth for three centuries, can be seen as a huge whirling storm. Around the storm dance smaller white ovals about the size of Earth.

Even the night side of Jupiter isn't quiet. In the darkness, Voyager's cameras saw shining layers of auroras far greater than Earth's northern lights, and they caught the flashes of titanic lightning bolts among the clouds.

Even more spectacular were the closeup views of Jupiter's moons. This was especially true of the four large "Galilean" satellites—Io, Europa, Ganymede, and Callisto—first seen by Galileo in 1610. These four Jovian moons are all different—different from Earth's moon, different from one another, and different from what scientists had expected.

Io, the innermost of the four, was the biggest surprise of the mission. It is a mottled red-orange world with more than 100 volcanoes. Seven of them were erupting violently, hurling long plumes of sulfur above the surface, as the Voyagers passed by.

Europa, the next moon outward, is an amazingly smooth world. It is crisscrossed by very long dark lines, which may be healed cracks in an icy crust.

Ganymede is the largest moon—larger even than the planet Mercury. It seems somewhat like our own moon. It has bright and dark regions and craters on its surface. But Ganymede is a lightweight world, so light that it must be a "snowball moon," made up of a mixture of ice and rock.

Callisto, the outermost large moon, is a brownish "snowball" that has the most intensely cratered surface of all the moons. Callisto's surface may have been shaped by a heavy meteorite bombardment that occurred at the very beginning of the solar system, 4,500,000,000 (billion) years ago.

Io is a red-orange moon with erupting volcanoes.

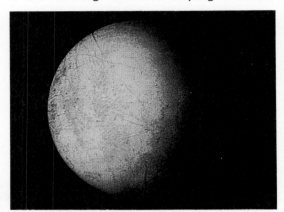

Europa is smooth, crisscrossed by long dark lines.

Ganymede is cratered and has bright and dark areas.

Callisto is Jupiter's most heavily cratered moon.

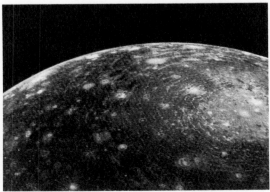

93

Callisto also carries what may be the largest meteorite impact crater anywhere—a multi-ringed basin big enough to hold most of the United States.

The Voyagers found something else circling Jupiter. They discovered a ring made up of tiny particles, much like the rings circling Saturn. But Jupiter's ring is too thin to be visible from Earth. And while scanning the ring, the Voyagers discovered another moon—the fourteenth known so far.

▶ A SMALL INFERNO

Jupiter is a frozen giant, but Venus is a small inferno. A thick yellow-white atmosphere shrouds the face of the world once thought to be Earth's twin. At the surface the temperature is hot enough to melt lead, and the atmospheric pressure is 90 times as great as Earth's.

Since December, 1978, the Pioneer Venus Orbiter has circled this hot world,

sampling the outer fringes of the atmosphere and sending radar beams through the clouds to map the unknown surface below.

Venus' atmosphere is unearthly—almost entirely carbon dioxide (96 percent), with minor amounts of nitrogen, water, and sulfur dioxide. The clouds that permanently hide Venus consist of five layers. On top is a very hazy layer of sulfuric acid "smog"; below this are three distinct layers of dense clouds. Below these clouds is another hazy layer, and then relatively clear air down to the scorching surface.

The thick clouds trap the sun's heat, and this solar energy then makes the atmosphere circulate. The Orbiter's instruments could see great swirls of clouds racing across the face of Venus. A great cloudy "Y" shape forms at the equator, stretches around the whole planet, breaks up into ripples, and forms again, all in a few days' time. Around Venus' North Pole is a huge whirlpool,

Swirls of clouds race across Venus and form a great cloudy "Y" at the equator.

94

Saturn seems to be a smaller, colder, less colorful version of Jupiter.

where a collar of cooler clouds surrounds a torrent of hotter air rushing inward and downward toward the planet's surface.

Seen dimly by radar, the surface of Venus looks like a place to teach geology to giants. On the hot, waterless surface is an enormously long, wide valley. It was not formed by a river but was probably ripped open by the same kind of strong crustal forces that shaped Earth. A huge plateau named Maxwell towers over the surface, dwarfing even the Earth's Himalaya mountains. And gigantic circular mountains may be the largest volcanoes in the entire solar system.

▶ THE RINGED PLANET

On September 1, a tired little spacecraft reached the end of a six-year journey and took the first close look at the distant ringed planet Saturn. Traveling by way of the asteroid belt and Jupiter, Pioneer 11 (now Pioneer Saturn) shot under the huge rings of Saturn, ducked behind the planet, and came safely out again. Its battery of instruments scanned the planet, the rings, and some of Saturn's moons.

The gaseous planet Saturn is so light that it would float in water if we had a bathtub big enough. Saturn seems to be a smaller, colder version of Jupiter. But where Jupiter is colorful, Saturn is a little dull. Saturn's clouds have no distinct colored bands, only varying yellow and brown hues in which some vague bands can be seen. Saturn's magnetic field is both weaker and more orderly than Jupiter's. It is much stronger than Earth's magnetic field but far weaker than scientists had expected.

Skimming along below Saturn's rings, Pioneer discovered two new rings. Then it took a quick glance at Saturn's largest moon, Titan. This moon intrigues scientists because it has a thick, orange-tinted atmosphere that may contain organic molecules, the building blocks of life. Pioneer's one picture of Titan shows a blurred, peach-colored globe. Better pictures are expected when the Voyager 1 spacecraft passes by Saturn on November 13, 1980.

BEVAN M. FRENCH
Discipline Scientist, Planetary Materials
National Aeronautics and Space Administration

95

SPACE BRIEFS

The 77-ton Skylab spacecraft was the first U.S. space station. It had circled Earth for more than six years. And it had been a home to three crews of U.S. astronauts. But by 1978, it was apparent to scientists that Skylab—the largest satellite ever put into space—was falling. The National Aeronautics and Space Administration (NASA) tried desperately to keep Skylab aloft until a space shuttle mission could push it into a higher orbit. However, NASA gave up the struggle, and for the first six months of 1979, Skylab dropped steadily. Each orbit was a little lower than the last. Tracked by powerful radars, Skylab's slow descent was marked by a flurry of concern about where it would enter the atmosphere and burn up—and if anyone would be harmed by its scattering debris.

On July 11, NASA made a final adjustment to Skylab's 34,981st orbit, hoping to bring the space station down over the South Atlantic Ocean, away from land. But as a NASA official said, "We had a tougher bird than we expected." Refusing to break up, Skylab crossed the South Atlantic intact and passed over the Indian Ocean. At last

Skylab did break up, and it dropped to a flaming, thundering death over Australia. It lit up the Australian midnight sky "like a train on fire," and shattered the silence with tremendous sonic booms. There was a worldwide sigh of relief when the scattered pieces crashed to Earth without causing any injury or damage.

Skylab scattered itself across Australia along a track about 100 miles (160 kilometers) wide and 2,000 miles (3,200 kilometers) long. A new "gold rush" started as hundreds of souvenir hunters dashed out into Australia's desolate scrublands to find pieces.

Although no one was injured by Skylab, at least two people had their lives changed by it. A baby born in India a few hours earlier was promptly named Skylab Singh. And a 17-year-old Australian carried a piece of Skylab by jet to the office of a San Francisco newspaper just in time to win a $10,000 prize.

▶ AND THE SOVIETS SET ANOTHER RECORD

Three days after Skylab had crashed to Earth, two Soviet cosmonauts set a new

This chunk of Skylab was one of many pieces that scattered across Australia when the huge space station broke up and crashed to Earth.

96

Soviet cosmonauts Valery Ryumin and Vladimir Lyakhov set a new space endurance record of 175 days.

record for continuous living in space. On July 14, Vladimir Lyakhov and Valery Ryumin, circling Earth in the Salyut 6 space station, broke the old endurance record of 140 days. That record had been set in 1978 by two other cosmonauts, also in Salyut 6.

Lyakhov and Ryumin stayed up a full 175 days and returned safely to Earth on August 19. Although they had some trouble at first with Earth's gravity, Soviet doctors concluded that they were in fine shape after almost six months in space.

Salyut 6 has become a near-permanent space station. Launched in 1977, it has already been lived in more than twice as long as Skylab was. Six crews have traveled to it and returned in two-person Soyuz spacecraft, and five automated Progress spacecraft have carried up supplies and mail. At the end of 1979, Salyut 6 was empty. But its high orbit (much higher than Skylab's) will keep it up long enough to be lived in by many future crews.

▶ SS 433—A "DISCO STAR"?

Quasars, pulsars, black holes—now perhaps our first "disco star." This very strange object—called SS 433—has been observed out near the edge of our galaxy. Astronomers are getting feverish trying to explain why the light from SS 433 changes from bluish to reddish and back again. Its red color indicates that it is moving away from Earth. But its blue color indicates that it is moving toward Earth. It seems that SS 433 is moving large amounts of matter around very fast. But how?

SS 433 may be something left over from a tremendous supernova explosion that took place about 40,000 years ago. One idea is that it really is a "disco star"—a small object like a neutron star or a black hole, surrounded by a flat disk of gas. Both star and disk are spinning so fast that gas is shot from the edge of the disk and into space—at one quarter the speed of light!

Don't expect the "disco fever" to end soon. Old records show that SS 433 has been doing its thing for at least 50 years.

▶ PLUTO: NOT SO FAR OUT

Want to win bets from your friends? Here's a good question: What's the farthest planet from the sun? Pluto, right? Wrong. On January 22, 1979, Pluto, moving along its unusually elongated orbit, actually passed inside the orbit of Neptune. It does this once every 248 years and remains there for twenty years. Now Neptune is the farthest planet from the sun. On March 14, 1999, Pluto will move outside Neptune's orbit and will again be the farthest planet out—for another 228 years.

BEVAN M. FRENCH
Discipline Scientist, Planetary Materials
National Aeronautics and Space Administration

97

THE UNENDING WAR WITH THE INSECTS

Insects are the most successful living things. There are more different kinds, or species, of insects than of all other living things put together. There may be as many as a billion billion insects living in the world right now.

Most insects are useful. They produce honey, wax, and silk. They pollinate plants. They are food for songbirds and other animals. Only about one species out of a thousand is troublesome, but those insects are very troublesome. Some bite us; some carry diseases like malaria and yellow fever; some eat things we value; some destroy our trees.

Since human beings developed agriculture about 10,000 years ago, insects have become even more troublesome. We grow crops in row upon row over thousands of acres. The insects that feed on our crops have the kind of food they need in quantities that they would never find in nature. And so they multiply enormously. When insects are particularly numerous and eat too much of our crops, people in the area face famine.

Because of all these things, there has been warfare between human beings and insects for a very long time. You can't kill insects with spears or arrows, or even with guns. But what about poison? Before World War II, plants were sprayed with Paris green or other mineral poisons. Such a poison didn't interfere with the plants as long as it stayed on the leaves. And it killed any insects that tried to eat the plants.

The rain, however, washed the plants and carried some of the poison down to the soil. There it was absorbed by the plants' roots, and it poisoned the plants. These mineral poisons were also deadly to human beings. Foods that had been sprayed with them had to be carefully washed before being eaten. And since mineral poisons were harmful to humans, they couldn't be sprayed directly on people to protect them from disease-carrying insects.

In 1939, a new kind of pesticide was discovered. It is known by the abbreviated name of DDT. DDT was cheap and odorless, and it seemed to kill insects without much bother to other forms of life. It could even be used directly on human beings. In 1943, a plague of typhus, spread by lice in clothing, was stopped in its tracks by the use of DDT. With the use of DDT and similar pesticides, it seemed as if the war against the insects had been won. There were, however, several problems.

For one thing, these pesticides didn't kill all insects of a particular species. Some just happened to have been resistant, or immune, to the pesticide. The resistant insects gave rise to young that inherited the resistance. Pretty soon, the pesticide was having a weaker effect. More of it had to be used . . . then still more.

Even though these pesticides seemed to have little effect on other creatures, the effect did build up as more and more was used. Birds began to die off and useful or pleasant species of insects, such as bees and butterflies, were affected. Because of these problems, DDT is no longer sold in the United States.

And so we are once again at war with the insects. Today there are a number of other strategies that we are using or that are being further developed:

• Instead of spraying whole fields, we can spray just where we know the insects are. In that way less pesticide can be made to do more work.

• We can take advantage of chemicals produced by the insects themselves. Insects have within their bodies substances, called hormones, that regulate growth. If the hormones are isolated and synthesized, they can be used as sprays to disrupt insect growth and kill them. This would affect only the insects that have these hormones, and no other species.

• Just as some insects are not affected by poison, some plants are not affected by insects. These plants can be grown and further bred for resistance.

• Insects have their enemies. They are eaten by other insects, by birds, by lizards, and so on. They can also be harmed by bacteria and viruses. If the proper insect enemies are introduced into an area, the numbers of insects could drop drastically.

SOME WAYS TO CONTROL INSECT PESTS

Spray just where the insects are.

Use hormones to kill certain kinds.

Breed plants that are insect-resistant.

Introduce insect enemies to an area.

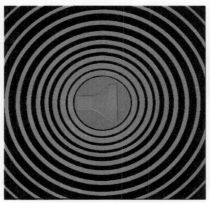
Send out ultrasonic squeaks.

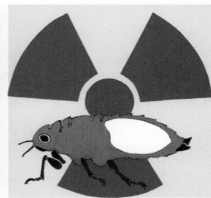
Use radiation to make insects sterile.

• Bats eat insects. They locate an insect by first emitting very shrill ultrasonic squeaks (squeaks that cannot be heard by humans). If there is an insect nearby, the sound "bounces off" it and creates an echo—telling the bat where it is. Naturally, insects instinctively avoid such a sound. Perhaps we could set up a device that would send out ultrasonic squeaks, which would keep insects away.

• Insects are attracted by certain chemicals. Female insects give off tiny quantities of chemicals called pheromones, which attract male insects. Scientists can now synthesize pheromones in the laboratory. Maybe they could place pheromones in certain designated areas where pesticides had been sprayed. Then, male insects would be attracted there and killed by the pesticides.

• Male insects can be subjected to radioactivity or to certain chemicals that make them sterile. The sterile males are then released into the environment. They are thus unable to fertilize the females' eggs. The eggs do not develop and no new insects are produced.

No doubt, still other strategies will be devised. And although each one may have its disadvantages, a combination of them would leave us in no danger of being destroyed by insects. On the other hand, it isn't likely that anything we do will lead to complete victory. The war between human beings and insects shows no signs of ending in the foreseeable future.

ISAAC ASIMOV
Associate Professor of Biochemistry
Boston University School of Medicine

The great inventor Thomas Edison created the first practical electric light bulb.

ONE HUNDRED YEARS OF LIGHT

One afternoon many years ago, a worker in Thomas Edison's New Jersey laboratory reported that an idea for a new invention wasn't working out. "Mr. Edison, we have tried a thousand things that have failed," the discouraged worker said. "We should give up."

Thomas Edison fixed his eyes firmly on the man and replied: "No, my good fellow, we haven't failed. We now *know* a thousand things that *won't* work."

That attitude of never giving up on a good idea may explain why Edison succeeded in developing the first practical electric light bulb, while other scientists failed.

It was on October 21, 1879, that Edison and his assistants unveiled their new invention—an incandescent light bulb. (An incandescent bulb is one in which a thread, or filament, is heated by electricity until it glows brightly.) Edison's first electric light bulb lasted only 40 hours. By today's standards that's not very long. But it was a record for that time. More important, the bulb invented by Edison worked well enough to usher in the age of electric lighting.

In 1979, people all over the world cele-brated the 100th anniversary of the creation of Edison's incandescent lamp. There were special ceremonies, exhibits, and scientific conferences. And on October 21, a centennial celebration for the famed inventor was held at the National Inventors Hall of Fame in Arlington, Virginia. The Inventors Hall of Fame was established in 1973, and Edison was the first inductee.

Edison's achievement was not his alone, however. Other scientists played an important role. As far back as the early 1800's, Sir Humphrey Davy, a noted British scientist, used electricity to produce light. Some 60 years later, a Belgian engineer designed an electric generator that could produce enough current to make electric lighting practical.

Still other researchers worked on the idea of an incandescent bulb. An English inventor named Joseph Swan developed a successful incandescent lamp using a carbon filament. But the carbon burned too quickly, and the bulb didn't give light for very long.

By the time Edison began his own work on the electric light, all the information necessary to make an incandescent lamp was known. But no one had come up with a filament material that was inexpensive and long-lasting.

That was to be Edison's achievement. He developed a filament that lasted more than a few hours. But it wasn't easy. Edison spent long hours trying all sorts of materials, including a whisker from an assistant's beard. Finally, the inventor found something that worked perfectly—a piece of his wife's sewing thread. When the thread was carbonized—heated until it turned into carbon—it proved to be an excellent filament, glowing for nearly two days.

Developing a practical electric light bulb that could replace gas and kerosene lamps was only the beginning. Edison's further accomplishment was the creation of an entire lighting system. He designed powerful electric generators, as well as switches, circuits, and just about every other piece of equipment needed to send electric current for lighting into homes and factories.

In time, tungsten filaments replaced the carbonized thread and bamboo wood used in the early light bulbs. And there have been other changes and improvements over the years. The original glass bulbs were hand blown, which was a long and costly process. Now there are machines that can turn out thousands of bulbs a minute. And today's bulb is sturdier, lasts longer, and gives off brighter light while using less electricity.

New light bulbs are constantly being developed. One that holds great promise for the future is a high-pressure sodium discharge bulb. In this bulb, metallic sodium is turned into vapor by using heat under high pressure. Electric current is then passed through the vapor, producing a strong, yellowish light.

The high-pressure sodium bulb is expensive to produce. If it were put on the market now, a single bulb would cost $15. But such a bulb might last from five to ten years, and it would use much less electricity than a normal incandescent bulb.

So as the electric light bulb celebrated its 100th birthday, work to improve it went on. If Edison were alive, he would surely approve of the long way it has come.

Edison's 1879 light bulb burned for only 40 hours. But it ushered in the age of electric lighting.

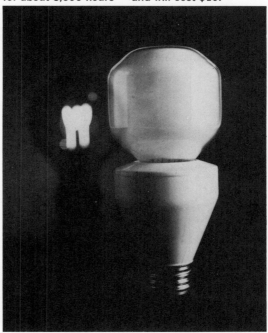

This light bulb that was introduced in 1979 will burn for about 5,000 hours—and will cost $10.

The most typical underground home is one that is dug into a hill.

LIVING UNDERGROUND

Elementary-school students in Reston, Virginia . . . Alice in Wonderland . . . 2,000 workers in Kansas City . . . early cave dwellers . . . thousands of Montrealers. All these people have something in common—part of their day was or is lived under the ground.

The children in Virginia go to Terraset Elementary School, a school that has been built inside a hill. The 2,000 workers in Kansas City have jobs in an industrial park that is 40 to 75 feet (12 to 23 meters) below the surface of the ground. The thousands of Montrealers are shopping in Place Ville-Marie, several blocks of stores buried under busy city streets. And they're not alone. All over the world, people are going underground to homes, schools, offices, factories, and shopping centers.

▶ WHY BUILD UNDER THE GROUND?

This revolutionary architecture isn't really new at all. The cave dwellers started it,
and underground structures have existed for centuries in China, Turkey, Spain, and Tunisia. But we are rediscovering something that was known thousands of years ago—that soil is an excellent moderator of temperature extremes. The soil surrounding an underground structure is like a big energy-conserving envelope.

If you dig deep enough into the earth, the temperature barely changes. At 10 feet (3 meters) down, the temperature stays about 50°F (10°C). So it never gets really hot or really cold in an underground house, no matter what the temperature is above ground.

That stable, moderate temperature is one of the major advantages of building homes and other structures under the ground. By eliminating the highs and lows of climate, the heating and cooling systems in an underground home do not have to work so hard. It takes a lot less fuel to maintain a comfortable temperature in an underground home

These underground apartments were built inside a sand dune in Florida. The giant windows look out over the sea and let light into the homes.

All you can see of this underground home is its sunken courtyard, which is surrounded by the rooms.

than it takes to warm up a conventional house in winter or cool it off in summer.

Many underground homes also have rooftop solar collectors, still another way to conserve energy. Going under can mean energy savings as high as 75 percent, some underground advocates claim. That means a drastic cut in your fuel bills. It seems that building underground is good for world ecology and for the homeowner's pocketbook, too.

And there are other advantages. When you live underground, there is very little outside maintenance of your home. Gone forever are the jobs of painting the outside of the house, repairing that frozen water pipe, and replacing shingles on the roof. (But you may have to *mow* your roof.)

If you're located a little too close to an airport, railroad, or busy highway, you won't be bothered by the noise. Thanks to sound-deadening properties of the soil, one of the first things you'll notice when you enter an underground house is how quiet it is.

An underground home is more fireproof than a conventional above-ground home. And if you live in an area that is hard-hit by storms and tornadoes, you will be comfortable down in your home as the weather rages above you.

But what if you enjoy the pleasure of looking out windows at trees and the sky? Will you miss the beauty of nature when your house is buried in the landscape instead of being perched up on top? What is it like to live in an underground house?

▶ LIFE UNDER THE GROUND

When most people think of "underground," they think of subways, spooky caves, or a basement. Words like damp, dark, and clammy come to mind. Images of bats, spiders, and slimy things are also associated with the underground. But underground homes are nothing like that. And because the term "underground" has an unpleasant sound to most people, architects use other words to describe subterranean homes. Labels such as "terratecture," "earth architecture," and "earth-covered" or "earth-sheltered" housing are used.

Inside underground homes, the air is fresh and dry. There is the same amount of light,

104

Pillow-shaped skylights are the only clues to this house buried in the Wisconsin landscape.

if not more, than in many above-ground homes. And you can look out at the same world that your friends in conventional homes see from their windows. To make this possible, architects have designed many unique features that provide daylight, fresh air, and above-ground visibility throughout the earth-covered homes.

There are actually several kinds of underground structures. In one kind, the earth is excavated and the structure is built below the surface. These homes use light shafts, skylights, or sunken courtyards open to the sky to admit natural light and air. If there is a sunken courtyard, all the rooms have windows and glass sliding doors that open onto it. This eliminates the feeling that you are underground. Forced ventilation and a dehumidifier keep the air inside fresh and dry.

Another kind of underground home is a structure that is built on the surface and then covered with earth. But the most typical underground house is one that is dug into a hill. The south side of the house is exposed. The north side and most of the east and west sides as well as the roof are buried in the hill.

This type of house is designed to take advantage of the sun's changing position in the winter and summer sky. South-facing glass windows and doors bring light and solar heat into the house from winter sun, low in the southern sky. Overhangs constructed over glass windows and doors are used to shade out the high summer sun. Movable shutters are also used to control the amount of solar energy that enters the house.

Of course, as with anything, there are disadvantages. The architecture is basically new and has not yet had a chance to withstand the test of time. Leaking roofs can be an expensive problem. And it's difficult to expand an underground home.

But people familiar with the benefits of underground living see it as the architecture of the future. For economic and ecologic reasons, more and more people are living in earth-sheltered homes. So the next time someone invites you to come *down* to their house, you may *really* be going down.

DIANE STORIN
Sponsoring Editor
Gateways to Science

105

A drawing of what Wolstenholme Towne may have looked like.

A VIRGINIA COLONY, REDISCOVERED

In 1619 some 200 people left England to begin a new life in North America. They traveled to what is now Virginia. There, on the banks of the James River, they built their town. It was named Wolstenholme Towne, after Sir John Wolstenholme, a prominent shareholder in the company that owned the land.

Life in the town was not easy. Many of the settlers died of starvation or illness. Then, in March, 1622, a group of Indians attacked the town, killing 58 residents. Most of the survivors fled down the river, to the colony of Jamestown. Wolstenholme Towne gradually decayed. Plants grew where houses once stood, and people forgot that the town had ever existed.

Today, Wolstenholme Towne is regaining its place in American history. In 1979, Ivar Noël-Hume, chief archeologist of the Colonial Williamsburg Foundation, announced that the town's site had been found and that many artifacts had been uncovered. Among the items found on the site were the only visored military helmets ever found in North America. These helmets were probably meant to protect the settlers in case they were attacked by hostile Indians. However, the helmets cut off side vision and prevented the wearers from hearing, so they were not very useful. Besides, says Noël-Hume, they were very hot: "When you wear one of those in the Virginia summer, you turn into a waffle in about ten minutes."

By studying postholes and other remains of buildings, the archeologists were able to determine the layout of the town. There were homes, stables, a fort, a large warehouse, and buildings where people worked or stored their crops. Although the original Jamestown settlement was begun earlier, nothing of its remains has ever been found. "Thus," says Noël-Hume, "the remains of buildings and artifacts unearthed at Wolstenholme provide us with our earliest evidence of life and death in colonial Virginia."

106

HUNTING FOR SUNKEN TREASURE

The tall sailing ship was laden with silver and gold. It was headed home to Spain when it hit Silver Shoals, a coral reef north of the island of Hispaniola. The year was 1641. The ship was the *Concepción*.

The *Concepción* was wrecked in the accident and sank into the sea. As the years passed it became covered by sediment, and coral grew over its anchor and cannon. People who hoped to recover the silver and gold searched in vain for the ship's remains. They knew the ship was there. But they didn't know its actual location in the long coral reef.

One of the treasure hunters was a Pennsylvanian named Burt Webber, Jr. Ever since he was a boy, Webber had been fascinated by tales of sunken treasure. When he was 16 years old, he learned how to scuba dive. When he turned 20 he began going on expeditions. But he always returned home empty-handed.

Eventually, Webber focused his attention on the *Concepción*. In 1977 he got a large ship and hired divers. He also hired aerial surveyors to make an accurate map of Silver Shoals. For five months he tried, unsuccessfully, to find the wreck. In 1978 he returned. This time he had a very special piece of equipment with him. It was a cesium magnetometer, an instrument that reacts to changes in the earth's magnetic field caused by the presence of iron.

Webber carried the magnetometer into the water and swam through the dense coral forest. Suddenly, lights on the instrument began to change color—an indication that iron was nearby. Webber and the other divers began removing sediment from the area, and then they found their treasure: coins of gold, tons of silver bars, Chinese porcelain, and much, much more.

It will be a while before all the treasure is found. But there is no doubt that Webber has made a very important—and very valuable—discovery. He has also proved an old saying: "When at first you don't succeed, try, try again."

Coins and jewelry found in the remains of the *Concepción,* which sank in 1641.

107

LEARNING MORE ABOUT OUR ANCESTORS

Who were the first humans on Earth? Where and when did they live? What did their ancestors look like?

These are the types of questions asked by paleoanthropologists—scientists who study the fossil remains of humans and humanlike creatures who lived millions of years ago. In 1979, paleoanthropologists announced some new findings in the story of early people.

Mary D. Leakey announced the discovery of humanlike footprints that were about 3,600,000 years old. They are the oldest footprints of humanlike creatures ever found. Leakey and her assistants uncovered the prints in northern Tanzania in Africa. They had been made by two creatures who walked through damp volcanic ash. When the ash dried and hardened, the footprints were preserved.

The prints were made by two creatures walking one behind the other. One was bigger than the other. It had feet that were 8.5 inches (21.5 centimeters) long. The other's feet were 7.3 inches (18.5 centimeters) long. Perhaps they were a male and a female, or a parent and child.

The footprints were very similar to those of people living today. But the creatures were not humans. Humans did not appear until about 2,000,000 years ago—some 1,600,000 years after these footprints were

made. How, then, do scientists know that the prints were made by ancestors of human beings?

There are two important differences between humans and apes. One is that humans walk upright. Studies of the footprints showed that the creatures that made them walked upright, as humans do. The second major difference is that humans have much larger brains. Many scientists believe that the development of the larger brain came after the ability to walk upright. The footprints found in Tanzania confirm this—they are far older than the oldest skulls large enough to be considered human.

Evidence of another ancestor of human beings was announced by Donald C. Johanson and Timothy White. They found fossilized bones of a humanlike creature in Ethiopia. The bones, which were about 3,500,000 years old, made up about 40 percent of the creature's skeleton. Thus, the scientists were able to reconstruct the creature, a female. The scientists called her Lucy. She was about 3½ feet (1 meter) tall. She walked erect and had a small brain. Later, in the same region of Ethiopia, the scientists found the remains of thirteen similar creatures.

In some ways, Lucy and her relatives resembled *Australopithecus africanus,* a crea-

These 3,600,000-year-old footprints were found in northern Tanzania. They were made by two creatures who walked upright. They are believed to be the oldest footprints of humanlike creatures ever found.

108

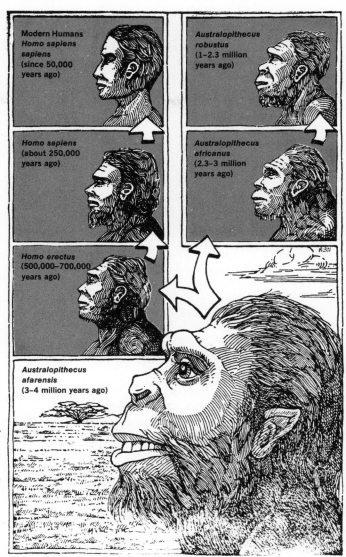

Modern Humans
Homo sapiens sapiens
(since 50,000 years ago)

Australopithecus robustus
(1–2.3 million years ago)

Homo sapiens
(about 250,000 years ago)

Australopithecus africanus
(2.3–3 million years ago)

Homo erectus
(500,000–700,000 years ago)

Australopithecus afarensis
(3–4 million years ago)

The bones of another humanlike creature were found in Ethiopia. Some scientists say that this creature is a new species, *A. afarensis,* and is the common ancestor of *A. africanus* and of modern humans.

ture that lived in eastern Africa between 2,000,000 and 3,000,000 years ago. Johanson and White named Lucy and her relatives *Australopithecus afarensis.* They say that this species is the common ancestor of *A. africanus* and of humans—that from *A. afarensis,* evolution proceeded on two paths. One path led to *A. africanus* and eventually died out. The other path led to modern people.

Not everyone agrees with Johanson and White. Some scientists believe Lucy should be classified as *A. africanus* rather than as a new species.

Also casting doubt on Johanson and White's theory are Mary Leakey and her son Richard, who is also an anthropologist. Richard Leakey says that he is prepared to accept that Lucy is a new species of *Australopithecus,* but that the common ancestor has not yet been found. He believes the common ancestor of the two paths existed much earlier—more than 4,000,000 years ago.

Such differences of opinion are common in anthropology. Only with further study and the finding of more fossils will the controversy be settled.

THE BIG THICKET

There is a mysterious wilderness in eastern Texas. It is a place of amazingly big trees, thick tangled underbrush, and dim spooky swamps where cypress trees sometimes grow right up out of the water. Hidden away among the dense growth are nooks of pleasant open farmland where people live in tiny communities. Birds twitter and tweet. All kinds of animals slither and scurry about. And the various plants are strange and beautiful. This wonderful place is called the Big Thicket.

Once upon a time the Big Thicket was a vast area. But oil drillers and lumbermen cut down large parts, and now it is threatened by land developers. Today less than one tenth of the wilderness remains. So in 1974 the U.S. Congress created the Big Thicket National Preserve to save about 84,500 acres (34,000 hectares) of this precious woodland.

The Big Thicket is precious because it is a naturalists' paradise. Scientists say it is a true "biological crossroads." Within its boundaries are temperate and subtropical habitats of jungle, swamp, woodland, plain, and desert. The Thicket contains samples of eight major kinds of ecological systems (plant and wildlife communities). This phenomenon does not occur anywhere else in the Western Hemisphere.

The northern part of the Thicket has tall beech and loblolly pine forests like those in the Appalachian Mountains—but there they grow in company with magnolia trees of the American southeast. The southern part of the Thicket is an eerie region of swamps, creeks, and bayous, much like Florida's Everglades. Between these two extremes are areas of hardwood trees growing amid dense palmettos; acid bogs and baygalls (tracts of swampy land); dry, sandy lands supporting yucca plants and cactus; two kinds of prairie; and two more kinds of pine forest.

If you visit the Big Thicket, you will be astounded at the great variety of wildlife. There are snakes, alligators, wild hogs, beavers, red wolves, bobcats, and whitetail deer. And among the smaller animals are raccoons, opposums, mink, squirrels, and rabbits.

There are also about 350 species of birds, among them the endangered American bald eagle, the red-cockaded woodpecker, and the Bachman's warbler. Colorful birds like the red cardinal and blue grosbeak can be seen if you keep a sharp eye peeled.

Of the 1,000 species of flowering plants in the Thicket, outstanding are the 30 species of wild orchid. But most amazing are the meat eaters. These plants draw insects and tiny animals into tubes or bladders where the plant digests the creature's meaty parts. The four meat eaters that are native to the Big Thicket are the bladderworts, the sundews, the butterworts, and the yellow pitcher plants.

The Big Thicket is a place of natural riches unmatched in North or South America. To preserve it helps keep alive a very special wonder.

Cypress trees rise from swamps . . . and stands of beech, loblolly, and magnolia grow side by side.

If you're alert, you may spot a bright red cardinal . . . or a hungry raccoon.

Flowering plants abound, like the grass-pink orchid . . . and the yellow pitcher plant.

EINSTEIN—SCIENTIST AND MAN OF PEACE

Albert Einstein was one of the greatest scientists the world has ever known. His theories revolutionized scientific thinking. His theories of relativity formed the basis of our understanding of gravitation and changed the way we view the universe. His explanation of the photoelectric effect led to the discovery of nuclear energy and to the development of lasers, television, and other technological wonders.

Einstein, an important public figure, was also a pacifist—a person who opposed war and supported disarmament. Einstein called for peaceful co-existence and co-operation between nations. "A war is not a parlor game," he said.

This amazing man was born in Ulm, Germany, on March 14, 1879. In 1979 people all over the world celebrated the 100th anniversary of his birth. There were special scientific gatherings, television programs, museum exhibits, new books, and postal stamps.

A bronze monument of Albert Einstein was unveiled in 1979 to commemorate his 100th birthday.

In Washington, D.C., on the grounds of the National Academy of Sciences, a bronze monument by Robert Berks was unveiled. It shows Einstein gazing into space. In the statue's left hand is a tablet containing three of Einstein's formulas. At the figure's feet is a circular map of the universe.

In Princeton, New Jersey, scientists gathered at the Institute for Advanced Study, where Einstein had worked during the last 22 years of his life. The scientists discussed some of the scientific mysteries that still remain to be solved. One of the subjects they discussed was the unified field theory. Einstein had spent many years trying to develop such a theory—one that would include both relativity and the quantum theory. Relativity deals with the stars and galaxies—the big "outer universe." The quantum theory deals with atoms and their particles—the tiny "inner universe." Einstein could not believe that different sets of equations should be needed to explain different aspects of the universe.

He also did not believe that probability (chance) played a role in the quantum theory. Einstein insisted that chance was not involved in the operation of the universe. "God does not play dice with the world," he said.

Most physicists disagreed with Einstein. They did not believe that a unified field theory was possible. Einstein died in 1955, without proving them wrong. But today there is new interest in the field theory, and some physicists suspect that the puzzle that so intrigued Einstein may eventually be solved.

Some scientists also believe that, in time, it may be proved that probability has no place in the quantum theory.

In remembering Einstein, a well-known physicist remarked: "His was a program that was not destined to be successful in his lifetime and may never be, but what he did gave a tremendous push to physical science throughout his whole working life. In a sense, all scientists are the children of Einstein in what they do from day to day.... In short, he lives."

EINSTEIN—THE INVENTOR

Did you know that Albert Einstein was also an inventor? He invented a refrigerator and an electric-eye camera.

On November 11, 1930, the U.S. Patent Office granted Einstein a patent for a refrigerator, or an icebox as it was sometimes called in those days. (It was an interesting coincidence that November 11 was Armistice Day, and Einstein was often hailed as a great peacemaker.) A novel feature of the refrigerator was the use of liquid butane, which turns into a gas to increase efficiency in the cooling operation.

Leo Szilard, a physicist, collaborated with Einstein on the invention. They sold the patent rights to the Electrolux Servel Corporation, which at that time was a large manufacturer of gas-operated refrigerators. Szilard tells the story that all the manufacturers wanted the patent. But they also wanted to advertise it as the "icebox Dr. Einstein has invented." Einstein would never have allowed them to use his name on an icebox, and so a refrigerator with the name Einstein on it was never sold.

On October 27, 1936, Einstein was granted a patent for an electric-eye camera, a camera operated by a photoelectric cell. The camera would enable people to get good pictures without having to worry about timing the exposure. The proper lens opening and exposure would be automatically set.

Einstein had won the 1921 Nobel prize in physics for his discoveries about the photoelectric effect, whereby light is converted into electricity. So it was not too surprising that he applied this knowledge to invent a photoelectric camera. It would use electricity generated by light to power its operation. Thus no battery was needed.

Einstein collaborated on this invention with Gustav Bucky, a radiologist. No one knows whether the two doctors sold the rights to the patent.

You may wonder why Einstein, who always seemed to be involved with complex mathematical formulas and theoretical physics, became interested in making practical inventions. This may have been because of his job as a patent examiner in the Swiss patent office in Bern. Appointed in

Einstein, during the years he worked in the Swiss patent office in Bern as a patent examiner.

1902, Einstein served there for over seven years. His job was to examine patent applications and decide whether to grant patents on them. During that period, Einstein produced some of his greatest ideas—"a series of scientific miracles," he called them. He had a drawer in his desk that he called his "theoretical physics office." He worked on his physics whenever he was finished with his duties of examining patent applications. It was while Einstein was employed at the patent office that he published his special theory of relativity.

Even after Einstein had left the patent office, he maintained a lively interest in patents and inventions. His son, Hans Einstein, said of his father: "It may be somewhat astonishing that a theoretically oriented mind as that of Albert Einstein would be interested in technical matters. But he thoroughly enjoyed learning about clever inventions and solutions, as he had always loved to solve certain types of puzzles. Maybe both, inventions and puzzles, reminded him of the happy, carefree, and successful days at the patent office in Bern, the days before the first World War and all that followed."

HARRY GOLDSMITH
Former patent counsel

113

LEFT-HANDED PEOPLE

Most people use one side of their body —eye, hand, and foot—more than the other. Usually, it's the right side. Certainly the great majority of us write and do almost everything best with the right hand. But nature isn't 100 percent consistent, and about 10 percent of the population do things with the left hand.

Today we don't think bad things about people who are "lefties." But earlier generations viewed them with suspicion and fear. Think about the word "sinister." What image comes to mind—Dracula or some loathsome beast? Well, the word sinister comes from the Latin word *sinister*, which means "left." Since left-handers were thought to be different and strange, many people decided that left-handedness should be changed. Even in this century, attempts were made to reteach lefties. There are still people who remember having their left hand tied down so that they would be forced to use their right hand. Fortunately, this practice stopped when it was discovered that forcing a person to switch hands could lead to stuttering and other disorders.

▶ **WHAT DETERMINES HANDEDNESS?**

The causes of handedness are found in the brain. In a right-handed person, the *left* side of the brain is dominant, while the left-handed person has the *right* side dominant. There is evidence that handedness is inherited, although scientists are not sure just how the trait is passed from parents to children. But scientists *have* discovered that the brain of a lefty is not as specialized as the brain of a right-hander and that lefties seem to use more of their brain than right-handers. One result of this flexibility is that many left-handed children grow up to become ambidextrous adults—they can use both hands equally well for writing and other tasks.

▶ **PROBLEMS, PROBLEMS, PROBLEMS**

Although we don't now try to change a person's handedness, a lefty does have some problems. Life is a series of adjustments. Tools, locks, zippers, jar tops, and many other everyday objects are made to be used with the right hand. Most desks with chairs attached are designed for right-handed writers. The lefty must twist his or her body and drag the writing hand across the page. And try to cut with a pair of scissors designed to be held in the right hand. Then there is the right-handed parent trying to show the left-handed child how to tie a shoe. And the knitter trying to understand instructions written by and for a right-handed knitter.

There are job problems too. In a symphony orchestra, for example, all violinists must use the bow with their right hand. A left-handed violinist seated next to a right-handed one could turn a musical event into a sword fight! Plenty of athletes are left-handed, but few have made their marks as quarterbacks, catchers, or boxers.

▶ FAMOUS LEFTIES

You might think at this point that lefties are losers. But the facts tend to prove just the opposite. Left-handers may be more creative than right-handers. This can't be proved for certain since people don't agree on just what creativity is and how it is measured. But a study at the University of Cincinnati showed that a significantly high percentage of instructors and students in the School of Architecture were left-handed. There also seems to be a large percentage of artists who are or were left-handed. Leonardo da Vinci, Michelangelo, and Pablo Picasso were lefties.

Lefties have also done well in the sports world. In tennis, five of the top players of this decade—Jimmy Connors, Manuel Orantes, Guillermo Vilas, Roscoe Tanner, and John McEnroe—are all lefties. Olympic medalists Mark Spitz, Dorothy Hamill, and Bruce Jenner are also lefties.

Baseball, especially, has had plenty of lefties—Sandy Koufax, Babe Ruth, Whitey Ford. As a matter of fact, the term "southpaw," which means a left-handed person, is believed to have been first used in Chicago in the 19th century to describe a left-handed pitcher. In the Chicago stadium, left-handed pitchers finished their windup with their throwing arm (the left) facing south.

The list of famous lefties can go on and on: Charlie Chaplin, Gerald R. Ford, Pelé, Judy Garland, Harry S. Truman, Benjamin Franklin, Ringo Starr. So if you are a lefty, be proud of it. There is even an organization

"Me 'n' Jackson are exactly the same age. Only he's different. He's LEFT-HANDED!"

just for you. Lefthanders International has more than 3,000 members. Its goal is to make life easier for the lefty. And there are also stores that cater to you, selling left-handed scissors, golf clubs, rulers, guitars, can openers, and notebooks.

▶ ARE YOU SURE YOU'RE RIGHT-HANDED?

Many people who consider themselves to be right-handed are not totally right-sided. Two tests can help determine if you have mixed tendencies, or so-called cross dominance.

1. Using pencil and paper, draw circles with both your left and right hands. If the circles are drawn clockwise by either hand, you have some left-sided tendencies.

2. Punch a small hole in a piece of paper. Keeping both eyes open, locate a small object about 10 feet (3 meters) away. Hold the paper with both hands at arm's length and sight the object through the hole by moving the paper slowly toward your face. If the hole repeatedly ends up in front of your left eye, you are probably left-eyed.

SCIENCE AND MAGIC

Here are two tricks that will entertain and puzzle your family and friends. They look like magic, but they are actually based on scientific principles. So, let's begin your act!

THE ACROBATIC COIN

WHAT YOU NEED

- A large coin
- An empty glass

WHAT YOU DO

1

Tell the audience you've got a challenge for them. Balance the coin on the edge of the empty glass. Ask if anybody wants to try blowing the coin across the top of the glass, over the other side of the rim. Let anyone try. If they don't know the trick, they are unlikely to hit on it by accident. Everyone will have a good laugh as the coin falls inside the glass or onto the table.

2

After a few tries, say that you'll show them how it's done. Bend down so your mouth is nearly on a level with the coin. (The glass should be at the edge of the table.) Then take a deep breath and blow with a burst of air just over the top of the coin and across it. If you've practiced beforehand, the coin will fly straight over the glass.

3

Let people try again if they wish. Almost certainly they will blow *up* or *down* on the coin—neither of which will work.

TIP

There is a knack to this trick: Aim your breath straight to the edge of the coin and blow, not steadily, but in one quick explosion of breath.

HOW IT WORKS

This trick is based on Bernoulli's principle, named after a Swiss scientist and mathematician, Daniel Bernoulli: When a fluid—such as air or water—is moving, its pressure goes down. Thus, the air that passes across the top of the coin has less pressure than the nonmoving air under the coin. There is less pressure pushing down on the coin from above than there is pushing up on the coin from below. This higher pressure underneath lifts the coin while the force of your breath pushes it over the glass.

Bernoulli's principle also accounts for the ability of an airplane wing to lift the plane and keep it up in the air.

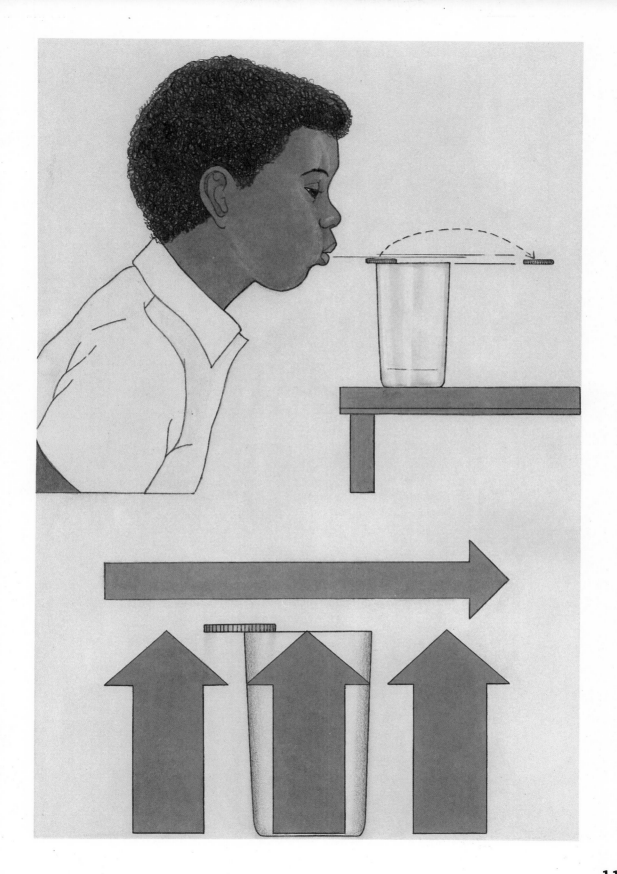

THE RICE BOWL MYSTERY

WHAT YOU NEED

- Enough uncooked rice to fill the bowl to the rim

- A long, wide, blunt-ended knife, like a cake knife

- A small-mouthed jar or bowl whose sides are wider than its mouth—a small fish bowl would be perfect

WHAT YOU DO

1

Ask your audience, "Have you ever heard of the rice bowl mystery?" Show the empty bowl. "Well, first fill up the bowl with rice." Do so until the rice starts to spill over the top. Then press the rice firmly down into the bowl with the palm and heel of your hand. Pack the rice all around the edge.

2

"Now we take a knife and plunge it into the bowl a few times to see if we can get hold of the rice with the blade." Plunge the knife down into the bowl one or two inches (2.5 or 5 cm) in different places. Do this ten times, pretending that you're having a hard time getting a grip.

3

"Oh, let's really bring it down. Maybe the rice will grab hold of the knife." With that, you plunge the knife down hard, more deeply than before, about six inches (15 cm) into the rice. The grains will take hold and you will lift the bowl straight off the table so that it is suspended in the air on the end of the knife!

4

You can ask a member of the audience to come up and hold the knife handle and see how it feels. Say something like, "It's done with mirrors!" That will throw them off the track.

TIP

Practice this trick a lot, and practice over a pillow! Remember to use short, quick stabs at first, a little way down and all around the surface of the rice. *Then* make one deep stab in the middle.

HOW IT WORKS

To understand how this trick works, you must know that there are lots of small spaces between the grains of rice in the bowl. When you stab the knife down, the grains are packed closer together. Each time you stab down, the grains gradually become packed tighter and tighter. When you plunge the knife all the way down, the tightly packed grains hold the knife so firmly that it can be used to lift the entire bowl.

CORN'S PRIMITIVE ANCESTOR

Thousands of years ago, when people first came to the Americas, they found many plants that grew nowhere else. One of these was a grasslike plant with large seeds that could be used as food. At first people simply gathered whatever seeds they could find and ground them to make flour. Eventually, they discovered that the seeds could be used to grow new plants. Each new plant, in turn, produced many seeds. A few seeds could be saved for planting and all the others could be eaten. This was a much more effective way of getting food than wandering around the countryside trying to find seeds.

Thus was agriculture born in the Americas. And the plant with the large seeds became one of the land's most important crops. The plant, of course, is corn.

Corn plants of today are very different from the corn plants of long ago. Both by accident and by design people changed corn. By crossbreeding two types of corn, they produced a third type that had some characteristics of both parents. By planting only seeds from healthy plants, they developed crops that were resistant to disease. As scientific methods were developed, corn was improved even more.

But what of the primitive plants of long ago? Do they still exist? "No," thought scientists. The plants, they believed, were extinct. Imagine, therefore, the excitement caused by a Mexican college student named Rafael Guzmán. In late 1978, he found a primitive form of corn growing in the mountains of southwestern Mexico. He told Hugh H. Iltis, a botanist at the University of Wisconsin, who soon found a second primitive form in the same area.

The primitive corn plants are perennials. They live for many years—unlike modern corn, which lives for just one growing season. If scientists can crossbreed the primitive forms with the modern forms, they may be able to create a type of corn with all the good characteristics of modern corn plus the long life of the primitive corn. This would make it less expensive to grow corn. Farmers wouldn't have to plow and seed their fields every spring. They would save money on energy and fertilizers.

Will scientists be able to achieve this? Dr. Iltis is sure it can be done—"but it will take a while, possibly ten years." That isn't very long when you consider that people have been eating corn for thousands of years.

Scientists are trying to crossbreed modern corn (above) with primitive corn (below) to create corn that will live for many years, not just one growing season.

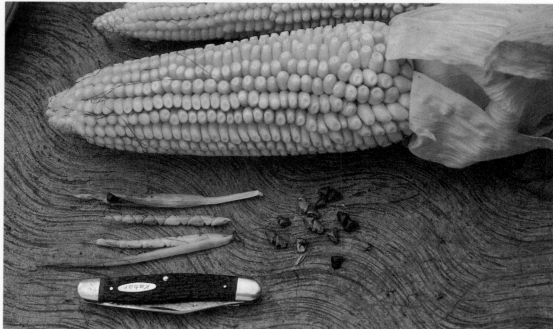

A drawing of the scientists' underwater canyon home.

LIVING UNDERWATER

What is the best way to learn about a place? "Visit it," may seem to be the obvious answer. But there is an even better answer: *live* in the place. This is exactly what scientists have been doing in a Caribbean canyon since 1978. What is unusual is that the canyon is underwater.

The canyon is located at the edge of St. Croix, one of the Virgin Islands that lie east of Puerto Rico. On the canyon floor, about 50 feet (15 meters) below the water's surface, rests the scientists' home. It is a bright yellow tubular structure about 16 feet (5 meters) long and 8 feet (2.5 meters) high. The scientists can look out at their surroundings. And, wearing scuba gear, they can easily swim out of their home and into the warm waters.

Usually, three or four scientists live there at a time. They don't have most of the conveniences that exist on land. But there are comfortable bunk beds, and for entertainment they have a radio and a tape recorder. Their meals consist of freeze-dried foods.

Some of the scientists who spend time in the canyon are biologists. They are interested in the plants and animals that live there. Other scientists are geologists who want to learn more about the sand and other sediment that covers the canyon floor.

The scientists have learned many new things about the canyon environment. For example, they were able to get a close look at a species of octopus that wasn't very well known. Previously, the octopus had only been seen near the water's surface. But the underwater scientists watched the octopus as it shot down through the water and into a home hidden on the ocean floor. This was the first time that anyone had ever seen this kind of octopus use a home.

The biologists recorded the comings and goings of parrotfish—small, brilliantly colored fish with parrotlike beaks. Schools of parrotfish would swim into the canyon in the early evening to sleep in caves in the canyon wall. When daylight came, the fish would leave the canyon. The scientists would follow, to see where the fish went and what they did during the day.

Geologists were interested in the effects of storms on the movement of sediment. They learned that stormy weather could cause major changes in the appearance of the canyon and could have a catastrophic effect on the organisms that lived there.

As one group of scientists finishes its work, it leaves. Another group comes to the canyon, to do new studies and to learn new things about this underwater world.

121

Three Mile Island became the focus of a controversy over the uses of nuclear energy.

NUCLEAR ENERGY: GOOD OR BAD?

On Wednesday, March 28, at 3:53 A.M., a pump failed at the Three Mile Island nuclear power plant, located near Harrisburg, Pennsylvania. Inside the control room, some of the 1,200 lights on the instrument panel blinked red. An electric alarm sounded a warning. This was the beginning of what was to become the worst nuclear accident in U.S. history.

In the days that followed, more information became known. Some radiation had escaped into the air. About half the 36,816 nuclear fuel rods in the reactor core were damaged. And a large hydrogen bubble had formed in the reactor. It could block cooling water from reaching part of the overheated nuclear reactor core.

On Friday, March 30, the governor of Pennsylvania advised pregnant women and preschool children to leave the area because of the high radiation levels. During the week that followed, thousands of people left. Within two weeks, most of them had returned. But the Three Mile Island accident had pushed the nuclear power issue into the front of people's minds. Could nuclear power fill the world's need for inexpensive energy, or did the dangers of nuclear power outweigh the benefits?

▶WHAT NUCLEAR ENERGY CAN DO

Nuclear energy cannot be used to fuel cars, heat homes, or melt the steel used in industry. But it can be used in power plants to generate electricity. When you flip a light switch, turn on a TV, or telephone a friend, you may be using electricity generated at a nuclear power plant.

Electricity is usually generated from steam. Here is how: Water is heated to produce steam; steam is used to drive an electric generator; the generator produces electricity. In most power plants, petroleum, coal, or gas fires provide the heat needed to produce the steam. The special feature of the Three Mile Island plant is that nuclear reactors supply the heat needed to produce the steam. Today, about 12.5 percent of the electricity generated in the United States comes from nuclear power plants.

▶OUT OF THE EARTH...

Nuclear power begins with uranium ore found in the earth's crust. As the ore comes from the earth, it is made up of two isotopes, or forms, of uranium. Uranium 235, which is used for nuclear fuel, makes up less than 1 percent. Uranium 238 makes up 99.3 percent. A series of physical and chemical

122

processes enrich the content of uranium 235 and change the ore into a powder from which uranium pellets are made. Let's take an imaginary trip to the Three Mile Island power plant and see how these tiny, pencil-thin uranium pellets provide energy in the fuel core of the reactor.

▶...TO THE POWER PLANT

Rising above the Susquehanna River, four huge cooling towers announce the presence of the nuclear power plant on Three Mile Island. As you get closer to the island, two high-domed containment buildings can be seen.

Inside the thick concrete walls of each containment building stands a steel bottle that is 40 feet (12 meters) tall. This is the nuclear reactor vessel. Deep inside this steel bottle, submerged under thousands of tons of water, thousands of tiny fuel rods make up the nuclear reactor core. Each fuel rod is filled with about 200 uranium pellets. One pellet can produce as much energy as a ton of coal.

There is a second set of rods, made of cadmium or boron, in the reactor core. These are the control rods. They are raised or lowered to speed up or slow down the rate of nuclear fission.

To start the nuclear reaction, the control rods are raised. The atoms of uranium 235 undergo fission (begin to break up), and produce an enormous amount of heat. In reactors like the one at Three Mile Island, water circulates through the core. This water absorbs heat from the uranium rods, and its temperature rises to 600°F (315°C). The water also becomes radioactive in passing through the core. The hot, radioactive water is pumped through a set of pipes, called the primary loop, into a chamber called a steam generator. Here the heat, passing out of the walls of the pipe, heats a second batch of water to the boiling point, producing steam. The steam flows through a secondary loop to a turbine to generate electricity. A third loop of water carries the excess heat to the cooling towers, where it passes into the air.

A computer is programmed to drop the control rods into the core if there is trouble in the reactor. If the temperature rises too high, an emergency core cooling system dumps thousands of gallons of water on the hot core. There is no danger that a nuclear plant can explode like an atomic bomb. But there can be steam explosions, which could release radioactivity into the air. The worst kind of trouble is a "meltdown" accident. If this happens, the fuel would melt through

DESIGN OF THREE MILE ISLAND REACTOR

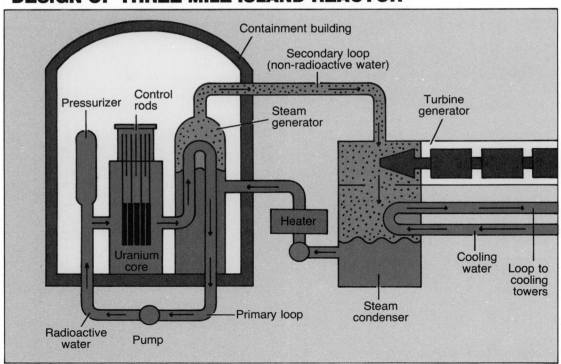

the floor of the containment building into the ground. There could be great loss of life, a great increase in the number of cancer cases, and contamination of land and water in areas far away from the nuclear plant.

Most people did not expect trouble at Three Mile Island. But on March 28 and the days that followed, a series of mechanical and human errors occurred. These included the failure of a reactor pump, stuck valves, and a serious loss of radioactive water coolant. Also, scientists were confused about the various alarms and instrument readings. At Three Mile Island, some of the safety systems were not as safe as people thought.

▶ THE FUTURE OF NUCLEAR ENERGY

The arguments about nuclear power are not new, but public debate has grown as a result of Three Mile Island. In many countries of the world, people have taken over reactor sites or marched in peaceful demonstrations to show their feelings about nuclear energy.

The supporters of nuclear energy say atomic plants are necessary to solve the energy problems of the world. They say nuclear energy offers clean, cheap, efficient power free of foreign control. To these people, the end of nuclear power means energy shortages and economic disaster. But critics of nuclear energy say the dangers that are a necessary part of a nuclear power plant make nuclear energy unsafe at any price. They say our energy problems can be solved with renewable natural resources like solar energy.

The nuclear power issues are complicated. The stakes are high. What exactly are the safety issues? Can they be solved?

Nuclear Waste Disposal. The safe disposal of nuclear waste is thought to be the toughest problem facing the nuclear industry. Each year one third of the fuel rods in a commercial reactor must be replaced. Most of the spent fuel rods are being stored temporarily in underwater tanks at the reactor sites. Scientists cannot agree how long-term isolation can be achieved. Some scientists suggest "burying" the wastes deep in the earth in salt mines, or in seabeds under the oceans. Others talk of disposal in Antarctic ice sheets. Still others suggest launching the wastes into space. The most promising solution seems to be burying the spent fuel rods in stainless steel containers deep in the earth. But so far no place has been agreed upon as a nuclear burial ground.

Opponents of nuclear energy say there is no way to be sure that any storage place will be safe for the thousands of years it takes for the radioactivity to decay to the point where it is no longer dangerous. Future generations will have to deal with the problem. Supporters of nuclear energy say we have the technology to solve all the problems of waste disposal.

Transportation. Nuclear fuel must be carried

The China Syndrome, starring Jack Lemmon and Jane Fonda, was a 1979 movie about an accident at a nuclear power plant. It opened just eleven days before the Three Mile Island accident, and some of the incidents of both dramas were amazingly similar.

from manufacturing sites to nuclear plants. Nuclear wastes must be carried to disposal sites. Opponents of nuclear energy say that trucks, trains, and boats carrying nuclear fuel or wastes can have accidents. Many cities and towns now ban the transportation of nuclear materials. Supporters of nuclear energy say that accident-proof containers are being developed for use in transporting radioactive materials.

The Nuclear Plant. Another safety issue is the nuclear plant itself. The nuclear plant is built to last about 35 years. Then it must be either torn down or sealed so that no radiation escapes. Thus the plant becomes part of the waste disposal problem.

Some people do not want nuclear plants to be located near densely populated areas. Other opponents point to the fact that some plants are located near geologically unsuitable areas. For example, the Diablo Canyon nuclear plant in California is a few miles from a geologic fault that may produce a serious earthquake. Plant officials say that the plant can withstand such an event.

Opponents of nuclear energy fear that the worst kind of accident—such as a meltdown — might occur at a nuclear plant. Supporters say that nuclear plant designers have anticipated such possibilities and have provided many back-up emergency systems.

Opponents also fear that terrorists may try to steal nuclear fuel or take over a nuclear plant. Supporters say that this is unlikely. And they point to the strong security systems protecting nuclear plants from sabotage.

Radiation. Nuclear plants do not pollute the air, but they do give off low-level radiation. Radioactive emissions are invisible, odorless, and tasteless. Unfortunately, not enough is known about how much radiation is safe. Scientists are concerned about the health risks connected with long exposure to low-level radiation.

Supporters of nuclear energy point out that there have been no known deaths from the operation of a nuclear plant. They say that human beings are exposed to radiation in the environment all the time. There is low-level radiation from cosmic rays and other natural sources such as concrete, granite, and coal and from manufactured

Canadians protest a proposed nuclear power plant— the world's largest—at Darlington, near Toronto.

sources such as TV sets and X rays, as well as from nuclear power plants.

Opponents say that many radioisotopes continue to radiate for very long periods of time, and they will remain with us for thousands of generations. They point out that low-level radiation effects are often felt by future generations. Cancer and genetic damage are two long-term effects of low-level radiation.

In October, in the midst of the controversy, a special presidential commission on the Three Mile Island accident released its report. It stated that basic changes would have to be made in the construction, operation, and regulation of nuclear reactors if the risks were to be kept at a minimum. It also stated that even if all the commission's recommendations were met, there was "no guarantee that there will be no serious future nuclear accidents."

There are no easy answers to the questions raised by nuclear energy. Until recently, the nuclear industry was booming. Now its future is in doubt. Will it recover from its current troubles? There is no way of knowing how the situation will turn out. But there is one thing we do know—we cannot take nuclear energy for granted again.

DIANE STORIN
Sponsoring Editor
Gateways to Science

125

THE U.S. GEOLOGICAL SURVEY

On a hot August day in 1869, a band of American explorers reached a point along the Colorado River in what is now the state of Arizona. The group of nine men had been exploring the river for 71 days—the first white men ever to venture this far down the Colorado. The long journey had taken its toll. Their clothes were no better than rags; the only food left to them was a little flour, some bacon, and coffee.

The leader of the tiny expedition was Major John Wesley Powell, a former Union Army officer who had become a professor of natural history. Despite the sorry state of his small band, Powell was determined to go on to complete the survey of the unknown reaches of the Colorado River and its mighty canyons.

On August 10, 1869, Powell wrote in his diary report: "We are three quarters of a mile in the depths of the earth and the great river shrinks into insignificance as it dashes its angry waves against the walls and cliffs that rise to the world above. . . . We have an unknown distance yet to run, an unknown river yet to explore."

But go on they did. And when the sur-

vivors completed their exploration a few weeks later, they had made the first significant survey of the Colorado River.

The Powell exploration was one of many mapping and surveying expeditions carried out by private scientific organizations and the U.S. Government in the 1800's. Often it was the U.S. Army that carried out this task. Powell's expedition had been jointly sponsored by the Illinois Natural History Society and the Illinois Industrial University. The U.S. Government contributed food and other supplies, and the Smithsonian Institution provided scientific instruments.

By the 1870's, the need for a federal bureau to map the country and locate mineral resources had become obvious. That need was filled by the creation of the U.S. Geological Survey—a part of the U.S. Department of the Interior—in 1879. One of the Survey's first directors was Major John Wesley Powell, who headed the Survey from 1881 to 1894. Under Powell, the Survey expanded its work to include geology as well as the study of mineral resources.

When the Geological Survey was first organized, it had only 38 employees and a

A Geological Survey scientist uses a data-gathering balloon to find out how mining affects air quality.

A Survey volcanologist monitors a volcanic crater in Hawaii, recording the temperature of the lava.

126

modest budget of about $100,000. In 1979, as the U.S. Geological Survey celebrated its 100th anniversary, it had grown into an organization that employed 13,000 scientists, engineers, and other staff people. And it now has a budget of over $600,000,000.

The Survey now uses space-age technology—such as satellite photos—to carry out its mission to provide information about the land and its water, mineral, and energy resources. But there is still plenty of work for earthbound scientists.

In California's Sierra Nevada mountains, a geologist dressed in a cowboy hat, jeans, and sturdy hiking boots works on a geological map of the region. In Hawaii, a scientist in a protective asbestos suit probes the crater of a volcano to determine the temperature of the bubbling lava. Off the coast of New Jersey, a team of conservationists checks oil rigs to make sure they are safe and are not polluting the ocean.

The work of these people illustrates the various activities of the U.S. Geological Survey. Basically, there are four main areas of research:

The Topographic Division draws detailed and accurate scale maps of the topography (mountains, lakes, valleys, and so on) of the United States and its possessions.

The Water Resources Division determines the location and the quality as well as the quantity of water available in rivers, lakes, and under the ground.

The Conservation Division surveys public lands to see if there are deposits of valuable minerals, such as oil, gas, and coal. Those lands having important mineral resources may then be leased to private companies that can extract the minerals.

The Geologic Division conducts research activities, including the preparation of geological maps that pinpoint the location of mineral deposits. The division also maps the ocean floors, giving special attention to the location of mineral resources.

On an international level, the Geological Survey provides technical assistance to developing nations. It works with other countries on joint scientific projects—usually through the scientific agencies of other nations or international organizations.

The Survey's work, as it enters its second century, has taken on a new importance. It is playing a vital role in the effort to conserve energy resources and to find new sources of energy. Today, as in the past, the U.S. Geological Survey aims to help the United States make the best possible use of its natural resources.

Survey geologists pan for samples of heavy metals, to inventory and evaluate Western mineral resources.

A Survey botanist takes a core sample from a pine, as part of a land-reclamation project in Montana.

127

HOLOGRAPHY: 3-D PICTURES

Two famous ballet dancers gracefully move in midair. They dance for hours, without ever touching the floor.

A bright red apple rests on a plate. Nearby is the *same* apple, half-eaten.

Are the dancers and apples real? They look real. You can walk around them, viewing them from all sides. But if you tried to touch them, you would find your hand moving through empty space.

Is it magic? No. You are looking at holograms—three-dimensional (3-D) pictures that are so real that many people think that something solid really is there.

The word "hologram" comes from two Greek roots: *holos,* which means "complete," and *gram,* which means "record." A hologram is a complete visual record of an object. It looks exactly like the original object. It appears to be a solid, three-dimensional object. But it isn't. It is made entirely of light. You can put your hand right through it.

The story of the hologram began in the late 1940's in the laboratory of British scientist Dennis Gabor. While working on improving the electron microscope, Dr. Gabor developed the theory of holography. But he couldn't make a hologram. To make a hologram a person needs a beam of coherent light—that is, light of a single wave length. It wasn't until 1960 that scientists found a way to produce coherent light. The device that does this is the laser.

Soon, scientists began to adapt the laser to Gabor's theories. The result was the birth of holography.

▶ **MAKING PICTURES WITH LASERS**

How do you make a three-dimensional picture with a laser beam? First, the laser beam is split into two parts. One part is aimed directly at a photographic plate. This plate is usually a glass slide that is coated with a photographic emulsion. It is a lot like the photographic film you use in a camera.

A hologram is a picture made entirely of light—but it looks as if something solid is there.

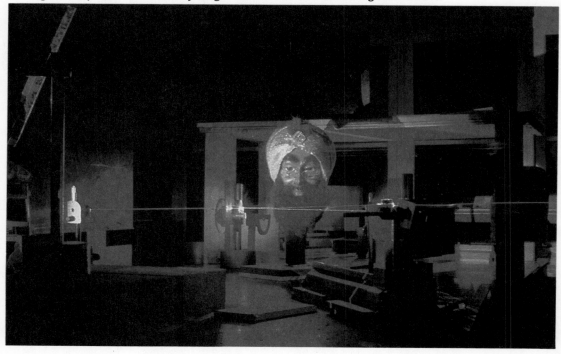

128

A laser device (*above*) is needed to produce holograms (*below*).

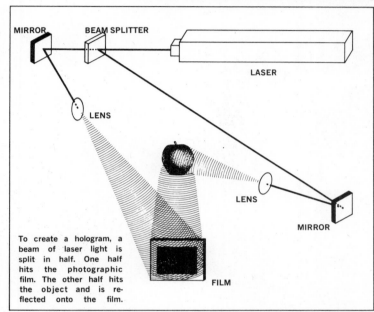

MIRROR BEAM SPLITTER LASER

LENS

LENS

MIRROR

To create a hologram, a beam of laser light is split in half. One half hits the photographic film. The other half hits the object and is reflected onto the film.

FILM

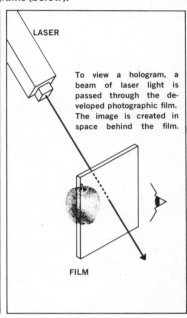

LASER

To view a hologram, a beam of laser light is passed through the developed photographic film. The image is created in space behind the film.

FILM

The second part of the laser beam is aimed at the object to be pictured. This beam strikes the object and is reflected onto the photographic plate. When the two beams meet on the plate, they interfere with one another. The pattern of this interference—a series of swirling lines that bear no resemblance to the object—is produced on the emulsion.

When the photographic plate is developed, the interference pattern is reproduced. In order to get an image of the original object, this pattern is exposed to a laser beam exactly like the laser beam used to make the pattern. Suddenly, behind the photographic plate, there is a floating image of the object. It is an exact replica, except that it is made only of light.

No description of a hologram can compare with actually seeing one. It's easy to think of a hologram as a kind of photograph. But it is very different from a conventional photograph.

First, as you have just learned, the way you look at a hologram is different from the way you look at a photograph. In a photograph, the image appears on the surface of a piece of paper. The hologram image appears in space, behind the photographic plate. Looking at a hologram is something like looking through a window. The window, in this case, is the photographic plate.

Second, what you see when you look at a hologram is different from what you see when you look at a conventional photograph. A hologram is thousands of times more detailed than a photograph. A photograph is a two-dimensional image of a three-

Kiss II, a holographic movie.

dimensional subject. A hologram is truly three-dimensional. It contains the whole image, not just one view.

Let's pretend that we are looking at a hologram of you. When we look at your hologram straight on, we see a front view. When we move to the right or to the left, the hologram reveals your profile. When we crouch down we can see under your chin. By stepping off to one side we can see objects that are located behind you—things that were hidden from view when we looked straight at you. In other words, looking at a hologram is like looking at the original scene.

▶ **HOLOGRAPHY TODAY**

The first holograms were projected from flat plates. Today, wraparound, or cylindrical, plates may be used. There are also holographic movies.

In the early holograms, laser light was needed to both produce and view the picture. But techniques have been improved and new methods have been developed. Today, it is no longer necessary to use coherent light to view a holographic image. Ordinary white light can be used. This makes holograms more available to the general public. It is no longer necessary to protect viewers from the potentially harmful laser rays. The cost of ordinary white light is much less than the cost of laser light. And with white light, it is possible to project the hologram either in front of or behind the photographic plate.

Almost from the beginning of holography, artists have been interested in using this technique as a medium of expression. Today an increasing number of painters, sculptors, and photographers are creating holographic art. Some create holographic portraits of people. Lloyd Cross made a holographic movie titled *Kiss II*. It shows a young woman suspended right in front of you. She winks and blows a kiss at you. A holographic movie by Rudie Berkout shows the opening of a lily blossom.

Exhibitions of holograms have drawn large crowds in many countries, including France, Germany, Sweden, Venezuela, Canada, and the United States. One of the best places to see holograms is the Museum of Holography, which is located in New

130

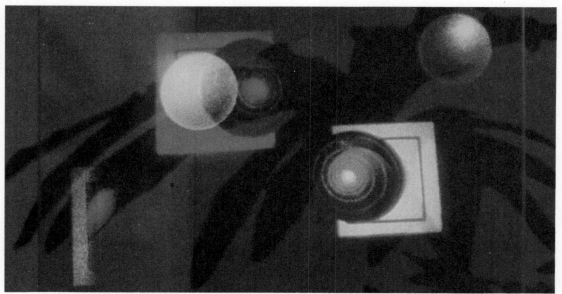

Today many artists are creating holographic art, like this geometric light sculpture.

York City. In addition to exhibits of holograms, the museum has films and lectures on holography. It also has special programs that travel to schools and to museums in other cities.

Holograms are also used in science and industry. The hologram is a valuable tool for studying how materials react to stress. For example, holograms are used to detect flaws in building materials, machine parts, and jet engine components.

Advertising and display companies use holograms in a variety of ways: to attract attention at conventions; to display objects that are not easily transported because of their weight, size, or fragility; and to display objects that are extremely valuable.

▶ **HOLOGRAPHY TOMORROW**

Scientists and artists agree that holography is still in its infancy. They compare holography today to photography a hundred years ago. They expect that techniques will continue to improve, and that in the future holography will play a much bigger role in our world than it does at the present time. Here are some possible applications of holograms:

Someday, instead of looking at photographs of a piece of jewelry, people sitting in their homes may be able to view a hologram of the jewelry. Dentists may make holograms of cavities and other dental problems, then use the holographic images to manufacture inlays and crowns.

Instead of using magnetic tape to store data in computers, holograms may be used. One small photographic plate would store the same amount of information that is currently stored on several hundred rolls of magnetic tape.

Holograms will extend our vision so that we will be able to see deep into the oceans or through dense fogs. Airplane pilots may look at holograms of important instruments while looking straight ahead through the cockpit window. Scientists may look through holographic microscopes to see cells as they really are—in three dimensions.

When a family sits down in front of the television set, they will watch the news, movies, and sports in three dimensions. If they have difficulty putting together a bicycle or a bookcase from a kit, they will hold up the enclosed hologram to the light, look at it from various angles, and get a complete view of the assembly process. When the children go to school, they will view holograms that show what distant places look like and how animals move.

And most probably, you will be telling your children what life was like when there were only those old-fashioned, two-dimensional photographs to look at.

131

FUN TO MAKE AND DO

With the help of an artist, these young people created this colorful wall mural in Berkeley, California. The artist transferred the outlines of their shadows onto the wall. Then the young painters filled in the details.

STUFFED SHIRTS

Do you have a favorite T-shirt that you have outgrown? Don't throw it away. Make it into a pillow that's both amusing and comfortable. Any kind of T-shirt can be made into a pillow—even a long sleeved shirt. You can use a shirt with a design printed on it or a plain shirt. You can even use a shirt that you have decorated yourself.

What to Use:

T-shirt
Polyester filling
Needle, thread, scissors

What to Do:

1. Thread the needle. Make sure to keep the thread double for extra strong seams.
2. Turn the T-shirt inside out.
3. Sew up the neck opening and the arm holes.
4. Sew up about one half of the bottom opening. (It's best if you close the sides, keeping the center part open.)
5. Turn the T-shirt back to its right side.
6. Through the opening in the bottom, stuff the shirt with polyester filling. Work with small amounts of filling at a time, spreading it evenly throughout the shirt.
7. When you have finished stuffing the shirt, sew up the opening in the bottom.

CORKY CREATURES

Here's a perfect activity for a rainy afternoon. Take lots of different-sized corks and turn them into people, animals, or plants. You can make creatures that are familiar. Or you can make creatures that exist only in the wonderful world of your imagination.

You'll soon discover that there are endless ways to put together the corks. A long series of corks makes a worm or a snake. A descending series of ever-bigger corks makes a pine tree. A face can be made by gluing small corks onto a large flat cork.

You can paint the corks with colored felt-tip pens. You can carve them into various shapes. You can create features by using sequins, braids, bits of felt, yarn, and other materials. These can easily be glued onto the corks. Colored pipe cleaners can be cut and shaped into arms, legs, antennas, tails, bristles, wings, and plant stems. To attach a pipe cleaner to a cork, punch a hole in the cork with a needle. Then stick the pipe cleaner into the hole. Toothpicks can be attached in a similar manner.

Have a pretty good idea of what your creature will look like before you glue the corks together. Once they are glued, it is difficult to change the basic structure. But there will still be time to add a polka-dot design, a mouth and eyes, a mane of yarn, or a red felt jacket. And don't let anyone tell you that a snake can't have feathery wings or sharp horns. In corky creatureland, such creatures do exist!

135

LET'S MAKE MONEY!

On Wednesday, Karen and Stan put up signs in nearby stores. They pushed notices under their neighbors' doors. Their message was clearly printed:

BIG YARD SALE
SPECIAL BARGAINS
Saturday, 10 A.M. to 4 P.M.
32 Chestnut Street
936-4025

On Thursday, they gathered all the items they hoped to sell—old comic books and magazines, used records, toys, seashells, and clothing they had outgrown. Their mother gave them some hats and jewelry she no longer wanted. Neighbors gave them tablecloths, towels, and some pots and pans.

On Friday, they bought lemons and cake mix. They made lemonade and cupcakes to sell to hungry buyers. They put price tags on all the items. Karen went to the bank and changed some dollar bills into nickels,

dimes, and quarters so they would have enough change. Stan gathered a supply of boxes and bags, which customers could use to carry home the items they bought.

Early Saturday morning, Karen and Stan set up two big tables on the lawn and neatly arranged all the items they hoped to sell. Against one table, they placed a large mirror, for people who tried on clothing.

Karen had a covered shoebox in which to keep the money they took in. Stan had a pencil and pad of paper, in case someone wanted a receipt.

The first customers arrived shortly after 10 A.M. Many other people followed. By late afternoon Karen and Stan had sold most of the items. They had taken in $28.40. After subtracting the cost of the lemons and cupcake mix, they had a profit of $25.63.

Marie, one of their friends, was also busy making money. She had made two dozen

There are lots of ways to earn money—such as making and selling things to eat and drink.

gingham aprons. On each, she had embroidered a border in a cross-stitch design. The fabric, thread, and embroidery yarn had cost her $41.18, or about $1.71 for each apron. Marie went around her neighborhood asking people if they would like to buy the aprons. In three hours she had sold all the aprons at $4.00 each. Her profit was $54.82.

Young people are discovering that there are lots of ways to make money. If you want to join the growing group of young entrepreneurs (business people), begin by answering the following questions:

1. What do I like to do? If you like to work with woodworking tools, you might build birdhouses. If you like to paint, consider making greeting cards or decorating stone paperweights. If you like animals, set up a dog-walking service or offer to take care of pets when families are away.

2. What do the people in my neighborhood want or need? The best way to learn your neighbors' needs is to ask them. How many have pets? How often do they need someone to take care of the pets? A pet-sitting service won't get much business if there are no pets nearby or if people take their pets with them when they travel.

3. Find out if anyone else is offering the same service or product that you plan to sell. Your neighborhood may not need two pet-sitting services—or five people selling aprons. Of course, if you can show that your service or product is better or cheaper than that of your competitors, then your business may prosper in spite of competition.

4. How much money must I spend? Getting started in a business may involve some expenses. If you plan to build birdhouses, you will have to buy wood, nails, and perhaps some tools. Do you have enough money to pay for these items? If not, can you earn the money? Or can you arrange to borrow the money from your parents?

▶ THINGS TO MAKE AND SELL

There are many items that may find a ready market in your community. To sell well, they must be made well. It also helps

To make extra money, this boy built his own newspaper and magazine stand from old orange crates.

to sell them at the right time. For example, people are more likely to buy heart-shaped sachets just before Valentine's Day than any other time of the year. If you want to make and sell sachets year-round, consider making different designs or scents for different seasons. A green felt pillow filled with pine needles has a wintertime appeal. A lacy sachet filled with rose petals is nice for Mother's Day gifts.

Here are some additional items you might make: macramé items, such as belts or holders for hanging plants . . . things to eat and drink, such as cookies, cakes, bread, lemonade, and mint tea . . . Halloween masks made from paper bags and decorated with yarn . . . greeting cards and stationary decorated with pressed flowers . . . personalized bookmarks made of felt, plastic, ribbons, or other materials . . . pomander balls . . . tie racks and shoeshine kits . . . a recipe book containing the favorite recipes of each family in your neighborhood . . . holiday candles

137

A group of youngsters in California set up a company called General Services. People phone and ask for help—and the kids provide the help. This can lead to such jobs as . . .

. . . decorated T-shirts . . . spice racks made from wood and baby food jars . . . fancy wastebaskets and tissue holders . . . beanbag toys . . . pot holders and pincushions . . . fireplace logs made from rolled-up newspapers . . . kites . . . jewelry . . . knitted or crocheted items such as hats, mittens, and pillows . . . a riddle and joke book . . . wall plaques of dried flowers or seashell designs . . . catnip toys and carpet covered scratching posts for cats . . . denim tote bags . . . felt eyeglass cases . . . decorated candlesticks made from air-dried clay.

▶THINGS TO RAISE AND SELL

If you have a garden, perhaps you would enjoy making money by using your "green thumb." Grow and sell vegetables, cut flowers, or herbs. Indoor gardeners can grow houseplants, as well as some herbs.

There may also be a market for certain animals. If you live in a community where people go fishing, raise worms for bait. If you prefer more cuddly animals, check with schools and pet shops—there may be a market for hamsters, guinea pigs, or gerbils. Tropical fish can also be raised and sold.

▶SERVICES TO SELL

Everyone who owns a car has the car washed occasionally. Some people do this themselves. Others are too busy and are very willing to buy the services of an ambitious youngster. If providing this service appeals to you, try to line up regular customers. This is easier than trying to find customers each day that you want to work. Customers prefer it, too. They don't have to look for someone every time their car needs washing. Of course, to keep regular customers, you must be reliable. If you have promised to wash a neighbor's car every other Friday, you must keep the appointment or risk losing a good customer.

If you are interested in the theater, put on a magic show or a comedy routine for the children in the neighborhood. Parents might wish to hire you to entertain youngsters at a

138

birthday party. If photography is your interest, line up people who want pictures taken of parties, family reunions, their homes, their pets, even their places of business. If you like to sew, find people who need skirts shortened or lengthened. If you know a lot about bikes, set up a repair and maintenance service.

Here are some other services that you may wish to offer: baby-sitting or taking young children to the movies or playground . . . toy repairing . . . fence painting . . . gardening work such as mowing, raking, and weeding . . . sidewalk sweeping . . . snow shoveling . . . cleaning services such as window washing or silver polishing . . . an errand service for people and businesses that do not have time to go to the post office, library, dry cleaners, or supermarket . . . newspaper delivery . . . berry picking . . . dog washing.

There are markets for just about anything and everything. If you want to make money, you can. Millions of kids are proving this every day.

. . . sidewalk sweeping . . .

. . . and car washing. Perhaps you and your friends can organize a similar service.

139

OLYMPIC GAMES

Do you know what a biathlon is? It's a competitive sport involving skiing and target shooting. Cross-country skiers carrying rifles make four stops along a 12.5-mile (20-kilometer) course. At each stop, they shoot at targets. The winner is the person with the fastest skiing time and the fewest number of missed targets.

The biathlon is one of the sports that are included in the Olympics. The Olympics are held every four years and are divided into Winter Games and Summer Games. The Games consist of eight winter sports and twenty-two summer sports. Most sports are divided into a number of events. Figure skating, for example, includes four events: men's singles, women's singles, pairs, and ice dancing.

1980 is an Olympic year. The Winter Games will be held in Lake Placid, New York; the Summer Games, in Moscow. Here is a game that will prepare you for the 1980 Olympics. The numbered column (on the left) lists the 30 Olympic sports. The lettered column (on the right) lists the same sports all jumbled up. See if you can match them.

Olympic Sport	Jumbled Name
1. alpine skiing	a. a bald hnl
*2. archery	b. a cherry
*3. basketball	c. hy liked cofe
*4. biathlon	d. mod ant lent hopern
*5. bobsled	e. wiggle hint fit
*6. boxing	f. croces
*7. canoeing	g. fret sang gukii
*8. cycling	h. dujo
9. equestian	i. fat rick led dan
*10. fencing	j. ginn fec
11. field hockey	k. glyccin
12. figure skating	l. gnatchiy
*13. gymnastics	m. gnobix
*14. handball	n. hit no sog
15. ice hockey	o. gonna ice
*16. judo	p. grow in
*17. luge	q. many git scs
18. modern pentathlon	r. mim wings
*19. rowing	s. sell a kabbt
*20. shooting	t. sob bled
21. nordic skiing	u. coin drinks ig
*22. soccer	v. string lew
23. speed skating	w. ton a bhil
*24. swimming	x. ugle
25. track and field	y. i coy cheek
*26. volleyball	z. wrap e tool
27. water polo	aa. rain queets
28. weightlifting	bb. yell all bov
*29. wrestling	cc. digs takes pen
*30. yachting	dd. a king nips lie

ANSWERS: 1.dd; 2.b; 3.s; 4.w; 5.t; 6.m; 7.o; 8.k; 9.aa; 10.j; 11.c; 12.g; 13.q; 14.a; 15.y; 16.h; 17.x; 18.d; 19.p; 20.n; 21.u; 22.f; 23.cc; 24.r; 25.i; 26.bb; 27.z; 28.e; 29.v; 30.l.

140

Here's another game. The Olympic sports with stars (*) on them are hidden in this search-a-word puzzle. Try to find them. Read forward, backward, up, down, and diagonally. If you wish, cover the puzzle with a sheet of tracing paper and circle each sport as you find it. One sport has already been circled for you.

B	A	S	K	E	T	B	A	L	L	B	I	B	S	F
F	L	R	S	C	I	T	S	A	N	M	Y	G	W	E
D	B	L	C	Q	K	N	J	Y	M	B	N	H	I	N
S	I	L	A	H	P	C	L	F	O	I	B	L	M	C
U	L	A	N	B	E	E	G	U	L	S	I	K	M	I
B	L	B	O	O	D	R	U	C	A	T	A	E	I	N
P	K	Y	E	X	A	N	Y	A	C	H	T	I	N	G
G	S	E	I	I	R	C	A	J	E	T	H	M	G	O
N	U	L	N	N	B	K	A	H	N	Y	L	A	F	D
I	C	L	G	G	R	O	W	I	N	G	O	C	E	U
T	H	O	V	S	L	T	C	M	A	P	N	T	R	J
O	F	V	E	D	M	D	H	R	U	A	I	G	N	C
O	S	T	A	K	F	U	A	B	O	B	S	L	E	D
H	E	R	B	G	N	I	L	T	S	E	R	W	E	R
S	O	C	C	E	R	W	B	U	H	L	B	D	A	O

141

STRING O' SPICE

This attractive, easy-to-make braid can be used to scent closets and drawers. Or use it to add a cheery touch in a kitchen or bathroom. Make it for yourself or as a present.

What to Use:

Yarn of three different colors
Patterned fabric
1 brass curtain ring

3 cotton balls
Cloves (powdered or whole)
Scissors and straight pins

What to Do:

1. Cut five 4-inch (10-centimeter) pieces of one of the colors of yarn.

2. Cut nine long pieces of each of the three yarns. Each piece should be $6\frac{1}{2}$ feet (2 meters) long.

3. Thread each long piece halfway through the brass curtain ring. Thread them one color group at a time, with the darkest color yarn in the center.

4. Tie one of the short pieces of yarn cut in step 1 around all the yarn, about 1 inch (2.5 centimeters) below the brass ring.

5. Braid the three strands (by color group) until about 4 inches (10 centimeters) of yarn are left unbraided. End the braid with the darkest color yarn in the center for interesting contrast.

6. Tie another of the short pieces of yarn around the bottom of the braid so that it will not unravel.

7. Comb or straighten the loose ends of yarn at the bottom of the braid. Shorten the extra-long ends so that this fringe looks neat.

8. Cut three circles from the fabric. Each circle should be about 5 inches (12 centimeters) in diameter. If possible, use pinking shears to cut the fabric; this gives a nice edge to the circles.

9. Place the circles upside down on a table. Put some cloves in the center of each circle. Cover the cloves with a cotton ball and gather up the edges of the circle as if to make a little bundle. Tie another of the short pieces of yarn in a bow around each bundle so that the cloves and cotton are securely held in the fabric. Then flare out the edges of the fabric, which will give the bundle a flat appearance.

10. Place one bundle near the top of the braid, one in the center, and one at the bottom. Pin each bundle to the braid.

142

AN A-MAZE-ING COASTER

Roller coasters have recently reached a new high in popularity. Here's a roller-coaster maze that may have you going around in circles trying to figure a way out.

Place a sheet of tracing paper over the maze. Begin at the arrow on the bottom and try to find your way around the coaster (to the arrow at the top). If you come to a blind alley, try a different-colored pencil and a different route.

The solution is on page 383.

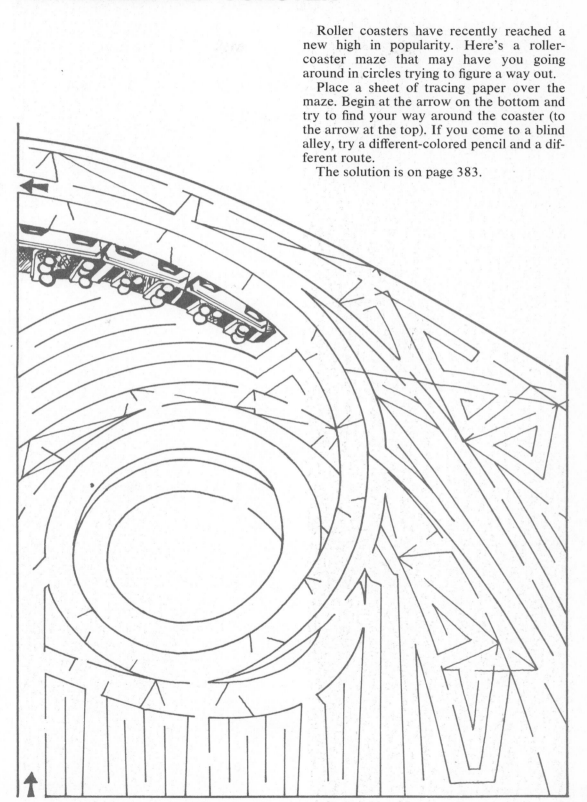

STAMP COLLECTING

Two subjects dominated the stamps issued around the world in 1979—the United Nations International Year of the Child and the history of postal service. The year was also one in which the value of rare stamps sought by collectors increased dramatically.

▶ **A YEAR FOR CHILDREN**

The year 1979 was declared the International Year of the Child (IYC) by the United Nations. That world organization and many individual countries issued stamps commemorating the event.

The United Nations issued two series of IYC stamps. One showed the face of a child as a child might have drawn it, while the other series showed children of all races beneath a rainbow. The United States honored IYC with a stamp that featured portrait sketches of four children, done in soft brown tones. One of the most endearing issues was released by Britain. It consisted of reproductions of illustrations from four beloved children's books—*The Tale of Peter Rabbit, The Wind in the Willows, Winnie-the-Pooh,* and *Alice's Adventures in Wonderland.* Ireland's issue featured designs drawn by children. And many other countries—from Bhutan in the Himalayas to Dominica in the Caribbean Sea—released stamps showing aspects of child care or scenes of children at play.

▶ **POSTAL HISTORY**

The year 1979 was also the 100th anniversary of the death of Rowland Hill, who introduced postage stamps in Britain in 1840. Britain, most of the countries of the Commonwealth of Nations, and many other countries as well marked the anniversary with special stamps.

In Hill's time, the cost of sending a letter depended on the distance it traveled. Postage was collected from the person who received it. Hill's idea was to charge a single rate of one penny for each half ounce of weight, paid in advance. To show that postage had been paid, a stamp would be fixed onto the letter. Hill's plan led to the first adhesive postage stamp, the Penny Black.

The stamps issued in Hill's memory generally showed his portrait, an early British stamp, the first stamp of the issuing country, or interesting items of postal history. Britain, for example, released stamps showing 18th- and 19th-century mail carriers and an air letter sheet showing the Penny Red stamp of 1841. Guyana's issue featured rare stamps from its colonial days.

The popular Europa series also took postal history as its theme for 1979. These stamps are issued by member nations in the Conference of European Postal and Telecommunications Administrations. Designs included early stamps, mail coaches, post riders, and objects that showed the development of telecommunications—from early telephones to satellites.

▶ **FLORA AND FAUNA**

In 1979 the United States released its first stamp showing endangered plants. The 15-cent commemorative issue, called Endangered Flora, featured four plants, shown together on one sheet. They were the trillium, the Hawaiian wild broadbean, the Contra Costa wallflower, and the Antioch Dunes evening primrose. Japan also included plants in its conservation issue. Two of the stamps showed a primrose and a type of butterwort.

Equally beautiful plants were subjects of stamps from many countries, although not all the plants were endangered species. The Canada violet, a delicate white flower, was shown in a Canadian issue. This stamp is one of a series depicting the country's natural beauty. There were stamps showing orchids, from Malawi, Singapore, and Surinam; plum blossoms, from Taiwan; and flowering trees, from Dominica.

But animals continued to be the favorite subjects for stamps. A remarkable issue from Brazil showed endangered species of South America. One was the manatee, a type of sea cow that is thought to have given rise to the legend of the mermaid. And Britain issued four dog stamps, showing a Welsh springer spaniel, an old English sheepdog, a West Highland terrier, and an Irish setter.

Le carnaval de Québec: The Quebec Carnaval
Canada 14

1979 STAMPS
FROM AROUND
THE WORLD

NIPPON 日本郵便
50
コウシンソウ   *Pinguicula ramosa*

UNITED NATIONS
INTERNATIONAL YEAR OF THE CHILD
31c

9p
The Tale of Peter Rabbit
The Year of the Child

10$\frac{1}{2}$p
The Wind in the Willows
The Year of the Child

USA 15c
Olympics 1980

Olympics 1980 Decathlon
USA 10c

11p
Winnie-the-Pooh
The Year of the Child

13p
Alice's Adventures in Wonderland
The Year of the Child

Martin Luther King Jr.
Black Heritage · USA 15c

9p
Old English Sheepdog

Brasil 79   12,00
XVIII CONGRESSO POSTAL UNIVERSAL – ALVARO A. MARTINS
Trichechus inunguis – Peixe-boi

2
中華民國郵票
REPUBLIC OF CHINA

Pennsylvania Toleware
Folk Art USA 15c

Emile Nelligan   Le vaisseau d'or
CANADA Postage Postes 17

Einstein
USA 15c

A TOPICAL COLLECTION OF TOYS

▶OTHER U.S. STAMPS

A tremendous group of stamps and postal stationery honoring the 1980 Olympic Games was begun in 1979. It was the largest group of U.S. postal items ever devoted to a single subject. Leading off the group was a 10-cent stamp featuring the decathlon. The first 15-cent issue was a block of four stamps, showing track and field, swimming, rowing, and equestrian events. Other items in the group were a 10-cent stamp showing a sprinter, a 31-cent stamp showing a high jumper, a 21-cent postal card featuring gymnastics, a 22-cent air letter sheet showing a discus thrower, and a 15-cent envelope featuring soccer.

Commemoratives marked the 50th anniversary of the birth of Martin Luther King, Jr., the civil rights leader, and the 100th anniversary of the birth of Albert Einstein, the scientist. King, who was assassinated in 1968, was shown in clergyman's robes, with civil rights marchers in the lower foreground. Einstein was sketched in an informal pose, in shades of brown.

A special U.S. stamp honored veterans of the Vietnam War. And more high-denomination stamps were released in the Americana Series to complete its theme of light. The 50-cent stamp showed an iron "betty" lamp; the $1 stamp, a candle holder used by early settlers; the $2 stamp, a kerosene lamp; and the $5 stamp, a railroad conductor's lantern. These stamps were designed so that when the block of four is put together, the lettering forms a frame.

Toleware, which was popular in the early days of the country, was another subject that was celebrated in a block of four stamps. Toleware objects were made of metal, coated with tin, and then painted or engraved with designs. The stamps showed two different coffee pots, a tea caddy, and a sugar bowl from Pennsylvania. They were part of a series on American folk art.

▶OTHER STAMPS FROM AROUND THE WORLD

Canada honored two writers with stamp issues. They were Frederick Philip Grove and Emile Nelligan. Grove was known for his novels of prairie life. His stamp showed a scene from one of his books, *Fruits of the Earth*. Nelligan, a poet of the early 20th century, was honored with a scene from his best-known poem, "The Golden Ship."

The Quebec Winter Carnival was featured on another Canadian stamp. It showed winter revelers grouped around Bonhomme Carnaval, the giant snowman whose melting ends the festivities. Other Canadian stamps focused on the country's spectacular national parks and the flags of the provinces and territories.

Four colorful stamps from Taiwan depicted temples and shrines surrounded by the island's beautiful scenery. The stamps were intended to acquaint people around the world with Chinese culture and to promote tourism.

Works of art were featured on other stamps. France reproduced an original painting by Salvador Dali in its art series. Sweden issued a sheet of miniatures showing Swedish art in the elaborate rococo style of the 18th century. And Malta pictured 17th-century tapestries in an attractive series of four stamps.

A series of stamps noting the start of the pontificate of Pope John Paul II was released by the Vatican in 1979.

Scotland, the birthplace of golf, issued an air letter sheet in honor of that game. One side of the sheet showed the Royal and Ancient golf course at St. Andrews. The other featured two well-known U.S. entertainers who were also golfers—Bing Crosby and Bob Hope.

▶A TOPICAL COLLECTION

One of the most interesting ways to collect stamps is to build a topical collection—a collection that focuses on one theme. Toys would be an excellent subject. You might start with Canada's 1979 Christmas issue, which featured antique toys. Sweden's 1978 Christmas stamps included an antique doll in a silk and velvet dress and a brightly colored, hand-carved wooden horse. Japan's New Year stamps usually depict toys—for 1979, the subject was a toy sheep made of clay. But whatever stamps you choose, a topical collection featuring toys is certain to include some of the most cheerful and colorful of the world's stamps.

CHARLESS HAHN
Stamp Editor, *Chicago Sun-Times*

147

TIRE CLIMBER

This tire climber is designed for school yards, community playgrounds, and other places where children get together to have a good time. All you need to do is find a spot for it, locate the materials, and convince some adults to put it all together.

The idea originated in Grand Island, Nebraska. Teachers at the Howard School came up with the idea and a parent drew up the plans. Most of the materials were donated, and the PTA paid for the items that had to be purchased.

What to Use:

2 telephone poles
1 steel pipe that is 4 inches (10 centimeters) in diameter
2 right angle braces; each one should be 1½ feet (45 centimeters) long
28 used tires (at least 6 in good condition)
heavy steel cable with turnbuckle, of the type used by telephone companies
cement, 3/16-inch chain, carriage bolts, nuts, washers, lock washers

What to Do:

1. Set the telephone poles about 5 feet (1.5 meters) deep into the ground. Pour cement around the bases to hold the poles upright.

2. Lay the steel pipe across the top of the telephone poles. Attach the pipe to each telephone pole with a right angle brace.

3. Attach the top row of tires first. Use the best tires for this row because they will be subject to the greatest stress. Bolt the

148

corner tires to the telephone poles. Attach each tire to the steel pipe with a loop of chain. Bolt the chain to the tire. Also attach each tire to its neighbors by means of chain. Usually, there are eight links of chain between tires, but this may vary a link or two so that the tires will hang evenly.

4. Work downward. Tires on the edges should be bolted to the telephone poles.

5. Beneath the bottom row of tires place a cable with a turnbuckle on one end to keep the tires taut at the bottom. (The bottom row of tires should be attached by chain to the cable.)

6. Make a hole in the bottom of each tire so that rainwater can drain.

7. Happy climbing!

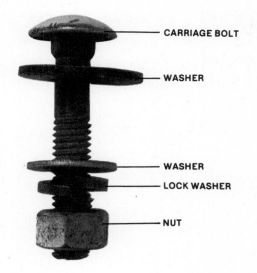

CARRIAGE BOLT

WASHER

WASHER

LOCK WASHER

NUT

Here is a diagram showing how to build a tire climber. The correct bolt is shown above.

149

MANY HANDS COOKING

from China
EGG FLOWER SOUP

Watch an egg turn into a flower. Chinese cooks say that the cooked shreds of egg afloat in this soup look like flower petals. With a few secrets of Chinese cooking, you can do it too.

One is to have all the ingredients out, measured, and ready to use *before* you start to cook. Another is to serve food right after cooking. Some foods look and taste better this way. Egg Flower Soup is one, so serve it promptly. (You may know this soup by another name — Egg Drop Soup.)

INGREDIENTS

1 tablespoon cornstarch
2 tablespoons cold water
1 egg
3 cups clear canned chicken broth
1 teaspoon salt
1 teaspoon chopped scallion or parsley

EQUIPMENT

measuring spoons
2 small bowls
fork
medium saucepan
mixing spoon
soup bowls

HOW TO MAKE

1. Put the cornstarch into one of the small bowls and gradually add the water, stirring it with the fork until you no longer see any lumps.

2. Break the egg into the other small bowl and beat it with the fork.

3. Pour the broth into the saucepan. Bring it to a boil over high heat.

4. Add the salt to the broth.

5. Give the cornstarch-and-water mixture a quick stir with the fork. Add it to the soup.

6. Stir the soup with the spoon until it thickens and becomes clear—about one minute.

7. Slowly pour the beaten egg into the soup. The egg will cook in the hot soup and form shreds.

8. When all the egg has been added, stir once. Turn off the heat.

9. Pour the soup into four soup bowls. Top the soup with the chopped scallion or parsley for decoration.

10. Pick up the bowl with both hands and sip the soup or eat it with a spoon.

This recipe serves 4 people.

150

from Puerto Rico
FRUIT POPS

Oranges, lemons, and bananas grow easily in Puerto Rico's sunny tropical climate. These tropical fruits are used for many of the island's drinks and desserts. In Puerto Rico, fruit ices bring relief from the heat, but you'll find fresh Fruit Pops delicious in any climate.

INGREDIENTS

1 cup sugar
2 cups water
3 oranges
3 lemons
2 bananas

EQUIPMENT

measuring cup
medium saucepan
mixing spoon
paring knife
fruit juicer and bowl to catch the juice
medium mixing bowl
fork
empty ice tray with dividers
toothpicks
paper cups (optional)

HOW TO MAKE

1. Measure the sugar and water into the saucepan and place it on the stove over medium heat.

2. Cook, stirring all the time, until the sugar dissolves (about 3 minutes).

3. Remove the saucepan from the stove and let the mixture cool for about 15 minutes.

4. Cut the oranges and lemons in half and squeeze the juice from them.

5. Peel the bananas and place them in the mixing bowl. Mash them with the fork.

6. Add the citrus juice to the mashed bananas. Mix well.

7. Pour the sugar-and-water mixture into the mixing bowl. Mix well.

8. Pour the mixture into an ice tray and place it in the freezer.

9. Freezing time varies from freezer to freezer. After 30 minutes, see if the pops are solid enough to hold a toothpick upright in each section.

10. Return the tray to the freezer until the pops are frozen—at least two hours.

11. The mixture can also be poured into paper cups and frozen. That way no toothpicks are needed.

This recipe makes 12 or more pops.

151

COIN COLLECTING

"Little friends may prove great friends," goes the moral to Aesop's fable "The Lion and the Mouse." Little friends in the form of coins and children were drawn together in 1979, which the United Nations proclaimed the International Year of the Child (IYC). The proclamation prompted nations around the world to issue coins on the theme of childhood. The year 1979 was also one in which the United States issued a new, small-size dollar coin. And silver and gold issues and rare collector coins reached new highs in value.

▶ **COINS FOR THE WORLD'S CHILDREN**

Nearly 30 countries issued coins commemorating IYC. More than a dozen—including Canada, Barbados, Bolivia, and China—issued gold coins. China's was the first gold coin from the Chinese mainland in more than half a century. It was a 450-yuan coin showing a young girl and boy growing a flower.

One of the most unusual issues was Hungary's 200-forint coin. On one side, it featured a design based on drawings by 4- and 5-year-old children. The other side showed the official IYC symbol.

To commemorate IYC: Hungary's 200-forint coin . . .

Bolivia issued a 200-peso silver coin that showed three Bolivian children playing native musical instruments. Iraq offered a pair of coins in different metals. The coins, one a silver 1-dinar and the other a nickel 250-fils, featured a profile of a child's head with the proclamation: "Children of Today, Heroes of Tomorrow."

India offered the widest range of coins on the IYC theme. It presented four coins—a

5- and a 10-paise in aluminum, a 10-rupee in copper-nickel, and a 50-rupee in silver. All four featured the "Happy Child—Nation's Pride" symbol developed by India for IYC. But the joy of childhood was perhaps best captured in Poland's issue, a 20-zlotych coin showing four dancing children.

. . . and Poland's 20-zlotych coin

Israel's 50-pound silver coin

Several other countries issued coins on the theme of children but not specifically related to IYC. Israel's 31st independence day commemorative, for example, was a silver 50-pound coin showing a mother playing with her two children. And Egypt issued two coins dedicated to the "Festival of the Teacher."

▶ **THE LITTLE DOLLAR**

The "little" dollar made its appearance in the United States in 1979. On July 2, the nation's new dollar coin, slightly larger than a quarter, was released. Public reaction ranged from criticism to indifference. Before the year had ended, this revolutionary new coin had probably caused almost as much controversy as the person whose likeness it bears, the 19th-century suffragette Susan B. Anthony.

The coin was the first regular U.S. issue

152

The "little" dollar coin from the United States

to portray an identifiable woman (at one time, there were many female forms representing "Liberty" on U.S. coinage). It was given an eleven-sided shape, to help distinguish it from the quarter. More than 700,000,000 pieces were minted, but as the year drew to a close, the Anthony dollar was rarely seen in circulation.

▶ BIG THINGS IN GOLD AND SILVER

The year 1979 was also one of big things—particularly in the price of gold. Gold prices rose to more than $500 an ounce in December. The upward trend of gold prices has fostered interest in gold coin issues. Canada, for example, has presented $100 gold collector coins each year since 1976, including 1979's IYC issue. In 1979 it introduced a 1-ounce bullion coin, known as the Gold Maple Leaf. The market value of this coin "floats" according to gold market levels.

Canada's 1-ounce gold bullion coin

U.S. Treasury officials were preparing for the first gold bullion issues in the United States—a series of medallions honoring American artists. The first medallions would be issued in 1980. But private industry took the lead in gold issues. In June, 1979, the Franklin Mint introduced gold bullion "coins" in quarter-, half-, and one-ounce weights.

Since 1967, South Africa has been marketing the Krugerrand. It has become the world's most popular gold bullion coin, and

it was produced in record numbers in 1979. In Britain, the gold sovereign was offered to collectors in a proof edition of 1979. Only 50,000 pieces were produced, so the coins were soon trading at high prices. And the Soviet Union released its third annual issue in a series of gold coins commemorating the 1980 Olympic Games, which will be held in Moscow.

Britain's gold sovereign proof edition

While gold was in the limelight in 1979, the performance of silver was no less spectacular. Silver prices soared from $6 an ounce in January to $18 an ounce in October. Collectors, speculators, and cookie-jar holders of U.S. silver coins from 1964 and earlier eagerly sold their holdings. Because the coins themselves were not valued as collector's items, many were melted down.

The Brasher gold doubloon

The record for the world's most expensive coin was taken by a gold doubloon issued in 1787 by Ephraim Brasher, a New York goldsmith. It sold for $430,000 at an auction in July. And other important sales were in the works. As the year ended, the sound of the auctioneer's gavel was becoming more and more familiar. And every time the gavel fell, the prices of scarce collector coins moved higher.

CLIFFORD MISHLER
Publisher, *Numismatics News*

153

A DECADE OF CRAFTS

As the 1970's drew to an end, definite trends could be seen in the crafts that were popular during the decade.

One trend came out of a growing awareness of the environment and what could be done to save it. This encouraged people to take a closer look at the world in which they live. As a result, there was a strong back-to-nature trend. People became interested in natural foods, natural products, natural colors. They were also interested in natural crafts—crafts that used materials like wool instead of synthetic fibers, and wood instead of plastics. Many of the finished items were left in their natural colors. If they were dyed, stained, or painted, the colors chosen were usually earth tones rather than bright colors. And if brighter colors were selected, flowers and herbs were often used to produce the dyes.

The fiber crafts (weaving, basketry, and macramé) were especially popular. Natural

The fiber crafts were very popular in the 1970's. Natural fibers were woven, twined, sewn . . .

154

fibers were used to create woven, coiled, twined, knotted, braided, crocheted, and sewn articles. The fibers were turned into pillows, clothing, wall hangings, planters, place mats, and many other practical and decorative items.

Woodworking, too, was a popular craft of the 1970's. Wood—a versatile, natural material—was sculpted, carved, painted, and assembled into many items. The technique of solar woodburning, which uses only a magnifying glass to concentrate the heat of the sun, was used to burn beautiful designs into the surface of the wood.

Another environment-oriented craft was "scrap crafting," which is the recycling or re-using of items to create beautiful and useful objects. Scrap pieces of leather, wood, glass, and fabric were the beginnings of some amazing craft projects. This popular method was also incorporated into many other craft techniques, such as découpage. Découpage is a paper craft in which cut-out pictures are glued onto a surface and thin layers of varnish are applied over them. Wall plaques, recipe boxes, and old storage trunks were just a few of the items that were découpaged.

. . . and coiled into useful and decorative items.

Solar woodburning was used to burn designs into wood.

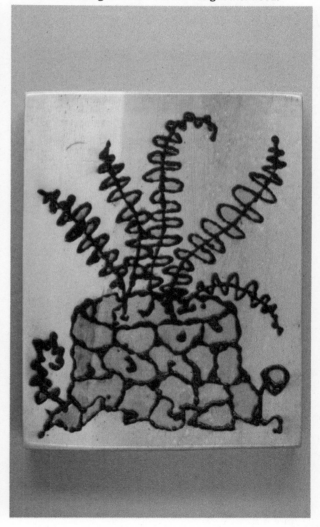

155

Folk-painting designs were often of people.

A piece of stained glass that is only decorative and not functional may today be classified as art.

There was also a great interest in decorative painting, especially to restore already-made articles. The styles included tole painting, folk painting, rosemaling, and stenciling. The designs that were used were usually scroll designs or scenes of people, birds, flowers, and fruits. The newest technique of folk painting was the "mud" method. In this technique, a design is painted using acrylics, and then a stain, with the consistency of mud, is applied over the painted surface. This adds the appearance of age as well as shading and contour to the designs.

Still another very popular craft was the making of miniature houses, rooms, and furnishings. In this craft, everything is reduced in an exact proportion. Many of these tiny reproductions were perfect in every detail.

Scrap crafting made use of old pieces of fabric and glass to create beautiful items.

Almost every technique used in making miniatures has been adapted from full-size construction crafts, such as woodworking, dollmaking, weaving, ceramics, decorative painting, and découpage.

Another trend of the decade was the reclassification of many crafts as art. These included some kinds of jewelry, glass, pottery, decorative painting, and weaving. What indicates the difference is not how these items are made but rather how they are used. An item such as a piece of stained glass serves only a decorative purpose, not a functional one. It may be classified as art. But if an item is useful beyond being beautiful—for example, a basket that decorates a wall but can also be used to hold something—then it is considered a craft.

As we enter the 1980's we are in the midst of an energy crisis. The sources of energy that we have depended on for many years—oil, coal, and natural gas—are slowly being depleted. This has led to a shortage in the supplies of gasoline, and so people are traveling less. More and more people are beginning to turn to crafts as a way of filling their leisure hours. At the same time, they are getting the satisfaction of creating things with their hands. The popularity of many of the crafts of the 1970's will undoubtedly continue in the 1980's. But as long as people continue to enjoy using their hands, new crafts will spring up to give pleasure.

WENDIE R. BLANCHARD
Managing Editor
Creative Crafts magazine

157

MUSICAL GLASSES

One of the most popular instruments of the 18th century was the armonica. Mozart wrote a lovely composition for it and four other instruments. Benjamin Franklin built a complicated armonica that was operated by a foot pedal. It consisted of different sized bowls placed on edge on a rod in a trough filled with water. As the player pumped the foot pedal, all the bowls spun around. By putting a finger on the rim of a spinning bowl, the player could produce a sound. Different bowls produced different sounds.

Many other people made armonicas in the 1700's. But their versions were much simpler and were known as musical glasses.

This instrument works on the same principle as organs, flutes, and harmonicas (an instrument invented later, about 1829). Each depends on the movement, or vibration, of columns of air. The longer the column of air, the lower the vibration—and the lower the sound.

To make an armonica, you need eight glasses, a pitcher of water, and a pencil. It's best to use identical glasses. And they must be made of glass—plastic will not work.

By filling each glass with varying amounts of water, you will be able to tune them to the notes in the musical scale: do-re-mi-fa-so-la-ti-do. The glass on the left-hand end of the row will be the first note. Since this is the lowest sound, it will contain the least water and the longest column of air. Tap the rim of the glass with a pencil. Does it sound like the "do" note? If the sound is flat, add water, a few drops at a time, until the note is in tune.

Next, fill the second glass from the left—the "re" glass—with a little water. Test the sound by tapping the edge. Adjust the amount of water until the sound is clear. Repeat this procedure with the remaining glasses. Each glass will contain more water than the glass on its left. Getting them in tune will involve a bit of work. But when the sounds are right, you will be able to play

This is a version of Benjamin Franklin's armonica, with a hand crank instead of a foot pedal.

158

a number of different songs simply by tapping the edges of the glasses.

A similar instrument can be made by filling a series of glass bottles with varying amounts of water. Bottles used for soft drinks or beer are ideal. Instead of tapping each bottle, you produce a sound by blowing across the mouth of the bottle. This causes the column of air in the bottle to vibrate, just as tapping the glass causes the air to vibrate.

It takes a little practice before you discover how to produce a nice sound. Begin by holding your lips tightly against your teeth. Extend your upper jaw a little beyond your lower jaw. Hold the rim of the bottle against your lower lip and blow downward across it. Adjust the position of the bottle and of your lips until you produce a strong, clear tone.

It's possible for you and your friends to make a small armonica orchestra. Each of you should make your instrument using containers of different shapes or sizes. In addition to glasses and bottles, try test tubes, canning jars, and other types of containers.

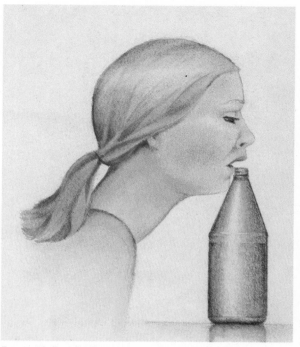

By carefully blowing across the mouth of a water-filled glass bottle, you can produce a musical sound.

You can make a simple armonica with eight glasses, water, and a pencil.

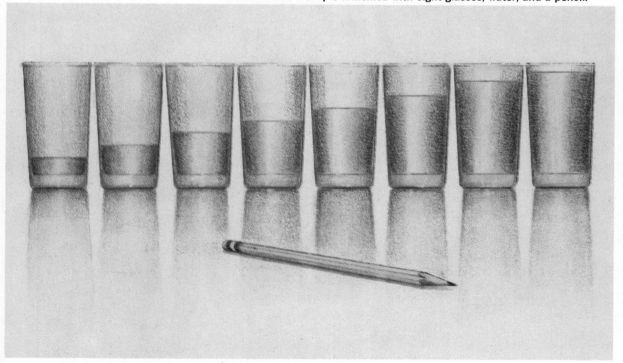

159

WORLD OF SPORTS

Puerto Rico, the host for the eighth Pan American Games, put on a dazzling opening ceremony.

BASEBALL

The Pirates' slugging first baseman, Willie Stargell, led them to victory in the World Series.

The Pittsburgh Pirates became baseball's champions in 1979, winning the World Series from the Baltimore Orioles, 4 games to 3. But it was a year during which Pittsburgh's success had been uncertain, from early spring until the last pitch was delivered in October. Their National League Eastern Division title wasn't achieved until the 162nd and last game of the regular season. They swept to the league pennant with three straight playoff victories over the Cincinnati Reds, but two of those contests were decided in extra innings. In the World Series, the Pirates were defeated in three of the first four games, then won three in a row to capture the trophy. Only three times in 75 previous World Series had the winner recovered from a 3–1 deficit.

In the fall classic, the Orioles won games one, three, and four by scores of 5–4, 8–4, and 9–6; Pittsburgh won game two, 3–2. But after game four, the Oriole bats fell silent, and the Pirates, powered by 38-year-old first baseman Willie Stargell, rolled to their three straight triumphs, 7–1, 4–0, and 4–1.

Overall, the whole 1979 campaign had brought surprising results. None of the four division titlists of 1978—the Los Angeles Dodgers and Philadelphia Phillies in the National League and the New York Yankees and Kansas City Royals in the American League—reached that success in 1979.

Three of the four division races weren't even settled until the final week of regular-season play. In the National League East, the Pirates nosed out the Montreal Expos by two games, largely because of five victories in six head-to-head encounters with Montreal during the month of September. In the National League West, a steady surge during the second half of the season provided Cincinnati with a final margin of a game and a half over Houston's Astros.

In the American League West, the California Angels topped Kansas City by three games. The Angels were winners for the first time in their 19 years of existence.

Only Baltimore, in the American League East, enjoyed an easy journey. The Orioles won 102 games (the most in the majors),

162

In August, Lou Brock of the St. Louis Cardinals got the 3,000th hit of his major league career.

A few weeks later, Carl Yastrzemski of the Boston Red Sox also joined the exclusive 3,000-hit club.

coasted along with wide margins, and finished with an eight-game bulge over Milwaukee. They then scored the necessary three victories in four playoff engagements with the Angels.

Stargell's key hits in the playoffs and World Series earned him Most Valuable Player awards in both those competitions. Stargell shared the National League's regular-season MVP honors with Keith Hernandez, the St. Louis Cardinals' first baseman, who led both leagues in batting with a .344 average. It was the first tie in the 49-year history of the balloting.

The American League's MVP honor went to Don Baylor, who contributed a league-leading 139 runs batted in to the Angels' division title.

The Cy Young Awards (for pitching) went to Baltimore's 23-game winner Mike Flanagan, in the American, and to Bruce Sutter, a Chicago Cubs' reliever, in the National. Sutter "saved" 37 games, tying the National League record.

1979 WORLD SERIES RESULTS

		R	H	E	Winning/Losing Pitcher
1	Pittsburgh	4	11	3	Bruce Kison
	Baltimore	5	6	3	Mike Flanagan
2	Pittsburgh	3	11	2	Don Robinson
	Baltimore	2	6	1	Don Stanhouse
3	Baltimore	8	13	0	Scott McGregor
	Pittsburgh	4	9	2	John Candelaria
4	Baltimore	9	12	0	Tim Stoddard
	Pittsburgh	6	17	1	Kent Tekulve
5	Baltimore	1	6	2	Mike Flanagan
	Pittsburgh	7	13	1	Bert Blyleven
6	Pittsburgh	4	10	0	John Candelaria
	Baltimore	0	7	1	Jim Palmer
7	Pittsburgh	4	10	0	Grant Jackson
	Baltimore	1	4	2	Scott McGregor

163

MAJOR LEAGUE BASEBALL FINAL STANDINGS

AMERICAN LEAGUE
Eastern Division

	W	L	Pct.	GB
*Baltimore	102	57	.642	—
Milwaukee	95	66	.590	8
Boston	91	69	.569	11½
New York	89	71	.556	13½
Detroit	85	76	.528	18
Cleveland	81	80	.503	22
Toronto	53	109	.327	50½

Western Division

	W	L	Pct.	GB
California	88	74	.543	—
Kansas City	85	77	.525	3
Texas	83	79	.512	5
Minnesota	82	80	.506	6
Chicago	73	87	.456	14
Seattle	67	95	.414	21
Oakland	54	108	.333	34

NATIONAL LEAGUE
Eastern Division

	W	L	Pct.	GB
*Pittsburgh	98	64	.605	—
Montreal	95	65	.594	2
St. Louis	86	76	.531	12
Philadelphia	84	78	.519	14
Chicago	80	82	.494	18
New York	63	99	.389	35

Western Division

	W	L	Pct.	GB
Cincinnati	90	71	.559	—
Houston	89	73	.549	1½
Los Angeles	79	83	.488	11½
San Francisco	71	91	.438	19½
San Diego	68	93	.422	22
Atlanta	66	94	.413	23½

*pennant winners

MAJOR LEAGUE LEADERS

AMERICAN LEAGUE

Batting
(top 10 qualifiers)

	AB	H	Pct.
Lynn, Boston	531	177	.333
Brett, Kansas City	645	212	.329
Downing, California	509	166	.326
Rice, Boston	619	201	.325
Oliver, Texas	492	159	.323
Molitor, Milwaukee	584	188	.322
Lezcano, Milwaukee	473	152	.321
Lemon, Chicago	556	177	.318
Kemp, Detroit	490	156	.318
Bochte, Seattle	554	175	.316

NATIONAL LEAGUE

Batting
(top 10 qualifiers)

	AB	H	Pct.
Hernandez, Saint Louis	610	210	.344
Rose, Philadelphia	628	208	.331
Knight, Cincinnati	551	175	.318
Garvey, Los Angeles	648	204	.315
Horner, Atlanta	487	153	.314
Templeton, Saint Louis	672	211	.314
Parker, Pittsburgh	622	193	.310
Winfield, San Diego	597	184	.308
Parrish, Montreal	544	167	.307
Mazzilli, New York	597	181	.303

Pitching
(top 5 qualifiers, based on ERA)

	W	L	ERA
Guidry, New York	18	8	2.78
John, New York	21	9	2.97
Eckersley, Boston	17	10	2.99
Flanagan, Baltimore	23	9	3.08
Morris, Detroit	17	7	3.27

Pitching
(top 5 qualifiers, based on ERA)

	W	L	ERA
Richard, Houston	18	13	2.71
Hume, Cincinnati	10	9	2.76
Schatzeder, Montreal	10	5	2.83
Hooton, Los Angeles	11	10	2.97
Niekro, Houston	21	11	3.00

Home Runs

	HR
Thomas, Milwaukee	45
Lynn, Boston	39
Rice, Boston	39
Baylor, California	36
Singleton, Baltimore	35

Home Runs

	HR
Kingman, Chicago	48
Schmidt, Philadelphia	45
Winfield, San Diego	34
Horner, Atlanta	33
Stargell, Pittsburgh	32

LITTLE LEAGUE BASEBALL

Little League baseball has developed into an international sport, played in dozens of countries. But the annual World Series, held in Williamsport, Pennsylvania, continues to be dominated by teams from the Far Eastern country of Taiwan. In 1979, the Taiwanese captured the championship for the eighth time since 1969.

In the championship game, the team from Pu-tzu, Taiwan, defeated the team from Campbell, California, 2–1. That final contest required two extra innings (beyond the regulation six). The winning pitcher, Dai Han-chao, actually hurled a no-hitter, but a first inning error gave the Californians their lone run. Dai struck out seventeen batters in the eight-inning finale.

Other Taiwanese also played important roles in the title game. Chen Chao-en delivered the home run that tied the score at 1–1. The winning tally in the eighth inning was scored by Lu Chang-kuen. He was awarded first base when hit by a pitch, advanced to third on a passed ball and a wild pitch, and romped home on a hit by Hou Chia-mou.

But for the Taiwanese, the high point in the tournament was the earlier 18–0 victory over the team from the U.S. Air Force Base at Aviano, Italy. In that game, Chen Chao-en pitched a perfect game. Not only did his opponents fail to reach base, but Chen fanned all eighteen batters he faced—a Little League record.

When the Californians scored against the Taiwanese in the title game, it was the first run allowed by Taiwan after eight consecutive shutouts, stretching back to preliminary competition in the Pacific region. Taiwan had blanked Puerto Rico, in addition to Aviano, at Williamsport; earlier, it had defeated the Philippines, Korea, Hong Kong, Guam, Indonesia, and Japan.

Campbell had advanced to the climactic championship by turning back the teams from North Little Rock, Arkansas, 8–3, and Grosse Point, Michigan, 8–5.

Taiwanese pitcher Dai Han-chao struck out seventeen batters in the eight-inning title game of the Little League World Series. Taiwan beat California, 2–1.

165

BASKETBALL

The Seattle SuperSonics, admitted to the National Basketball Association just ten years earlier, soared to the professional championship in 1979. Thus, the NBA crowned a new titleholder for the tenth straight year.

In the final playoff series, the Sonics foiled the defending titlists, the Washington Bullets, 4 games to 1. The Sonics captured four straight after losing the opening engagement. A year earlier, the results had been quite different. The same teams had met in the final series in 1978. But Washington had won the seventh and deciding game. This time, the Bullets, with a 3–1 deficit, made their last stand on their home court in Maryland. This is normally an advantage. But they were unable to check the overpowering Sonics. While the Sonics trailed by eight points early in the second half, they rallied for a 97–93 decision.

The Sonics were led by two versatile performers in the playoffs—Dennis Johnson and Gus Williams. Williams was the leading scorer with an average of 28.6 points per game. Johnson averaged 22.6, but he was also rated the outstanding defensive guard in the league. He and Jack Sikma bottled up the Washington offense, and Johnson was voted the most valuable player in the series.

The NBA playoffs were true to form in that the final series paired the teams with the best regular-season records. Washington topped the Eastern Conference, and Seattle led the Western. But both teams were involved in difficult journeys to the championship round, particularly the Bullets.

Washington was carried to seven-game play by the Atlanta Hawks and the San Antonio Spurs. Playing against the Spurs, the Bullets were forced to recover from a 3–1 games deficit. In 33 years of NBA playoffs, only two previous teams had survived that handicap in a seven-game series. The last of Washington's three straight triumphs was a spine-tingling 107–105 decision.

Wes Unseld of the Washington Bullets guards Seattle's Lonnie Shelton in the NBA playoff finals. The SuperSonics won the title series, 4 games to 1.

166

NBA FINAL STANDINGS

EASTERN CONFERENCE

Atlantic Division

	W	L	Pct.
Washington	54	28	.659
Philadelphia	47	35	.573
N.J. Nets	37	45	.451
N.Y. Knicks	31	51	.378
Boston	29	53	.354

Central Division

	W	L	Pct.
San Antonio	48	34	.585
Houston	47	35	.573
Atlanta	46	36	.561
Cleveland	30	52	.366
Detroit	30	52	.366
New Orleans	26	56	.317

WESTERN CONFERENCE

Midwest Division

	W	L	Pct.
Kansas City	48	34	.585
Denver	47	35	.573
Indiana	38	44	.463
Milwaukee	38	44	.463
Chicago	31	51	.378

Pacific Division

	W	L	Pct.
Seattle	52	30	.634
Phoenix	50	32	.610
Los Angeles	47	35	.573
Portland	45	37	.549
San Diego	43	39	.524
Golden State	38	44	.463

NBA Championship: Seattle SuperSonics

COLLEGE BASKETBALL

Conference	Winner
Atlantic Coast	North Carolina
Big Eight	Oklahoma
Big Ten	Michigan State; Iowa; Purdue (tied)
Ivy League	Pennsylvania
Mid-American	Toledo; Central Michigan (tied)
Missouri Valley	Indiana State
Pacific Ten	UCLA
Southeastern	Tennessee
Southern	Appalachian State
Southwest	Arkansas
West Coast Athletic	San Francisco
Western Athletic	Brigham Young

NCAA: Michigan State

National Invitation Tournament: Indiana

Ann Meyers, who had been a four-time all-American guard at UCLA, scored a first for women's sports by signing a contract with the NBA's Indiana Pacers. But Meyers did not make the team, and she later signed with the New Jersey Gems of the Women's Basketball League.

Seattle romped past Los Angeles in five games. But the Sonics' meeting with the Phoenix Suns wasn't decided until the final few seconds of the seventh game, resulting in a 114–110 verdict for Seattle.

In college basketball, Michigan State University emerged from a 40-team tournament as champion of the National Collegiate Athletic Association (NCAA). In the final, the Spartans overcame previously undefeated Indiana State, 75–64. During the regular season, Indiana State was ranked No. 1 in the nation, with a 26–0 record. But in the final, the Spartans thwarted the Sycamores' All-American, Larry Bird, mainly through the efforts of Earvin (Magic) Johnson. Johnson was voted the game's MVP.

Women's college basketball greatly increased in popularity during the year. The winner of the AIAW championship tournament was Old Dominion (Virginia). The Virginians defeated Louisiana Tech in the final, 75–65. (AIAW stands for Association for Intercollegiate Athletics for Women.)

FOOTBALL

Professional football's 14th Super Bowl matched two teams with remarkably different histories—the Pittsburgh Steelers, highly successful in recent years, and the Los Angeles Rams, the victims of long-term frustration. The Steelers were bidding for their fourth NFL championship in six seasons (no other team has won more than two Super Bowl engagements). The Rams, winners of seven consecutive division titles, were involved in the climactic contest for the first time. The Steelers won, 31–19.

Ironically, Los Angeles had reached its previously unattainable goal of playing in the Super Bowl after a regular season record of 9–7 in the National Conference West—the least impressive among the league's six division winners. The other division titlists were Dallas (11–5) and Tampa Bay (10–6) in the National Conference; and Pittsburgh (12–4), Miami (10–6), and San Diego (12–4) in the American Conference.

Except for the continued domination by Pittsburgh, the 1979 campaign produced surprising results. None was more startling than the playoff round leading to the conference championships. Favorites fell in three of the four games—the Houston Oilers winning over the San Diego Chargers, 17–14; Tampa Bay Buccaneers over the Philadelphia Eagles, 24–17; and Los Angeles over the Dallas Cowboys, 21–19. The last was the biggest shocker because Dallas, a perennial playoff entry, had been a Super Bowl participant the previous year.

Only the Steelers marched merrily along. With an awesome offense powered by quarterback Terry Bradshaw, and with an equally strong defense called the "iron curtain," the Steelers overwhelmed the Miami Dolphins, 34–14, in their first playoff game. They then turned back a stubborn but injury-riddled Houston club, 27–13, in the American Conference championship game.

In the Pittsburgh-Houston title match, Bradshaw threw touchdown passes to Bennie Cunningham and John Stallworth; Rocky Bleier ran for another score; and

Quarterback Terry Bradshaw (12) provided strong offensive power for Pittsburgh, and helped the team beat Houston in the American Conference title game.

Matt Bahr kicked two field goals. Meanwhile, the Steeler defense limited the league's leading rusher, Earl Campbell, to 15 yards. The only Oiler touchdown resulted from an intercepted pass and a 75-yard run by Vernon Perry, who had intercepted four passes a week earlier against San Diego. Toni Fritsch's two field goals gave Houston six additional points.

Los Angeles moved into the Super Bowl with a 9–0 triumph over Tampa Bay in the National Conference championship game, as Frank Corral booted field goals of 19, 21, and 23 yards. The Rams' defense stifled the Buccaneers' attack, while Vince Ferragamo's passing and the running of Wendell Tyler and Cullen Bryant advanced the Rams steadily within field goal range. Ferragamo, a substitute quarterback, also engineered the stunning upset of Dallas by firing three scoring passes. The decisive pitch was a 50-yard play with two minutes remaining.

Overall, Tampa Bay furnished the most astonishing reversal in recent memory. An expansion team assembled only four years earlier, the Buccaneers had lost 26 consecutive games during their first two seasons. In 1979, they fell only one victory short of reaching the Super Bowl.

Individual honors during the regular season were shared by Dan Fouts, San Diego quarterback, and Houston's Earl Campbell. Fouts broke Joe Namath's single-season record by passing for 4,082 yards. Namath's mark was 4,007. Campbell led the league in rushing for the second consecutive year, with 1,697 yards.

In the Canadian League, the Edmonton Eskimos won the Grey Cup, symbolic of the championship, with a 17–9 victory over the Montreal Alouettes.

An impressive performance in the Sugar Bowl made the University of Alabama a unanimous winner in all the polls that rated the nation's college teams. With power and balance on offense and defense, the Crimson Tide swept through Arkansas on New Year's Day (1980), 24–9, to gain the lead in the balloting over Southern California.

It was Alabama's 12th victory of the campaign without a defeat, and the 21st in a row over a two-year period. Southern Califor-

Running back Cullen Bryant aided in the Ram's defeat of Tampa Bay for the National Conference title.

nia's 17–16 triumph over Ohio State in the Rose Bowl was the Trojans' 11th success without a defeat, but they had been tied once during the regular season.

Prior to the bowl skirmishing, Alabama and Ohio State each had been listed at the top of one of the two major polls, with identical 11–0 records. Also high in the voting were Southern California (10–0–1) and Florida State (11–0). And meriting consideration were Oklahoma, Nebraska, Houston, and Arkansas. Each had a 10–1 mark and all were involved in the bowl competition.

Alabama's perfect slate removed its competitors from national championship contention, particularly since previously unbeaten Florida State fell before Oklahoma, 24–7, in the Orange Bowl. In the Cotton Bowl, Houston defeated Nebraska, 17–14.

Southern California added to its long list of Heisman Trophy winners when running back Charles White was overwhelmingly selected as college football's outstanding player of 1979. White led the nation in rushing, with 1,803 yards gained. And he ended his collegiate career in the Trojan's one-point Rose Bowl victory by scoring the decisive touchdown with 1:32 minutes left to play. White established two Rose Bowl records—times carrying the ball (39) and yards gained (247).

169

The 1979 Heisman Trophy winner (best collegiate player): Charles White of Southern California.

COLLEGE FOOTBALL

Conference	Winner
Atlantic Coast	North Carolina State
Big Eight	Oklahoma
Big Ten	Ohio State
Ivy League	Yale
Mid-American	Central Michigan
Pacific Ten	Southern California
Southeastern	Alabama
Southern	Tennessee-Chattanooga
Southwest	Houston; Arkansas (tied)
Western Athletic	Brigham Young

Cotton Bowl: Houston 17, Nebraska 14
Gator Bowl: North Carolina 17, Michigan 15
Orange Bowl: Oklahoma 24, Florida State 7
Rose Bowl: Southern California 17, Ohio State 16
Sugar Bowl: Alabama 24, Arkansas 9

Heisman Trophy: Charles White, Southern California

NFL FINAL STANDINGS

AMERICAN CONFERENCE

Eastern Division

	W	L	T	Pct.	PF	PA
Miami	10	6	0	.625	341	257
New England	9	7	0	.563	411	326
N.Y. Jets	8	8	0	.500	337	383
Buffalo	7	9	0	.438	268	279
Baltimore	5	11	0	.313	271	351

Central Division

	W	L	T	Pct.	PF	PA
Pittsburgh	12	4	0	.750	416	262
Houston	11	5	0	.688	362	331
Cleveland	9	7	0	.563	359	352
Cincinnati	4	12	0	.250	337	421

Western Division

	W	L	T	Pct.	PF	PA
San Diego	12	4	0	.750	411	246
Denver	10	6	0	.625	289	262
Oakland	9	7	0	.563	365	337
Seattle	9	7	0	.563	378	372
Kansas City	7	9	0	.438	238	262

Conference Champion: Pittsburgh Steelers

NATIONAL CONFERENCE

Eastern Division

	W	L	T	Pct.	PF	PA
Dallas	11	5	0	.688	371	313
Philadelphia	11	5	0	.688	339	282
Washington	10	6	0	.625	348	295
N.Y. Giants	6	10	0	.375	237	323
St. Louis	5	11	0	.313	307	358

Central Division

	W	L	T	Pct.	PF	PA
Tampa Bay	10	6	0	.625	273	237
Chicago	10	6	0	.625	306	249
Minnesota	7	9	0	.438	259	337
Green Bay	5	11	0	.313	246	316
Detroit	2	14	0	.125	219	365

Western Division

	W	L	T	Pct.	PF	PA
Los Angeles	9	7	0	.563	323	309
New Orleans	8	8	0	.500	370	360
Atlanta	6	10	0	.375	300	388
San Francisco	2	14	0	.125	308	416

Conference Champion: Los Angeles Rams

1980 Super Bowl Winner: Pittsburgh Steelers

Fuzzy Zoeller triumphed in the Masters.

Jerilyn Britz won the U.S. Women's Open.

GOLF

PROFESSIONAL		AMATEUR	
	Individual		**Individual**
Masters	Fuzzy Zoeller	**U.S. Amateur**	Mark O'Meara
U.S. Open	Hale Irwin	**U.S. Women's Amateur**	Carolyn Hill
Canadian Open	Lee Trevino	**British Amateur**	Jay Sigel
British Open	Severiano Ballesteros	**British Ladies Amateur**	M. Madill
PGA	David Graham	**Canadian Amateur**	Rafael Alarcon
World Series of Golf	Lon Hinkle	**Canadian Ladies Amateur**	Stacy West
U.S. Women's Open	Jerilyn Britz		
Ladies PGA	Donna Caponi Young		
	Team		**Team**
World Cup	United States		
Ryder Cup	United States	**Walker Cup**	United States

The Montreal Canadiens and the New York Rangers battled it out
for the Stanley Cup. The Canadiens took the series, 4 games to 1.

HOCKEY

There were some anxious moments in Montreal as the 1979 National Hockey League season rushed toward a conclusion. But in the end, the usual happened. The Canadiens captured the Stanley Cup, the symbol of supremacy in the world of war on ice.

Simple statistics tell the story of the Canadiens' remarkable run of success. They won the cup for the fourth straight time; they have won 22 Stanley Cups since 1916; and they have missed the playoffs only once since 1948.

In the 1979 championship series, the Canadiens were confronted by a surprising foe, the New York Rangers. The Rangers had finished third in their division, hadn't won the cup since 1940, and were in the final for only the third time since then. In the opening game at Montreal, the Rangers scored a 4–1 victory. But that was their final hour of glory. Montreal evened the series on its home ice, 6–2; twice defeated the Rangers in New York's Madison Square Garden, 4–1 and 4–3 (in overtime); and back in the Montreal Forum closed out the competition, 4–1.

The real concern about the fate of the Canadiens had come with their semifinal series with the Boston Bruins. Montreal was dangerously close to elimination in that seven-game scramble. In the seventh game, trailing 3–1, they rallied for two goals in the third period. Then they fell behind again, 4–3, with 3 minutes, 59 seconds remaining. The clock showed 74 seconds left to play when Guy Lafleur's goal tied the score. And 9 minutes, 33 seconds into the overtime period, Yvon Lambert's tally won it for Montreal.

Montreal had a sizable list of outstanding performers—Ken Dryden, Lafleur, Lambert, Serge Savard, Larry Robinson. But the Conn Smythe Trophy for the most valuable player in Stanley Cup play went to Bob Gainey, the 25-year-old left winger who scored 6 goals and 16 points during the playoffs.

While the Canadiens retained their title, the Rangers will be remembered as the year's Cinderella team. For a long time, the Rangers had not been among the top NHL teams. Regrouped under a new coach, Fred Shero, the Rangers reached the final by winning playoffs from the Los Angeles Kings in 2 straight games; the Flyers, 4 games to 1; and the New York Islanders, 4 games to 2. The Islanders, with record scorer Mike Bossy, had the best record in the league during the regular season. Their only two playoff triumphs over the Rangers were produced in overtime.

In the World Hockey Association's seventh season, the Winnipeg Jets captured their third Avco Cup by defeating the Edmonton Oilers, 4 games to 2. Immediately after that, the WHA disbanded as a professional league. Four of its teams—Winnipeg, Edmonton, the New England Whalers, and the Quebec Nordiques—are to be absorbed by the National Hockey League.

Bob Gainey of the Canadiens was named the most valuable player in the Stanley Cup series.

173

Bryan Trottier of the Islanders took the most valuable player award for regular season play.

NHL FINAL STANDINGS

CAMPBELL CONFERENCE

Patrick Division

	W	L	T	Pts.
N.Y. Islanders	51	15	14	116
Philadelphia	40	25	15	95
N.Y. Rangers	40	29	11	91
Atlanta	41	31	8	90

Smythe Division

	W	L	T	Pts.
Chicago	29	36	15	73
Vancouver	25	42	13	63
St. Louis	18	50	12	48
Colorado	15	53	12	42

WALES CONFERENCE

Norris Division

	W	L	T	Pts.
Montreal	52	17	11	115
Pittsburgh	36	31	13	85
Los Angeles	34	34	12	80
Washington	24	41	15	63
Detroit	23	41	16	62

Adams Division

	W	L	T	Pts.
Boston	43	23	14	100
Buffalo	36	28	16	88
Toronto	34	33	13	81
Minnesota	28	40	12	68

Stanley Cup: Montreal Canadiens

WHA FINAL STANDINGS

	W	L	T	Pts.
Edmonton	48	30	2	98
Quebec	41	34	5	87
Winnipeg	39	35	6	84
New England	37	34	9	83
Cincinnati	33	41	6	72
Birmingham	32	42	6	70
*Indianapolis	5	18	2	12

*team disbanded

Avco Cup: Winnipeg Jets

OUTSTANDING PLAYERS

Scorer	Real Cloutier, Quebec
Rookie	Wayne Gretzky, Edmonton
Goalie	Dave Dryden, Edmonton
Most Valuable Player	Dave Dryden, Edmonton
Sportsmanship	Kent Nilsson, Winnipeg
Defenseman	Rick Ley, New England
Avco Cup Play	Rich Preston, Winnipeg

OUTSTANDING PLAYERS

Calder Trophy (rookie)	Bobby Smith, Minnesota
Conn Smythe Trophy (Stanley Cup play)	Bob Gainey, Montreal
Hart Trophy (most valuable player)	Bryan Trottier, N.Y. Islanders
Lady Byng Trophy (sportsmanship)	Bob MacMillan, Atlanta
Norris Trophy (defenseman)	Denis Potvin, N.Y. Islanders
Ross Trophy (scorer)	Bryan Trottier, N.Y. Islanders
Venzina Trophy (goalies)	Ken Dryden and Michel Larocque, Montreal

Tai Babilonia and Randy Gardner won the world pairs figure-skating championships—the first Americans to win the title in 29 years.

ICE SKATING

FIGURE SKATING

World Championships

Men	Vladimir Kovalev, U.S.S.R.
Women	Linda Fratianne, U.S.
Pairs	Tai Babilonia / Randy Gardner, U.S.
Dance	Natalja Linichuk / Gennadij Karponsov, U.S.S.R.

United States Championships

Men	Charles Tickner
Women	Linda Fratianne
Pairs	Tai Babilonia / Randy Gardner
Dance	Stacey Smith / John Summers

SPEED SKATING

World Championships

Men	Eric Heiden, U.S.
Women	Beth Heiden, U.S.

SKIING

WORLD CUP CHAMPIONSHIPS

Men	Peter Luescher, Switzerland
Women	Annemarie Proell Moser, Austria

U.S. ALPINE CHAMPIONSHIPS

	Men	Women
Downhill	Sepp Ferstl	Irene Epple
Slalom	Cary Adgate	Cindy Nelson
Giant Slalom	Phil Mahre	Viki Fleckenstein

CANADIAN ALPINE CHAMPIONSHIPS

	Men	Women
Downhill	Ken Reid	Loni Klettl
Slalom	Raymond Pratte	Kathy Kreiner
Giant Slalom	Peter Monod	Judy Richardson
Combined	Dave Murray	Marie Dufresne

SOCCER

In Soccer Bowl-79, the Vancouver Whitecaps defeated the Tampa Bay Rowdies, 2–1.

NORTH AMERICAN SOCCER LEAGUE FINAL STANDINGS

NATIONAL CONFERENCE

Eastern Division

	W	L	GF	GA	Pts.
New York	24	6	84	52	216
Washington	19	11	68	50	172
Toronto	14	16	52	65	133
Rochester	15	15	43	57	132

Central Division

	W	L	GF	GA	Pts.
Minnesota	21	9	67	48	184
Dallas	17	13	53	51	152
Tulsa	14	16	61	56	139
Atlanta	12	18	59	61	121

Western Division

	W	L	GF	GA	Pts.
Vancouver	20	10	54	34	172
Los Angeles	18	12	62	47	162
Seattle	13	17	58	52	125
Portland	11	19	50	75	112

AMERICAN CONFERENCE

Eastern Division

	W	L	GF	GA	Pts.
Tampa Bay	19	11	67	46	169
Ft. Lauderdale	17	13	75	65	165
Philadelphia	10	20	55	60	111
New England	12	18	41	56	110

Central Division

	W	L	GF	GA	Pts.
Houston	22	8	61	46	187
Chicago	16	14	70	62	159
Detroit	14	16	61	56	133
Memphis	6	24	38	74	73

Western Division

	W	L	GF	GA	Pts.
San Diego	15	15	59	55	140
California	15	15	53	56	140
Edmonton	8	22	43	78	88
San Jose	8	22	41	74	86

Soccer Bowl-79: Vancouver Whitecaps

Seventeen-year-old Jesse Vassallo and 14-year-old Mary Meagher set new world swimming records at the Pan Am Games. (Later in the year, Meagher broke her own record.)

SWIMMING

WORLD SWIMMING RECORDS SET IN 1979

EVENT	HOLDER	TIME
	Men	
200-meter freestyle	Sergei Kopliakov, U.S.S.R.	1:49.83
400-meter freestyle	Vladimir Salnikov, U.S.S.R.	3:51.41
800-meter freestyle	Vladimir Salnikov, U.S.S.R.	7:56.43
200-meter individual medley	Jesse Vassallo, U.S.	2:03.29
	Women	
200-meter freestyle	Cynthia Woodhead, U.S.	1:58.23
1,500-meter freestyle	Kim Linehan, U.S.	16:04.49
200-meter breaststroke	Lina Kachusite, U.S.S.R.	2:28.36
200-meter butterfly	Mary Meagher, U.S.	2:07.01

Twenty-year-old John McEnroe became the youngest winner of the U.S. men's singles tournament.

TENNIS

During 1979, the International Year of the Child, youth did indeed prevail in the world of tennis. Tracy Austin, a 16-year-old high school junior from California, became the youngest player ever to win a U.S. singles championship. To make her conquest even more impressive, Austin took the final match in two straight sets (6–4, 6–3) from Chris Evert Lloyd. Lloyd, the reigning U.S. champion, had won the title the four previous years.

At that same tournament at Flushing Meadow, New York, 20-year-old John McEnroe became the youngest U.S. men's titlist in 31 years. On the way to the championship, McEnroe eliminated the defending titlist, Jimmy Connors. He then won the final match from fellow New Yorker, Vitas Gerulaitis (7–5, 6–3, 6–3).

Across the Atlantic earlier in the summer, the slightly older players held off the surge of the youngsters in the century-old Wimbledon competition. Sweden's Bjorn Borg scored a record fourth straight victory in the men's singles. He won his title by surviving a spectacularly close final match against the American with the cannonball delivery, Roscoe Tanner (6–7, 6–1, 3–6, 6–3, 6–4).

Martina Navratilova, the Czechoslovakian who had defected to the United States, triumphed in Wimbledon's women's division for the second consecutive year. She turned back Chris Evert Lloyd in straight sets (6–4, 6–4). She reached the final with a semifinal victory over Tracy Austin, a result that was later reversed in the U.S. Open.

A historic milestone at Wimbledon was reached by Billie Jean King when she teamed with Navratilova to win the doubles title. It was King's twentieth Wimbledon championship—bringing her total to six singles, ten doubles, and four mixed doubles. This passed the record that she had shared with 87-year-old Elizabeth Ryan, who had died during the 1979 tournament.

TOURNAMENT TENNIS

	Australian Open	French Open	Wimbledon	U.S. Open
Men's Singles	Guillermo Vilas, Argentina	Bjorn Borg, Sweden	Bjorn Borg, Sweden	John McEnroe, U.S.
Women's Singles	Chris O'Neill, Australia	Chris Evert Lloyd, U.S.	Martina Navratilova, U.S.	Tracy Austin, U.S.
Men's Doubles	Wojtek Fibak, Poland / Kim Warwick, Australia	Gene Mayer, U.S. / Sandy Mayer, U.S.	John McEnroe, U.S. / Peter Fleming, U.S.	John McEnroe, U.S. / Peter Fleming, U.S.
Women's Doubles	Betsy Nagelsen, U.S. / Renata Tomanova, Czechoslovakia	Betty Stove, Netherlands / Wendy Turnbull, Australia	Billie Jean King, U.S. / Martina Navratilova, U.S.	Betty Stove, Netherlands / Wendy Turnbull, Australia

Davis Cup Winner: United States

British runner Sebastian Coe broke three world track records in 1979.

TRACK AND FIELD

WORLD TRACK AND FIELD RECORDS SET IN 1979

EVENT	HOLDER	TIME OR DISTANCE
	Men	
200-meter run	Pietro Mennea, Italy	19.72
800-meter run	Sebastian Coe, Britain	1:42.40
1,500-meter run	Sebastian Coe, Britain	3:32.10
1-mile run	Sebastian Coe, Britain	3:49.00
110-meter hurdles	Renaldo Nehemiah, U.S.	13.00
	Women	
200-meter run	Marita Koch, E. Germany	21.71
400-meter run	Marita Koch, E. Germany	48.60
400-meter hurdles	Marina Makeyeva, U.S.S.R.	54.78
Javelin throw	Ruth Fuchs, E. Germany	228' $\frac{3}{4}$"

SPORTS BRIEFS

The air was calm. The sea was smooth. The conditions were just right for the *Gossamer Albatross* to fly across the English Channel on June 12, 1979. Bryan Allen, a champion bicyclist from California, climbed into the plane at Dover, England. The *Gossamer Albatross* rose gently into the air. To keep the propeller turning, Allen had to steadily churn the pedals in the plane's cockpit. Finally, after three hours, Allen landed safely at Cape Gris-Nez, France—having made the first human-powered flight across the English Channel. If pilot Bryan Allen was a hero, so too was the plane. Made of light but strong space-age materials, the *Gossamer Albatross* weighed about half the weight of its pilot. And to take advantage of all possible lift, it had a wingspan wider than a DC-9's. But even so, Allen was exhausted by the time he landed in France, 22 miles (35 kilometers) from Dover. "I sure don't want to do that again," he said, grinning.

Naiads were mythological spirits that lived in lakes and streams. The water was their home. Diana Nyad, who pronounces her name the same way, is also at home in the water. The New Yorker is a world-record-holding marathon swimmer. She has swum around Manhattan island, in the Suez Canal, and across the North Sea. And in 1979, after two previous unsuccessful attempts, Nyad became the first person to swim the 60 miles (97 kilometers) from the Bahamas to Florida.

Willie Mays, the great baseball center-fielder, played the game with grace and joy. From 1951 to 1973, he roamed outfields like a gazelle, and he made more putouts than any outfielder in history. But Mays, the former Giant and Met, was more than just graceful. He played with an explosive power that propelled 660 home runs, third behind only Henry Aaron and Babe Ruth. In 1979, his talent was rewarded, and Willie Mays, the "Say-Hey Kid," was elected to the Baseball Hall of Fame, in Cooperstown, New York.

Gilles Villeneuve is not afraid to take chances. Seated behind the wheel of his Formula One Ferrari racing car, he attacks race courses with verve and audacity. His bravery and skill made Villeneuve one of the best Grand Prix drivers of 1979. During the year, the 27-year-old driver from Quebec, Canada, won several important races, including the U.S. Grand Prix.

Marci Papadopoulos left the audience gasping at the 1979 U.S. Baton Twirling Championships. The 14-year-old Californian twirled her way to victories in all five events: solo, strut, dance-twirl, two-baton, and three-baton. Earlier in the year, Marci had performed at the First World Baton Twirling Demonstrations in Venice, Italy. Marci and other enthusiasts would like to see baton twirling become an Olympic sport.

Two important international competitions took place in 1979. One was the World Cup II track meet held in Montreal, Canada, in the fall. It had many people looking forward to the 1980 Olympics, since most of the world's top track and field athletes were there. A woman sprinter from the United States stole the show. Twenty-two-year-old Evelyn Ashford (*above*) won the 100-meter and 200-meter dashes, beating world-record holders each time.

The other competition was the Soviet Spartakiade, held in Moscow during the summer. It, too, gave athletes preparing for the Olympics a chance to show their stuff. Spartakiade was an exhibition as well as a competition. In addition to the regular Olympic sports, spectators watched group demonstrations, such as this living sculpture formed by platforms of young gymnasts (*right*).

183

THE PAN AMERICAN GAMES

The Pan American Games are held every four years, and they are the Western Hemisphere's preliminary to the Olympics. In July, 1979, the eighth Pan Am Games were held in San Juan, Puerto Rico. More than 4,400 athletes from 33 countries and territories participated in 25 sports.

The Games were a spectacular success for the United States, whose athletes collected a record 263 medals. The huge haul included 126 golds. Cuba, a steadily rising power in international athletics, finished second with an overall total of 146, including 65 golds. Canada was third with 135 medals, 24 of them gold.

The water sports proved to be an awesome showcase of U.S. talent. U.S. swimmers and divers captured 33 of a maximum 36 golds. They established Pan Am records in 21 events and broke 3 world records. The U.S. swimmers won 20 consecutive events before a pair of Canadian girls, Anne Gagnon and Joanne Bedard, snapped the long string by finishing first and second in the 200-meter breaststroke.

The U.S. swim team was led by 15-year-old Cynthia "Sippy" Woodhead. She placed first 5 times, the most for any athlete in the Games. Woodhead accounted for 1 of the 3 world records in the water events—with a clocking of 1:53.43 in the 200-meter freestyle. The second world mark was a magic moment for the island spectators, for it was produced by a native-born Puerto Rican, Jesse Vassallo. Seventeen-year-old Vassallo, as a resident of California, was representing the United States in the Games. He captured the 200-meter individual medley, covering the distance in 2:03.29. The third world-record breaker was the youngest U.S. swimmer, 14-year-old Mary Meagher. She swam the 200-meter butterfly in 2:09.77.

U.S. track and field performers finished on top in 25 of 39 events, with women contributing 11 of those victories. The major upset in that competition was the double defeat of Alberto Juantorena of Cuba.

No athlete in the Games was more distinguished than Juantorena, who had scored a rare twin triumph in the 1976 Olympics—in the 400- and 800-meter runs. In San Juan, the Cuban was defeated by Tony Darden of the United States in the 400 and by

The eighth Pan Am Games were held in Puerto Rico, with more than 4,400 athletes participating.

Cynthia Woodhead led the U.S. swim team to five first-place finishes and also set a world record.

184

In track and field competition, Cuban runner Silvio Leonard won the 100- and 200-meter dashes.

Canadian women, led by Monica Goermann, won four of the six golds in the women's gymnastic events.

James Robinson, also of the United States, in the 800. But the Cuban runners upheld their honor when Silvio Leonard took the golds in the 100- and 200-meter dashes.

The exciting gymnastic events were dominated by the Cubans and the Canadians. The Cuban men won all 8 golds. And the Canadian women won 4 of the 6 golds. Two U.S. high school girls were the surprising winners of the other 2 golds.

Cuba's powerful boxing brigade, led by Olympic heavyweight champion Teofilo Stevenson, went home with 5 of the 11 gold medals in that sport. In freestyle wrestling, the U.S. delegation did remarkably well, finishing first in all 10 events.

Roller skating and softball were new additions to the Pan Am Games. In roller skating, which turned out to be one of the most popular events, the United States and Argentina accounted for all the first-place finishes. In softball, the U.S. women's team captured the gold with a 2–0 win over Puerto Rico in the final game. The Canadian men's team won the championship match from the heavily favored U.S. team, 1–0.

FINAL MEDAL STANDINGS

	Gold	Silver	Bronze	Total
United States	126	92	45	263
Cuba	65	49	32	146
Canada	24	44	67	135
Mexico	3	6	28	37
Argentina	12	7	17	36
Brazil	9	13	14	36
Puerto Rico	2	9	11	22
Venezuela	1	4	7	12
Dominican Rep.	0	5	7	12
Chile	1	4	6	11
Colombia	0	1	8	9
Panama	0	3	1	4
Jamaica	0	3	0	3
Guyana	0	2	1	3
Peru	0	1	2	3
Ecuador	0	0	2	2
Bahamas	0	1	0	1
Virgin Islands	0	0	1	1
Neth. Antilles	0	0	1	1
El Salvador	0	0	1	1
Belize	0	0	1	1

185

ORIENTEERING—AN UNUSUAL RACE

You're in the woods beside a stream. You have a map and a compass. You're trying to reach a clearing that the map says is near the stream. But the stream winds and twists several times between you and the clearing. Should you follow the stream with all its twists and turns? Or can you get to the clearing faster if you set off in a straight line through the woods? Speed is important because there are other people who are trying to get to that clearing before you do. You're in a race!

This may sound like an unusual kind of race. In most races, everyone has to follow the same course. But in this race, you work with a map and a compass, and you choose your own route. And that's just part of the fun of the unusual and challenging sport called orienteering.

Orienteering gets its name from the fact that you must orient (relate) yourself to your surroundings at all times—or you'll probably get lost. In order to become oriented, you and the other competitors are given a special map at the start of the race. The map is a topographical map of the area you'll be racing in. It shows woods, hills, streams, ponds—everything having to do with the lay of the land. The map also shows a series of "control points." These are places you must reach in a specific order during the race. At each control point is a hole punch. You must punch your entry card so that the judges will know you've been to that point. The first one to reach the finish line is the winner.

To be a good orienteer, you've got to know how to read a "topo" map. The next control point may be right through those woods, but you might have to slosh through a mosquito-infested swamp to get there. Maybe you should follow the winding stream instead. And many of the control points are very carefully hidden, so that you don't just stumble on them by luck. You've got to know what you're doing.

As if all that weren't enough, some of the tougher orienteering races are run over courses that are 10 miles (16 kilometers) long. So the sport involves a real physical challenge as well as the mental challenge of reading maps and compasses and making navigational decisions.

Orienteering is not quite as hard as a wilderness survival test. But it's also no walk in the woods. It's a sport that provides challenge and fun. Do you have your compass? Your map? Ready—go!

186

The unusual sport of orienteering involves reading maps and compasses and making decisions.

ROLLING ALONG—THE SKATING CRAZE

They make you feel taller and faster. They let you swoop like the wind or spin like a top. You can dance on them, race on them, and play hockey on them without ice. These are just some of the reasons that millions of people have been lacing on roller skates.

So many people took up skating in 1979 that it became one of the fastest-growing pastimes ever to roll across North America. Some skate makers were selling more than 300,000 pairs a month.

The skaters seemed to be everywhere. They visited roller rinks in greater numbers than ever before. They took to their wheels on the streets and sidewalks of cities and towns. Some workers skated to and from their jobs. Some even skated while on their jobs, rolling along hallways in office buildings. Dancers in roller discos did their twisting and turning on skates. Rock singers and movie stars had their pictures taken on skates. Young children and grandparents rolled gently through parks. Daredevils risked their necks in roller acrobatics.

▶THE NEW SKATES

Roller skates have been around for more than 100 years. Why have they suddenly become so popular? Mostly because of the new wheels. The wheels, made from a plastic called polyurethane, were first used widely on skateboards. Attached to roller skates, the polyurethane wheels are a lot quieter than metal wheels and a lot stronger than wooden wheels.

With the new wheels, people moved outdoors for the kind of skating that before could only have been done on the smooth surfaces of rinks. And at the same time, indoor skating began to move to a disco beat. Since disco dancing and roller skating became popular at about the same time, it was only natural to want to do both at once.

The comfortable ride provided by the new wheels also allowed people to skate great distances—to travel to and from work, to see the sights, or just to get some exercise. Some skaters traveled up to 100 miles (160 kilometers) at a time. And a roller-skating marathon in Long Beach, California, attracted entrants ranging in age from 6 to 60. The fastest racers covered the 26.2-mile (42.2-kilometer) course in just under an hour and a half.

The skates became pretty fancy, too. Gone were most of the old clamp-on models. In came the new shoe-type skates. A good but plain pair cost about $75. Special models went for a good deal more—for example, cowboy-boot skates were priced at $200. A pair of motorized skates could speed a skater along at about 30 miles (48 kilometers) per hour and travel 220 miles per gallon (94 kilometers per liter) of gas. They cost about $150.

▶**FAD OR SPORT?**

Not everyone was happy about the roller-skating craze. In fact, some joggers and bicyclists were pretty upset when the skaters arrived on the scene. There was not always enough room in the parks or on the roads for everyone. And with all the joggers, cyclists, and skaters jockeying for space, people who just wanted to take an old-fashioned walk were often out of luck. Some cities and towns tried to calm things down by passing laws saying when and where people could skate. But it was not clear whether or not these limits would slow the growth of skating's popularity.

Some people believed that the fun would not last anyway, that skaters would tire of the pastime once the newness wore off. But there are signs that skating will be more than just a passing fad. At the 1979 Pan American Games, the Western Hemisphere's international athletic competition, roller skating became an official event. For the first time ever in the Games, skaters competed for medals in races and dance events.

Skaters are now trying to have the roller races and dancing made part of the Olympic Games. If they succeed, skating will have been accepted as a full-fledged sport. And skates will be part of the scene for a long time to come.

Disco dancing and roller skating—it was only natural for people to do both at the same time.

In 1979 roller skating became, for the first time, an official event at the Pan American Games.

GIVE THAT CARROT A SPEEDING TICKET!

Which is faster: A carrot or a can of sardines? Of course that's an odd question. But odder still is the fact that hundreds of people got the chance to find out in 1979. For during the year, art and oddness were wonderfully combined at the second Artists' Soap Box Derby, held in San Francisco. Instead of the traditional "soap boxes"—square wooden boxes mounted on wheels—the artists came up with some of the most outlandish "vehicles" imaginable: a sleek, speedy carrot with a green parachute trailing behind; a huge sardine can that zipped along on hidden wheels; and even a camera that had to be quick as a flash.

A total of 87 artists brought their creations to the derby, which was sponsored by the San Francisco Museum of Modern Art. The event was held at a hill in the city's McLaren Park. The spectators were awed, amused, and sometimes afraid as one or two of the vehicles went out of control and headed toward the crowd. But even if the vehicles were not especially built to be crash-proof, they certainly showed a lot about artistic design.

Imagine, for example, a two-stick orange popsicle—on wheels. Popsicles are made to be split in half, and partway down the hill, that's exactly what this one did. Each half coasted the rest of the way by itself. The derby may have begun with 87 vehicles, but it finished with 88.

Among the other entries was a huge bug, decorated with colorful metals and plastics, bright beads and buttons, a TV antenna, and bowling trophies. Another artist fashioned a fabulous fish, festooned with flattened aluminum cans. And one sculptor created a figure of a man lying on his stomach with his arms stretched ahead of him. The arms "held" the front wheel, and the driver sat on the man's back and maneuvered with a steering wheel that was mounted between the shoulders.

Transportation—or art—may never be the same again.

191

LIVING HISTORY

If you collect old toy soldiers, you can hold history in your hands.

GUARDIANS OF THE FIELDS

Scarecrows are among our best friends. Throughout the ages they have played a special role in the development of agriculture. Since the time that the soil was first tilled, people have relied on scarecrows to help protect their crops against hungry birds and other animals.

Almost every group of people, from nearly every land, has used scarecrows to protect their crops. The colonists who first came to the New World were familiar with scarecrows, but they were surprised to find the Indians using similar forms to keep intruders out of their cornfields. And it is fascinating to see how often scarecrows portray the characteristics of their national origin. For instance, the colorful figures guarding the rice and vegetable patches in Japan differ a great deal from those found in Europe or America because they are dressed in typical Japanese garb.

▶ **FROM STICK FIGURES TO PIE PANS**

The earliest planters soon learned that if they put a figure resembling a person in their fields, it would scare off crows and other pests. At the same time it would relieve the planters from the monotonous duty of keeping constant watch over their crops.

At first, farmers simply drove stakes into the ground and over them hung pieces of cloth that would flap in the breeze. It was hoped that unwelcome visitors would be deceived into thinking that the farmers were standing guard. It was a clever idea and it fooled the crows—at least for a while.

As the years went by, it seemed that the birds had grown wiser and bolder. So farmers began draping stick figures with old clothing to make them appear more realistic. To amuse themselves, the farmers also tried to make the figures look humorous as well as frightening. This was the beginning of an artistic tradition that has continued to this very day.

In great-grandfather's time, nearly every garden had its homemade crop guardian. Some of them were given affectionate names like Slim Jim, Clyde, the Green Lady, or just plain Boogie-man. They

194

ranged from ordinary stick figures to charming creations designed to show off the previous season's discarded fashions. The most traditional scarecrow was a jolly fellow wearing a tattered coat and faded overalls, stuffed with straw. Its head usually had a funny face and was crowned with a floppy hat. Some, however, were so elegantly dressed that watchdogs had to be chained to them at night to prevent tramps from sneaking up and exchanging their ragged coats for the field watchers' fancier garments.

These trusty helpmates are not as common today as they used to be. Modern farming methods have made scarecrows unnecessary because many seeds are treated with chemicals to prevent birds from digging them up. But you can still spot them in fields along back country roads—although they may just consist of lines of dangling aluminum pie pans that flash and glitter in the sun.

Unfortunately, a scarecrow's end is not a happy one. They seldom last more than a single season. The sun fades them and harsh winds gradually tear them to shreds. When the harvest is over, they are tossed aside and forgotten. But with the coming of the next spring, a new scarecrow usually appears on the same spot.

Do scarecrows really work? Many gardeners insist they do. Others are not so sure, but they enjoy building them just the same. Almost everyone agrees that they make the landscape more interesting, and their presence adds a touch of nostalgia for those who love to remember the good old days. It seems that as long as people continue to earn their living from the soil and struggle to prevent their ancient enemies, the crows, from robbing the fields, scarecrows are here to stay.

▶ A HOMESPUN ART FORM

Scarecrows are truly romantic figures and have long been favorite subjects for poets,

196

painters, and writers. They are mentioned in the Bible and have appeared in such favorite stories as *The Wizard of Oz*. They have also become a part of our folklore. One enchanting tale tells of a boy who built such a fearsome field figure that crows brought back the corn they had stolen the year before!

Nowadays experts consider scarecrows a contemporary folk art form. Some of the more interesting figures have been uprooted and taken to cities for exhibition. And some of the best are preserved in permanent folk art collections along with quilts, weathervanes, and cigar-store Indians. In recent years scarecrow contests have been held at county fairs, with prizes awarded for the most original and artistic designs.

You might like to try this folk art form. Young people are excellent scarecrow makers. It is a challenge to put together frightening and humorous life-sized images. Let your imagination run wild and you'll come up with wonderful creations. All it takes are some old clothes and a couple of sturdy sticks, one long enough to stand upright in the ground and the other attached at right angles to form a cross. This becomes the skeleton over which the clothes are draped—so the scarecrow will look like a real person when it shakes and flutters in unexpected gusts of wind. The head can be made from whatever object happens to be at hand—a rusty bucket, a plastic pumpkin left over from last Halloween, a piece of wood with a face sketched on, flower pots, even punctured basketballs.

The scarecrow's homespun character has not changed much over the years. It is still the universal symbol of country living. Above all, these scary creatures are fun to make and delightful to behold in their natural settings. They represent an exciting folk art activity in which we can all indulge our fancies.

AVON NEAL
Author, *Scarecrows*

THE OAK ISLAND MYSTERY

Almost everyone has dreamed of finding hidden treasure. For the archeologist, treasure may be the artifacts of a lost civilization. For the deep sea diver, treasure may be a sunken ship filled with gold coins. But for many others, the dream is to find a treasure map leading the way to a chest filled with gold and jewels.

For almost 200 years people have been digging for treasure on Oak Island. They haven't found it yet, but the dream doesn't die. So strong is the dream that fifteen separate expeditions have tried to find the treasure. Six people have died, and more than $2,000,000 has been spent.

Tiny Oak Island lies in the Atlantic Ocean off the coast of Nova Scotia, Canada. Its name was derived from the huge oak trees that once dotted the small, windswept island. In 1795, Daniel McGinnis, a teenager, was exploring the island when he noticed a long depression in the ground. Nearby stood an oak tree, with a branch

Perhaps pirates buried their loot on Oak Island . . .

sawed off directly over the depression. It looked as if a rope could have been slung over the branch and used to haul something out of the hole. Daniel went home and returned with two friends and some tools.

They began to dig and soon excavated a pit, with walls of smooth, hard clay. At about 10 feet (3 meters) their shovels struck wood. They must have been excited when they brushed away the earth and found that they were standing on a floor of very old oak logs. They removed the logs and began to dig again. They found nothing until they reached 20 feet (6 meters), when they struck another platform. At 30 feet (9 meters), you guessed it, another platform. Disappointed, the boys abandoned their digging. But it certainly seemed as if *someone* had gone to a lot of trouble to bury something in the tunnel—or the "money pit," as it has come to be called.

Nine years later, McGinnis and his friends returned to dig again. And, again, every 10 feet (3 meters) they found a platform. At 90 feet (27 meters) they found a flat stone carved with marks they could not read. Later, experts tried to decipher the symbols. Some said they read, "Forty feet below, two million pounds." But McGinnis and his friends were never to find the treasure. The day after finding the stone, they returned to find much of the tunnel filled with water. Eventually, they gave up the search.

In 1850 another group tried to solve the mystery of Oak Island. All they were able to solve was the origin of the water that continually flooded the tunnel. First they noticed that the water was salty and that its level rose and fell with the tides. Exploring the ocean's edge, they found stone-lined flood tunnels that went from the water line into the wall of the main tunnel, just 98 feet (30 meters) below the surface. Even odder was a huge, apparently man-made blanket of coconut fiber, grass, and seaweed that they found buried along the beach. The blanket acted as a gigantic sponge, taking in water at high tide and pouring it into the flood tunnels at low tide. Thus the main tunnel stayed continually flooded. It looked like the original builders had booby-trapped the tunnel so that no one would ever find their treasure!

Over the years other expeditions tried to find the treasure, excavating deeper and deeper into the tunnel. They, too, were frustrated in their attempts. The only things found so far include pieces of metal and wood, a copper coin dated 1713, and a scrap of parchment.

What makes people risk their lives and spend years working in a pit? What do they think they will find? There are many theories. Most revolve around gold and jewels. Some think that the treasure consists of French Queen Marie Antoinette's jewels. It is known that her maid escaped to Nova Scotia during the French Revolution.

Others think that the tunnel contains the lost treasure of the Incas. Impossible! you say. Remember the coconut fiber that was found? The nearest coconut tree grows 1,500 miles (2,400 kilometers) south of Nova Scotia. Perhaps ships carrying Incan gold were blown off course by hurricanes, and the gold was buried in Nova Scotia.

But most of the searchers believe that at the bottom of the mystery lies pirate treasure. It is known that in the late 1600's, there were many pirate ships in the waters between the Caribbean and Nova Scotia. And there is some evidence that points to Captain Kidd having buried his loot on Oak Island.

A Montreal businessman says the tunnel is a communal pirate bank. The main tunnel was dug first. Then each pirate who wanted to use the bank dug a secret tunnel out and up from the main tunnel. These tunnels came to within 30 feet (9 meters) of the surface. Pirates hid their treasure in these tunnels. Then the flood tunnels were dug and the main tunnel was flooded. When a pirate wanted to claim his treasure, he just had to dig down 30 feet (9 meters) to his private bank. All he needed to know was its exact location. Similar pirate banks have been found in Haiti and Madagascar.

To this day, no one has succeeded in finding any treasure. Said one prospector, "I saw enough to convince me that there was a treasure buried there. And enough to convince me that no one will ever get it!" But the search goes on.

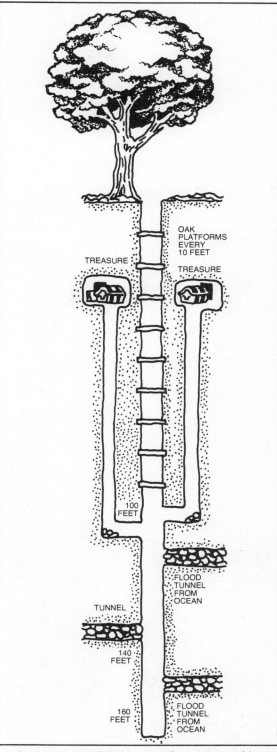

. . . in a "money pit" that was really a communal bank.

199

CHARLESTON: HARBOR OF HISTORY

Early in 1670, a small group of tired travelers stepped onto the marshy shore of what is now South Carolina. They had left their native England the previous summer—the first of several groups of people who would build a new community in this semitropical land so far from home.

The new community was named Charles Towne, in honor of King Charles II of England. But soon the people realized that it would be easier to defend their community if it were moved to a peninsula of land between the Ashley and Cooper rivers. The town officially relocated in 1680. In the 300 years since then, it has grown into one of North America's most beautiful cities.

The years were not, however, quiet ones. The city knew tragedy as well as triumph, poverty as well as wealth, sadness as well as joy. It was menaced by pirates, involved in wars, thrashed by hurricanes, struck by fires and earthquakes. Many of its citizens died in epidemics of smallpox and yellow fever.

▶ A CITY OF "FIRSTS"

Charles Towne (renamed Charleston in 1783) has had many "firsts" in its history. The first American naval victory of the Revolutionary War occurred in its harbor. On Sullivan Island, one of several islands in the harbor, stood a log fort made of trunks of palmettos, a type of palm that may reach heights of 90 feet (27 meters). On June 28, 1776, a group of patriots led by Colonel William Moultrie repelled a British fleet bent on capturing the city. The Americans were greatly outnumbered and had so little gunpowder that they had to suspend firing for two hours. But the palmetto logs absorbed the British gunfire, and the Americans suffered little loss. Surprisingly, the patriots were able to inflict great damage on the British, and by the time darkness fell, they had left in defeat.

In 1829, the federal government began to build another fort in the Charleston harbor. It was named for General Thomas Sumter, who was also a hero of the Revolutionary War. In 1860, South Carolina seceded from the Union, but Fort Sumter remained under federal control. It soon became a symbol of the growing difficulties between the southern, Confederate states and the northern, Union states. At 4:30 A.M. on April 12, 1861, Confederate soldiers fired at the Union forces that occupied Fort Sumter. It was the first shot of the Civil War, which lasted four years and caused many deaths and much suffering.

Another "first" occurred in Charleston

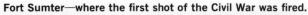

Fort Sumter—where the first shot of the Civil War was fired.

200

The historic district—where magnificent houses of yesterday are still lived in today.

harbor on February 17, 1864. A submarine designed by Horace L. Hunley torpedoed and sank a Union ship, the *Housatonic,* that was blockading the harbor. It was the first submarine in the world to sink an enemy ship in time of war.

The first fire insurance company in America was located in Charleston. Organized in 1736, it was known as "The Friendly Society for the Mutual Insurance of Houses Against Fire." Its fire fighters carried buckets and ladders as they rushed to put out fires in the wooden houses. Unfortunately, in 1740 a huge fire destroyed half the city—some 300 houses and many stores—and ruined the insurance company.

America's first local Chamber of Commerce and the first museum society were formed in Charleston in 1773. And artificial ice was first made there, in 1851.

▶ **A CITY WHERE HISTORY LIVES**

For Charlestonians of today and for people who visit this city, perhaps the most important "first" is a law that protects historical districts and buildings—the first such pro-

tective law in the United States. More than 1,000 buildings are now protected under this law. The magnificent houses of the 18th and 19th centuries remain as they were when wealthy merchants lived in them. The houses are still lived in today, some by descendants of the people who built them.

Many of Charleston's attractions are open to the public. You can visit an imposing three-story house where President George Washington once stayed. You can go to St. Michael's Episcopal Church, Charleston's oldest church building. One pew in the Church is much larger than the others—it was enlarged for Washington, who had very long legs.

You can see a full-scale replica of Hunley's submarine and visit Fort Sumter. In houses, museums, and shops you can see fine furniture, silver, and ironwork made by master artisans. All of these features link the Charleston of today with its past. It truly is a city where history lives.

JENNY TESAR
Sponsoring Editor
Gateways to Science

201

MESSAGES FROM THE PAST

The following objects have something interesting in common: an alarm clock, a safety pin, a toothbrush, a pair of bifocals, and a penny. All these objects were buried in a time capsule in 1938. And they will remain buried until 6939—nearly 5,000 years from now.

A time capsule is a fascinating way to "send a message" to the future. Some people of the 20th century want the people of future centuries to know what our life was like. And so they have buried time capsules—containers filled with objects, books, and pictures that tell the story of the 20th-century world. The time capsules are sealed inside the earth with instructions that they be opened at a certain time, usually thousands of years later.

The 1938 time capsule is about to be buried.

This practice of sending messages to people of the future actually goes back to the days of the ancient Egyptians and Babylonians. They would seal inscriptions and statuettes into the foundations of temples. And today, following that ancient custom, the cornerstones of buildings are often hollowed out to hold objects of the time.

But the term "time capsule" was first used for the container that was buried in 1938. In that year the people of New York City were preparing for a world's fair, which would be held in 1939. As part of the celebration, scientists of the Westinghouse Electric Corporation assembled this first time capsule. They came to the fairgrounds and buried it 50 feet (15 meters) below the earth.

The time capsule was made of Cupaloy, a metal of almost pure copper, which would not wear down or disintegrate over the centuries. Cigar-shaped, the capsule was about 7 feet (2 meters) long and as thick as a telephone pole. It contained dozens of common items, such as the ones mentioned earlier. But a lot more went into the capsule. There were also samples of fabrics, such as rayon, silk, and wool; samples of metals, such as aluminum, iron, and manganese; and samples of nonmetallic materials, such as cement, rubber, and asbestos. There were seeds of wheat, corn, cotton, alfalfa, and barley; a Bible; and an electric wall switch. And perhaps the two most interesting items of all were a newsreel film and an essay in microfilm. The newsreel showed interesting events and personalities of the time. The microfilm (film with microscopic-sized letters) contained more than 10,000,000 words and 1,000 pictures detailing the culture, science, industry, religion, and education of the world of 1938.

▶ AS THE WORLD CHANGES ...

A good sampling of the 20th-century world was buried in that 1938 time capsule. But a lot happened in the years that followed. The world changed a great deal. And so when another world's fair came to New York City in 1965, the scientists at Wes-

202

tinghouse decided to bury a second time capsule, right next to the first, that would show some of the changes of those 27 years.

Into that second capsule went a 50-star U.S. flag (in 1938 the U.S. flag had had 48 stars), a credit card, a bikini bathing suit, contact lenses, and an electric toothbrush. The capsule also contained something that would have truly astounded the people of 1938—a piece of a U.S. spacecraft that had carried an astronaut into space.

In addition to human beings venturing into space, the most important scientific event of the years between 1938 and 1965 was the dawn of the atomic age. So the 1965 capsule included some objects representing the world of atomic energy, such as a sample of radioactive carbon and a film strip about the USS *Nautilus* (the first atomic-powered submarine).

Later, time capsules were featured as part of two more world's fair celebrations: Expo 67 held in Montreal, Canada, and Expo '70, at Osaka, Japan. The 1967 capsule is to be opened in 2067; the 1970 capsule, in 6970.

▶ YOUR OWN TIME CAPSULE

Most of these time capsules will not be opened for thousands of years. But not all capsules need be buried that long. You can make your own time capsule, which you can bury for five years or even one year. What would you put in your time capsule? Here are some suggestions:
- a picture of yourself
- a newspaper from the day on which you bury the capsule
- a note containing your height and weight (you will be interested to see how you have grown)
- a lock of your hair (you will want to see if it gets darker or lighter)
- a tracing of your hand
- a note telling a little about yourself, what you did on the day you buried your capsule, and what you think you will be like on the day you open your capsule
- a sample of your handwriting
- the name of your best friend or your favorite book, song, or TV show

If you bury your time capsule outdoors, you'll need a waterproof container, such as a large glass jar with a tight-fitting lid. If you decide to hide your time capsule indoors, any cardboard box will be good enough.

In either case, make sure that your time capsule is well hidden. Leave a note to yourself to remind you where you hid it and when to open it. When you do open it, one year or five years from now, you'll be excited to receive messages from *your* past.

DANIEL J. DOMOFF
Consulting Editor
Educational Developmental Laboratories

203

LITTLE TOY SOLDIERS

The auctioneer held her gavel poised in midair, ready to close the bidding on the item just put up for sale.

"Two hundred is bid," she announced to the crowd gathered at the Phillips auction gallery in New York City. "Is there any advance over two hundred?"

There was a moment of hesitation. Suddenly a hand shot up in the back of the auction gallery.

"Two-twenty!" the auctioneer cried, a note of excitement in her voice. Another hand went up—then another.

"Two-forty . . . Two-sixty," declared the auctioneer, jabbing the gavel in the direction of each bidder.

In a matter of seconds the bidding had jumped to $300. Finally, the auctioneer brought down her hammer, signaling that the lot had been "knocked down," or sold. The sale price was $325.

What was the item that had commanded so much interest? A valuable old print? A

rare book? A delicate porcelain tea set? Guess again. Actually, the lot consisted of ten tiny toy soldiers—a set of medieval Knights of Agincourt, made by the English firm of W. Britain. (In the 1950's, the same toy soldiers had sold for less than $20.)

Other toy soldiers were sold that day for equally high prices. A set of six cavalrymen made in France 30 years ago sold for $225. A group of ancient Roman soldiers, put out by a German company in the 1920's, went for $420.

Some of the toy soldiers were still bright and shiny in their thick coats of enamel paint. Others were frayed and bent, battle-scarred veterans of childhood war games on living-room floors.

Fifty years ago, miniature warriors like these could have been bought for just a few pennies each. Only twenty years ago, similar figures were still being sold in department stores for a few dollars a set.

But no more. Most of the firms that produced high-quality lead soldiers either have gone out of business or have shifted to making toy soldiers out of cheaper materials such as plastic. As a result, the lead soldiers your dad and granddad played with are worth their weight in gold. They have become highly prized collector's items.

▶WHY COLLECT TOY SOLDIERS?

In the past few years, thousands of people around the world have joined the ranks of toy soldier collectors. It is estimated that there are about 10,000 toy soldier enthusiasts in the United States and Canada. And there are many more thousands in European countries like Britain, France, and West Germany.

(Still another group of military buffs collects what are called military miniatures. These are detailed, lifelike models that were never meant to be played with. They are considered miniature works of art by their owners.)

Why the sudden interest in toy soldiers? And why are collectors willing to spend hundreds and even thousands of dollars on their hobby? Part of it has to do with nostal-

Antique toy soldiers like these medieval Knights of Agincourt have now become collector's items.

gia—fond memories of childhood playthings. Collectors also point to the fine workmanship of the old lead soldiers, which were cast and painted by hand and not by machines.

But there's also another reason. Because toy soldiers—as well as other old toys—are increasing in value at a fast rate, they are considered a good investment. Some businessmen are buying toy soldiers as a hedge against inflation. As one of them put it: "My stocks may go up or down, but my toy soldier collection is worth more each year."

▶HOLDING HISTORY IN YOUR HAND

Most collectors are attracted by the pageantry of their miniature armies, dressed in the colorful uniforms of centuries past. A shelf full of kilted Scottish Highlanders, scarlet-coated British guardsmen, or galloping French hussars is an eye-dazzling spectacle. Said one collector, "When I pick up one of my toy soldiers, I am holding history in my hand."

Although there has been a recent explosion of interest in toy soldiers, they have been popular playthings for several thousand years. Tiny figures of fighting men, made out of clay, wood, and bronze, have been found in ancient Egyptian, Greek, and Roman tombs. Archeologists believe the figures were both religious objects and children's toys.

During the Middle Ages, the sons of wealthy noblemen used wooden models of knights to stage mock tournaments. Strings and pulleys enabled the children to send the knights crashing into each other so that their lances actually broke, as in a real joust.

Later on, toy replicas of soldiers and military equipment were used to educate the sons of princes and kings in the art of warfare. These royal playthings were made of gold or silver. As a young prince, the 17th-century French King Louis XIII had a magnificent set of 300 toy soldiers made of silver. This beautiful set was passed on to his son, the future Louis XIV, and something new was added. The soldiers were mounted in such a way that they could actually move around and fight battles.

Most toy soldiers of the 1600's and 1700's were made of metal. But many other

These camels and their riders are examples of the fine workmanship of toy soldiers made in the past.

materials were used, including wood, cork, and wax. There were even toy soldiers that could be eaten! Made of sugar and flour, they were hardened in molds until they could be painted. Like their civilian counterpart, the gingerbread man, they were very popular. The Russian Czar Peter III, as a boy, had a whole collection of these pastry soldiers. One time, he discovered that a rat had raided his military cookie jar and had eaten part of his army. According to a popular account, Peter was so furious that he had the rat court-martialed and executed.

Up until the end of the 18th century, toy soldiers were very expensive, and only the rich could afford them. Then, in 1775, a German firm in the city of Nuremberg began to mass produce toy soldiers made out of tin. The German-made soldiers were thin, two-dimensional figures called "flats"—as opposed to three-dimensional, or "round," figures.

Flat figures dominated the toy soldier scene for nearly one hundred years. The Nuremberg firms were soon joined by toy makers in other German cities. By the 1840's, German flats were being exported to other parts of Europe.

The most famous of the German toy sol-

205

dier makers was Heyde of Dresden. Beginning in the 1870's, the firm produced a wide range of three-dimensional, or round, figures. Boxed sets of Heyde figures were shipped all over the world and were popular in the United States as well as in Europe. Heyde figures covered all periods of history, from the armies of ancient Greece and Rome to the combat troops of World War I. There were German marching bands in spiked helmets, artillery units with cannon, and cavalrymen that were detachable from their horses. The Heyde firm continued making toy soldiers until World War II, when its Dresden factory was bombed out.

For the past 150 years, the French firm of Mignot has produced boxed sets of solid lead toy soldiers. Naturally, the emphasis is on French troops. But their catalog lists soldiers of all periods and armies—from ancient Egyptians to Union and Confederate troops of the U.S. Civil War. The Mignot Company is now the oldest toy soldier manufacturer in the world.

The toy soldiers made by Heyde and Mignot were solid figures—that is, metal through and through. But in 1893 an English toy maker named William Britain came up with a method of making lead soldiers that were hollow on the inside.

Little toy soldiers cover the entire sweep of history —from Attila the Hun *(above)* to Chinese troops who fought in the Boxer Rebellion of 1900 *(below).*

By far the most popular of the old toy soldiers are the hollow-cast figures made by W. Britain.

These hollow-cast figures were cheaper to produce than the solid toy soldiers of other makers. Thus, the W. Britain Company was able to undersell its competitors. By 1905, W. Britain was turning out 5,000,000 castings a year, representing 100 different British fighting units.

Britain's lead soldiers quickly became popular. Many a young boy awoke on Christmas morning to find a set of Britain's toy soldiers "with movable arms" (a feature added in 1897) under the family tree. By the time World War I began, in 1914, Britain's figures were being shipped to people all over the world.

Britains Ltd., as the company was later known, kept growing and adding to its line of toy soldiers. But although it became the biggest and best-known toy soldier firm in the world, it never relaxed its high standards. Each new set was carefully researched, and each figure was hand-painted. The company switched over to plastic in the mid-1960's because of cost factors.

Several firms in the United States began producing lead soldiers in the early 1900's. The most noted of these was the McLoughlin company, which made soldiers of the world. In the 1940's and 1950's a firm called Comet put out a well-designed line of solid figures under the name Authenticast. But none of these firms ever rivaled Britains in production or popularity.

The old toy soldiers have now become museum pieces or expensive collector's items. But new toy soldier firms have sprung up in Britain and the United States to meet the needs of toy soldier buffs. Many of these newcomers offer lead soldiers made in the traditional way—hand-painted in glossy enamels and even with movable arms. Although they're less expensive than the old soldiers, they are not cheap. A set of four to eight figures may cost anywhere from $20 to $40—sometimes more.

But for true toy soldier collectors, the new figures can never replace the Britains, Mignots, and Heydes of earlier generations. "There's nothing like the look and feel of the lead soldiers I played with as a kid," commented one devoted Britains collector. "They're in a class by themselves."

HENRY I. KURTZ
Author, *Captain John Smith*

207

THE RETURN OF THE ZEPPELIN

On August 29, 1929, a huge, blimplike shape rose majestically over Lakehurst Naval Air Station in New Jersey. A crowd of people cheered—the *Graf Zeppelin,* the largest airship of its day, was beginning its round-the-world flight. (An airship, like a balloon, rises because it is filled with gas that is lighter than air. But unlike a balloon, an airship can be steered and has propellers to move it forward.)

The *Graf Zeppelin's* flight was the first round-the-world flight by an airship. On board were several dozen passengers from many different countries. The stately zeppelin moved through the air at just over 70 miles (113 kilometers) an hour. During the following weeks it circled the globe, returning to Lakehurst 21 days, 5 hours, and 54 minutes after its first takeoff. Thousands were on hand to greet the returning airship, for this was a historic occasion. It not only marked the first round-the-world trip by a passenger-carrying airship, it also heralded what many believed would be the era of the zeppelin.

But ten years later, zeppelins were almost gone from the skies. A series of fatal crashes and explosions had killed public enthusiasm for travel by airship.

Now, a half century later, people are once again talking about using airships to carry cargo and passengers all over the world. In 1979, which was the 50th anniversary of the *Graf Zeppelin's* world tour, the U.S. Senate's Science, Technology and Space Committee heard testimony from zeppelin enthusiasts. The airship supporters spoke of building a new fleet of zeppelins that would be capable of carrying much bigger loads than even the largest airplane. One scientist suggested creating an airship that would be a cross between a helicopter and a zeppelin. This type of sky ship could transport such things as ready-to-assemble buildings and oil-drilling rigs to remote areas where there are no airfields.

Another scientist favored a fleet of giant zeppelins to transport freight across the length and breadth of the United States. Each of the monster airships would be 1,300 feet (396 meters) long—almost twice the size of the *Graf Zeppelin*—and could carry a cargo load of 500 tons. Supporters say that such airships could make the New York to Los Angeles run in only 36 hours. That's more than two days faster than trucks take to do the job.

Furthermore, zeppelins use far less fuel than either trucks or planes carrying the same amount of freight. As the cost of oil continues to soar, this could help cut energy costs.

▶**FROM BALLOONS TO ZEPPELINS**

The use of balloons and airships to carry people and things goes back nearly 200 years. In 1783, a team of Frenchmen made the first successful manned balloon flight. Two years later, an American named John Jeffries and his French companion J. P. Blanchard made the first balloon crossing of the English Channel.

The problem with these early balloons was that there was no way to steer them. Once aloft, they just drifted with the wind. Throughout the early 1800's, enterprising balloonists tried everything from oars to hand-powered paddle wheels to propel balloons. In 1852, a balloonist named Henri Giffard attached a propeller powered by a small steam engine to his balloon, and the first real "aircraft" was born.

Later designers used electric motors, and in 1898 a Brazilian named Alberto Santos-Dumont became the first man to fly an airplane that used a gasoline engine. These early airships were called dirigibles—a term that comes from the Latin word to steer. The cigar-shaped bag was kept inflated by the gas inside—usually hydrogen. If the bag was punctured, it would deflate.

By the late 1800's, designers had created the rigid airship, in which the skin of the bag was stretched over a metal framework. The rigid airship kept its shape whether there was gas inside or not. The most famous rigid airships were those designed by Count Ferdinand von Zeppelin of Germany. The first in a long line of zeppelins was put into the air in 1900. Soon German zeppelins

The *Graf Zeppelin*, in 1929. Today people are once again thinking about using airships.

were being used to carry passengers to different parts of Europe. Some were even used in World War I to drop bombs on enemy targets.

After World War I, the zeppelins became a popular form of air travel. Each year they became bigger and more luxurious. The biggest had huge lounges and dining areas.

In 1928, Germany built the *Graf Zeppelin,* named in honor of Count Zeppelin. It was the largest airship built up to that time—more than three times as long as a 747 passenger jet of today. The *Graf Zeppelin* was used to inaugurate a transatlantic passenger service from Europe to the United States.

The first flight to the United States took place in the fall of 1928. Carrying 20 passengers and a crew of 40—including Dr. Hugo Eckener, the head of the German Zeppelin Transport Company—the great airship glided over the Atlantic. Midway to North America, however, the zeppelin ran into a rain squall. The big airship was buffeted about, fabric was ripped from the tail fin, and it seemed that the first flight across the Atlantic might end in tragedy.

In the control cabin, Dr. Eckener watched as the craft began to drift. The engines were stopped as volunteers from the crew crawled out onto the enormous tail to make repairs. As the dangerous work progressed, a rain shower hit the zeppelin and it began to lose altitude and drop toward the ocean. It was a frightening moment. Eckener was afraid that if he started the engines while the crewmen were still outside, the motion would sweep them off the

tail to their deaths. When the big craft was only 300 feet (90 meters) above water, the command to start engines was given. The crewmen making repairs saw what was happening and crawled to safety.

The *Graf Zeppelin* proceeded without further incident to the United States. There it was greeted by tumultuous crowds in every city it flew over.

The *Graf Zeppelin's* transatlantic flights and its round-the-world tour started a new boom in zeppelin building and travel. Britain and the United States joined Germany in building passenger aircraft. It seemed that zeppelins were the wave of the future.

Then came a series of accidents, in which dirigibles crashed and lives were lost. The worst of these disasters occurred in 1937, when the German airship *Hindenburg* exploded and burst into flames as it was being moored at Lakehurst Naval Air Station. Thirty-six people were killed, and with them died the hopes and dreams of zeppelin enthusiasts in Europe and the United States.

Now it appears that rigid airships may stage a comeback. Defenders of the airship point out that the reason for earlier accidents was the use of hydrogen, a gas that is highly flammable and dangerous. By using a slightly heavier gas called helium, the danger is eliminated, and airships would be as safe as—and perhaps even safer than—other forms of air travel.

So the next time you look up into the sky, that strange object you see may not be a bird, a plane, or even Superman. It may just be a zeppelin majestically gliding through the air.

Trois Rivières is Canada's second oldest city. The three outlets of the St. Maurice River, separated by small islands, gave Trois Rivières (Three Rivers) its name.

TROIS RIVIÈRES

Halfway between Montreal and Quebec City, in Canada's Quebec Province, there is another city that has its own special meaning in Canada's past and present life. This city is Trois Rivières, which means "Three Rivers" in English. Because Trois Rivières is mainly a place of industry and commerce, it is sometimes forgotten when the beauties of Quebec, Canada's French-speaking province, are being described. But it has a small Old French section of great charm, and the story of Trois Rivières' role in Canada's history and economy is fascinating.

Trois Rivières is Canada's second oldest city (after Quebec City). It lies on the northern bank of the great St. Lawrence River, 78 miles (125 kilometers) southwest of Quebec City and 83 miles (134 kilometers) northeast of Montreal. The city was founded at a very important spot—the place where the St. Maurice River enters the St. Lawrence from the north.

The St. Maurice River and its valley led to the growth of Trois Rivières. A long and turbulent river, the St. Maurice starts far to the north, in the foothills of the Laurentian Mountains. The valley and its watershed are rich in forests, which in turn are full of wild fur-bearing animals. These resources gave rise to Trois Rivières' two main enterprises: the fur trade in long-ago times, and the timber and paper industries in the 19th and 20th centuries. The St. Maurice River was the water highway that was used to bring both the furs and the logs downriver to Trois Rivières.

▶ EARLY TIMES

Jacques Cartier, the French explorer, first saw the site of Trois Rivières in 1535. After that, French seamen came to buy fur pelts from the Indians. A trading post grew up, and then a fort was built to protect the post from attacks by the Iroquois Indians. The fortified settlement at Trois Rivières became the gateway to the vast North American trading empire that the French were setting up. Roman Catholic missionaries came too, to convert the Indians. In the mid-17th century the settlement was a bustling center, filled with French traders, explorers, missionaries, and Indian traders.

Many great French explorers lived in Trois Rivières. Among them were Radisson and Groseilliers, who explored Lake Superior and Hudson Bay; Jean Nicolet, the discoverer of Lake Michigan; and the La Vérendryes (father and son), who explored the Rocky Mountains.

Trois Rivières' first great period ended about 1665 when the center of the fur trade shifted to two other river ports. But even so, Canada's first "heavy industry" was started about 7 miles (11 kilometers) north of Trois Rivières in the 1730's. This was an ironworks, Les Forges du Saint-Maurice, the first in North America. It flourished until about 1850. In its heyday, this big forge provided jobs for 300 people. It made horseshoe nails, plowshares, anchors, cast-iron heating stoves, anvils, flatirons, caldrons, kettles, and tools of all kinds. And in wartime it made cannonballs. Now the forge and its buildings are in ruins, but it is being gradually restored. It is one of the fascinating places to see in a search for Trois Rivières' history.

The past can also be found in the city itself. A bad fire in 1908 destroyed most of the Old French section. But a cluster of buildings survives, showing the architecture of the early days. The chief building is the Ursuline Convent, built about 1700. It has massive, stark walls with clean, graceful

lines. Several large houses of about the same period are to be seen nearby. One, Tonnancour House, built in 1690, is the city's oldest.

▶TREES, PULP, AND PAPER

By the 1840's, Trois Rivières had been in a long period of decline. Then an upsurge in logging in the St. Maurice valley brought the city back to life. Lumber mills sprang up, and soon millions of cords of lumber were being shipped to Europe and the United States. At the end of the 1880's, when ways to make paper from wood pulp were perfected, the pulp and paper industry grew rapidly in many parts of Quebec. Big pulp and paper mills were built at Trois Rivières. Today the city makes more newsprint (the paper used in newspapers) than any other place in North America. And there is even a school of papermaking, run by the Quebec Department of Youth, that trains young people to take their place in this big industry.

Paper is not the only product of Trois Rivières, whose activities and prosperity are constantly growing. Textiles and rubber and electrical products are also manufactured and are helping to spark the economic advance of this whole part of Quebec.

The Ursuline Convent, built about 1700.

Trois Rivières' forge, the first in North America.

The Loch Ness Monster, at Busch Gardens, is only for the bravest riders.

ROLLER COASTERS—SCARE MACHINES

Charles Lindbergh, the first person to fly across the Atlantic Ocean alone, called it a "greater thrill than flying an airplane at top speed." James Irwin, who went to the moon on Apollo 15, said that it was "rougher than Saturn V." A Harvard University student liked it so much that he did it for 110 hours. What are these people talking about? A trip on an SST? Being shot from a cannon? Sky diving? No. What they are talking about is a ride on a roller coaster.

Roller coasters have been around for about three hundred years. But they have had their ups and downs in popularity. In the early 1920's a new one opened up almost every week. In the 1950's most of them had been plowed under by bulldozers. In the 1970's a great revival of interest was once again taking place.

About 30 have been built since 1972, and most of these are humdingers. Nestled in amusement parks across the country, they are designed to scare a rider just to the point where the stomach jumps out of its usual resting place and up into the throat. The heart drops to somewhere around the knees. Only the autonomic nervous system keeps

the rider breathing. Fans travel the country looking for a scarier ride. And fiendish designers sit in back rooms trying to invent the ultimate scare.

▶ICY BEGINNINGS

The first coasters were built in St. Petersburg, Russia, in the 17th century. Ice-covered wooden slides with an angle of about 50 degrees provided a slick, fast surface for sleds. Riders climbed to the top of a 70-foot (21-meter) platform and then shot down the slide—it must have been much like a modern bobsled ride. The French redesigned the rides and called them Russian Mountains. They adapted the sleds to run on wheels instead of runners. Thus ice wasn't needed and the rides could be enjoyed year-round.

By the latter part of the 19th century the popular coasters had spread to the United States. The first one in the United States was actually a converted railroad. Originally a series of open cars, it had carried coal from mines at the top of Mt. Pisgah in Pennsylvania to Mauch Chunk at the foot of the mountain. As a coaster, it took the riders up

212

to the top of the mountain and then sent them down again. It wasn't fast, but the scenery was very beautiful.

In 1884, LaMarcus A. Thompson, an engineer, built a device much like the Mauch Chunk railroad. He built it at Coney Island, an amusement park in Brooklyn, New York. Wheeled cars moved along hills and valleys of tracks. Since the cars had no power, men pushed them to the top of an incline. Then the cars plunged to the bottom on their own. People lined up to take a five-cent ride on the new invention. It is estimated that the owner took in about $700 a day. Soon other amusement-park owners were begging Thompson to build rides.

By 1920 most amusement parks had some kind of roller coaster. The parks boomed and coasters were a big part of their business. In 1927, at Crystal Beach, outside Buffalo, New York, the Cyclone opened. It was billed as the "most fearsome coaster ever built." Almost 75,000 people went to see the Cyclone on opening day. The park owner had a first-aid station to minister to fainting riders. Soon there were Cyclones in parks around the country. At Playland, in Rye, New York, an especially terrifying roller coaster was built. It was 90 feet (27 meters) high. The tracks were a series of loops. In one loop, the car plunged underground. It was the first coaster to go underground, adding an extra thrill to the ride.

As the 1920's drew to a close, economic depression settled over the United States. Many people were jobless. Attendance at amusement parks dwindled because people just didn't have the money for rides and other amusements. Parks that had been jammed with laughing people were now almost empty. Roller coasters stood idle and many were torn down. Soon roller coasters became just a memory.

Walt Disney remembered amusement parks as shabby, dirty places. But he went ahead and built Disneyland, in Anaheim, California, a "theme park" with activities for every possible taste. Most of the Disneyland rides are based on Disney characters like Mickey Mouse and the other creatures made famous by the Disney movies and comic books. Disney characters are also the theme of Walt Disney World in Florida.

The idea of the theme park became very popular in the 1960's and 1970's. And the people who visit these theme parks want the thrill and excitement of roller coasters. With modern technology and the computer, they are getting the fantastic rides they demand. Park owners are spending millions of dollars for computerized steel monsters that rise and dip and loop and do corkscrew turns.

▶ HOW A ROLLER COASTER WORKS

The feeling of riding on a roller coaster is the feeling of sudden shocks. You are slowly brought to the top of a steep incline. Then, suddenly, you are dropped. Your body falls through space. Again you are

The first coasters were built in the 17th century in Russia. Riders on sleds shot down huge, ice-covered wooden slides—like a bobsled ride.

brought to the top of another incline, and you slow almost to a standstill. Then you rush down in an incredible burst of speed.

People who ride a roller coaster have a definite feeling of falling because they are, in fact, falling. The force that drives the coasters is the force of gravity and nothing else. There are no motors or engines attached to the cars. The coaster is mechanically towed to the top of the first and highest hill of the ride. As it is pulled up, enough energy is stored in the coaster to make it run all the way around the track. The coaster falls down the first hill. When it hits the bottom it has enough speed to make it to the top of the next hill. Because the coaster is losing energy, the next hill is made smaller than the first. This is repeated until the coaster comes to a stop at the end of the ride.

Because the roller coaster runs on the force of gravity, engineers can calculate exactly how fast the cars will move and how far they will go. This allows coaster designers to create rides that go through tunnels and loops and turns without unexpected stops or speed ups. Some of the loops and turns look dangerous, but they really aren't because special safety devices are used. In addition, centrifugal force—the force of spinning—pins riders in their seats. If you want to see how centrifugal force works, put some water in a pail and swing the pail by its handle around and around over your head. Even when the pail is turned upside down, the water doesn't spill because centrifugal force holds the water against the bottom of the pail.

▶ BUT ARE THEY SAFE?

With a ride that could be dangerous—as a roller-coaster ride could be—operators have to be very concerned with safety. Modern coasters have very sophisticated equipment. The cars are made from high-impact molded plastic. Each rider is provided with shoulder straps. It is unlikely anyone could fall out of a car unless he or she was doing something foolish like standing up or showing off.

A main safety concern is that a car could break away or that part of the track could collapse. To try to prevent this, all parts of the ride are inspected often. Periodically, joints and other metal parts subjected to stress are x-rayed. X rays can detect weaknesses in the metal.

Of course, accidents are possible, and oc-

The Big Bend, at Six Flags Over Texas, is another good coaster ride for people who are seeking thrills.

214

The Corkscrew, at Knott's Berry Farm in California. The loops and turns may look dangerous to you, but special devices are used to keep riders safe.

casionally they do occur. But a roller coaster is generally much safer than the family car.

▶ **COASTERS THAT CHALLENGE THE BRAVEST**

Just why do some people search out scary rides? Some say they go just for the thrill of it. One expert on amusement parks says people seek out thrills on scary rides because there are very few thrills left in everyday life. An official at Disneyland says that it goes back to a basic instinct for survival—the rider knows that the ride isn't *really* dangerous, but it gives the rider the feeling that he or she has survived a terrifying experience.

If you are one of those people who are looking for the ultimate scare, here are some roller-coaster rides that you definitely shouldn't miss:

Loch Ness Monster. Named for the mysterious Scottish sea monster, this ride is hard to miss at Busch Gardens in Williamsburg, Virginia. It features a 114-foot (35-

meter) drop, during which the rider travels in total darkness through a tunnel.

Colossus. Said to be the world's largest roller coaster, it is located at Magic Mountain, a park in northern California. At one point the rider plunges 105 feet (32 meters). At the bottom of this drop, the car is traveling at 65 miles (105 kilometers) per hour.

Mind Bender. Located at Six Flags Over Georgia, in Atlanta, this one really does bend the mind. There are three loops, so that a person is completely upside down three separate times. The speed approaches 60 miles (97 kilometers) per hour. And all this happens in just 90 seconds.

Space Mountain. Located at Walt Disney World, in Florida, this coaster is more than a ride. The ride begins inside the top of a mountain. It is pitch dark. Eighty film projectors and 150 speakers subject riders to dazzling visual and sound effects as they zip through the dark.

JOHN VICTOR
President, Program Design, Inc.

215

YOU CAN BANK ON IT!

"A penny saved is a penny earned," goes the old saying. But these antique mechanical coin banks give a bonus—they perform a clever or amusing trick each time a coin is deposited in them. They date from between 1870 and 1890. At that time, mechanical banks made of iron and tin were great favorites with children. Today they have become expensive collector's items. But new mechanical banks—usually made of plastic—are now being made. So in addition to saving your pennies, perhaps you should think about saving your banks.

Novelty Bank, 1872. A coin is placed on the man's tray. The door is closed. The man swivels around and deposits the coin behind the cashier's tray.

Uncle Sam Bank, 1886. A coin is placed in Uncle Sam's hand. A lever behind his umbrella is pushed. He drops the coin into his satchel, at the same time opening and closing his mouth as if he were talking.

Girl Skipping Rope Bank, 1890. A coin is placed between the squirrel's paws (at right). The bank is wound with a key and a lever is pushed. The girl skips rope and moves her head, arms, and legs.

Trick Dog Bank, 1888. A coin is placed in the dog's mouth. A lever is pushed. The dog leaps through the hoop and deposits the coin in the barrel. The dog is then placed back into position.

Jonah and the Whale Bank, 1890. A coin is placed on Jonah's back. A lever is pushed and the coin is deposited in the whale's mouth. The mouth opens and closes a number of times after the coin is swallowed.

Taxco is a small, picturesque city in southwestern Mexico.

TAXCO—THE CITY BUILT ON SILVER

It's almost daybreak in Taxco, a small city in southwestern Mexico. The usual morning symphony begins: Cocks crow. Here and there a donkey brays. The multitude of dogs continue their refrain of barking, which has lasted through most of the night. And the bells of the churches herald a new day.

As the sun rises, Taxco emerges as a pyramid of white and pastel houses, red tile roofs, and church steeples clinging to the side of a mountain. Among the buildings are trees with red, orange, and purple blossoms. Bright red flower pots filled with geraniums and other plants claim nearly every bit of space on iron-grilled window sills and balconies. Narrow cobbled streets climb and wind through the maze of colonial dwellings. Some of the streets are so steep and narrow that they can be ascended only on foot or on a donkey.

There is definitely an Old World look to Taxco. But there is something more. Taxco is actually built on silver. Ore is mined from under the city itself and from the surrounding hills. Artisans craft the refined metal into silverware and jewelry. And more than 200 silver shops sell the exquisite silver items that have made Taxco world famous.

▶ HOW THE SILVER CITY GREW

In 1521 a Spanish expedition led by Hernando Cortes conquered the capital of the Aztecs on the site of present-day Mexico City. Soon afterward, Cortes sent out a party of soldiers to look for tin to mix with copper in order to make cannons. The Spaniards traveled to an Indian Village called Tlachco, in the mountains far to the south. The metal they found there was not tin—it was precious silver.

The discovery of silver drew Spanish colonists to Tlachco. Soon they had built a town, which they named Taxco, near the Indian village. Productive veins of silver were discovered. But for more than 200 years, Taxco was known to outsiders as just a small stopover on a burro trail between Mexico City and Acapulco.

In the 1700's, José de la Borda, who had come from France to seek his fortune in silver, discovered the rich San Ignacios vein.

218

The beautiful silver creations that have made Taxco famous can be found in stores throughout the city.

He amassed a fortune and poured his wealth into Taxco. He paid for the construction of cobbled streets, bridges, aqueducts, and the famous baroque church of Santa Prisca.

Mining declined after the San Ignacios vein had been depleted. Taxco became a poor, sleepy little town. But because it was picturesque and pleasant, it attracted a number of artists and writers. One of these writers was an American named William Spratling, who helped to shape the destiny of the mining town.

In 1929, Spratling came to Taxco to write a book about life in a small Mexican town. Soon he began to wonder why the silver that was mined in Taxco was exported, and the finished silver products crafted abroad. Why, he thought, can't the silver be crafted in Taxco?

Spratling had a good eye for design. But he had no skill in silversmithing, and the only silversmiths around were a few folk artists who made simple trinkets for the tourist trade. So he went to a nearby town and persuaded two experienced goldsmiths to come to Taxco to work in his own shop.

Design was the key element in the objects that Spratling's shop made. Aztec and other Indian designs were used in jewelry and or-

namental objects. *Las Delicias,* as Spratling's shop had come to be called, prospered as the demand for his products increased. He began to hire local youths with artistic ability to be trained as apprentices in design and silversmithing.

In 1931, a highway that ran through Taxco was completed, and many travelers began to pass through the Silver City. Visitors stopped to admire and buy the superior silver creations of William Spratling.

By 1940, *Las Delicias* employed over 300 artisans. Some of them eventually became independent designers and set up their own shops. Today, Mexico leads all the countries of the world in the production of silver. And Taxco silver designs are heralded as among the very best.

It starts to get dark early in Taxco as the sun sinks behind the crest of the mountain on which the city is built. One by one, the lights in houses come on, and then the streetlights. Well before midnight the town has gone to bed. Except for a little revelry here and there—and the incessant barking of the dogs—Taxco sleeps over its veins of silver as it has for centuries.

JOHN TEDFORD
Cumbre publishing company, Mexico

219

WORLD OF YOUTH

The year 1979 was declared the International Year of the Child. And countries all over the world honored their children.

A CELEBRATION OF CHILDREN

Children are the world's greatest resource. They grow up to become scientists and farmers, teachers and explorers, presidents and doctors, and many other important people. But in too many parts of the world, children are not treated like a precious resource.

At a factory in Colombia, young children carry heavy loads of bricks. At a garbage heap in the Philippines, a boy looks for bits of metal, glass, and other objects that he can sell. In a carpet factory in Morocco, girls spend their days tying thousands of tiny knots. In a coal mine in India, children pull machinery through low tunnels. On a farm in California, children pick box after box of asparagus.

More than 55,000,000 children under the age of 15 work. Most work at jobs that are unpleasant, unhealthy, and unsafe. These children do not work because they want to. They work because they have to. Without the money they make, they and their families might starve. Almost all their money goes for food. Sometimes they save enough to buy a new shirt or pair of pants. If they are lucky, they own more than one set of clothing. Many never have shoes—or footballs or bicycles or skates or television sets.

There are other sad statistics. In the poorer countries, some 12,000,000 children under the age of 5 died in 1979. Most of these deaths could have been prevented if the children had received proper food and medical care. Millions of other children will survive to live another year. But many of them will not get enough food to eat, will not have proper medical care, will not have a chance to go to school, will get jobs that pay very little.

Even in wealthy countries, many children are in trouble. Those who live in city slums rarely have the opportunities that are enjoyed by children of higher-income families. Those who are part of migrant families that pick crops may work seven days a week at the height of the growing season. In other families, there is enough money but not enough love. Some children are beaten and otherwise abused by their parents. Some be-

222

come drug addicts or run away, often into a world of crime. Some even commit suicide. And these problems seem to be getting worse. In one wealthy country, the suicide rate of children between 5 and 15 years of age doubled in the past ten years.

A Belgian priest, Canon Joseph Moerman, believed that adults should do something about children's problems. He suggested a special Year of the Child. During this year, he said, people everywhere could try extra hard to help children.

The United Nations adopted Moerman's idea. It declared 1979 the International Year of the Child. One goal of the year was to make people more aware of children's needs. Another goal was to get governments to pass laws and develop programs that would help children.

World reaction to the U.N. call for action was encouraging. Special commissions for the International Year of the Child were set up in 121 nations. Each commission decided what its own country's problems were. It decided what kinds of programs would best help the children in the country.

International groups made important contributions. The World Bank, a U.N. agency, published a "World Atlas of the Child." This is a useful reference book. It also shows how much work must be done. Here are some facts from the book:

• The largest number of children are in the poorest countries.

• The number of children in most poor countries will be almost twice as large in the year 2000 as it was in 1975.

• A child born in 1975 in a poor country could expect to live about 43 years. In comparison, a child born that same year in the United States or Canada could expect to live more than 70 years.

• In a typical poor country, 58 percent of the children go to primary school. Only 9 percent go to secondary school. In countries such as Canada and the United States, almost 100 percent of the children go to primary school, and 79 percent go to secondary school.

Obviously, all the problems faced by children cannot be solved in one year. The International Year of the Child was just a beginning. But it made people all over the world aware of the problems faced by children. And to millions of children, it brought hope that their lives would improve.

THE RIGHTS OF A CHILD

The year 1979 was also the 20th anniversary of the Declaration of the Rights of the Child. This declaration was adopted by the United Nations on November 20, 1959. The ten principles are an appeal to individuals, organizations, and governments to recognize and meet the special needs of children everywhere.

Every child has the right to affection, love, and understanding.

Every child has the right to adequate nutrition and medical care.

Every child has the right to free education.

Every child has the right to full opportunity for play and recreation.

Every child has the right to a name and nationality.

Every child has the right to special care, if handicapped.

Every child has the right to be among the first to receive relief in times of disaster.

Every child has the right to be a useful member of society and to develop individual abilities.

Every child has the right to be brought up in a spirit of peace and universal brotherhood.

Every child has the right to enjoy these rights, regardless of race, color, sex, religion, national or social origin.

224

Children are people

International Year of the Child 1979

<u>Every Child has the Right to:</u> affection, love and understanding...

The child, for the full and harmonious development of his personality, needs love and understanding. He shall, wherever possible, grow up in the care and under the responsibility of his parents, and in any case in an atmosphere of affection and of moral and material security; a child of tender years shall not, save in exceptional circumstances, be separated from his mother. Society and the public authorities shall have the duty to extend particular care to children without a family and to those without adequate means of support. Payment of State and other assistance towards the maintenance of children of large families is desirable.

Every child has the right:
1 to affection, love and understanding...
2 to adequate nutrition, housing, medical care and recreation... 3 to free education, to learn to be a useful member of society and develop individual abilities...
4 to an opportunity to develop physically, mentally and morally in freedom and dignity... 5 to a name and nationality....
6 to special care, if handicapped...
7 to be among the first to receive relief in times of disaster... 8 to be brought up in a spirit of peace and universal brotherhood... 9 to protection against neglect, cruelty and exploitation... 10 to enjoy these rights, regardless of race, colour, sex, religion, national, or social origin...

Children are people

International Year of the Child 1979

<u>Every Child has the Right to:</u> an opportunity to develop physically, mentally and morally in freedom and dignity...

The child shall enjoy special protection, and shall be given opportunities and facilities, by law and by other means, to enable him to develop physically, mentally, morally, spiritually and socially in a healthy and normal manner and in conditions of freedom and dignity. In the enactment of laws for this purpose the best interests of the child shall be the paramount consideration.

Every child has the right:
1 to affection, love and understanding...
2 to adequate nutrition, housing, medical care and recreation... 3 to free education, to learn to be a useful member of society and develop individual abilities...
4 to an opportunity to develop physically, mentally and morally in freedom and dignity... 5 to a name and nationality....
6 to special care, if handicapped...
7 to be among the first to receive relief in times of disaster... 8 to be brought up in a spirit of peace and universal brotherhood... 9 to protection against neglect, cruelty and exploitation... 10 to enjoy these rights, regardless of race, colour, sex, religion, national, or social origin...

225

PICTURES FROM A SMALL PLANET

These colorful paintings are from an international exhibit that celebrated the International Year of the Child. Called Pictures from a Small Planet, the exhibit showed the world—in paintings—as children view it. It was sponsored by the United States Committee for UNICEF (*United Nations International Children's Emergency Fund*).

The works of art were selected from UNICEF's 10,000-piece permanent collection, which includes the work of children between the ages of 5 and 15 from countries all over the world. The judges selected pictures that expressed the special regional or national character of the young people's cultures. Yet, in spite of vast cultural differences, the young artists focused on universal subjects—play, school, holidays, work, and family. It seems that in terms of the interests and concerns of children, ours is after all a small planet.

Procession in the Street, by Sevgul Bora, Turkey

Making Hay, by Amy Hankee, 8, United States

Parade, by Francesca Bionda, 8, Italy

A View of a Town, by R. Q. Mensah, 13, Ghana

Going to the Country, by Hernan Trujillo, 10, Puerto Rico

228

Loaded Truck, by Krassimir Ivanov, 7, Bulgaria

Blue Night Sky, by Bui-thi Phuong-ly, 10, Vietnam

Stuffed worm, Czechoslovakia

Wooden animal, Nigeria

CHILD'S PLAY

Since ancient times, toys have enchanted young people. However simple or sophisticated the toys may be, they are prized as miniature imitations of the surrounding world. They teach us about life, and they capture our imaginations.

During the International Year of the Child, an exhibit that showed children's toys and games from all over the world was sponsored by UNESCO (*U*nited *N*ations *E*ducational, *S*cientific and *C*ultural *O*rganization). Most of the toys were created by children themselves. The 900 toys exhibited focused on three themes—toys and play in the psychological development of the child; play and the child's relationship to the community; and play in education. The toys on these pages were some of the highlights of the exhibit.

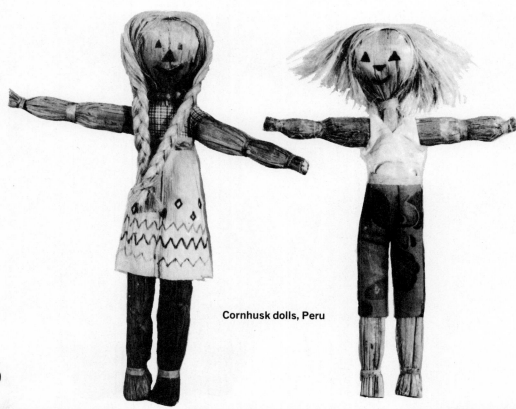
Cornhusk dolls, Peru

230

Knitted lion, Italy

Wire cyclist, Congo

Stuffed camel, Ireland

Kite, Japan

231

YOUNG HEADLINERS

Ron Keeva Unz, a 17-year-old from California, won first place in the 1979 Westinghouse Science Talent Search. More than 1,000 high school seniors submitted original research projects in hopes of winning the top award, a $12,000 scholarship. Unz plans a career as a theoretical physicist or a mathematician. His winning project dealt with the effects of gravitation on electromagnetic interactions.

Young people made their views heard on Capitol Hill in 1979. This group of schoolchildren from the Washington, D.C., area testified before a congressional subcommittee on May 1, Save the Children Day. They told the lawmakers the problems that most concern them—energy, pollution, inflation, war, and smoking.

These young people may have found the answer to the energy crisis—child power. They are Jonathan and Alexandra Gurr, shown operating a washing machine made from a bicycle and a garbage can. The machine was displayed at ACT 79, a fair held in Washington, D.C., in April. All the displays were part of a movement called appropriate technology, which seeks small-scale solutions to big problems like energy and pollution.

Eight-year-old Ricky Schroder of New York climbed his way to stardom in 1979. Ricky played the son of a broken-down boxer (Jon Voight) in the movie *The Champ*. While the film was Ricky's first, he had gotten experience by acting in television commercials. One of his most valuable talents turned out to be his ability to cry on cue.

JACKIE PARKER—FLIGHT CONTROLLER

At 18 years of age, Jacquelyn Parker accomplished a first in the history of space flight. In September, 1979, she was the youngest person ever to become a full-fledged NASA flight controller. Stationed at the Johnson Space Center in Dallas, Texas, Jackie worked as part of a team that monitored computors.

With lightning speed, these computers communicate vital statistics about manned space flights and the health of the astronauts on board. This computer system is the nerve center of a space mission. And flight controllers live every minute of a space flight right at the computer console.

NASA has been a part of Jackie's life for many years. Her father worked in the NASA Experiments Office until his retirement in the 1960's. And if you had asked Jackie a few years ago what she wanted to be, she'd have replied "an astronaut!"

Flying is Jackie's favorite hobby. A week after starting flying lessons, she soloed. At 17, she received her pilot's license—about a week before she learned to drive a car. Then she became interested in aerobatics—flying stunts including loops, dives, and rolls.

Jackie rocketed her way through school. She completed high school in less than a year and entered college at 14. She studied math and computer science at Florida Technological University (now called the University of Central Florida) and graduated only three years later, at 17. After she graduated, she worked for a summer as an intern computer systems analyst for NASA. She quickly impressed everyone with her analytical skills and went on to become the youngest NASA flight controller ever.

But Jackie would still like to be *aboard* a space flight. In fact, she was one of 1,700 women to apply for NASA's astronaut program. Though she wasn't selected on her first try, Jackie isn't discouraged. She vows that someday she'll be in orbit.

REID RONDELL: A TEENAGE STUNT MAN

After-school activities for Reid Rondell are certainly not typical for a teenager. He jumps off the roof of his house, leaps from a telephone pole in the backyard, fights with friends, and gets into motorcycle wrecks. For the young Californian, however, it's just an ordinary afternoon of practicing for his job as a Hollywood stunt man.

When a television or movie star has a risky role to play, Reid often steps in to do the job. On one episode of *Family,* he "doubled" for Kristy McNichols in a bicycle crash. And Reid took the place of one of Charlie's Angels to skateboard through traffic on a busy street. He's also climbed a dangerous cliff on *Young Dan'l Boone* and been pulled from the ocean by a helicopter for a *Baretta* show. Most recently, Reid went to Africa to work on a new Tarzan movie. He dressed as an ape and swung on vines through the jungle.

Reid's specialty is the "high fall." In fact, he got started in stunt work at age 10 by falling from some boxes on a TV show. Since then he's fallen from buildings as high as 40 feet (12 meters). Reid lands on a big air bag, and he has never been hurt.

Reid's teacher is his dad, who is also a stunt man. They work together to make the action look real. One stunt they do perfectly is called the "car hit." As the cameras roll, Reid's dad is driving a car and "accidentally" runs into Reid. With perfect timing, Reid flips onto the hood, bounces off the windshield, and falls into the street.

Of course, these are not things that just anybody can do. *You* should certainly not try them. Doing stunts safely takes a lot of skill and practice. To keep in shape for such strenuous work, Reid exercises every day with push-ups and sit-ups. He also practices flips and falls on a trampoline.

Reid likes the challenge of doing different stunts, and he likes the pay. His salary depends on the kind of stunts he performs. But for every day he's on a film set, Reid gets at least the same minimum wage as any older stunt man—$225.

Reid is willing to take the risk because he's had the proper training from his father and other stunt men. And after graduation, performing stunts will be a full-time career.

MICHELE AND TOM GRIMM
Authors, *What Is a Seal?*

235

GIRL SCOUTS AND GIRL GUIDES

For Girl Scouts in the United States, energy conservation was a prime concern in 1979—just as it was for everyone else throughout the nation. In St. Paul, Minnesota, the St. Croix Girl Scout Council opened a solar heated office building. These Scouts are being shown how the solar heating system works.

Girl Guides in India teach the wives of fishermen to write in Sanskrit, one of the oldest languages in the world. The Guides themselves come from small villages. Their training has helped them return to their homes and teach other women to improve their lives.

236

Girl Scouts in Paraguay were trained to work with blind children. Here, they are taking blind children to a zoo. They are helping the youngsters enjoy an experience that many sighted children take for granted. The Scouts answer such questions as, "What makes that sound? Is it feathered or furred? What color is it?"

In September, 1979, Girl Guides from Finland spent six days and nights camping in Lapland, an area where the climate is often cold and harsh. Girl Guiding has helped them to develop discipline, self-reliance, and *sisu*—the Finnish word for determination.

237

CHILDREN'S VILLAGE

The city of Toronto, Canada, has a children's amusement park like no other you've ever seen. Although it is called Children's Village, it is not a village at all but an enchanting place to play. Here you can do things that you may have daydreamed about but never before had the real chance to do.

You can climb a pink plastic mountain called King of the Castle, bounce up and down on a giant air mattress, walk along a scary net-enclosed bridge high up above the ground, squirt water on yourself and your friends, crawl through a pipe, go hand over hand on a ladder over water, and slide down a long chute into a splashing pool.

You will not find any mechanical rides or gadgets at Children's Village. You won't ever be able to sit back and let your thrills be made for you, as would happen on a ferris wheel or merry-go-round. Your whirling you must do yourself, just as you must do your own climbing, swinging, leaping, and bouncing.

One half of Children's Village is called Waterplay, and it has 15 water games to choose from. In Waterplay you can really let yourself go. But you won't drown, for the water is never more than 6 inches (15 centimeters) deep. Everyone is allowed to squirt water on everyone else, using pumps worked by foot pedals. These pumps are also used to play the "funny faces" game, in which water is pumped up through tall pipes (or "necks") and comes out the mouths and noses of the "faces." In Waterplay there are also curving slides that land you in a splashing pool.

The other half of the Village is called Land Play, and its games are under a big, orange canopy. One of the most popular games is the Net Climb. Nylon net is hung at different levels from wooden posts. After

The Waterplay area has 15 water games for you to choose from.

you mount the nets one by one, you will reach a tree-high hut. Next you set out from the hut across a swinging rope bridge enclosed in net—and at last you reach a lookout tower beyond.

Children's Village is designed for young people who love to go into intriguing "play places" and to climb up fascinating things. And there is often some special treat waiting. If you scramble up the King of the Castle mountain, you will get to ring the bell of a ship's telegraph. When you go inside the orange caboose, you'll find that hot dogs, hamburgers, and french fries are served. If you enter the Lion's Mouth, walking along on his huge tongue, you'll soon find yourself in Soda Fountain Mountain. And, after getting soaked playing all the games in Waterplay, you can go inside a big, brightly colored bird and get gently blown dry.

Children's Village is part of a big recreation and culture park called Ontario Place, which covers three small islands in Lake Ontario. Ontario Place has many attractions for both adults and children—including theaters, movies, shops, restaurants, and rides. But Children's Village is for kids only!

You must do all your swinging yourself.

The Net Climb is one of the most popular games in the Land Play area.

239

YOUNG PHOTOGRAPHERS

Photography is a way of capturing a passing moment. But it can be much more, as the young people who took the pictures on these pages seem to know.

These pictures won prizes in the 1979 Scholastic/Kodak Photo Awards program. Like all excellent photographs, they add something of their own to the scenes they capture. Seen through the lens of the camera, cattails and power lines form intricate patterns traced in black against the sky. A firecracker becomes a sparkling, magical snake. And a face peering through a window tells a wordless story all its own.

One of this year's contest winners put it this way: "Photography has changed the way I view the world."

Peek-A-Boo,
by Janet Edwards, 18, Cypress, California

Water Lilies, by Kate Faust, 15, West Helene, Arkansas

Cattails, by Pete Larkin, 18, West Des Moines, Iowa

Bottoms Up, by James Taskett, 17, Webster, New York

241

It's Only A Paper Moon,
by DeeDee Woods, 17, Phoenix, Arizona

Strawberries, by Cammie Warner, 17, Pacific Palisades, California

242

City Sunset,
by Howard Castleberry, 17, Austin, Texas

Sparkler Trails, by Tom Scott, 17, Barberton, Ohio

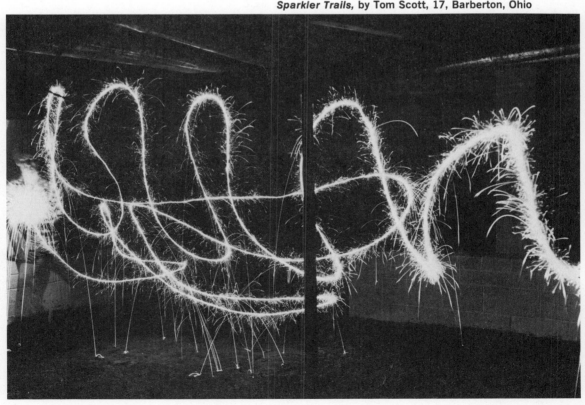

BOY SCOUTS

In 1979, U.S. Scouts and Explorers were drawn in increasing numbers to the High Adventure Programs. Activities included scuba diving, wilderness survival, mountain search and rescue, panning for gold, archeology, and horseback riding.

There are many programs that help inner-city Boy Scouts to participate in out-of-doors activities, like hiking and camping out.

Canadian Venturers are active in many outdoor events. In 1979, they skied and put up snow shelters and camped out.

In the summer of 1979, Scouts attended an international encampment in Sweden. Here, they are getting a lesson in spinning yarn.

Cub Scouting programs, for boys ages 8 through 10, included lessons in bicycle safety. The 50th anniversary of Cub Scouting will be marked in 1980 with a year-long series of activities.

Winners of the 1979 Cub Scout Physical Fitness Contest: Keven Armstrong, 10; Derek Schiffman, 9; Greg Weichers, 8. The five-event competition consisted of softball throw, push-ups, sit-ups, standing broad jump, and the 50-yard dash.

The Order of the Arrow is a service-oriented camping brotherhood of the Boy Scouts of America. In 1979, more than 4,000 members of the OA attended a convention at Fort Collins, Colorado. Activities included dance, song, athletic, and cooking competitions.

Young people with handicaps can participate in a number of Scouting programs. They can be members of units that consist mainly of boys without handicaps. Or they can be members of units especially for the handicapped.

BE A CLOWN!

When a circus comes to town, excitement crackles through the air. Acrobats somersault from swings and perches far above the ground. Animal trainers snap their whips at snarling lions and tigers. Fearless riders perform handstands on the bare backs of galloping horses.

All these acts are wonderful, but the most fun happens when a tiny car lurches its way into the center ring. It looks hardly bigger than a toy. Perhaps one person, crouched over, could fit inside. Suddenly the door opens, and out pops a clown! She cartwheels happily away—and a moment later another clown leaps out of the tiny car. Before you know it, out falls another clown, and still another, and then even more clowns, all jumping and tumbling out of the midget automobile. There are dozens of them: white-faced clowns, tramp clowns, pink-faced clowns—some with floppy shoes or big yellow buttons or shiny red noses. They run all over the circus, playing jokes and doing tricks and making people laugh.

How can all those clowns fit into that little car? Only the clowns know, and they won't tell you. It's their secret. To find out the answer you would have to become a clown yourself. And becoming a clown is not easy. Many of the very best clowns have gone to school to learn their trade.

One of the most famous circuses in the world is the Ringling Brothers and Barnum & Bailey Circus. This circus runs Clown College in Venice, Florida. Each year thousands of would-be clowns apply to take the eight-week course. But only about 60 people are accepted. They have to demonstrate a lot of laugh-making talent in order to get into Clown College.

Once in school, students learn everything that a clown must know—acrobatics, juggling, balancing, doing magic, riding elephants, and walking on stilts. They even study the history of circuses and of clowning. Most important, perhaps, the students learn costuming and how to put on makeup. Makeup is very important because no two

248

clowns ever look alike. Each clown must develop his or her own special clown face.

There are three basic types of clowns. "Whiteface" clowns might have big red noses on their white-painted faces. They are usually happy-go-lucky types who wear baggy, oversized costumes that are bright and colorful. "Auguste" (OW-guhst) clowns usually have pink or reddish faces. They are often foolish types who fall all over themselves, do everything wrong, and get hit in the face with pies. "Character" clowns look the most like real people, but their comic makeup might emphasize certain features, such as a large nose or a heavy, dark mustache. Character clowns may dress as police officers, farmers, doctors, and so on.

The students at Clown College study hard. They take their clowning very seriously. "You have to work at being funny," says one. The best of the students are offered jobs with the Ringling circus. Only 20 or 30 a year are chosen. In the spring and summer months they travel all over with the circus.

For many clowns, clowning becomes a way of life. A clown who calls himself Prince Paul has been with the Ringling circus for over 30 years. He enjoys making people laugh. That's why he decided to make clowning his career.

One of the most famous clowns of all time was called Weary Willie. Willie took on the character of a tramp. He was very sad-looking, and he always dressed in tatters and rags. Somehow, even though he looked so sorrowful, he always made people laugh. The tramp Weary Willie was really a man named Emmett Kelly. Sadly for the circus, and for all who love clowns, Kelly died in 1979, at the age of 80. By a strange coincidence, he died on the same day that the Ringling Brothers and Barnum & Bailey Circus opened its show in New York City. For Emmett Kelly especially, clowning was more than a career. It was his life.

If you think you would like to make clowning your career, you can write to Clown College to ask for a tryout. The address is:

Clown College
P. O. Box 1528
Venice, Florida 33595

While you're waiting to hear from Clown College, you had better sharpen your gags. Remember, a lot of other people are trying to become clowns too!

At school, students learn how to create their own special clown faces—and noses are especially important.

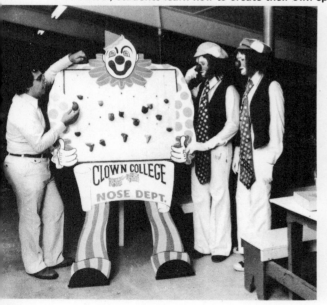

249

STUDENT LAWMAKERS

How are laws made? You can begin to find answers to that question by reading books and articles about the lawmaking process. You can also ask your parents, teachers, and other adults. But seeing and hearing answers are often not enough. The best answers come from doing.

Some of you may be lucky enough to join one of the student model congresses that are held every year around the United States. At a model congress, students learn how laws are made by becoming lawmakers for a day. They research and propose their own bills. The bills are debated, with speakers for and against. Some bills are defeated in debate, while others survive and become "laws." Some model congresses follow the same rules as the U.S. Congress. Others follow the rules of their own state legislatures.

In addition to learning how laws are made, the students are able to express their own opinions and thoroughly enjoy themselves. The following is an example of one specific model congress, held by Rhode Island high school students every year.

Students at a New England model congress, held every year in Massachusetts, vote on bills submitted to their mock senate and house of representatives.

250

Speaker: "Now we move on to Senate Bill Number 22, *A Commission to Study Nuclear Power in Rhode Island.* Will the author please come forward?"

Senator James: "The purpose of this bill is to inform the public of their choices before they commit themselves to any type of energy development program."

Representative: "I move that we now open debate."

Representative: "I second the motion."

Speaker: "It has been moved and seconded that we open debate on Senate Bill Number 22. All in favor please say 'aye'... all opposed please say 'nay'... debate has been opened."

It would seem as if this were a formal session of Congress, in Washington, D.C. But, in fact, these are the voices of Rhode Island high school students. They have assembled at the Rhode Island State House in Providence for a three-day "mock state legislature." It is called Model Legislature and it closely resembles an actual Rhode Island state legislature session. It is so true to life that the student participants don't even feel as if they are pretending. They *are* the senators, representatives, pages, and lobbyists involved in making laws for the people of Rhode Island. In 1979 the Model Legislature covered such issues as rescinding the state ratification of the Equal Rights Amendment (ERA) and regulating the sale of handguns.

That session in Providence was the finale of what is a year-long program. The year begins with each school being allotted a fixed number of "seats" in the mock legislature. Because the program is so popular, the students are chosen to fill the seats in a variety of ways—from drawing straws to competing in speaking contests. Once the seats are filled, other students can still become pages (who act as aides and messengers) or lobbyists (who try to get votes for certain bills).

Then a leadership competition is held. Each contestant tries out for the top positions in the legislature by giving a short extemporaneous speech on a current issue. A panel of judges awards leadership positions to the twenty most outstanding speakers. The student speaker of the house and president of the senate are chosen in this way.

Rhode Island students participating in their Model Legislature ponder the bills on the agenda.

Fall and winter are filled with busy preparations. Participants have their party affiliations determined through a political questionnaire. And about 65 bills are written by the students, according to a special Model Legislation format. They can choose just about any topic that is of interest to them. The bills are assigned to committees for deliberation. Not all bills will be presented to the Model Legislature.

Finally, the all-important weekend arrives. The floor session is officially convened on Saturday. Throughout the day, bills are introduced, debated, and voted on. Often, guest speakers such as the governor and real state legislators address the students. At the end of the day, a list of all bills passed into Model Legislature law is read. At that time, too, the scholarship winners are announced. (Some Rhode Island colleges have set up Model Legislature scholarship programs.) The session then formally comes to a close. But for some participants, the program may be just the beginning of a political career.

Speaker: "It has been moved and seconded that we adjourn this session of the Rhode Island State Model Legislature. All in favor signify by saying 'aye'. All opposed signify by saying 'nay.'

Legislature: "NAY!"

LAURIE J. MASSE
1979 member
Rhode Island State Model Legislature

251

THE CREATIVE WORLD

In 1979, the marvelous muppets starred in their first film, *The Muppet Movie.*

THE MARVELOUS MUPPETS

Marionettes and puppets have been delighting audiences for centuries. "Marionette" means a figure on strings, operated from above. "Puppet" is a more general term, covering all kinds of puppets—hand, rod, and string. The word "marionette" is said to have come from the name of Mary, mother of Jesus, since early marionette shows were religious in nature. "Puppet" is closely related to the old word "poppet," meaning doll.

Now we come to a very special word—"Muppet," which is a specially coined blending of the words "marionette" and "puppet." And Muppets are also very special characters. Most Muppets are puppets, but they can also be huge, good-natured ogres with human performers inside them. They can even be zany objects, like a singing hamburger or a talking bust of Beethoven. Some of the Muppets are modeled after animals—Kermit the Frog, Miss Piggy, Fozzie Bear, Rowlf the dog, for example. Others, such as Statler, Waldorf, and Bunsen Honeydew, are like cartoon humans. And still others don't belong to any species known—on this planet, at least.

The first Muppets were seen in 1955 on a local television station in Washington, D.C. One cast member was a perky frog, made from a woman's old green coat, with two halves of a Ping-Pong ball for eyes. Perhaps you've already guessed his name. It's Kermit the Frog, and he's the only one of the original Muppets who's still on active duty. He's also the only Muppet who appears on both "Sesame Street" and "The Muppet Show," which have different Muppet casts. He works lots of Muppet TV "specials" too.

The Muppets were soon invited to appear on nationally viewed television shows such as "Today," "Tonight," "The Ed Sullivan Show," and "The Jimmy Dean Show." And from the very beginning, they were part of the concept of "Sesame Street." In 1976, "The Muppet Show" was first aired, and in 1979 the Muppets starred in their first movie, *The Muppet Movie*.

The Muppets have won many television and recording awards. These include the 1978 Emmy Award as the Outstanding Comedy, Variety, or Music series, a top honor in American television. Superstar Kermit has been especially singled out for honors. Did you know that he's the only frog ever to have been praised in the Congressional Record, the official record book of the U.S. Congress? He also has a balloon in his image in the famous Macy's Thanksgiving Day Parade, and he's an honorary policeman in Lafayette, Indiana.

The people who build and perform the Muppets are proud of their awards, but what they prize most is not an award but a reward. That's the satisfaction of knowing that the Muppets and their wacky, way-out humor are seen everywhere and are pleasing people of all ages—from 1 to 101.

JIM HENSON
Creator of the Muppets

Big Bird, the big muppet of "Sesame Street."

255

THE MASTER QUILT MAKERS OF HAWAII

Quilts are among the most colorful and beautiful examples of folk art. The craft began in Europe hundreds of years ago. When Europeans settled in the American colonies, some of them brought quilts with them. And others remembered the quilts they had seen in Europe.

Once the settlers had established themselves in America, many of the women began to make quilts to brighten up their new homes. The women created their own designs, cut out the shapes from bits of fabric, then carefully stitched the shapes together to make a large cloth. By the 1800's, quilting was a highly developed art in the United States.

Beginning in 1820, missionaries from New England traveled to Hawaii. Their purpose was to convert the Hawaiians to Christianity. But it wasn't long before the missionaries' wives had introduced the Hawaiian women to the art of quilting.

Before that time, the Hawaiians did not know how to sew. They did not have needles and thread. They made their clothes and their bedding from tapa, the pounded bark of trees. Some of the tapa sheets were decorated with geometric designs made by using stencils dipped in red dyes.

The missionaries established boarding schools for Hawaiian children. The girls at some of these schools were taught how to sew and how to make quilts. The first quilts made by the students followed typical New England designs of that period. These same patterns were used by Hawaiian women as they learned how to use needle and thread.

Before long, however, the Hawaiians began to create their own designs. According to legend, the first such quilt was made by a young woman who had put a sheet in the sun to bleach it. Later, when she returned to get the sheet, she was fascinated by the pattern of shadows cast on the sheet by nearby tree branches. She took some red material and cut it in the design made by the branches. Then she sewed the red cloth onto the bleached sheet and quilted it.

"My Beloved Flag"

"The Beautiful Unequaled Gardens of Eden and Elenale"

256

In many ways, the young woman's quilt resembled the tapa sheets, which were also white with red designs. This was true of many of the early Hawaiian patterns—they combined aspects of the tapa with techniques and ideas taught them by the New Englanders. The result was an art form that is distinctively Hawaiian.

Many of the quilts have patterns that include items found in Hawaii. For example, some patterns depict breadfruit, pineapple, and other plants native to the islands. Some patterns are patriotic. One quilt has the royal crown of Hawaii in the center. Around it is a red, white, and blue design based on the Hawaiian flag. Still other quilts mark important events. "The Pearl of the Pacific" was made to commemorate the discovery of pearls in Hawaii. "Birth of Puu Kiai" marked the birth of a volcano.

Very few quilt designs included people, birds, or other animals. Showing such subjects was thought to be unlucky. One exception is the quilt "The Beautiful Unequaled Gardens of Eden and Elenale," made around the beginning of the 20th century. On the right side of this quilt, Adam and Eve are seated underneath a tree. A devil, in the form of a snake, is wound around the tree. Above the tree is an angel holding an open book. On the left side of the quilt are two figures in royal dress. They are Elenale and Leinaala, the main characters in a popular Hawaiian story. According to the story, Elenale rescued Leinaala from a witch. He took her to live in a beautiful garden. The person who made the quilt must have seen a similarity between the Garden of Eden and the garden of Elenale.

The Hawaiians carefully guarded their work until the quilts were finished. They didn't want anyone to steal their designs. When a woman finished a quilt, she showed it to everyone. Then, if anyone made a quilt with the same design, everyone would know the design was stolen. Stealing a design was considered a very bad thing to do. It was like taking away some of the person's soul or power.

Today, the people of Hawaii are continuing to make beautiful quilts. New designs are still being created—designs that are as beautiful and imaginative as those created many years ago.

"The Garden Island"

"Crowns and Kahilis"

257

Jane Fonda (best actress) and Jon Voight (best actor) in *Coming Home.*

1979 ACADEMY AWARDS

CATEGORY	WINNER
Motion Picture	*The Deer Hunter*
Actor	Jon Voight (*Coming Home*)
Actress	Jane Fonda (*Coming Home*)
Supporting Actor	Christopher Walken (*The Deer Hunter*)
Supporting Actress	Maggie Smith (*California Suite*)
Director	Michael Cimino (*The Deer Hunter*)
Foreign Language Film	*Get Out Your Handkerchiefs* (France)
Song	"Last Dance" (*Thank God It's Friday*)
Documentary Feature	*Scared Straight!*
Documentary Short	*The Flight of the Gossamer Condor*
Cinematography	Nestor Almendros (*Days of Heaven*)

Christopher Walken (best supporting actor) in *The Deer Hunter* (best picture).

Maggie Smith (best supporting actress) and Michael Caine in *California Suite*.

HAPPY BIRTHDAY, MOMA

"In encouraging the creation and enjoyment of beautiful things, we are furthering democracy itself. That is why this museum is a citadel of civilization."

U.S. President Franklin D. Roosevelt spoke these words in 1939 in a nationwide radio broadcast. The occasion was the opening of the Museum of Modern Art's new building in New York City. The museum—today known as MOMA—was only 10 years old at that time. But it was already an important force in helping people become aware of 20th-century art.

In 1979, MOMA celebrated its 50th anniversary. During the half-century since its founding, it has become the home of the world's most important collection of modern art. MOMA's collection contains more than 100,000 items. Included are many famous paintings and sculptures—works by Van Gogh, Matisse, Rodin, Picasso, Pollock, and Calder, to name but a very few. Also included in the collection are masterpieces from other fields of art—drawings, prints, photographs, architectural materials, industrial and graphic designs, and films.

In addition to displaying items from its collection, the museum has many temporary exhibitions. Some of these help introduce people to the work of young artists, to new trends in art, or to new ideas.

▶ SOME MAJOR EXHIBITIONS

Among the most popular exhibitions are "retrospectives." A retrospective show focuses on the work of an individual artist or a specific art movement. For example, a 1977 retrospective, called Cézanne: the Late Work, included 124 oils and watercolors. All were painted by Cézanne between 1895 and 1906, the last years of the French artist's life. Cézanne was perhaps the most influential person in 20th-century painting.

That exhibition brought together paintings from all over the world. Some were lent by museums. Others were lent by private collectors. The show gave many people their first—and perhaps only—chance to see and study all the major work from this radical period of Cézanne's life.

The Architecture of the École des Beaux-Arts was another MOMA retrospective,

Still Life With Apples, from Cézanne: the Late Work.

260

held in 1975. It focused on the 19th-century work of students of the famous architecture school (*école*) in Paris. Some 200 beautifully detailed drawings and photographs introduced viewers to the school's excessively ornamental style. Beaux-Arts ideas dominated architecture in Europe and North America from the 1860's to the 1930's. Many public buildings—including libraries, museums, and courthouses—were built in this style. Gradually, however, Beaux-Arts ideas were replaced by modern architecture, with its simpler lines. Beaux-Arts was ridiculed and, eventually, ignored. The MOMA show was important because it helped the people of today learn about this once powerful architectural style.

One of the major exhibitions of the 50th anniversary year was called Ansel Adams and the West. Adams is one of the best-known landscape photographers of our time. Most of the 153 black-and-white photographs in the MOMA retrospective showed scenes from Yosemite National Park and the High Sierras of California. In each photograph, there is a dramatic play of light and shadow. The style is distinctively Adams'— a blending of nature's awesomeness and the photographer's technical artistry.

As MOMA enters its second 50 years, it is planning to expand its quarters. It is continuing to acquire new masterpieces and to help us learn about the artists of our century. Like all great museums, it is preserving the treasures of yesterday and today for the world of tomorrow.

A drawing of a beaux-arts museum, from The Architecture of the École des Beaux-Arts.

High Country Crags and Moon, from Ansel Adams and the West.

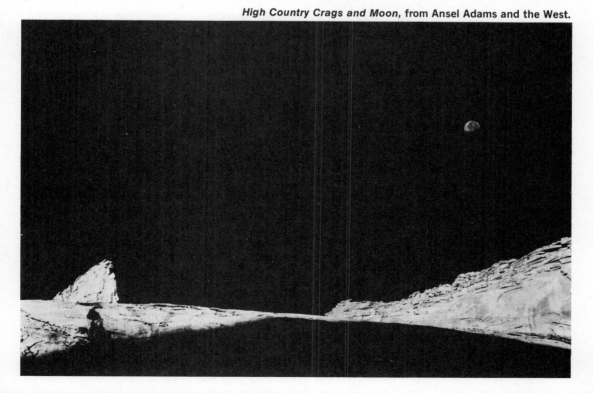

SOUSA MARCHES ON

Hurrah for the flag of the free!
May it wave as our standard forever
The gem of the land and the sea,
The banner of the right.

Let despots remember the day
When our fathers with mighty endeavor
Proclaimed as they marched to the fray
That by their might and by their right
It waves forever.

Words written by John Philip Sousa
to accompany *The Stars and Stripes Forever*

A drum major blows his whistle and raises his baton. Snare drums rattle, cymbals clash, and the brassy blare of trumpets and trombones splits the air as a marching band steps off briskly. The listener hears the familiar strains of *Semper Fidelis* . . . or *The Washington Post* . . . or *El Capitán*.

It could be any one of these or a hundred other rousing marches composed by the man who has been called "The March King"—John Philip Sousa, whose 125th birthday was celebrated in 1979.

During his lifetime, Sousa won honors and fame as a composer and conductor. People in every corner of the globe have thrilled to the sound of his marches, particularly *The Stars and Stripes Forever*—which may be the most popular march ever written.

But Sousa was more than just a band leader who wrote marches. He was, in the words of one critic, "the people's musician"—a gifted composer who wrote light operas, waltzes, and popular songs that delighted people everywhere.

Yet few Americans know much about this outstanding musical figure. That's unfortunate, because Sousa's life was a true American success story. He was born in Washington, D.C., on November 6, 1854. Both his parents were immigrants. His father, Antonio Sousa, had been born in Spain, but actually came from a Portuguese background. His mother was German.

John grew up in Washington during the Civil War years, and his earliest memories were of military parades. In his autobiogra-

phy, *Marching Along,* Sousa recalled: "From childhood I was passionately fond of music and wanted to be a musician. Washington was, in those Civil War days, an armed camp, and there were bands galore. Strange is the boy who doesn't love a band. I loved all of them, good and bad alike."

Sousa's parents encouraged his musical interest, and he was enrolled in a music school when he was 6 years old. There he learned to play violin, alto and baritone horns, and other instruments. He quickly won every medal offered by the school. By the age of 13, he was such a good musician that he was offered a job with a circus band. Sousa jumped at the chance—what young boy wouldn't? But his father wouldn't hear of it, and instead arranged for him to join the U.S. Marine Band—which he himself had played in.

Sousa stayed with the Marine Band for five years and then left to conduct a vaudeville theater orchestra and continue his musical studies. He also began to compose his own music.

In 1880, when he was only 26, Sousa was appointed conductor of the U.S. Marine Band. He quickly molded the band into a first-rate musical organization. The band's

This may be the most popular march ever written.

262

John Philip Sousa at Great Lakes Naval Station in 1918.

concerts, which featured classical music as well as marches, became popular events.

Then, in 1892, a group of businessmen offered him financial backing if he would leave the Marine Corps and organize a band of his own. He accepted the offer and the Sousa Band was born.

Sousa's band soon became famous throughout the world. It performed at the Chicago World's Fair in 1893, made four successful European tours between 1900 and 1905, and then went on a round-the-world tour in 1910. Wherever he went, Sousa and his stirring music were warmly applauded.

Throughout these years, Sousa the composer was active. He produced ten comic operas (including *The Bride Elect, El Capitán,* and *The Free Lance*), more than 50 songs, two overtures, and a dozen suites for band and orchestra.

Of course, his most famous musical works were his marches. There is a special quality about a Sousa march, a joyous lilt that makes it more than just parade music. Perhaps this is due to the fact that Sousa wrote marches to celebrate particular occasions or groups of people. *The Washington Post* was composed as musical background for the awarding of prizes to schoolchildren participating in an essay contest. *King Cotton* celebrated a Cotton States Exposition in Atlanta, Georgia. And *Pride of the Wolverines* was intended as a musical salute to Detroit, Michigan.

The most stirring march of all, *The Stars and Stripes Forever,* was Sousa's tribute in words and music to the American people. The inspiration for this march came to Sousa in the fall of 1896, while he was traveling by ship from Europe to the United States. Later he wrote that he "paced the deck with a mental brass band playing the march fully a hundred times during the week I was on the steamer."

The Stars and Stripes Forever was an instant hit. It became so popular in the United States that some people tried to have it adopted as the national anthem. Today it is played at almost every patriotic celebration.

Sousa demonstrated his own patriotism by serving as a bandmaster in two wars—the Spanish-American War and World War I. He actually served in three branches of the military services—the Army, the Navy, and the Marines.

Sousa remained active as a musician up until his death, at the age of 78, in 1932. A few years earlier, he had written: "I hope that, long after my marches have been forgotten, the clarion call of America which I tried to make the keynote of my compositions will continue to inspire her children with undying loyalty."

Sousa's marches have not been forgotten, however. They continue to entertain and inspire people all over the world. Nearly 50 years after his death, Sousa marches on.

HENRY I. KURTZ
Author, *Captain John Smith*

263

THE MUSIC SCENE

Disco music rose to new heights in popularity in 1979. Millions of discomaniacs were bumping and thumping around the dance floors of the more than 10,000 discotheques in North America. And the over-18 crowd was not the only one at discos. Younger teenagers also decided to make the scene. They joined the crowds at the after-school discos that were sprouting up in small towns and large cities everywhere.

If the discos were to continue their mad pace, the one ingredient they needed was music. And recording artists, musicians, producers, and record companies were more than willing to comply with the overwhelming demands. Disco music suddenly became a mixed bag of voices and singing styles. Some of the best-known names in the music world began to turn out the popular disco sound. Rod Stewart wailed and crooned "Do Ya Think I'm Sexy?" Diana Ross recorded "The Boss." Cher joined in with her hit single "Take Me Home." Barbra Streisand recorded "The Main Event," the theme song from her latest motion picture. Arthur Fiedler, the late conductor of the Boston Pops Orchestra, recorded *Saturday Night Fiedler,* a disco "symphony." Broadway's musical comedy star Ethel Merman surprised the music world with her *Ethel Merman Disco Album*. And there was even a *Mickey Mouse Disco* album.

Donna Summer and Gloria Gaynor continued to reign as the disco queens. Donna hit the charts with "Hot Stuff," "Bad Girls," and *Greatest Hits—On the Radio—Volumes I & II*. This album featured many of her familiar old standards—disco and ballads. Gloria Gaynor kept everyone dancing with her breathless rendition of "I Will Survive," from the album *Love Tracks*.

The Bee Gees, whose song hits for the *Saturday Night Fever* film had ignited the disco explosion, continued as chart-toppers

Gloria Gaynor continued to reign as one of the disco queens.

264

A very popular disco group of the year was the Village People.

with "Love You Inside Out," from their hit album *Spirits Have Flown*. Chic, who sold over 4,000,000 copies of "Le Freak," maintained their disco dominance with "I Want You" from *C'est Chic* and "Good Times" from *Risque*.

Disco also helped send new recording artists to the top of the charts. Anita Ward, a 22-year-old substitute schoolteacher, climbed into the number-one position with "Ring My Bell." Twenty-four-year-old Amii Stewart, an actress–dancer, sang "Knock on Wood" onto the charts. "Makin' It" certainly made it for actor–musician David Naughton—it was his very first single record. Sixteen-year-old France Joli, a Canadian singer, scored an immediate hit with her "Come to Me." And a new Peaches and Herb went right to the top of the Top Ten charts with "Reunited." Their *2 Hot!* was also successful.

Group action also joined in the disco phenomenon. The Electric Light Orchestra followed their hit "Share a Little Love" from their *Discovery* album with "Don't Bring Me Down." Sister Sledge contributed to the bounce and beat of disco with "He's the Greatest Dancer," from their top-selling album *We Are Family*. The Doobie Brothers did their share by recording a hit single, "Minute by Minute." But the title of "fastest rising group" in the music business belonged to the Village People. Those six men, all from the Greenwich Village area in New York City, recorded several of the best-selling disco records and albums of the year. Their *Village People, Macho Man,* and *Go West* albums all made the charts. "Macho Man," "Y.M.C.A.," "In the Navy," and "Sleazy," were hit singles.

Disco had certainly made its mark on the music scene. But toward the end of 1979, an anti-disco movement began to take shape. A Chicago FM disk jockey even started a campaign to "destroy" disco music. He smashed disco records on his morning radio show while his station promoted a "Disco Demolition Night" that drew thousands of participants to a local ball park. One of the most obvious signs of a decline in disco

Billy Joel hit the Top Ten charts with "My Life."

Dionne Warwick came out with a new album, *Dionne*.

popularity was the drop in audience ratings for disco radio stations. By the end of the year, some recording artists who had specialized in the disco sound began to look for new directions.

▶ OTHER SOUNDS, OTHER STYLES

There was also an audience for soft or pop rock in 1979, and it was growing. This fact was confirmed by the continuing popularity of several established groups and the re-appearance of familiar singing stars. Cheap Trick's hit single "I Want You to Want Me" was included in their album *Cheap Trick At Budokan*. Supertramp hit the Best Seller charts with "Goodbye Stranger," a cut from their *Breakfast in America* album. Dr. Hook's "When You're in Love With a Beautiful Woman" from *Pleasure and Pain* and Little River Band's "Lonesome Loser" from *First Under the Wire* were resounding successes. All these songs mixed the Beatle tunefulness with studio sophistication, high energy, and a rock beat. Following in the same mold was the Cars' "Let's Go," from *Candy-O*. One of the music world's fastest rising groups, the Knack, hit the charts with "My Sharona" and "Good Girls Don't," from their *Get the Knack* album.

Solo artists also had their middle-of-the-road hits. Anne Murray followed "You Needed Me" and "I Just Fall in Love Again" with "Broken-Hearted Me." Melissa Manchester gave us "Don't Cry Out Loud," Maureen McGovern had a hit with "Different Worlds," and newcomer Ricki Lee Jones struck a major chord with the blues-styled pop hit "Chuck E's in Love." Longtime favorite Billy Joel hit the Top Ten charts with his haunting "My Life." Another favorite, Barbra Streisand, used 1979 not only to record disco but to introduce two new albums, *Greatest Hits, Volume 2* and *Wet*.

It was also comeback time for several artists. Dionne Warwick suddenly re-appeared on the music scene, after an absence of sev-

266

Judy Collins went pop with *Hard Time for Lovers.*

Deborah Harry reached fame as lead singer of Blondie.

eral years, with "I'll Never Love This Way Again" and a brand new album, *Dionne.* Instrumentalist Herb Alpert returned to the music charts with the Latin-flavored, melodic "Rise." Some all-time favorites also returned with new styles. Folk singer Judy Collins turned to pop with *Hard Times for Lovers,* while soul singer Ray Charles made increasing use of such Broadway show tunes as "Some Enchanted Evening" in his live concerts.

Perhaps the most publicized comebacks were made by two established names, Elton John and Alice Cooper. Elton re-appeared after two years with a new image—he abandoned his oversized glasses and flashy outfits. On his new album, *A Single Man,* he recorded songs written with a new collaborator, Gary Osborne. Another album, *Victim of Love,* began climbing the charts almost the moment it was released. Alice Cooper came back to the world of music teamed up with Bernie Taupin (Elton John's old partner). Together they produced

a new album, *From the Inside.* It included the single "How You Gonna See Me Now."

Two of the best-known groups of recent years, the Eagles and Fleetwood Mac, brought their names to the fore again with new singles. The Eagles' hit single was called "Heartache Tonight," and Fleetwood Mac introduced "Tusk."

Rock music could also be heard at its best in the masterful Neil Young album, *Rust Never Sleeps.* And one of the hottest rock groups to hit the music scene in some time was Blondie, with most of the publicity being centered on the lead singer, Deborah Harry. While she was being hailed as the Marilyn Monroe of punk rock, the group's "Heart of Glass" hit the 2,000,000 sales mark.

▶DYNAMIC DUOS

The unique pairing of songwriter–singer Neil Diamond and the versatile Barbra Streisand proved to be one of the best ideas of the year. This magical, musical feat pro-

267

Kenny Rogers was a three-category winner of the Country Music Association Awards.

vided the record-buying public with "You Don't Bring Me Flowers." The two singers had recorded the song separately. An imaginative disk jockey simply "wove" both renditions together, producing a very big hit.

Because of the success of the Diamond-Streisand combination, another attempt was made to bring together two strong musical forces. This time, Barbra teamed up in the recording studio with disco queen Donna Summer. The outcome was their almost-instant success with "No More Tears (Enough Is Enough)." And duets didn't stop there. Under the theme "sweetheart pop," Roberta Flack and Donny Hathaway recorded "The Closer I Get to You"; Kenny Loggins and Stevie Nicks sang "Whenever I Call You Friend"; and Diana Ross and Michael Jackson rendered "Ease on Down the Road."

▶ MUSIC FROM TV AND THE MOVIES

Both televison and motion pictures offered interesting fare for rock fans in 1979. "Elvis!," the story of the legendary rock singer, and "Heroes of Rock 'n' Roll" gave TV audiences a glimpse of some of the figures who made rock history. Movie audiences saw *The Wiz,* a not-very-successful

film version of the black Broadway musical that was based on *The Wizard of Oz.* One of the more successful films of the year was *Hair.* This musical extravaganza was the wide-screen version of the very popular Broadway musical of the 1960's.

Television also brought recording fame to several artists. An appearance on TV's "The Gong Show" led to a recording contract for Cheryl Lynn and her first album, *Got to Be Real.* Suzi Quatro, the actress who played Leather Tuscadero in the TV series *Happy Days,* revived her singing career with "Stumblin' In," a Top Ten single. *Saturday Night Live,* one of TV's most popular shows, also contributed to the music scene. John Belushi and Dan Ackroyd, who performed as a singing act on the show under the name the Blues Brothers, moved to the recording studio. Their first effort, *Briefcase Full of Blues,* became an immediate success.

▶ A LITTLE BIT OF COUNTRY

In the country music field the nationally televised Country Music Association Awards ceremony brought recognition to several recording artists. The Charlie Daniels Band won in three categories. One award was for its hit "The Devil Went Down to Georgia"; another was for Instrumental Group of the Year. And Daniels himself won the Instrumentalist of the Year award.

Kenny Rogers was also a three-award winner. He was voted Male Vocalist of the Year, and his best-selling *The Gambler* was named Album of the Year. In addition, his duet with Dottie West, "Till I Can Make It On My Own," earned them the Duo of the Year award. Popular Willie Nelson was named Entertainer of the year.

The country music world lost one of its legendary figures in 1979. Mother Maybelle Carter, of the famous Carter Family, died at the age of 69.

▶ THE WORLD AROUND THEM

Much of the 1970's has been generally viewed as a period in which rockers and the young generation were self-absorbed, interested more in themselves than in the world around them. But in 1979, a new wave of involvement seemed to have taken hold. Suddenly the music people were becoming more interested in the social and political issues confronting the world.

In January, the Bee Gees, along with several other recording stars, staged a benefit for UNICEF at the United Nations in New York City. (UNICEF is the United Nations International Children's Emergency Fund.) The proceeds of the record sales were to be donated to the children of the world through relief organizations.

Later in the year, a number of well-known musicians gave a series of antinuclear concerts. Called MUSE (Musicians United for Safe Energy), the concerts were held on five successive evenings at Madison Square Garden in New York City. Among the superstars who contributed their talents to the concerts were Bonnie Raitt, Jackson Browne, Graham Nash, Bruce Springsteen, James Taylor, the Doobie Brothers, and Crosby, Stills & Nash. The money was to be used to campaign for solar energy.

It looked to some people who follow the music scene as if the "me" decade of the 1970's might become the "we" decade of the 1980's.

ARNOLD SHAW
Author, *The Rock Revolution* and
52nd St.: The Street of Jazz

1979 GRAMMY AWARDS

Record of the Year	"Just the Way You Are"	Billy Joel, artist
Album of the Year	*Saturday Night Fever*	The Bee Gees, David Shire, Yvonne Elliman, Tavares, Kool & The Gang, K. C. & The Sunshine Band, MFSB, Trammps, Walter Murphy, Ralph MacDonald, artists
Song of the Year	"Just the Way You Are"	Billy Joel, songwriter
New Artist of the Year		A Taste of Honey, artist
Pop Vocal Performance—female	"You Needed Me"	Anne Murray, artist
Pop Vocal Performance—male	"Copacabana"	Barry Manilow, artist
Pop Vocal Performance—group	*Saturday Night Fever*	Bee Gees, artist
Rhythm and Blues Vocal Performance—female	"Last Dance"	Donna Summer, artist
Rhythm and Blues Vocal Performance—male	"On Broadway"	George Benson, artist
Country Vocal Performance—female	*Here You Come Again*	Dolly Parton, artist
Country Vocal Performance—male	"Georgia On My Mind"	Willie Nelson, artist
Original Score for a Motion Picture	*Close Encounters of the Third Kind*	John Williams, composer
Score from an Original Cast Show	*Ain't Misbehavin'*	Thomas Z. Shepard, producer
Classical Album	*Brahms: Concerto for Violin in D Major*	Itzhak Perlman, with Carlo Maria Giulini conducting the Chicago Symphony
Recording for Children	*The Muppet Show*	Jim Henson, artist

WHAT DO YOU SEE IN THIS PICTURE?

Sir Anthony Van Dyck was a famous portrait painter who lived in the 1600's. Because of his ability to portray strong likenesses of people, Van Dyck won countless commissions to do portraits of the wealthy, aristocratic people of his day. The artist gave his subjects such casual elegance and grace that they resembled a social ideal. This talent won him the title of the "cavalier painter." Cavaliers, representing the cream of society, were gallant, courteous gentlemen clad in laces, colorful satins, and plumed hats.

Van Dyck spent most of his later life in England, where he painted many pictures of King Charles I and his family. Look at Van Dyck's painting *The Children of Charles I*. The picture shows the King's three children, who all became rulers themselves—Charles II; Mary, Princess of Orange; and James II. Doesn't it look as if they could step right out of their portrait and speak to you?

The Children of Charles I has a formal, dignified air about it. Bright light falls on the rich costumes of the three children, who are dressed according to the fashion of the day. Both Charles and little Jamie wear floor-length dresses, as did most young boys of their time. The rich lace trimming and handsomely textured fabric of the children's attire properly bespeak royalty.

Because the painting features much ornamentation and curving lines, its style is called baroque. The deliberate brush strokes reveal a knifelike precision. The colors in the picture—running from muted blue to mellow cream to sumptuous scarlet—add to its effect, as does the dark background used for contrast. The children's facial expressions show earnest attention. As is typical of Van Dyck's work, the painting probably flattered its subjects.

Van Dyck arranged the figures to show that Charles was the heir to the throne. Charles stands slightly apart from the other children and looks directly out at the viewer. The dog gazes affectionately at him. And the rich color of Charles's clothes also highlights his figure.

Throughout much of the painting is a flo-ral motif. You can see it in the large, pale rose blossoms against a white-clouded sky in the background, the bud in the ruddy hair of the princess, and the carelessly scattered blooms at her feet. The exotic Turkish rug adds richness to the grouping.

The retriever, with its carefully drawn sleek coat, gives balance to the picture. Look how the curve of the dog's back subtly corresponds to the curve of little Jamie's full skirt. The dog, with the hand of the future monarch on its head, also suggests the English aristocracy's love of the hunt.

The Children of Charles I presents a romaticized portrayal of the three figures. The artist's gift for making his subjects appear grand and noble established a distinctive style in portrait painting that was to last for 200 years in England.

For all Van Dyck's popularity in England, he was not himself English. He was born on March 22, 1599, in Antwerp, in northern Belgium. His father was a silk merchant, and his mother was an exquisite embroiderer. As a small child, the gifted boy astonished his parents by creating excellent pieces of art.

As early as 10 years of age, Van Dyck was serving an apprenticeship. At the age of 16, he was already teaching pupils of his own. A few years later, Van Dyck was established as the most treasured assistant in the studio of Peter Paul Rubens, the Flemish master. He was strongly influenced by Rubens' style and use of warm colors.

Italy, the treasure house of the art world, beckoned Van Dyck in 1621. There he studied the works of the great painters. He especially admired Titian, and his Italian works reflect this influence. In Italy, Van Dyck won marvelous success, leaving outstanding portraits in Bologna, Florence, Rome, Genoa, Sicily—wherever he visited.

Van Dyck returned to Antwerp in 1627 for about five years. He painted some of his finest religious works during that period.

Then, in 1632, King Charles I of England summoned the Flemish artist to his country and made him court painter. The art-loving king knighted the portrait painter that same year. The English court welcomed the talented artist. Van Dyck rode about the countryside in his coach-and-four, enjoying his thoroughbred dogs and elegant clothes.

Members of the aristocracy clamored to have their portraits done. Van Dyck painted about 350 portraits of the English nobility, including 38 of King Charles. Van Dyck had so many opportunities to paint people that it is said he often did only the principal figure. Then he rushed off to another client, leaving his assistants to fill in the background and other such details.

Van Dyck lived in England until his death, in 1641. He was survived by his widow, the Scotch Lady Mary Ruthven, and an 8-day-old daughter. Today, more than 300 years after his death, art lovers everywhere treasure the legacy of Sir Anthony Van Dyck.

LOUISE D. MORRISON
The Harpeth Hall School (Nashville, Tennessee)

The Children of Charles I

271

SCULPTURES IN THE SAND

Anyone can become a sculptor at the beach. All you need is sand, seawater, and a subject. You can create almost anything.

Some very unusual sculptures are often made when there's a sand sculpture contest. A number of coastal cities sponsor contests, including Long Beach in southern California. The Great Sand Sculpture Contest is held there every summer, and the beach-front is usually crowded with sculptors and spectators. Contestants—of all ages—are allowed two hours to create their master-pieces. As many as twelve people are allowed to work on one sculpture. But it must be built within an area that measures 20 square feet (1.9 square meters).

According to the contest rules, you can make a sculpture using only sand and seawater and natural materials found on the beach, such as seashells and seaweed. You can use shovels and buckets of water, but the building has to be done by hand. Frames or molds cannot be used to support or shape the creations of dampened sand.

Many of the contestants design small clay models at home and bring them to the beach to copy. Others make sketches of what they are going to sculpt.

Because sand castles are so common, they are judged in a separate category. Ribbons are awarded to those with the most artistic design and originality. The other sculptures are judged for humorous qualities, as well as for design and originality. As you can imagine, it's always difficult for the judges to pick the winners.

In a recent contest, 40 sand castles and sculptures were completed. One that made everyone laugh was a lady on roller skates who had fallen down and dropped her ice cream cone. The favorite subjects were animals, including a fat tunafish riding in a boat, a sunbathing pig, and a lazy lion. And there were ocean creatures of all kinds—a smiling whale, a shy sea serpent, and even a beautiful mermaid.

Some of the winning creations are shown on these pages. Next time you're at the beach, see how creative you can be by making a castle or sculpture of sand.

MICHELE AND TOM GRIMM
Authors, *What Is a Seal?*

Animals—like this sunbathing pig—are a favorite subject in sand sculpture contests.

272

You, too, can create an unusual sculpture like this tunafish in a boat.

Some sculptures win prizes because of their humorous qualities, like this poor lady on roller skates.

PEOPLE IN THE ARTS

Jon Voight, winner of the 1979 Academy Award for best actor, is a perfectionist. He wants every character he plays to be realistic. His first important role was in the 1969 film *Midnight Cowboy*. His 1979 Oscar was for his portrayal of a Vietnam War veteran confined to a wheelchair in *Coming Home*. His next film was *The Champ*, in which he played a former prizefighter who returns to boxing to prove himself to his young son. Despite his success, Voight still attends drama classes regularly to improve his acting.

Aleksandr Godunov, a 30-year-old soloist with the Soviet Union's Bolshoi Ballet, defected in August while the company was touring the United States. Godunov was among the most prominent of the Bolshoi's principal dancers. He said he decided to stay in the United States so that he would have freedom as an artist. Godunov's wife, Lyudmila Vlasova, also a Bolshoi dancer on the tour, made headlines, too. U.S. officials detained the plane on which she was to fly home until they were satisfied that she was returning of her own free will.

The beautiful soprano voice of **Beverly Sills** has captivated opera lovers all over the world. But in 1979, Sills retired from her career as a singer. As she ended one career, however, she began another. Sills became general director of the New York City Opera. Managing an opera company is a complex and often tricky job. It involves fund raising, choosing operas to be performed, and hiring singers. Sills wants to see the company perform operettas as well as operas. But her major goal is to continue to popularize opera. "Bubbles," as her family and fans call her, wants more and more people to love opera as much as she does.

Steve Martin—that "wild and cra-a-azy guy" with an arrow through his head—is one of the hottest comedians around. He started early. When he was a boy he performed magic tricks for Disneyland visitors. By the time he was 21, he was writing comedy material for TV stars. Before long, he was on television himself. His fan club has been growing ever since. His concerts, records, and movies are big hits. So is his book, *Cruel Shoes*, which provides important information on such concerns as "How to Fold Soup" and "What to Do When the Dopes Come Over." Whatever Martin does, he draws lots of laughs. "But," as he sings during each performance, "the most amazin' thing to me is I get paid for doin' this."

FUN TO READ

An illustration from *The Girl Who Loved Wild Horses,* by Paul Goble. The book was the winner of the 1979 Caldecott Medal.

THE OLD LADY NEXT DOOR

Dave and I were busy dusting Poco with flea powder when we saw Mrs. Carson limping up her front walk. She was lugging the battered old suitcase she always carried when she went to visit her daughter in Chicago.

Dave quickly handed me the can and loped across the lawn that joined the two yards.

"Let me help you, Mrs. Carson."

That's what I like about Dave. He isn't as good-looking as some guys, with his long hawk-face and sandy lashes that match his hair, but he has a heart like a marshmallow. You can count on him when your dog gets lost or you need someone to bring you your homework when you have the flu.

Poco wriggled and snuggled up against me. He's like a baby, with great big appealing eyes that make you let him jump up beside you on the sofa, which you shouldn't do. He follows me wherever I go.

When Dave came back, he was grinning broadly.

"That's the old-ladyist old lady I ever saw," he said. "Like the grandmothers in books. She says 'dearie' and 'bless my soul' and things like that."

"And bakes ginger cookies," I sighed happily.

Mrs. Carson and I had become good friends, and her cookie jar always seemed to be full of something delightful.

"My grandmothers are more like—well, more like my mom," Dave continued. "They wear snappy clothes and go to the beauty parlor to have their hair done."

"Mine, too. And Grandma Pierce just bought a pantsuit. She says it's more comfortable when she's driving the car."

We giggled a little, and then we agreed that we wouldn't want to change our grandmothers because they were fun in a lot of ways, even if they didn't do much baking.

278

That evening at dinner I started to tell Mom and Dad how Dave and I had decided that Mrs. Carson was the most grandmotherly old lady we knew. But Dad started talking first, and his story knocked everything else out of my head.

"There was a bank robbery over at Weston about noon today," he said. "It was the same young punks who've pulled four other robberies in the last six months—the man they call Stocking-face and his girl friend, Goldilocks. They got away with over a hundred thousand dollars."

My head swam. I couldn't imagine having that much money. It was like something in a movie, with Stocking-face running like a deer for the getaway car, and Goldilocks dashing along beside him, her blond hair blowing in the wind.

"It must be terribly exciting to rob a bank," I said.

Mom and Dad looked at me as if I'd used swear words.

"Why, Joannie!" Mom was breathless. "You act as if you think it was fun, or a game."

I was embarrassed, and I felt myself blushing. "Oh, I know it's wrong," I said hastily. "I just thought that—well, I guess it seems like an adventure to them."

"It didn't seem like an adventure to the people in the bank," said Dad grimly. "One woman fainted, and the teller who gave them the money had a heart attack. Luckily they got him to the hospital in time."

I nodded meekly. Of course, I'd never even steal a candy bar from a grocery store, much less rob a bank. But I couldn't get over the sneaky feeling that Stocking-face and Goldilocks must enjoy their adventures.

I was still thinking about them when I went to bed that night. The idea of a bank robbery taking place in a small town just fifteen miles away was so exciting that my thoughts kept crowding out sleep.

As I flipped over for the umpteenth time, I heard a car door slam outside. Then there was a murmur of voices coming from the direction of Mrs. Carson's house.

Mom always says I have the curiosity of a whole litter of cats. I jumped out of bed and went to the window, which looks down right on Mrs. Carson's front porch.

A man and woman stood there, and they were kissing. There was a full moon, and I could see them outlined clearly. The woman wasn't Mrs. Carson, because she was too young and straight. I could see that her short hair was bright red and very curly.

The door opened, and they went inside. I wondered who they were. Then I remembered that Mrs. Carson had mentioned once that her daughter had red hair. But why would her daughter come to visit her the very day she had returned from visiting her daughter? And who was the man? I knew I wouldn't find any answers standing at the window, so I went back to bed.

My curiosity bump made me go to see Mrs. Carson the next day. I took her half of one of Mother's cherry pies, because she'd given me so many treats. She greeted me at the door, looking happy and excited.

"Well, bless your bonny heart!" she exclaimed over the pie. "What a lovely time for me to have it. My daughter came last night, so we can share it. She said that after I left her, she got so homesick for me that she just had to follow me home. Now wasn't that sweet? Her fiancé drove her down in her car, but he had to leave this morning."

I saw that there was a small blue car in the driveway, so everything seemed to be explained.

Mrs. Carson tucked a wisp of gray hair behind one ear. "I'll call Vivian. I want her to meet you. I've told her all about my good neighbors."

She went to the back of the house and a few minutes later came tiptoeing back, smiling gently.

"She's sleeping, poor dear. They got in so late that she's all tuckered out. You'll meet her another day."

I hoped I would, because as I said, I'm awfully curious. But several days passed before I met her. One morning I saw that the newsboy had tossed Mrs. Carson's paper so crookedly that it landed behind a bush, and I was afraid she wouldn't notice it. So I went over, picked it up, and carried it to the door.

It was Vivian who opened the door instead of her mother. She was awfully pretty. Her hair was a soft golden red, and her skin was peachy. She had on a thin, pale-green robe that sort of floated around her. The only trouble was that she had on more makeup than I'd ever seen on anybody before. Her mouth was so red and smeary it looked like crushed strawberries. Blue eye shadow and about three layers of false eyelashes almost hid her eyes, but I could see that they were blue, like Mrs. Carson's.

She smiled at me, and she had a nice smile.

"You must be Joan," she said. "Mother has told me about you. She's at the grocery just now. Won't you come in?"

I shook my head. "I'm going swimming with Dave this morning—he's the boy who lives down the street. I just thought I'd bring Mrs. Carson's paper. The boy threw it behind a bush, and I thought it might be lost."

I told Dave about Vivian while we were resting after our swim at the pool.

"It's funny that a nice old lady like Mrs. Carson would have a daughter who looks like she's already to act in a show. I wonder what she thinks of Vivian."

"Probably thinks she's the greatest thing that's happened since they invented ice-cream cones," laughed Dave. "Mothers don't see too well when they look at their daughters."

I knew that was true, and I was sure that Mrs. Carson would want to spend a lot of time visiting with Vivian. So I stayed away

280

and left them alone until the day the newsboy threw the paper behind the bush again. I fumed about how careless he was getting and then went to pick it up.

This time I walked around to the back of the house, because it was late afternoon, the time when Mrs. Carson was usually in her kitchen.

As I rounded the corner of the house, I heard voices, one of them a man's.

"It's time for us to clear out, Viv," he was saying. "I can't stick it anymore. I've got a contact with a private plane just across the state line. He can fly us across the Mexican border tonight. Then, kid, we're home free."

"OK." Her voice sounded hard, not at all the way it had been when she talked to me. "We'll do away with the old lady, huh?" And they both screamed with laughter.

By this time I was near the edge of the open kitchen window, and by looking in slantwise, I could see Vivian and the man sitting at the kitchen table.

Then Vivian said, "I won't have to do the Goldilocks bit any longer, either."

She opened a drawer in the table and pulled out a blond wig, twirling it around her finger until the hair spun out like a cloud.

For a minute I couldn't believe what I'd heard. I was so scared I felt like a block of ice. Vivian was Goldilocks who robbed banks! The blond wig was a disguise! Now they were planning to run away, and before they left they intended to do away with Mrs. Carson. She must have caught on to what they were doing.

I raced for home, making as little noise as I could. All I could think of was that I had to get help for that poor old woman before it was too late.

It was Mother's day to work at the Social Service Center where they help people find jobs and places to live. The house was empty. I hurried to the phone and dialed Dad's office. I heard the phone ring for a long time, and then a woman's voice answered lazily.

When I asked for Dad, she sniffed. "Sorry, this is the cleaning woman. The office just closed, and all the big shots have gone home."

I tried the Social Service Center. Again the phone rang and rang, but this time no one ever answered. I hung up and nibbled my nails for a few minutes, wondering what to do. I finally thought about what I should have done in the first place. I started to dial the police.

I was only halfway through when I heard the front door open and a voice called, "Joannie, dear! Are you there?"

It was Mrs. Carson. I hung up the phone and ran into the hallway. I simply hugged her, I was so relieved.

"Thank goodness, you're safe! I was just trying to call the police!"

She blinked at me. "The police? Why, what for, dearie? What's wrong?"

I blurted it all out, though I felt terrible having to tell her something like that about her daughter.

Her eyes got bigger and bigger, and she began to moan.

"Oh, it can't be true! I know Viv's always been a little wild, but she wouldn't hurt her own mother!"

Suddenly she sagged against the wall, clutching at it. I thought she was going to fall.

"Take me home!" she gasped. "I want to lie down. Help me, Joannie!"

"But they're over there!" I protested. "You can lie down here!"

"No, no!" Her hands were clasped over her chest, and she looked awful. "They went to the store a few minutes ago and won't be back for at least an hour. Take me home, Joannie. We can lock the doors and call the police from there."

She pitched forward, and I caught her, bracing myself to keep her from falling. I decided I had to do things her way, or she might have a heart attack. I led her out and across the yard, then into her own front door.

As soon as we were inside, an amazing thing happened. She pulled herself away from me, whirled, and locked the door.

"Well, I see you got her." The man was standing in the living-room doorway, a nasty grin on his sharp face.

"Sure," she said. "What do you think I am, a dope?"

The voice was coming from Mrs. Carson, but it wasn't Mrs. Carson's voice. It was Vivian's. Vivian had masqueraded as her mother to trap me! If I hadn't been so upset when she came to the house, I would have seen that something was wrong. The gray wig was a little lopsided, and the gray-brown makeup on her face was patchy, as if it had been put on in a hurry. But no, there was still something wrong. She still looked almost exactly like Mrs. Carson.

All the pieces of the truth suddenly came together like a clap of thunder. There had never been a Mrs. Carson, any more than there had been a Goldilocks. Vivian had played both parts. I remembered that I had never seen Mrs. Carson and Vivian together. When Vivian had said they could do away with the old lady, she had meant that she wouldn't have to play that role any longer.

Stocking-face was glaring at Vivian. "Well, maybe you are a dope. If you hadn't taken off your makeup to do that daughter bit, we might not be in this jam."

"Don't you think I got tired looking like a hag? I wanted to be pretty for you, Gus. I knew how bored you were, hiding all the time." Vivian's voice was wheedling.

"OK, OK, so we'll take care of it."

I'd been listening in a sort of trance, as if it were all a movie. All of a sudden I realized that I was in danger. Since Mrs. Carson——I mean Vivian——had locked the front door, I made a dash for the back. Stocking-face caught me neatly and gave me a ringing slap.

"None of that! We can't let you get out there and tell what you heard."

"You shouldn't have snooped." Vivian pulled off the gray wig and began wiping the makeup from her face. "Did you think we didn't hear you running away from the window, like an elephant? You're a silly girl."

"What are you going to do with me?" I squeaked.

"Tie you up nice and tight. They'll find you sooner or later, I guess, but not until we're well on our way."

I was scared silly, but at least, I thought, they were not going to hurt me. I changed my mind about that pretty soon. Stocking-face dragged me into the bedroom and tied me to a chair. He pulled the ropes so tight that they bit into my flesh.

"You're hurting me!" I wailed.

He grinned. "Now ain't that too bad?"

There was something in his face that made shivers creep down my spine. I could see that he liked hurting me. Vivian was standing in the doorway, and she laughed. She was enjoying it, too.

All at once I remembered how I'd had a sort of half-romantic feeling about these two as adventurers. I knew now that they weren't the least bit dashing and glamorous. They were just plain mean. They lived by taking what belonged to others and hurting anyone who got in their way.

Stocking-face thrust a roll of rags into my mouth and tied it in place. It made it hard for me to breathe.

Then they left, and before long I heard the sound of their car driving away. I wondered how long it would be before someone

found me. I had to breathe in gasps, and my jaws were beginning to get sore.

I waited and waited. I could see through the window, and it was beginning to get dark. Dad and Mom must be home by now. Surely they were looking for me. But would they think to look here? I'd told Mom that I was leaving Mrs. Carson alone to visit with her daughter. They'd probably call all my girl friends, and Dave, and all the places they knew I was in the habit of going.

Every once in a while I tried to pull against the ropes that held me, but it hurt so much that I quit trying. Finally, I was so tired that I just sagged back and cried until the bandage around my mouth was wet. Then I dropped off to sleep.

When I woke it was dark, and I heard a yipping sound outside. It kept up for a long time, the sound of a small dog whose bark was too fierce for his size. It was Poco, who had probably seen me go into the house earlier and was now calling in his dog language for me to come out.

Then there was something else.

"Quiet fellow. Is she in there?"

If was Dave's voice. Of course they would have called Dave to help look for me.

"Joannie, are you in there?"

I tried to spit out that awful gag, but of course I couldn't. Dave was knocking at the door, and I was in a panic for fear that if I didn't answer he would go away. I thought of what I could do. The idea scared me, but I knew I had to do it. I pushed my feet hard against the floor and flung myself backward. As I had expected, I hit the floor with a crash.

My head hurt terribly, but in a few minutes Dave was there picking me up.

"For Pete's sake!" he kept saying. "For Pete's sake!"

You can imagine the excitement when Dave led me home, and I told my story.

Mother said, "It's unbelievable!" And Dad called Goldilocks and Stocking-face a name he had never used before.

Of course, they called the police right away. An alert was sent out in time to catch the robbers before they had crossed the state line.

Police Chief Clark came over the next day and explained the whole thing to us.

"Those two had a smooth scheme worked out. Goldilocks rented a house as a respectable old woman so that they could store their loot until it was safe to take it out of the country. Each time they committed a robbery, Stocking-face would drop her off somewhere, usually at a railway station, carrying the money in an old suitcase. She'd go into the rest room, make up as an old lady, and come out looking like the most harmless kind of traveler in the world. The times when the old lady was supposed to be visiting her daughter were the times when they staged their holdups."

"And she carried the money home in that awful-looking suitcase!" I gasped.

Dave came in about then, carrying a paper bag.

"I thought you might like some ginger cookies," he said. "You know, in memory of your old friend Mrs. Carson."

I was tempted to throw the ice pack at him——the one I was holding against the knot on my head.

Then he opened the bag and began to take out the most luscious-looking chocolate-covered cream puffs I've ever seen. You can't imagine how pleased I was. I'm not sure I'll ever want another ginger cookie again.

285

POETRY

THE FROG

Be kind and tender to the Frog,
    And do not call him names,
As "Slimy-Skin," or "Polly-wog,"
    Or likewise, "Uncle James,"
Or "Gape-a-grin," or "Toad-gone-wrong,"
    Or "Billy-Bandy-knees;"
The Frog is justly sensitive
    To epithets like these.

No animal will more repay
    A treatment kind and fair,
At least, so lonely people say
Who keep a frog (and, by the way,
    They are extremely rare).

HILAIRE BELLOC (1870–1953)

THE EAGLE

He clasps the crag with crooked hands;
Close to the sun in lonely lands,
Ringed with the azure world, he stands.

The wrinkled sea beneath him crawls;
He watches from his mountain walls,
And like a thunderbolt he falls.

ALFRED, LORD TENNYSON (1809–1892)

A pin has a head, but has no hair;
A clock has a face, but no mouth there;
Needles have eyes, but they cannot see;
A fly has a trunk without lock or key;
A timepiece may lose, but cannot win;
A corn-field dimples without a chin;
A hill has no leg, but has a foot;
A wine-glass a stem, but not a root;
Rivers run, though they have no feet;
A saw has teeth, but it does not eat;
Ash-trees have keys, yet never a lock;
And baby crows, without being a cock.

CHRISTINA ROSSETTI (1830–1894)

MEMORY

My mind lets go a thousand things,
Like dates of wars and deaths of kings,
And yet recalls the very hour—
'Twas noon by yonder village tower,
And on the last blue noon in May—
The wind came briskly up this way,
Crisping the brook beside the road;
Then, pausing here, set down its load
Of pine-scents, and shook listlessly
Two petals from that wild-rose tree.

THOMAS BAILEY ALDRICH (1836–1907)

THE MIDDLE WAY

A white swan swimming to the shore beyond
Parts with his breast the cherry-petalled pond.

RÔKA (1671–1703)

THE MONTHS

January brings the snow,
Makes our feet and fingers glow.

February brings the rain,
Thaws the frozen lake again.

March brings breezes loud and shrill,
Stirs the dancing daffodil.

April brings the primrose sweet,
Scatters daisies at our feet.

May brings flocks of pretty lambs,
Skipping by their fleecy dams.

June brings tulips, lilies, roses,
Fills the children's hands with posies.

Hot July brings cooling showers,
Apricots and gillyflowers.

August brings the sheaves of corn,
Then the harvest home is borne.

Warm September brings the fruit,
Sportsmen then begin to shoot.

Fresh October brings the pheasant,
Then to gather nuts is pleasant.

Dull November brings the blast,
Then the leaves are whirling fast.

Chill December brings the sleet,
Blazing fire, and Christmas treat.

SARA COLERIDGE (1802–1852)

LIGHTLY STEPPED A YELLOW STAR

Lightly stepped a yellow star
To its lofty place,
Loosed the Moon her silver hat
From her lustral face.

All of evening softly lit
As an astral hall—
"Father," I observed to Heaven,
"You are punctual!"

EMILY DICKINSON (1830–1886)

SAILING HOMEWARD

Cliffs that rise a thousand feet
Without a break,
Lake that stretches a hundred miles
Without a wave.
Sands that are white through all the year,
Without a stain,
Pine-tree woods, winter and summer
Ever-green,
Streams that for ever flow and flow
Without a pause,
Trees that for twenty thousand years
Your vows have kept,
You have suddenly healed the pain of a
traveler's heart,
And moved his brush to write a new song.

CHAN FANG-SHENG (4th century)

NIGHT MAGIC

Silently shadows deepen
As the sun slowly descends in the sky.

The darkness comes
In a mysterious midnight blue.

The stars glisten
On the rolling hills

While the moon casts
Silvery shadows through the evening.

Everything is suddenly still
In the mysterious mist of night.

The world is asleep
Having dreams of tomorrow,

And then gradually, the darkness is broken

Which brings a new day.

MARIE RAGLAND
age 12
Annandale, Virginia

MY REFLECTION

I like to look at my reflection
in the lake.
It's a picture of me,
that's no mistake.
When I smile it smiles,
when I grow it grows.
Is it real?
Who knows?
My reflection stays
as long as I do.
And when I come back
it's always there, too.

STACEY WAGONER
age 11
West Lafayette, Indiana

CONSIDER

Birds swoop gracefully
On the invisible tightrope
From tree to tree.

SUZANE SWINNERTON
age 11
Caldwell, Idaho

POMEGRANATE

Rubies and garnets in a lemon shell.
Crunch, crunch, crunch,
Squirting raspberry juice
Behind my teeth;
Trickling down my tongue;
Inhaling the musty smell of fall.

KATHLEEN LINDHOLM
age 10
Los Angeles, California

SEASON RIDDLES

When I hear my first robin
And hear it sing,
Then I know that it is spring.

If it's time for picnics
In a park that's near,
I know for sure
That summer's here.

When the weather is chilly
And I hear geese call,
Everyone says it's the
Start of fall.

When cold and icy north winds blow,
It's winter time and
Time for snow.

MIA CRADEUR
age 11
Opelousas, Louisiana

WISE OWL

Oh, to be an old owl,
Sage and silent,
Sitting on his bough.

Waiting, watchful,
Proud, majestic,
Knowing all
But telling little—
Oh, to be an old owl.

Nocturnal owl
Glides through
The night
A menacing shadow.

Dear owl,
Are you what they say you are,
Wise,
Or
Are you
Just a bird?

DAVID GADD
age 12
Papatoetoe, New Zealand

MUSIC

Everything is silent in the woods—
Everything apart from the music.
The music made by the flowers,
The ferns,
The trees.
The flowers are trumpets,
Blowing in the wind.
The ferns are harps,
Playing while the fairies dance.
The trees are drums
With their branches beating the trunks,
Waving and blowing in the wind.

LESLEY SMYTH
age 11
Esher, Surrey, England

TOMORROW

Tomorrow is mysterious
like a book you haven't finished.
Tomorrow is slow
like a turtle in a race.
Tomorrow is a thought
that is just like a dream.
You can think about tomorrow all day,
and you will never know
what is going to happen.
Tomorrow just won't come
until tomorrow.

BRAD PALMER
age 10
Columbus, Ohio

A LONELY DROP OF WATER

A lonely drop of water is going to flood
    your eye.
Down the tear trickles.
Your eye reddens.
Your mother comes to comfort you.
The gloom you have stored up inside you
    is ready
To burst out, and float away.
You are now free from misery.

You go out to play.
You see a dewdrop hanging onto its
    mother.
The dewdrop lets go.
It snuggles itself in the ground.
All is well.

LARA HURLEY
age 10
Charlton, Massachusetts

Charlie Burnett & the Spring Flood

Charlie Burnett grew up in Old Shawneetown, Illinois—a village on the north bank of the Ohio River just below the mouth of the Wabash, where the Midwest slowly eases into the South. His father died when Charlie was still a baby. Miss Lizzie, his mother, had to turn their home into a boardinghouse to support them. It was such a busy place that she had little time to spend with her son. As soon as Charlie was old enough, he had chores to do, too. Instead of going to the levee after school with the other village boys—to fish or skip pebbles or simply watch the boats on the river—he had to go home to help his mother with the boarders' supper. So Charlie was often lonely.

Sometimes Miss Lizzie grew sad seeing Charlie in the kitchen when the other boys were playing outside. When she hugged him and said, "You run along, Charlie honey! Go out and play with your cousin Billy. We'll manage here!" Charlie just shook his head. "No, thank you, Ma'am," he told her. "I reckon I'd rather stay here and finish what I'm doing."

The fact of the matter was that Charlie was a little scared of his cousin, because Billy often tagged along after Harry Fawcett, the twelve-year-old town bully. Charlie still smarted with the humiliation of his last encounter with Harry and his gang. He had been sitting in the side yard shelling peas, with his mother's apron tied around his neck, when Harry and his crew, including Billy, had come by.

"Why, Miz Burnett, how sweet you *do* look today," Harry exclaimed as he caught sight of Charlie. Then he vaulted the picket fence, knelt before the younger boy, and clasped his hands to his heart, simpering, "Oh, my darling, won't you be mine?"

While his followers laughed uproariously, Harry jumped up and kicked the pan out of Charlie's lap, scattering peas in every direction. Then he ran away with his snickering cronies.

So even when Charlie had free time, he spent it by himself. He often thought that if he could only have a pet, he wouldn't feel so lonesome. But that was impossible. A puppy would bark and disturb the boarders. A cat? No, Miss Sophie in the front bedroom sneezed at the very mention of a kitten.

Then one day Zack, the hired man, solved the problem. He found a baby rabbit whose mother had been shot and brought it home. Charlie was overjoyed. Zack fixed a pen in the yard, where Sam the Rabbit could stay during the day, and a snug box next to the big range in the kitchen where he could spend the nights and stay in bad weather. As Charlie went about his afternoon chores, Sam followed him, hippety-hoppety, wherever he

290

went. If Charlie sat down, Sam crouched beside him and twitched his nose. They shared carrots and secrets, and Charlie wasn't lonely anymore.

Often in the spring, when snow melting in the faraway Appalachian Mountains turned lazy tributaries into rushing torrents, the broad Ohio rose higher and higher against its banks and levees. In a rainy season there was a good chance that the river would spill over and flood the countryside. That year the winter had been hard in the eastern mountains, and so, early in the spring, Shawneetown prepared itself. Townsmen worked in shifts, piling sandbags to raise the height of the levee. Watchmen mounted on horses stood guard above the town, ready to spread the alarm of a flooding crest. Householders moved their family treasures to the upper stories of their homes.

Most houses in Shawneetown had porches with galleries above them, and most families owned rowboats. These boats were carried up and lashed to the gallery railings, so that they could be stocked with food and blankets when the time came. Then, if the waters flooded their lower floors, the townspeople could row to the safety of the schoolhouse hill and spend a sociable day or two camping out in the school building until the water subsided.

The children of the town looked forward to flood time with as much excitement as if it were the Fourth of July. No school! No chores! Just a round of songfests and parlor games and picnicking. Because Charlie was planning to take Sam along this year, he expected he would have more fun than usual.

As the town braced itself for the Ohio's cresting, word came that the Wabash, too, was swollen with rain and would soon add its peak load to that of the larger river. All able-bodied men were pressed into service to reinforce the levees. Women and children were given orders to prepare food and be ready to hurry to their upper floors as soon as the church bell rang.

But before the emergency measures could be put into effect, the cresting rivers collided. They smashed through the earthworks above the town. A wall of chocolate-colored water surged down Main Street before the alarm could be sounded. Charlie and Miss Lizzie were in the kitchen filling a last hamper with food, when the rushing water pushed against the back door and swung it open.

"Run, Charlie! Run for the stairs!" cried his mother, grabbing the basket and pushing her son ahead of her. They reached the landing just as the water swirled through the dining room into the hall and spilled out over the parlor window sills. They stopped to gasp for breath.

All of a sudden, Charlie shrieked, "Sam!" In the rush he had forgotten the rabbit penned into its box beside the stove, waiting for Zack to carry it upstairs at the last minute. He leaped up to rescue the pet. Before he could take a step downstairs, however, his mother grabbed him by the suspenders and held him fast. He wriggled to get free, but Miss Lizzie locked her arm about his waist and called for Miss Sophie to help her hold him. The force of the water was enough to carry the heavy brass umbrella stand out the front door. A nine-year-old boy would have no chance of holding his footing in the millrace of the front hall.

A washtub and an old stool bumped through the dining room

doorway and out into the frothy stream like awkward boats. A chair and logs from the woodbox followed. Then, to Charlie's horror, Sam's box floated past the foot of the staircase, with Sam huddled in a corner, his ears flat against his body. Through the front door it swung—and out to sea. Miss Lizzie and Miss Sophie had to hold on tight to restrain the frantic boy.

At the schoolhouse that evening the party went on as expected, but Charlie was too numb with grief to enjoy it. When the songfest began, he hung back until Miss Lizzie pushed him up front to the row of stools reserved for the schoolchildren.

"Now," said Miss Sophie, at the piano, "what shall we sing?"

"Please, Ma'am," called a sugary voice from the row behind Charlie's, "can we sing 'My Bonny Lies Over the Ocean'?" It was Harry Fawcett. A chorus of suppressed snickers followed the request.

Miss Sophie banged a chord for silence, then started to play the popular tune. Her pounding had hardly begun when Charlie heard a sob from the boy next to him. It was his cousin Billy.

"Look at the sissy!" came Harry's stage whisper from the row behind. "Bawling over his old cat!"

Charlie suddenly remembered that Billy had a cat named Bonny. She must have been lost like Sam. How cruel of Harry Fawcett to ask for that song!

In his anger, Charlie forgot his own sorrow. He jumped up and turned to the row behind him. "You bully!" he yelled at Harry. "Picking on somebody when he's feeling bad. You . . . You . . . You. . . ." Charlie couldn't think of anything mean enough to say, so he swung his fist into Harry Fawcett's eye.

Mrs. Burnett had to apologize to Mrs. Fawcett for Harry's black eye. For a while Charlie suffered the disapproval of the ladies who supervised the young people. But among the children of Shawneetown, he became a hero.

When the waters went down and the people returned to clean the mud out of their houses, Zack found Sam's box caught in a parapet over the door of the town bank. But Sam was not in it. Bonny was not found either.

It wasn't long afterward that Billy came looking for his cousin Charlie. "A little old raccoon had a nest in a tree in our yard," he said slowly. "I guess she got carried away, but there's a couple of baby coons alive in the nest. If you like, I reckon we could bring them up together."

Charlie hesitated, but only for a moment. He saw that the raccoons—and even Billy—needed a friend as much as he did. So he took the homeless baby from his cousin. Then, with the flip of a penny to help them decide, Charlie named his raccoon Ohio, and Billy named his Wabash—to remind them of the biggest spring flood Shawneetown had ever seen.

ANNE MALCOLMSON
Author, *Yankee Doodle's Cousins*

Black Tuesday

October 29, 1979, was the 50th anniversary of an event that affected the lives of millions of people. On that day in 1929, a day still remembered as Black Tuesday, the U.S. stock market suffered the worst day in its history. By the end of that grim day, stock prices had dropped by a fantastic $14,000,000,000. The Crash of '29 marked the end of an era of prosperity and unbounded optimism. It also marked the beginning of the Great Depression that quickly spread from the United States to other parts of the world.

The decade that led up to the Crash of '29 is often called the Roaring Twenties. It was a time for letting loose after the lean, hard years of World War I. People listened to a new type of music called jazz and did the high-kicking steps of the Charleston, the lastest dance craze. And a new invention called radio was sweeping the country.

But most of all, the Roaring Twenties were years when Americans believed that prosperity was here to stay. The automobile industry was booming and the stock market was enjoying the biggest boom in its history. The prices of stocks issued by the country's major companies doubled, tripled, and then soared out of sight.

People everywhere were jumping on the get-rich-quick bandwagon. And because there were no strong federal controls over the stock market, speculators could do pretty much as they pleased. Small-time speculators bought stock on margin—a kind of installment plan where you could put up a small part of the stock's price and pay the rest later. Rich and powerful speculators formed pools, pushing prices down when they wanted to buy and driving prices up when they wanted to sell.

Some business experts warned that such practices would eventually lead to a collapse of the market. But many investors paid no attention to the prophets of doom. They preferred to listen instead to the prophets of profit. The result was that most stockholders were caught off guard when the bubble burst and the stock market came crashing down in 1929. Many lost everything they had.

In the wake of the Crash of '29, the federal government stepped in and passed the Securities and Exchange Act. Margin buying was curbed and the manipulation of stock prices was made almost impossible. Thanks to the tough rules established by the Securities and Exchange Commission, most experts believe there will never be another stock market crash like the one in 1929. But, of course, no one can be sure.

What follows is a dramatized account of the stock market crash of 1929 as seen through the eyes of a young newspaper reporter. It is a story that ends with the day that will always be known as Black Tuesday.

Tommy Baxter walked briskly into the newsroom of *The New York Chronicle* shortly before 11 A.M. on a gray Monday morning. He was a slim young man with an alert, smooth-featured face, wire-rimmed glasses that made him look a bit older than his 24 years, and a half-grown mustache. The budding mustache, a shade lighter than the wavy brown hair on his head, was something he had recently added—an effort to make himself look more mature.

Baxter waved to several men sitting at the copy desk, then flopped into the wooden swivel chair at his own desk. He checked the bulletin board on the wall to see if there were any messages. There was nothing new. But for just a moment his eyes lingered on a clipping he had put up two years earlier, in 1927—the year the *Chronicle* had hired him as a cub reporter. The clipping was yellowed, but the big, bold headline was sharp and clear: BABE BLASTS NUMBER 60, BREAKS HOME RUN RECORD.

Tommy Baxter sighed as he reread the story. That was one of the biggest events of the decade, and he had played a part in covering it. True, it was a small part. By a stroke of luck, Baxter had been at Yankee Stadium the September day that Babe Ruth had made baseball history by smashing a home run into the right field bleachers. That clout was number 60 for the Babe—the most homers ever hit by a ballplayer in a single season. Baxter had gotten to write a sidebar story—an interview with the fan who had caught the record-breaking home run ball.

Since then he had covered nothing bigger than a car smashup or a water-main break. For the past month, he had been on what all the *Chronicle* reporters sarcastically called the "Death Watch"—writing obituary notices. He felt quite frustrated.

Baxter's thoughts were interrupted by a pat on the back. He looked up and saw the smiling face of Hal Stewart, another junior reporter. Stewart dropped some papers on Baxter's desk. "One for you and one for me," he said cheerily.

Baxter grimaced. "More obits, I suppose."

"Yep," replied Stewart. "A vice-president of a Wall Street bank died of a heart attack. Poor guy, he probably owned 10,000 shares of Radio."

"What's wrong with Radio?" asked Baxter.

Stewart made a sour face. "Don't you read the newspapers, Tommy? Last Thursday it dropped nearly twenty-five points in one day."

Baxter shook his head. "Wow, that's pretty bad. How come you know so much about the market?"

"Why man, everyone's in the market," Stewart replied. "I have twenty shares of American Can. Don't you have any stock?"

"Nope," said Baxter. "I can't afford it on my salary."

Stewart looked surprised. "Well, buy on margin like everybody else. Just put down ten percent of the cost and your broker lends you the rest. Then when the stock goes up you sell, pay back your broker, and walk away with a nice fat profit."

"What happens if the stock goes *down* instead of up?"

Stewart scowled. "I can see you're one of those doom and gloom types. Sure, the market declined last week. But I feel . . ."

Before he could finish, one of the news editors motioned to Baxter. "Tommy, get over to the city desk. The chief wants to talk to you." The "chief"—as he was known in the newsroom—was Barney Rice, the city editor.

Baxter found Barney Rice at the city desk. The fat stub of a cigar was clenched firmly between his teeth. A green eye shade shielded his eyes from the glare of the overhead lights.

Rice looked up, pulled the cigar out of his mouth and said gruffly, "Baxter, what do you know about the stock market?"

"Not much, chief—only what I've been reading the last few days," the young reporter admitted.

"Well, you better be a quick learner," the city ed growled. "The regular beat reporter just called in sick. Which means I need a good news hound who can find out what's going on down there and phone in the info to a rewrite man. Lots of color, good human interest. Can you handle it?"

Baxter's head was whirling. Wow, a real story, he thought to himself. "Sure Mr. Rice, I can handle it."

"Remember kid, this is page-one stuff," Rice cautioned. "Don't let me down."

Moments later, Baxter was walking down the steps to the Times Square subway station. He stopped at a newsstand and picked up a copy of the *New York Herald*—he liked to keep up with the competition—and a candy bar, just in case he wouldn't have time for lunch. He handed the vendor a dime, and the man took out two cents for the paper and another two cents for the candy. The reporter pocketed a penny of his six cents change and dropped the nickel into the turnstile to pay his fare.

A downtown express train was rumbling into the station and he hopped aboard. Barney Rice had given him a file of background stories and the name of a stockbroker who would help him get on the floor of the New York Stock Exchange.

Baxter leafed through the pile of papers. The clippings contained statements from prominent businessmen and financial experts. In one story, the chairman of the National City Bank of New York was quoted as saying, "I know of nothing fundamentally wrong with the stock market." A leading economist at Harvard had given a speech stating that stock prices had reached "a permanent high plateau." Other business leaders stated flatly that the market's slump was temporary and that people should buy more stock while prices were at bargain levels.

There were a few experts, however, who urged caution in

buying stocks. One influential investment report predicted that big investors would unload their stock as prices declined, leading to a loss of confidence in the market and panic selling.

Baxter shoved the clippings into his pocket and looked around the subway car. Most of the people had their newspapers opened to the stock market quotations. Of course, he knew that a lot of Americans owned stocks—more than a million, it was said. And he knew that businesspeople considered the market an important indicator of the economy's health. When stock prices went up, things were good. But he hadn't realized just how many ordinary Americans were interested in the market.

The train screeched to a halt at the Wall Street station, and Baxter got off. He walked quickly to the offices of Morris, Sawyer, and Campbell—the brokerage house where Barney Rice had a friendly contact.

It was 12:30 P.M. and the office was crowded with people who had dropped by during their lunch hour to check the latest stock prices. While waiting for the broker he was supposed to speak to, Baxter looked around. Over on one wall, he could see a large board on which were posted that day's prices for the major stocks. Clerks were busy putting up cards with the last prices received over the ticker-tape machine, which could be heard tapping away in another part of the room. Baxter saw that nearly all the leading stocks had dropped off a few points since the market had opened at 10 A.M. He took out his notebook and began to jot down a description of the scene. As he did, a man in a blue pinstripe suit walked up and introduced himself.

"I'm Ernie Blackman. And you must be the reporter from the *Chronicle*."

Baxter nodded. "That's right. My name's Tom Baxter. Barney Rice said you'd be able to fill me in on what's happening and maybe get me onto the floor of the Exchange."

"I hope so," Blackman said, sighing heavily. "Things are pretty hectic. We're having a hard time keeping track of prices because the ticker is over an hour late."

Baxter interrupted, pointing to the procession of numbers marching across the board in the front of the room. "You mean those stock prices are not up-to-the-minute?"

Blackman shook his head sadly. "Not even close. For all I know they could be up twenty points or down fifty by now. The only way I can get the latest price of a stock is to call one of our people on the floor of the Exchange. But the lines are so tied up it's hard to get through. Now you know why everyone looks so grim—they're getting panicky."

Baxter looked at the crowd of people around him. Many were puffing nervously on cigarettes. Some were shouting at clerks to get them the price of a particular stock. "Now's the time to buy," one man was saying. "You can pick up the best stocks for

297

half of what they'll be selling for in a few months." A second man shouted, "You're a fool. I'm bailing out now while I can still get a decent price for my stock."

Baxter turned to Ernie Blackman. "Just how bad are things?" he asked. "I thought the banks had stepped in last week to help prop up the market."

"That's true," Blackman replied. "Six of the biggest banks in the country put up nearly two hundred and fifty million dollars last Thursday to buy stock so the market wouldn't collapse."

Blackman looked around to see if anyone was close enough to hear him. Then he pulled Baxter aside. "This is strictly confidential—don't quote me directly—but the banks are quietly dumping most of the stock they bought last week. They think the worst is yet to come."

Blackman went on to say that many brokerage houses were unloading stock held on margin—because their customers didn't have the cash to make the additional margin payments.

By now, Baxter was anxious to get on the floor of the Exchange. Blackman walked the newsman over to a large, marble building at the corner of Wall and Broad streets. Over the Greek columns decorating the front of the building were the words "New York Stock Exchange."

Inside they were met by Don McGraw, the floor broker for Morris, Sawyer, and Campbell. A cheerful man with a pleasant manner, McGraw handed Baxter a badge with a name and number on it. "Put this on," he instructed.

"But this is a broker's badge," Baxter protested.

McGraw chuckled. "I know. It belongs to a friend of mine who just retired. It's the only way I can get you on the floor. Don't worry, no one will bother you if you act like you belong."

Baxter followed McGraw onto the trading floor of the Exchange—an enormous room about five stories high and almost as long as a football field. The first thing the young reporter noticed was the noise. A steady roar of voices mixed with the clackety-clack of the tickers and the snap and whooshing sounds of the pneumatic tubes used to send orders and other messages from one part of the floor to another. There were people everywhere—brokers hurrying from one trading booth to another; uniformed pages plucking slips of paper from brokers' hands and scurrying off to deliver transaction reports to the clerks who recorded them.

McGraw paused at the Morris, Sawyer post to pick up some more buy and sell orders. A clerk was on the phone reporting the most recent transactions to the firm's office. McGraw pulled out a leather cushioned seat attached to a spring mechanism.

"This is what they mean when they talk about a 'seat on the Exchange' " he explained. "My firm paid over three hundred thousand dollars for this seat. The funny thing is, I never get a chance to sit on it. I'm too busy running around."

During the next hour, Baxter followed McGraw from one

horseshoe-shaped trading post to another. He watched as the floor broker made a sale or a buy. Each transaction was like a mini-auction—with the broker who had a sell order offering the stock at one price, and a broker with a buy order offering to take the stock for a lower price. But on this day very few brokers were buying. Most were trying to sell.

"Some of my customers are still bullish," McGraw remarked.

The reporter looked puzzled, and McGraw managed a weak laugh. "There are two kinds of animals on Wall Street—bulls and bears," he explained. "The bulls are people who expect stock prices to go up, so they buy. Bears, on the other hand, believe prices are going down, so they sell. Right now the bears are running wild. But maybe the bulls will come roaring back."

They didn't, as Baxter and McGraw soon found out. By the time the gong sounded at 3 P.M., signaling the end of trading on the floor, the market had suffered another day of staggering losses.

It was late in the afternoon when the reporter phoned in his report to the *Chronicle*. A rewrite man took down the details—the scene in the broker's office, the attitudes of the people, and the chaos on the floor of the Exchange. When Baxter had finished filing his story, Barney Rice got on the line.

"Nice going, Baxter," said the city editor, "terrific stuff."

"Thanks, chief," Baxter said, feeling very pleased with himself. Then he added, a bit timidly, "Maybe you'll let me write the story myself one of these days."

"Sure, kid," Rice replied. "But right now I want you to keep on top of this. Be back at the Exchange when it opens tomorrow. I want reports every two hours—it sounds like things may get worse."

The following morning Baxter was back at the Exchange. In the moments before the opening gong sounded, he stood on a balcony overlooking the great hall. Below him, the Exchange's seven hundred brokers and two thousand clerks, pages, and other employees took their places. The young reporter could feel the tension in the air—a frightening sense of uncertainty.

The electric gong sounded, signaling the opening of the Exchange on this cool and overcast Tuesday, October 29. As Baxter watched from his perch, the hall exploded into activity. He could see brokers charging wildly from one booth to another, sometimes in groups, like flocks of frightened geese.

The large screen began to flash the opening prices. Baxter hastily scribbled them in his notebook. Standard Oil down 7¾ . . . Radio down 10¼ . . . Westinghouse down 14½ . . . It was obvious to the young reporter that a disaster was in the making.

As the brokers on the floor saw the opening prices on the screen, their activity became more frenzied. A giant backlog of sell orders had accumulated overnight, and now the brokers were frantically trying to sell before prices dropped even lower. Baxter hurried downstairs and through the doors leading to the floor of the Exchange.

The steady roar of shouting men was almost deafening. All around him, a blurry mass of people rushed about. Everywhere, brokers were trying to sell. But there were hardly any buyers. The paper profits on which tens of thousands had built their dreams of wealth were evaporating.

As the morning dragged on, the panic spread. Huge blocks of stock were dumped on the Exchange by big investors, banks, corporations, and the stockbrokers themselves. With the situation becoming desperate, the mood on the floor turned ugly. Baxter paused at one trading post where a score of brokers were involved in a pushing, shouting, and shoving match. All of them were trying to sell the same stock to a lone buyer in the middle of the crowd.

Just before noon, Baxter spotted Don McGraw slumped on one of the jump seats at his firm's post. His face was pale and weary. When he saw Baxter, he lifted his arm in a halfhearted greeting. "Well, Tommy, I finally got to sit on my half-million dollar seat on the Exchange."

Baxter patted him on the shoulder. "It's pretty bad, isn't it?"

"It's bad all right," said McGraw. "If this were a ship, I'd say head for the lifeboats."

The day wore on, and the chaos continued. By the time the Exchange finally closed at 3 P.M., the rout was complete. Baxter noted the preliminary figures—more than sixteen million shares had been traded, the most on any one day in the history of the market. Brokers he spoke to estimated total losses at $10,000,000,000 to $15,000,000,000.

After phoning in a report to the *Chronicle* city desk, the reporter left the Exchange and headed up Wall Street. Thousands of people jammed the streets. Many were stockholders; others were just curiosity seekers. Rumors were circulating that stockbrokers were jumping out of windows—but those proved untrue. Still, there were casualties. At one brokerage office, a man was being carried out on a stretcher. He had suffered a heart attack after learning of his losses. At another office, two hysterical women were being gently escorted out. All around him Baxter saw people who looked like shell-shocked veterans of some terrible battle. For them, this had been a day of shattered dreams and lost fortunes.

It was nearly 5 P.M. when Baxter walked into the newsroom of the *Chronicle*. The clackety-clack of typewriters and the sounds of friendly voices were a welcome change from the mad uproar of the Exchange. Friends waved at him. It felt good to be back.

At the city desk, Barney Rice chewed on a cigar while Baxter gave him a rundown of what he had seen. "Sounds like good stuff," Rice said when he had finished. "Why don't you write it up."

"Me . . . write it?" Baxter stammered.

Rice nodded. "Sure, kid. What you saw, what you heard, what it was like down on Wall Street today. Just the way you told it to me. Now get to work—we've got a deadline, y'know."

Baxter shoved a piece of paper in his typewriter and sat staring at it for a couple of minutes. Then the words began to come. He wrote about the people he had met on Wall Street. The broker who had given him the inside story . . . Don McGraw finally getting to use his expensive seat on the Exchange . . . the stunned investors watching their dreams of riches destroyed. When he had finished, he brought the story to the city desk.

The young man waited while the city editor read what he had written. Rice's face was expressionless. Finally, he read the last page and looked up. "Fine story, Baxter. Looks like you earned yourself a by-line. Now go on home. I want you to be nice and fresh tomorrow so you can do a followup."

But Baxter was too keyed up to go home. Instead, he followed his story down to the composing room. He watched as it was set in type, and then as the columns of lead slugs were placed in page forms. And he waited until the first edition started rolling off the presses.

Baxter broke into a broad grin as he looked at page one. There, right under the lead news story about the collapse of the market, was his story. "CHRONICLE REPORTER'S EYE-WITNESS ACCOUNT—THE WILD SCENE AT THE EXCHANGE" blared the headline, and under it, in bold type, the words "By Thomas Baxter."

Good things can happen even on the worst of days, he told himself. Then he tucked the paper under his arm and headed home. For Tommy Baxter and millions of other Americans, the day they would call Black Tuesday had come to an end.

HENRY I. KURTZ
Author, *John and Sebastian Cabot*

LOOKING AT BOOKS

THE WESTING GAME

On Halloween, a teenage girl goes into a deserted house on a dare—and finds the body of an eccentric millionaire. Sixteen people are named as his heirs, but they must play a strange—and dangerous—game to determine who will inherit the fortune. Will it be the Chinese restaurateur? The two Greek boys? The black lady judge? The girl named Turtle? Or the person who isn't even supposed to be in the game? This fast-paced mystery by Ellen Raskin was awarded the 1979 John Newbery Medal, the highest award for a book for young people.

DRACULA, GO HOME!

Larry was taking a shortcut through the cemetery when he saw the evil-looking man dressed all in black. "I knew he was Dracula the moment I saw him," Larry tells us in this mystery written by Kin Platt. Larry is scared. But he is also curious, especially when the man checks into the hotel where Larry is working for the summer. The strange guest never comes down to meals and leaves the hotel through the window. Larry does some detective work in his spare time, gets bitten on the neck while he is asleep, and discovers the man is very nasty indeed.

hold fast

Michael has just turned 14 when his parents are killed in an automobile crash. He leaves the small Newfoundland community that was his home and goes to live with relatives in St. Albert, a city some distance away. This story by Kevin Major tells of Michael's struggle to survive in his new and very different environment. He must deal with such people as the loud-mouthed Kentson, who makes fun of the way Michael talks, and with his uncle, who rules life at home with an iron hand. But Michael develops close friendships, too. The Canada Council awarded *Hold Fast* a Children's Literature Prize.

THE GIRL WHO LOVED WILD HORSES

This book, written and illustrated by Paul Goble, won the 1979 Caldecott Medal for excellence in illustration. It tells of a young Indian girl and her special understanding and love of horses. One day there is a terrible storm and all the horses gallop away. The girl jumps on one of them and is carried far from her home. There she meets a beautiful spotted stallion, the leader of all the wild horses that roam the hills. The girl lives with the horses for a year before her people find and rescue her. Although she is happy to see her parents, she feels she belongs with the horses. Because her family loves her, they let her leave. But once a year she returns to visit her family and brings them a colt.

The Bewitched Cat

Once upon a time a very poor man and his wife lived in a lonely hut in the woods. They owned but a kettle, a griddle, a cat, and three sons. What the two eldest boys were called I don't know, but the youngest was named Per.

When their parents died, the three boys were to divide what was left. The eldest son took the kettle; the second son got the griddle. Having no choice, Per was given the cat for his own.

Very soon after, the three sons took their worldly goods and set off to try their luck. The eldest went toward the north, carrying the kettle under one arm. The second son walked toward the east, the griddle in his knapsack.

Per, the youngest, looked at his cat, which was white of fur and gentle of manner, and said, "How can I leave you behind in this hut to waste away your life?" Then he walked toward the south, and the cat followed him.

When Per had walked for some distance over the field and through the forest, the cat said, "Sit down on the moss under this pine, and I shall go hunting. Whatever I capture, you must take to the King's farm that lies on the hill yonder."

The cat showed the boy an opening through the trees from which he could see a high hill, on the crest of which was spread a farm with many log buildings of dark brown color.

"In that farmhouse lives a King," explained the cat. "He is both sad and sour. All day long he sits in one chair, and he believes only what he sees with his very own eyes."

"Why should I go to visit such a King?" asked the lad.

"To me, he is both near and dear," answered the cat. With this remark, the little creature darted off into the shadows.

306

Per did not have to wait long before the cat returned, riding between the horns of a reindeer.

"You, who are so small and weak, how could you capture this large animal?" asked Per.

"The less you ask the more you learn!" was the cat's reply. "Listen with care to all I say: lead this animal to the King's farm and straight into the kitchen. When the King comes to view it, tell him the reindeer is a gift from Sir Per. You must not tell who Sir Per really is nor where he lives. Keep faith and all will go well for you!"

Per promised, then led the reindeer in the direction of the hill. When he came to the main house he walked straight into the kitchen, followed by the great animal. No one stopped him, for all were astonished.

At once servants ran to tell their master. "A real live reindeer stands in the middle of your kitchen. The boy with him says the animal is a gift."

"Stuff and nonsense!" sputtered the King.

All the same he got to his feet and went to look.

When he beheld the animal, he asked Per, "Who is the generous man who sends me so fine a gift?"

"Sir Per and none other."

"Who is Sir Per?"

"My master, and a very good master is he."

"Where does he live?"

"That I dare not answer."

"Stuff and nonsense!" sputtered the King. "But at least you deserve a meal for your trouble."

So a supper was brought the boy, and when his hunger was sated and his legs rested he returned to the woods. There under a pine he found his cat carefully licking her paws.

Per told all that had taken place. At the end, the little creature remarked, "One gift breaks ice, magic's in thrice!"

Not another word would she say to explain.

On the second day, the cat went hunting again and this time she came riding back on the horns of a hart.

All took place as before, and Per led the animal to the King's farm and straight into the kitchen. When the old man saw this second gift, he was less sour than on the first day. This time he wanted more than ever to know who Sir Per really was and where he lived. The lad kept his promise as before and told nothing except the name of his master.

When he returned to the woods, he found his cat carefully cleaning her ears.

Of course Per related everything that had taken place, and the little creature remarked, "Two gifts warm the heart, now a third must take part!"

Not another word would she add.

307

On the third day when the cat went hunting, she came back riding between the antlers of an enormous elk.

"You, who are so small and weak," cried the lad, "how could you capture this great creature?"

"The more you ask the less you learn!" replied the cat. "Give this elk as you have given the reindeer and the hart. Say the same words and keep the same silence."

Per promised as he had promised on the two previous days, and soon he was making his way to the King's farm.

When the servants saw the huge elk standing in their kitchen, they rushed to the King and shouted, "A real live elk stands in front of your fire. This, too, is a gift from Sir Per."

"Nonsense and stuff!" sputtered the King. All the same he ran to look. When his very own eyes beheld the enormous animal standing in his kitchen, he was so amazed and excited he did not know if he was standing on his right foot or his left.

Again the King asked who Sir Per really was and where he lived. Again the lad kept silent.

Then the King exploded. "Since I can't learn who your master is, nor where he lives, tell him to come to us. We'll give him a welcome he won't forget!"

Now when Per returned to the woods he found his cat asleep under the pine. He wakened her and related all that had taken place. The cat asked, "But why do you look so sad?"

"What shall we do about Sir Per's visit to the King?"

"You must act the part of Sir Per," answered the cat.

"How can I visit the King in the guise of a lord when I have nothing to wear but the rags on my back?"

"No fear and no tear!" warned the cat. "Wait here for three days while I go to the valley where Glede Castle lies."

With this, she darted off into the forest and was lost to sight.

When, indeed, the cat returned, she came riding in a gilded coach drawn by prancing horses, tawny and white. This coach was laden with clothes for Per; never before had he seen their match. They jingled and dripped with gold and were studded with gems.

"When the King asks whence this raiment comes, reply, 'From Glede Castle, but what I have at home is finer far than what you see here.'"

Well disguised and adorned like a prince, the lad rode to the King's farm. There he was welcomed by servant and master, for all believed him to be Sir Per and none other.

"Whence comes such finery?" asked the old King. "I have not seen the like anywhere."

"This is good enough for journeys abroad, but what I have at home is finer far than this."

"This home of yours, exactly where is it and what is its name, Sir Per?"

308

"The name of my castle is Glede, and it lies in a faraway valley," replied the young lad.

The King looked startled, then said, "That is the very castle I dreamed of when I was young, but when my queen died and my little girl vanished, I stopped dreaming. Perhaps, Sir Per, you will take me there?"

"Gladly," the lad replied, and so it was agreed.

When Per returned to the forest, he found his cat sunning herself on a high branch of the pine. He called to her and she leaped down and sat beside him on the moss while he related all that had taken place.

"But why do you look so sad, Per?" she asked.

"How shall I take the King to a castle I myself have never seen?"

"Wait and see! Magic's in three!" the cat replied, and not another word would she add.

The next day, dressed and disguised as Sir Per, the lad rode to the farm. When he met the King, he cried, "Now let us journey to that faraway valley where Glede Castle lies."

"What I see I believe, but nothing more!" mumbled the old King, and he slammed his crown on his head. Off they rode, Per leading the way in his coach. But the cat was nowhere to be seen, for she was running far ahead, preparing their way.

When the procession had traveled for some time, it passed a flock of sheep whose wool was so long it caressed the hill where they grazed.

The cat had already said to the shepherd, "When the King asks who owns these sheep, you must say they belong to Sir Per." And the shepherd had agreed.

When the old King was riding past, he caught sight of the sheep and cried, "Whose strange sheep are these?"

"They belong to Sir Per," the shepherd replied.

When the procession had traveled a still longer distance, they came to a herd of cattle with coats so sleek they shone like silk.

Here again the cat had prepared the way.

When the King came riding by and beheld the fat, sleek animals, he cried, "Whose fine cows are these?"

The cowherd replied as the cat had taught, "They belong to Sir Per, of course."

When the procession had traveled still farther, they came to a herd of horses, perfect in form, smooth of coat, and beautifully matched in color.

The cat, always running ahead, had prepared the way even here, so when the King cried out, "Whose wonderful horses are these?" the answer came, "They belong to Sir Per. Indeed, what does not?"

At this the King sputtered, "Does Sir Per own the realm and everything in it?"

No one bothered to answer. Whereupon the old man fell into a dark silence and said not a word for the rest of the journey.

At length and at last, the King's procession came to the far-away valley where flowers still bloom when summer has died elsewhere in that northern land. In the midst of the valley rose Glede Castle, and its gates were three: brass and silver and gold. The walls shone like crystal, and its turrets gleamed like gold.

An old servant with snow white hair, wearing silver livery, opened the gates and welcomed them with many a courtly bow.

Once inside the castle, the old King and Sir Per walked from room to room. Each was more spacious than the last. Finally they reached a hall decked for a feast.

Here at last the cat appeared. When the old King caught sight of the pretty white animal seated at the head of the table, his eyes grew wide with wonder.

But Per said not a word.

The cat bade them all be seated, and they ranged themselves round the great board, which was aglint with silver and glass and glowing with candles. No sooner had servants carried in rare dishes and spread them before the guests than a loud thumping sound was heard at the gates. All stopped as if frozen with fear.

Excusing herself, the cat darted out of the hall. Her velvet feet carried her swiftly to the gate. It opened slowly by itself, and this is what she saw: a troll shaped like a man but twice as tall and three times as broad. His head was as large as a boulder.

His eyes were dark holes under the cliff of his brow. His black hair was a tangled mass. His mouth was a shadowy cave.

The troll kept up a hideous roar: "Who sits in my castle? Who drinks my mead? Who eats my meat?"

"Be silent!" commanded the cat. "You'd better turn around, for at your back you will see one far stronger than you."

The troll turned just in time for a strong shaft of sunlight to strike him full in the eyes. As everyone knows, no troll of darkness can live in the sun.

As the beam shot into his eyes a dreadful change took place: he became even larger than before. Bigger and bigger he grew, until his head seemed to fill the sky. Then with a loud explosion his whole body flew into bits, and within a few moments all that was left of him was a cloud of dust settling slowly to the ground.

"One, two, three! Fate ended thee!" whispered a voice. But it was the voice of the cat no longer. Most curious of all, a change had come over the little creature just as the troll had exploded.

Instead of the little animal with white fur and velvety paws, there stood at the castle gate a lovely blond maiden in a robe of blue and silver, wearing a crown of white flowers in her hair. Golden lashes shadowed her blue eyes.

This beautiful young maiden walked slowly back into the castle. When she entered the banquet hall and the old King beheld her, his mouth fell open and he sputtered, "But this is my very own child. My own long-lost daughter, Aldora."

The girl walked swiftly toward him and put her arms around his neck. In a clear sweet voice she confirmed what he had said.

"Yes, you are indeed my father. When my mother died, a wicked troll snatched me away. When I refused to marry him he turned me into a white cat and cast me out into the dark forest. But I had the good fortune to find Per. When Per's parents died and we two went wandering, I knew you and I, Father, would meet again once more."

"So," the King cried, "it was you, Daughter, who sent Per to lift me from my sorrow and bring me to this castle?"

"Through Per and through no one else do we meet again," the Princess replied, "and he has captured my heart."

"B—but," stammered Per, "how can I woo a lady like you? You deserve a lord or a prince!"

"How ridiculous!" laughed the Princess. "To me you are both lord and prince."

The sound of her laughter was so full of music that the fiddlers caught the key at once and broke into a wedding dance.

Then and there the time of their wedding was set.

When the wedding took place soon after, guests came from east, west, north, and south. They made merry for seven days and seven nights so that castle and valley rang with their joy.

a Norwegian story from *Scandinavian Stories*
by MARGARET SPERRY

312

THE NEW BOOK OF KNOWLEDGE
1980

The following articles are from the 1980 edition of *The New Book of Knowledge*. They are included here to help you keep your encyclopedia up-to-date.

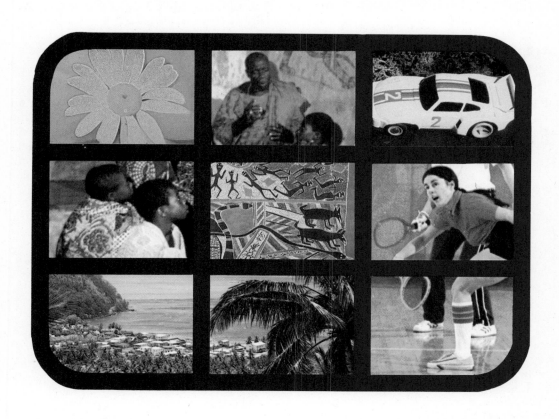

Typical radio-controlled aerobatic (stunt) plane being readied for flight.

AIRPLANE MODELS

No one knows who built the first model airplane. Models of birds, carved from wood and able to fly like gliders, have been found in ancient Egyptian tombs. Early inventors such as Leonardo Da Vinci (1452–1519) built models of their concepts of "flying machines." But the modern hobby of model-airplane building did not really begin until after World War I. The war proved that the airplane was an exciting and practical way to transport people and products. The romance of air travel, together with a natural creative desire, led many people of all ages into the hobby of building miniature models of real airplanes.

▶ NON-FLYING MODELS

The easiest-to-build and least expensive model airplanes are constructed from plastic kits. They are made up of highly detailed, pre-molded plastic parts, which need only to be glued together and painted to produce a very realistic model of an airplane. They are simple to build, but serious modelers have been known to spend hundreds of hours in research and construction. They try to duplicate, as nearly as possible, an actual aircraft—perhaps one flown by a specific pilot in a particular battle. Many modelers go one step further. They build realistic settings, complete with trees and shrubs, buildings, and even miniature people, to create museumlike displays for their airplanes.

In the days before plastic kits, it was common practice to carve models from blocks of wood. That type of construction is mostly limited now to experienced modelers who wish to duplicate an airplane for which no kit is available. It is quite enjoyable to whittle an airplane from a piece of wood. And it is good practice for going on to the next step in model building.

▶ FLYING MODELS

This is the part of model-airplane building where the real excitement begins. An airplane is not truly an airplane unless it flies.

There is great variety in the types of models built for flight—from the simplest hand-launched glider to very complicated radio-

314

controlled helicopters. Some are scale models of real airplanes. But others are special aircraft designed for contests in which the models are judged for flight duration, precision maneuvers, or speed.

Flying models are classified according to the way they are controlled in flight. The three categories of flying models are free flight, control line, and radio control.

Free Flight

The very early model airplanes were all free-flying planes—that is, once they were launched, there was no way to control their flight. Free flight remains a very popular activity today. To many modelers there is nothing quite so beautiful as the sight of a model drifting freely on a gentle breeze.

But it is not fun to lose a model if it flies too far. The wise free-flight flier sets the rudder on the airplane to produce a gentle turn, which keeps the model flying in circles overhead.

Free-flight models can be divided into three types—gliders, rubber-powered, and engine-powered.

Gliders are relatively simple models. They are launched into the air either by being thrown or by being towed on a string (much like a kite) and then released for free flight. The towline is attached to a hook on the bottom of the glider. When it reaches altitude, the line is slackened, allowing it to slide off the hook. The glider is then free to soar like a bird.

Rubber-powered models have propellers that are turned by wound-up rubber bands. When the rubber unwinds, it turns the propeller, which pulls the airplane forward through the air. Some rubber-powered models are very small, with wingspans of no more than 30 centimeters (12 inches). Others have wingspans of close to 2 meters (6 feet). A very special type of rubber-powered model is designed to be flown in large rooms indoors. These super-lightweight models are capable of flying for almost an hour at a time.

Engine-powered models, also called gas models, are powered by small engines similar to those used in lawn mowers but small enough to fit in the palm of your hand. These miniature engines produce a great deal of power for their small size. They are capable of flying a model airplane to amazing heights. Once the model rises high enough, the motor is shut off by a timing mechanism, and the airplane is free to glide gently back to earth.

Free-flight models have one disadvantage. They require large open spaces in which to fly. This was one of the factors that led to the invention of a means of controlling the flight in a small area.

Control Line

Control-line airplanes are flown in circles at the end of two thin steel wires connected to a handle that is held by the pilot. The two wires are usually about 20 meters (65 feet) long. They are attached to a mechanism inside the airplane that controls the up-and-down direction of flight. By moving the handle, pilots can make the airplane do loops, figure eights, and other stunts. They can also control the takeoff and landing.

Control-line airplanes are all powered by engines. There are contests for stunt flying, speed flying, and racing and for scale models.

Radio Control

Remote-control airplanes are the most realistic because they can be controlled in flight without wires or connections of any sort. Every maneuver that a real airplane makes can be duplicated by a radio-controlled model. Sometimes it is difficult to tell whether a model plane or a real plane is in the sky.

To understand how radio control works, think of your radio or television set. Somewhere outside your house there is a radio or television station transmitting radio waves through the air. You cannot see them or feel them or hear them. But your radio or television is designed to receive these waves and turn them into sound and pictures. Different kinds of radio waves are sent out on different channels, and you can tune your receiver to pick up these waves.

In a radio-control system for model airplanes, there is a transmitter, a receiver, and small electric motors (called servos) to move the airplane's controls. The pilot, using a hand-held transmitter, moves various levers and buttons to transmit different signals on different channels. Inside the airplane, the receiver picks up these signals and actuates the servos to move the controls that steer the plane.

On simple radio-controlled models, the only control is the rudder, which steers the airplane right or left. On the most complex models, all the controls of a real airplane are duplicated, including retractable landing gear, engine throttle, sky-writing smoke in stunt planes, bomb-dropping in war planes, parachute drops, and just about anything else you can think of.

Radio-controlled models come in all types and sizes. There are gliders with wingspans of more than 3 meters (over 10 feet) that can soar for hours when the skillful pilot takes advantage of rising air currents. There are racing planes that fly at almost 200 kilometers (125 miles) per hour. Aerobatic airplanes can loop, roll, spin, and do everything a real air-show plane can do. And there are helicopters that hover and fly backward and sideways just as the real ones do.

Scale models have such amazing details that it is almost impossible to tell them from the real thing. In fact, radio-controlled models can be so realistic in appearance and flight that many have been used in motion pictures when it would have been too dangerous or expensive to use real aircraft. Perhaps you have seen one of these movies and never even realized that you were watching a model airplane.

A scale model rocket.

▶ROCKETS

As the space age has developed, model rockets have become an exciting part of the modeling hobby. But model rockets are not strictly model airplanes. They are not toys, either. They are miniature missiles powered by real solid-fuel rocket motors.

Model rockets are generally constructed of a basic cardboard tube for the body, with a balsa wood or plastic nose cone and balsa tail fins. There are many kits available, and it is best to start with a kit. They are properly designed and built to be completely safe in operation. A homemade rocket can be dangerous.

The rocket motor itself is a small cylinder that fits into the rear of the rocket body. Model-rocket motors are dangerous when they are not used properly. In certain places it is necessary to have a license to purchase them. For example, in California you must be at least 14 years of age to get a license. Your local hobby shop can give you full details on how to get a license.

Model-rocket motors are ignited by wires, attached at one end to the rocket and at the other end to an electric ignition device placed some distance away for safety. When electricity flows through the wires, the ignition wire in the rocket motor gets hot, just as the wires in a toaster do. This causes the rocket fuel to burn. When the fuel burns, the rocket does not go off like a firecracker. Instead, a hot, rapidly expanding gas is released. The gas shoots out through the motor nozzle at a very high speed and pushes the model rocket with a great deal of thrust (power).

A single rocket motor burns for just a few seconds. But it will push the model rocket to altitudes of more than 90 meters (over 325 feet). Multistage rockets use two or more motors, burning one after the other, to get to much greater heights.

Just before the motor burns out, the last little bit of gas pressure actually blows out through the front of the motor. This causes the nose cone of the rocket to pop off and release a parachute. The model rocket then comes down very gently on its parachute, ready for another blast-off.

As with airplanes, model rockets can be scale models of actual rockets and missiles.

316

Construction plan and materials for model of U.S. Army Air Force P-51 Mustang. The completed model, also shown, can be flown either by rubber-band power or a small gas engine.

Or they can be original designs made up by the builder. Contests are often held on military bases, where the models can be tracked by radar to determine how high they fly.

▶ **YOU CAN DO IT, TOO**

When the model-airplane hobby first started, very little equipment was available in stores. Now, most cities and towns have well-stocked hobby shops, and construction kits are available for all types of airplanes.

The most common construction material is still lightweight balsa wood. But plastics are also popular, especially for complex shapes such as engine cowlings (housing for the engine) and wing tips. Some flying models are all plastic and are almost ready to fly right out of the box.

If you are just becoming interested in model airplanes, the best way to begin is with a well-proved kit of a simple airplane. It is not wise to start off with a big, complex model just because it looks exciting. Start with a model that is within your ability to build, and you will soon progress to that big, fancy airplane. Try to get advice from an experienced modeler. Read some of the model magazines that are available on newsstands and in hobby shops. If you wish to join a model-airplane club, your local hobby shop will know if there are any clubs in your area. The Academy of Model Aeronautics in Washington, D.C., and the Model Aeronautics Association in Ontario can give you information on flying-model contests.

Above all, be patient. If you work carefully and neatly, all your airplanes will fly like birds!

DON TYPOND
Editor, *Model Airplane News*

317

Dolly Parton

Willie Nelson

Chet Atkins

COUNTRY AND WESTERN MUSIC

Country and western is a native American music. Its origins lie in the folk songs of the English, Scottish, and Irish people who settled in the southeastern United States. By the early 1800's, the sentiments and rhythms of their songs had changed to suit the rugged, challenging country in which they lived.

In its early stages, this music was called hillbilly music—a reference to the "hill country" of the Appalachian Mountains. Songs were passed from family to family and friend to friend. But for the most part, the music remained within its own community. In small towns and among close-knit families, it was one of the main sources of entertainment. Often, small bands made up of two fiddlers and two guitarists played very fast, complex, and delicate melodies for lyrics that were sung in high, close harmonies. This style came to be called bluegrass music. Over the years it was blended with other styles—blues, jazz, and the sentimental ballads of the southwest—until it became what we know as country and western.

From the beginning, country and western was a music of struggle and determination. The songs celebrated hard work and good fun, and they told tales of romantic and financial troubles.

▶EARLY COUNTRY AND WESTERN STARS

During the 1930's and 1940's, the popularity of country and western music began to spread all over the United States.

The first wide exposure given to country and western performers came from two main sources—the radio and the Grand Ole Opry, in Nashville, Tennessee. On radio, such singers as Jimmie Rodgers, Roy Acuff, and Ernest Tubb could reach many more listeners than they could in person. The Grand Ole Opry—a huge, barn-shaped music hall—presented country and western shows every Saturday night. It made Nashville the center of country and western.

Western movies also contributed to the rise of country and western music. Popular heroes such as Gene Autry and Tex Ritter displayed the musical talents that had started them in show business.

By the late 1940's, there was a large, devoted audience for country and western music, and many popular singers recorded hit records. Country and western stars and their bands criss-crossed the country in buses, playing hundreds of one-night shows.

One of the first major stars of country and western was Hank Williams. He was an important figure not only because he was an exciting performer, but also because he

Johnny Cash

wrote many of his songs. Before Williams, most country and western singers had either adapted traditional folk and country songs or used songs written by professional songwriters. Williams wrote songs about loneliness and isolation as well as about good times. Most of his songs were either slow, mournful ballads or fast, jumping tunes that were accompanied by piano. These fast-paced songs came to be known as honky-tonk music. Other performers who specialized in honky-tonk were Lefty Frizzell, Webb Pierce, and Ray Price.

As country and western grew in popularity throughout the 1950's, some radio stations began broadcasting only country and western music. It offered new kinds of songs—songs that told exciting stories about heroes and common people and were sung with sincerity. Johnny Cash's "I Walk the Line," Johnny Horton's "Battle of New Orleans," and Marty Robbins' "El Paso" were among the most popular. The 1950's also saw the rise of women as important country and western performers. Kitty Wells and Wanda Jackson were among the leading female singers of the time.

▶PROGRESSIVE COUNTRY MUSIC

During the 1960's, country and western took full advantage of the newest technology of the recording industry. Per-

formers used orchestral string sections and brass instruments—trumpets, saxophones, French horns. Oddly enough, it was a guitarist who pioneered these changes. Chet Atkins, who had accompanied nearly every country and western performer, became Nashville's most acclaimed record producer. His elaborately orchestrated records sold in the millions. This new sound was called "progressive country."

The key to the success of the progressive sound was smoothness and polish. Many older performers thought this new sound was an undignified attempt to appeal to the large pop music audience. But young artists like Charlie Pride—country and western's first black star—and Buck Owens recorded strings of hit songs using the new methods.

▶COUNTRY AND THE "OUTLAWS"

The progressive sound remained popular during the 1960's and 1970's. Singers such as Tanya Tucker and Bill Anderson recorded popular story-songs by writers such as Tom T. Hall. Many leading singers—Dolly Parton, for example—wrote their own songs. Around this time, country and western became popular throughout the world. Olivia Newton-John, an Australian, became well known as a performer.

As happens with any vital, growing musical form, there were those who disagreed with the main trends. Some younger performers believed that much of country's original strength had been in its rough energy and lack of restraint. They felt that the calm, progressive sound denied the music this sort of energy. These young performers also enjoyed rock music, and rock's loud volume and beat began to find its way into the new country music.

These dissenting artists were referred to as "outlaws" because they made their music outside the usual Nashville recording studios. The most prominent outlaws included Waylon Jennings and Willie Nelson.

Country and western music in all its forms—from bluegrass to the outlaws' country rock—continues to evolve and flourish. And the number of people attracted to it is increasing all the time.

KEN TUCKER
Music Critic, Los Angeles *Herald Examiner*

FEDERAL BUREAU OF INVESTIGATION

What do kidnappings, bank robberies, airplane hijackings, and cases involving foreign spies have in common? They are all federal crimes—crimes against national laws rather than state or local laws. And as federal crimes, they are investigated by a kind of national police force, the Federal Bureau of Investigation (FBI). Although it is part of the United States Department of Justice, the FBI is one of the most important, powerful, and influential police agencies in the world. Many other countries have imitated the FBI and have depended on it for help and advice.

The FBI has several basic responsibilities. One is to enforce hundreds of federal laws. FBI agents try to capture people who have committed crimes and to gather evidence that can be used against them in court. The agents often testify during the trials of the people they have investigated.

The FBI also protects the national security of the United States from foreign spies. It is the job of the Central Intelligence Agency (CIA) to gather information on other countries and analyze what is happening there. But it is the FBI's job to try to prevent agents of other countries from doing the same to the United States. Therefore, FBI agents often investigate officials sent to the United States by other governments, to make sure they are not trying to harm the United States (for example, by stealing secret details of how U.S. weapons are made).

Another of the FBI's responsibilities is to investigate people who are named to important government jobs. The FBI often checks on the background of these people to find out whether they are loyal to the United States and worthy of being trusted by the public.

▶ SERVICES OF THE FBI

One way in which the FBI has obtained a great deal of influence is by providing helpful services. Its Identification Division, for example, has the largest fingerprint file in the world. With millions of fingerprint cards, it is able to help identify hundreds of thousands of fugitives and other criminals every year. Through the use of fingerprints and other information, the FBI's Disaster Squad also helps identify the victims of plane crashes and other disasters.

The FBI Laboratory, started in 1932, was a pioneer in applying scientific principles to the solution of mysterious crimes. Sometimes, with as little as a bit of cloth and a chip of paint, it can come up with details of where someone has been. Or by studying a bullet, it can discover where and when a gun was bought.

The FBI's National Crime Information Center (NCIC) is a computerized file that contains details on hundreds of thousands of crimes and criminals. It permits the fast and easy exchange of information among police in all the states of the United States and some other countries. By using NCIC, a police officer who stops someone for speeding in Pennsylvania, for example, can find out within a few minutes whether the person is driving a car stolen in California. But one problem with NCIC (as with the fingerprint file) is that the information is not always up-to-date. This can lead to a person's being arrested by mistake.

At the FBI National Academy in Quantico, Virginia, local police officers take short courses in various aspects of law enforcement. In return, police departments are often willing to go out of their way to help the FBI solve difficult cases. The FBI also collects and publishes statistics on crime in the United States.

▶ FBI AGENTS

The bureau, as the FBI is often called, has about 8,500 special agents and more than 10,000 other employees. They work at FBI headquarters in Washington, D.C.; in 59 major field offices and hundreds of smaller "resident agencies" around the United States; or in a few offices overseas. Men and women between the ages of 23 and 35 are eligible to apply to become special agents. But applicants must have a college degree and some other experience or skill (for example, as a teacher, police officer, lawyer, accountant, or laboratory scientist). People who have a special ability with languages or who have worked for the FBI as clerks are often accepted without any other special experience.

The 15-week training course for agents includes classes on legal matters and on how to interview witnesses, as well as physical-fitness training and lessons in how to shoot a gun. Only after they have been assigned to a field office do agents begin to specialize in some area of the FBI's work.

▶HISTORY

The FBI was founded in 1908 as a small branch of the Department of Justice. Since then, the bureau has been through many ups and downs. Around the time of World War I, it participated in a "red scare," in which many innocent citizens of the United States and new residents from other countries were arrested and unjustly accused of being Communists.

The appointment of J. Edgar Hoover, a young lawyer, as director in 1924 helped change the course of the FBI. Hoover eliminated corruption in the staff and stopped the practice of investigating people for political reasons. In the 1930's, when there was a national crime wave, Congress passed many laws that gave the FBI new responsibilities. For example, when bank robbery became a federal crime, the bureau began to pursue bank robbers across state lines. During World War II, at the direction of President Franklin D. Roosevelt, Hoover's FBI made a major contribution to the U.S. war effort, catching German spies and conducting special missions in Latin America.

Hoover was a genius at building the FBI's reputation. Agents, called G-men, were thought of as supermen. (The G came from "Government.") Children went to bed wearing "junior G-man" pajamas, and their parents read about the bureau's accomplishments in the newspaper every day. Impressive statistics on the FBI's work convinced many people that the more the country spent on the FBI, the more it saved.

Hoover stayed as director a total of 48 years. After World War II he resumed the practice of using the bureau for political purposes. It was later discovered that he used the bureau to gather information on his personal enemies. The FBI played a major

A state police officer operates a computer linked with the FBI's National Crime Information Center.

part in the anti-Communist internal security scare of the 1950's. In the 1960's and early 1970's, the bureau engaged in illegal wiretapping and other tactics (sometimes with the knowledge of higher officials and sometimes not) to deal with the civil rights movement and the opposition to U.S. involvement in Vietnam.

After Hoover died in 1972 at the age of 77, the FBI was at the center of a number of scandals. Special congressional investigations revealed that Hoover and others had abused their power and authority. Several former FBI officials were themselves charged with crimes. Under the supervision of the Justice Department, directors who followed Hoover began to put the bureau back on the right track. In 1979, Congress and the Justice Department wrote a new "charter" for the FBI, setting out what it could and could not do in the future.

SANFORD J. UNGAR
Managing Editor, *Foreign Policy* magazine

321

RACKET SPORTS

When you think of racket (or racquet) sports, you probably think of tennis or badminton. But in recent years, other racket sports have become increasingly popular. These include squash, paddleball, racquetball, and platform tennis.

Racket sports are played for competition as well as for fun and exercise. The governing bodies of the various racket sports organize tournaments. There are competitions for young people as well as national men's and women's championships.

Almost all racket sports come from a game that was invented in France in the Middle Ages. It was called court tennis because it was first played by monks in the monastery courtyards. Gradually, the game was adopted by kings and nobility. It was from court tennis that today's racket and paddle games developed.

▶ SQUASH RACQUETS

Squash was invented in England during the mid-19th century by students attending an exclusive school called Harrow, located outside of London.

They named the game squash because of the sound the ball made as it was hit against the walls. In addition, the ball was softer or "squashier" than the one used for another, more difficult game called hard racquets.

Squash arrived in the United States in 1882. The first court was built at St. Paul's School in Concord, New Hampshire. From there it spread to other schools, colleges, universities, and many private clubs.

Squash is a game of speed, power, and finesse.

Equipment

The wooden racket weighs between 227 grams (8 ounces) and 284 grams (10 ounces). It is 69 centimeters (27 inches) long. It has a hitting surface that is 17 centimeters (6¾ inches) in diameter and is strung with nylon or gut.

The ball is hollow. Its diameter is 4.4 centimeters (1¾ inches). For years, the ball was made of hard, black rubber. It was a rather dead ball. But in 1976, the "70+" ball was introduced to bring liveliness to the sport. This ball is slightly smaller, lighter, bouncier, and more like the "English" or "International" ball that is used in every country except the United States, Mexico, and parts of Canada.

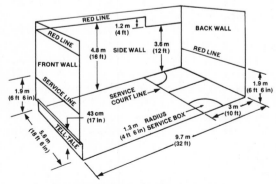

DIAGRAM OF A SQUASH RACQUETS COURT

322

The Court

The official four-walled American singles court is 9.8 meters (32 feet) long, 5.6 meters (18½ feet) wide, and 4.9 meters (16 feet) high at the front wall. Running along the lower part of the front wall there is a sheet of metal 43 centimeters (17 inches) high. This sheet of metal, called a tell-tale, clangs when hit with a ball. Hitting the tell-tale is the same as hitting into the net on a tennis court. You lose the point.

There is also a doubles court on which two teams of two players compete. This court is 7.6 meters (25 feet) wide by 13.7 meters (45 feet) long.

Rules and Play

The object of squash is to hit the ball against the front wall so that it rebounds to an area in the court where the opposing player cannot return it to the front wall. The opposing player must hit the ball before it bounces twice on the floor. The basic idea is the same in racquetball and paddleball. The ball can hit many walls and still be in play, as long as the player returns it to the front wall before it bounces on the floor a second time.

To win a match, you must win three out of five games. Fifteen points usually wins a game. But if the score is tied at 13-all or 14-all, the game may be extended up to a maximum of 18 points. Points can be won whether or not you are serving.

There are red lines on the floor and walls, within which the ball must bounce to remain in play. If you hit outside these lines or into the tell-tale, you lose the point. If you interfere with your opponent's shot, a let is called, and the point has to be played over. If you get in the way of your opponent on purpose, you lose the point.

▶**PADDLEBALL**

Paddleball is an outgrowth of handball, which was brought to the United States by Irish immigrants in the late 1880's. The one-wall variety is especially popular in New York City. When recreational parks were built in the 1930's, most of them included paddleball courts.

Four-wall paddleball was the creation of a physical education teacher at the University of Michigan in the 1930's. He wanted to keep his tennis team active during the winter months, so he made up a game employing a short paddle and a rubber ball to be played on the university's indoor four-wall handball courts.

Equipment

The official paddle is made of rock maple. It is about 20 centimeters (8 inches) wide and 41 centimeters (16 inches) long and weighs about 454 grams (16 ounces). A leather thong is attached to the end of the handle, and it must be worn around the player's wrist at all times. There is no limit on the number or size of holes that may be drilled into the face of the paddle. The holes are to reduce wind resistance. The same paddle is used for both one- and four-wall games.

The ball for four-wall paddleball is about 5 centimeters (2 inches) in diameter and is made of rubber. The one-wall ball is livelier and slightly smaller—4.8 centimeters (1⅞ inches) in diameter.

The Court

The courts are the same sizes as handball courts. The four-wall court is 6.1 meters (20 feet) wide and high and 12.2 meters (40 feet) long. The back wall, which is often constructed of tempered glass for spectator viewing, must be at least 3.7 meters (12 feet) in height. The walls are made of either cement blocks or plastic panels. The floor is usually made of wood.

The one-wall court is 6.1 meters (20 feet) wide and 10.4 meters (34 feet) long, with the front wall measuring 4.9 meters (16 feet) high. The court is often made entirely of concrete.

Rules and Play

The basic idea of paddleball is the same as that of squash. But in paddleball, the ball may hit the ceiling and there is no tell-tale.

To win a match, you must win two out of three games. The first and second games are won by the first player who scores 21 points in each. If a third game is required to decide the match, an 11-point game is played. Only the person serving can score points.

In the single-wall version, the players are

allowed to transfer the paddle from one hand to the other when making returns. Most one-wall paddleballers have learned to hit the ball equally well and hard using either hand.

There is one difference in scoring between one-wall and four-wall paddleball. In one-wall, the winning side must win by a margin of at least two points. So, for example, final scores of 22-20 or 23-21 are not unusual.

▶RACQUETBALL

This very simple game is an offshoot of paddleball. It became one of the fastest-growing sports in the United States during the 1970's. Invented by a Connecticut tennis teacher in the 1940's, the sport was first played in community centers and other places that already had handball courts.

Equipment

The loosely strung racket looks like a miniature tennis racket. It is made of either aluminum, fiberglass, carbon, or a combination of these materials. It is approximately 46 centimeters (18 inches) long and 23 centimeters (9 inches) wide at the broadest part

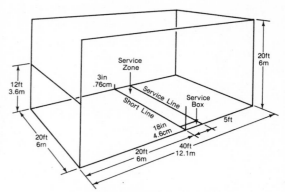

DIAGRAM OF A RACQUETBALL COURT

of the hitting head. Rackets vary in weight from 241 grams (8¼ ounces) to 276 grams (9¾ ounces). The diameter of the rubber ball may not be larger than 6.3 centimeters (2½ inches) or less than 5.7 centimeters (2¼ inches). The ball weighs 40 grams (1.4 ounces).

The Court

The four-wall and one-wall courts are the same sizes as the paddleball courts.

Rules and Play

The basic idea of racquetball is the same as that of squash and paddleball. Just as in paddleball, the ball may hit the ceiling, there is no tell-tale, and you must win two out of three games to win a match. Twenty-one points decides each of the first two games. If a third game is required to decide the match, an 11-point game is played. Only the person serving can score.

Because of the liveliness of the ball, power has become the key to being an effective racquetball player. The hard-driven kill shot, or roll-out, which is hit just above the floor on the front wall, is frequently an outright winner.

You can hit any ball harder with a strung racket than with a solid-faced paddle. Racquetball is the same as four-wall paddleball except that racquetball is a faster game simply because of the racket.

▶PLATFORM TENNIS

The roots of this sport are to be found in Scarsdale, New York. In 1928, the first court was built at a private home. It was

Like the other racket sports, racquetball is an enjoyable game that is also an excellent form of exercise.

Platform tennis is one of the fastest-growing sports in the United States.

constructed of wood and raised off the ground so that the sport could be played outdoors during the winter months. The sport quickly spread to country clubs that needed a cold-weather activity in order to stay open all year.

Equipment

The oval-faced paddles contain many holes about 1 centimeter in diameter. The paddles are made of either rock maple, plywood, plastic, or aluminum. They are about 43 centimeters (17 inches) long and 20 centimeters (8 inches) wide and vary in weight from 397 grams (14 ounces) to 510 grams (18 ounces).

The ball is either yellow or orange and made of solid sponge rubber. It is about the same size as a tennis ball.

The Court

The overall playing deck is about 9.1 meters (30 feet) wide and 18.3 meters (60 feet) long. The lines within which the ball must land are identical to badminton—6.1 meters (20 feet) by 13.4 meters (44 feet). The framework surrounding the court is 3.7 me-

ters (12 feet) high and has steel wire screening attached to it. The net that divides the court in half is 86 centimeters (34 inches) high in the center and 94 centimeters (37 inches) at the net posts. The court is usually made of wood or aluminum.

Rules and Play

Scoring is the same as in regular tennis, but only one serve is allowed. "Tiebreaker" sets start when each player has won six games.

The fundamental strokes for squash, racquetball, and paddleball are hit with a loose wrist. But the platform tennis stroke is very much like the more firm, locked-wrist motion of regular tennis. It is not necessary to hit the ball with great power. This is because of the shortness of the court, and because balls that are hit beyond the boundaries of the court may be returned after they have rebounded off the screens that surround the court.

Platform tennis is a unique combination of tennis and the wall games such as squash.

DICK SQUIRES
Author, *The Other Racquet Sports*

325

SOLOMON ISLANDS

Northeast of Australia, in the Pacific Ocean, there is a double chain of large and small islands separated by a scenic water corridor. These are the Solomon Islands, which became an independent nation in 1978. They form one of the largest island groups in the Pacific, but they are sparsely populated. Bougainville and several smaller islands in the north are geographically part of the Solomon Islands chain, but politically they are a part of Papua New Guinea, an independent nation.

▶THE PEOPLE

Life in the inland villages is very isolated because travel through the dense jungles is difficult. People grow their own food and seldom see anyone who lives more than a short distance away. Most people have settled along the coasts, where travel is easier. Solomon Islanders formerly went to sea in huge wooden dugouts that could hold as many as a hundred people. These canoes, which are often elaborately carved and inlaid with mother-of-pearl, are being replaced by motorboats.

Most Solomon Islanders are Melanesians. Some Polynesians inhabit small, outlying islands, and a few Europeans and Chinese live on the coastal lowlands. Many Solomon Islanders speak English. Melanesian pidgin (a simplified form of English) is the most widely understood language. But more than 60 different dialects are spoken.

Most of the people are Christians, and schools are generally run by missionaries. In addition to numerous primary schools, there are secondary schools, teacher-training institutes, and technical schools. The University of the South Pacific, on Fiji, has an extension center in Honiara.

▶THE LAND

Most of the islands are part of the neighboring continental rock structure or are of volcanic origin. A few smaller islands are coral atolls. Guadalcanal, the largest island, is made up of a chain of rugged mountains that extend to the shoreline. Mount Popomanasiu (formerly Mount Lammas), the nation's highest peak, is on this island. It rises to 2,440 meters (8,005 feet). Most people live along the northern coast, where there are many large coconut plantations. Honiara, the nation's capital and chief port, is there. Malaita is the most populous island. Other large islands are Choiseul, New Georgia, Santa Isabel, San Cristobal, and the Santa Cruz group.

The Solomon Islands lie close to the equator and have a tropical climate. The weather is usually damp and hot. The average temperature is 28°C (82°F), and it is warm throughout the year. The coastal regions receive about 3,000 millimeters (120 inches) of rain a year. Twice that amount falls in the interior rain forests and on the windward coasts.

The rugged and mountainous interiors of most of the islands are covered with some of the world's most impenetrable tropical jungle. The tropical jungles teem with a wide variety of birds and insects. Colorful parrots, cockatoos, and pigeons are some of the many birds. Irridescent green and blue bird-wing butterflies and the giant Queen Victoria butterfly, with a 23-centimeter (9-inch) wingspan, are common. Eagles, the black and white hornbill, frigate birds, snakes, sharks, bonito fish, and dolphins were sacred to pagan Solomon Islanders.

FACTS AND FIGURES

SOLOMON ISLANDS is the official name of the country.

CAPITAL: Honiara.

LOCATION: Pacific Ocean, east of Papua New Guinea. **Latitude** — 5° S to 13°S. **Longitude** — 155° E to 171° E.

AREA: 28,446 km² (10,983 sq mi).

POPULATION: 200,000 (estimate).

LANGUAGE: English (official), Melanesian pidgin, many local Austronesian and Papuan dialects.

GOVERNMENT: Constitutional monarchy. **Head of state**—governor-general. **Head of government**—prime minister. **International co-operation**—Commonwealth of Nations, United Nations.

NATIONAL ANTHEM: "God Save Our Solomon Islands."

ECONOMY: Agricultural products—copra, taro, bananas, sweet potatoes, manioc, sugarcane, tobacco, palm oil, cocoa, rice, spices. **Industries and products**—timber, food processing, beverages, handicrafts, household goods. **Chief minerals**—gold, bauxite, phosphates. **Chief exports**—copra, timber, palm oil, processed fish, marine shells, cocoa, spices, crocodile skins. **Chief imports**—petroleum, machinery, durable consumer goods. **Monetary unit**—Solomon Islands dollar.

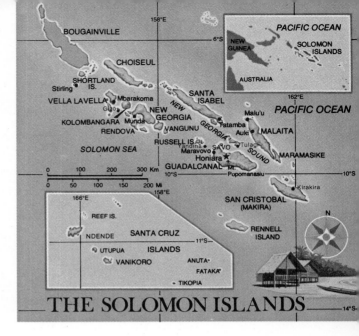

THE SOLOMON ISLANDS

▶ THE ECONOMY

Most Solomon Islanders are farmers. They grow a wide variety of tropical fruits and vegetables and raise pigs and fowl for their own use. The main commercial crop is copra, which is produced from coconuts. The growing of other commercial crops and the raising of cattle are being encouraged to lessen the dependence on copra.

Timber from the dense forests is an important export. Marine shells, used for making buttons and jewelry, are also exported. There are bauxite and phosphate deposits and traces of gold on Guadalcanal.

Fishing is important. Coastal people may trade their fish to inland farmers for a more varied diet. And the canning, freezing, and smoking of fish for export is the most rapidly growing industry. Other new factories produce furniture, beverages, and processed foods for local use. The traditional arts of wood carving and mother-of-pearl inlay are still practiced. The government is encouraging the development of tourism. Popular places to visit are the bird sanctuary on Savo and traditional villages on Malaita.

There are few towns. Most important are the ports of Honiara, Gizo, Munda, Yandina, Tulagi, Auki, and Kirakira. It is difficult to build roads in the interior, but regular air and boat services link the islands with one another and the outside world.

▶ HISTORY AND GOVERNMENT

Little is known of the early history of the Solomon Islands. The first inhabitants may have come from Southeast Asia. Some of the islands were visited in 1568 by the Spanish explorer Álvaro de Mendaña de Neyra, who named them after the biblical King Solomon. He and Pedro Fernandes de Queirós unsuccessfully attempted to establish a colony there in 1596. The islands then remained isolated for many years. The English naval officer Philip Carteret and the French explorer Louis de Bougainville rediscovered the Solomons in 1767 and 1768. During the 1800's, European missionaries, traders, and whalers visited or settled there. Many islanders were taken to work on plantations in Queensland and on Fiji, and there was much hostility toward Europeans.

Germany claimed the northern islands in 1885, but transferred most of them to Britain in 1900. Many of the southern islands became a British protectorate in 1893. After World War I, some of the northern islands became part of the Australian territory of New Guinea. Later, these islands became part of the nation of Papua New Guinea.

The Japanese occupied many of the islands in 1942. Some of the most decisive battles of World War II took place on Guadalcanal, Savo, and New Georgia. Solomon Islanders aided the American forces. During the war, many people on Malaita became involved in an anti-British movement called Marching Rule. The movement declined in 1952, when the first of several local councils in the protectorate was established on Malaita and given control of local services. Additional measures of self-government were granted later, and the islands became independent in 1978.

A governor-general, who symbolically represents the British crown, is head of state. The prime minister, selected from among the members of parliament, is head of government. Parliament members are elected by popular vote. The chief concerns of the new government are to preserve the region's Melanesian heritage while developing the economy, expanding education, and integrating islanders of different backgrounds into a single nation.

HAROLD M. ROSS
University of Illinois

327

TUVALU

Tuvalu, formerly known as the Ellice Islands, is an island nation in the southwestern Pacific Ocean, north of Fiji and south of Kiribati. The name "Tuvalu" means "cluster of eight." But the country is actually made up of nine islands—people from the original eight islands settled on the small island of Niulakita in relatively recent times. Tuvalu became an independent country in 1978.

▶THE PEOPLE

The number of people in Tuvalu is large for the small land area, and many Tuvaluans leave the country to find work on other islands. Almost all Tuvaluans are Polynesians, but there are a few Europeans and a small number of Micronesians. The islands speak a Malay-Polynesian language, Tuvaluan, which has distinct northern and southern dialects. English is widely spoken, and Samoan is understood by many older people.

Religion plays an important part in everyday life. Most people belong to the Tuvalu Church, a Protestant sect that grew out of the London Missionary Society in Samoa. Some recent religious minorities are the Seventh-Day Adventists, Jehovah's Witnesses, and Bahais.

Loyalty to the home island and ties of kinship are important. Each island has one main village. Traditional island and village chiefs today are concerned largely with the preservation of local culture.

▶THE LAND

The islands are scattered across 1,300,000 square kilometers (500,000 square miles) of ocean, linked only by ship and radio. Funafuti, the site of the nation's capital, is the most densely populated. Other large islands are Vaitupu, Niutao, and Nanumea. The smaller islands are Nanumanga, Nui, Nukufetau, Nukulaelae, and Niulakita.

The nine low-lying islands are partly covered by tropical vegetation and coconut plantations. Some of the islands are true coral atolls (ring-shaped islands surrounding lagoons). Others are reef islands (ridges of rock, coral, or sand at or near the surface of the water). Some of the atolls have large lagoons, as on Funafuti, Nukufetau, and Nukulaelae. Lagoons are an asset because they are good places to fish, using lines, nets, or spears, in all but the roughest weather. Small motorboats and canoes are used within the lagoons or outside the reefs. Larger vessels are used for transportation among the islands. An airport links Funafuti to the rest of the world.

The climate is warm and humid, with an average daily high temperature of about 30°C (86°F). Westerly storms are common from November to February, but hurricanes causing great destruction are rare. Rainfall is generally quite high, averaging 3,000 milimeters (120 inches) a year. But rainfall varies with the seasons, and there are occasional shortages. Most islands have wells for emergency use, but most of the water supply comes from rain collected from roofs and stored in cisterns. Rationing of water is sometimes imposed during droughts.

▶THE ECONOMY

The two basic economic activities in Tuvalu are farming and fishing. Few plants can survive the salty air, brackish ground water, and poor, sandy soil. So people rely on hardy trees such as coconut palms, pines, and breadfruit. The coconut palm is particularly important. The nuts provide food, oil, and juice, and the husks can be used for fuel or for making string. The sap of the tree can

---

FACTS AND FIGURES

TUVALU is the official name of the country.

CAPITAL: Funafuti.

LOCATION: Pacific Ocean, north of Fiji and south of Kiribati. **Latitude**—5° S to 10° S. **Longitude**—175° E to 180° E.

AREA: 26 km² (10 sq mi).

POPULATION: 8,000 (estimate).

LANGUAGE: Tuvaluan and English.

GOVERNMENT: Constitutional monarchy. **Head of state**—governor-general. **Head of government**—prime minister. **International cooperation**—Commonwealth of Nations.

NATIONAL ANTHEM: *Tuvalu mo te Atua* ("Tuvalu and the Almighty").

ECONOMY: **Agricultural products**—coconuts, taro, pandanus (screw pine), breadfruit, bananas. **Industries and products**—copra, fishing. **Chief exports**—stamps, copra. **Chief imports**—food, petroleum, machinery. **Monetary unit**—Australian and Tuvaluan dollars.

be made into molasses, and the leaves and trunks are used for building and for making baskets. The flesh of the coconut is dried to make copra. Pits are dug and filled with organic matter for planting bananas, papayas, and root crops such as taro.

Pork and chicken are eaten on special occasions, but the chief source of protein is fish. Men do most of the fishing, casting nets or lines from canoes. Both men and women use nets or spears to fish on the reefs.

Co-operatives owned by the villages run stores and sell crops. Many Tuvaluans work for the government, particularly in the capital of Funafuti, which has grown rapidly in recent years. People with cash incomes eat mainly imported foodstuffs.

Copra was once the leading export. More revenue now comes from the sale of stamps, foreign aid, and the earnings of Tuvaluans abroad. Tourism and commercial fishing offer the best prospects for future economic development.

▶HISTORY AND GOVERNMENT

Tuvalu was formerly called the Ellice Islands. According to Tuvaluan traditions, the original inhabitants of the islands came from Samoa and Tonga many years ago. The Spanish explorer Álvaro de Mendaña de Neyra sighted the islands in the 16th century. But the people had limited contact with Europeans until the mid-19th century. From 1850 to 1870 the islands were raided by Peruvian and Australian slave traders.

Gradually traders, whalers, and missionaries began to visit the islands. The first missionaries were Samoans, who used the Bible in the Samoan language. By 1890 almost the entire population was Christian. The early pastors reorganized village government in accordance with Samoan customs. They took over many of the powers of the traditional chiefs, and some pastors became laws unto themselves. Pastors still have great authority, but they no longer control the government or the educational system of the islands.

In the late 1800's, the Ellice Islands became a British protectorate. In 1915 they became part of the Gilbert and Ellice Islands colony, still administered by Britain. During World War II, the Ellice Islands as-

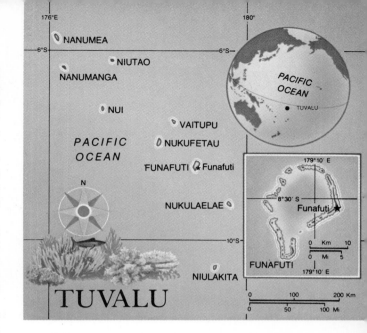

sumed strategic importance for assaults on the Japanese-held Gilbert Islands. The United States established bases on several of the islands, and many Tuvaluans joined in the war effort.

In the postwar years, Tuvaluans were employed in large numbers in the administration of the colony. But they did not want to be dominated by the more numerous Gilbertese, and Tuvaluans began to demand separation from their neighbors. The Ellice Islands broke away from the Gilbert Islands in 1975 and became known as Tuvalu. Full independence from Britain was achieved in 1978.

The head of state is the governor-general, a native Tuvaluan who represents the British monarch. Island councils elected by universal suffrage control village affairs. Each island elects one or two members to the national legislature. The members select a prime minister from among themselves, and the prime minister selects the cabinet.

Tuvalu faces many economic problems, particularly the strain that the steadily growing population places on its limited resources. But the government and the people point to their strong social organization, their high literacy rate, and their peaceful traditions as signs of hope for the future.

HAROLD M. ROSS
University of Illinois

MICHAEL R. GOLDSMITH
University of Waikato (New Zealand)

329

ANTIGUA AND BARBUDA

Beautiful beaches, calm waters, and sunny skies make the Caribbean nation of Antigua and Barbuda a popular resort. The country is part of the Leeward Islands in the Lesser Antilles. It includes the islands of Antigua and Barbuda and tiny, uninhabited Redonda.

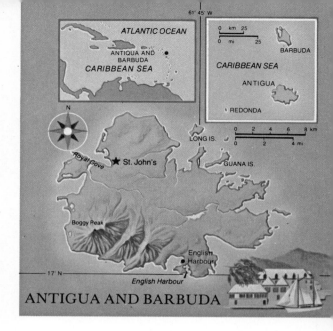

ANTIGUA AND BARBUDA

▶ THE LAND

Antigua, the largest island, is mostly flat, with rolling green hills, tropical vegetation, and many gardens. The nation's high point, Boggy Peak, rises to 405 meters (1,330 feet) in western Antigua. The capital, St. John's, is on Royal Cove in Antigua, the nation's chief harbor. The wooded island of Barbuda, north of Antigua, is noted for its superb beaches of pink and white sand.

The country is relatively dry, with rainfall averaging only 1,070 millimeters (42 inches) a year. Additional water for human use is provided by desalinization plants. Temperatures range from 22 to 30°C (71 to 86°F).

▶ THE PEOPLE AND THE ECONOMY

Over 90 percent of the people are of black African descent. The rest are of British, Portuguese, Lebanese, or mixed ancestry. English is the official language. Most of the people live on the island of Antigua.

Tourism is the chief economic activity.

FACTS AND FIGURES

ANTIGUA AND BARBUDA is the official name of the country.

CAPITAL: St. John's.

LOCATION: Caribbean Sea. **Latitude**—17° N to 18° N. **Longitude**—61° W to 62° W.

AREA: 442 km² (171 sq mi).

POPULATION: 17,000 (estimate).

LANGUAGE: English.

GOVERNMENT: Constitutional monarchy. **Head of state**—British monarch, represented by governor-general. **Head of government**—prime minister. **International co-operation**—United Nations, Commonwealth of Nations, Caribbean Community (CARICOM). Organization of American States (OAS).

ECONOMY: Agricultural products—cotton, vegetables. **Industries and products**—tourism, rum, wine, textiles, handicrafts, assembled equipment. **Chief exports**—beverages. **Chief imports**—machinery, petroleum, foodstuffs, raw materials. **Monetary unit**—Eastern Caribbean dollar.

Sugar was the mainstay of the economy until the mid-1960's, but the nation has since ceased to be a sugar producer. Cotton and vegetables are grown, and a number of light industries have recently been established.

▶ HISTORY AND GOVERNMENT

Christopher Columbus visited the island now known as Antigua in 1493. The islands were first settled by Arawak Indians from Venezuela. But there were few Indians left when British settlers from nearby St. Christopher (now St. Kitts) arrived in 1632. The islands were briefly under French control during the 17th century. Historic Nelson's Dockyard, built on English Harbour in 1764, served as headquarters for the English admiral Horatio Nelson.

Tobacco, the first commercial crop, soon gave way to sugar. Many black Africans were brought to the sugar plantations as slaves. They were freed in 1834, when slavery was abolished in the British colonies. In 1967, Antigua became one of the West Indies Associated States, with full internal self-government. Plans for full independence were made in 1979.

The British monarch, represented by a governor-general, is head of state. A prime minister is head of government. The legislature has two houses, one elected by universal adult suffrage and the other appointed.

HOWARD A. FERGUS
University of the West Indies (Montserrat)

SAINT KITTS–NEVIS

The Caribbean nation of St. Kitts–Nevis is rich in history. St. Kitts (formerly St. Christopher) was the first British colony in the West Indies. It was known as the "Mother Colony" of the British Caribbean because colonizing parties went from there to the other islands. A well-preserved British fort, built at Brimstone Hill on St. Kitts in 1791, came to be known as the Gibraltar of the West Indies. Nevis was the birthplace of the American political leader Alexander Hamilton. Neighboring Anguilla was once linked to St. Kitts–Nevis. But it broke away in 1969 and has chosen to remain a dependency of Britain.

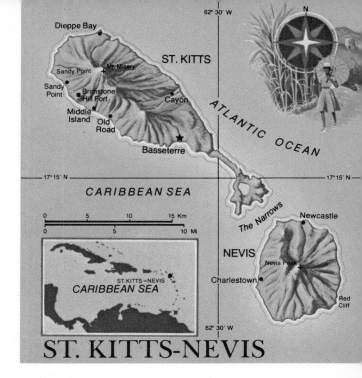

ST. KITTS-NEVIS

▶THE LAND

St. Kitts–Nevis is in the Leeward Islands of the Lesser Antilles. Mountain ranges occupy the center of St. Kitts, rising to a high point of 1,156 meters (3,792 feet) at Mount Misery. St. Kitts has a narrow peninsula in the southeast where salt ponds and lovely beaches are found. Volcanic Nevis rises sharply from palm-studded coral beaches to tall, green, cloud-capped Nevis Peak.

St. Kitts–Nevis is fanned by cool northeast trade winds for most of the year. This makes the tropical climate very pleasant. Rainfall is abundant, and the soil is fertile.

FACTS AND FIGURES

ST. KITTS-NEVIS is the official name of the country.

CAPITAL: Basseterre.

LOCATION: Caribbean Sea. **Latitude**—17° 20′ N. **Longitude**—62° 48′ W.

AREA: 261 km² (101 sq mi).

POPULATION: 48,000 (estimate).

LANGUAGE: English.

GOVERNMENT: Constitutional monarchy. **Head of state**—British monarch, represented by governor-general. **Head of government**—prime minister. **International co-operation**—United Nations, Commonwealth of Nations, Caribbean Community (CARICOM), Organization of American States (OAS).

ECONOMY: Agricultural products—sugarcane, coconuts, cotton, livestock. **Industries and products**—tourism, malt, beer, rum, textiles, clothes, handicrafts. **Chief mineral**—salt. **Chief exports**—sugar, food, beverages. **Chief imports**—petroleum and petroleum products, machinery, foodstuffs. **Monetary unit**—Eastern Caribbean dollar.

▶THE PEOPLE AND THE ECONOMY

Most of the people are of African descent. There are a number of people of European and mixed descent. More than three fourths of the people live on St. Kitts, where the capital, Basseterre, is located.

St. Kitts has been an island of sugar plantations since the mid-1600's. The government now manages the plantations and a sugar refinery. A greater variety of crops is grown on Nevis. Tourism, light industry, and handicrafts are other sources of income.

▶HISTORY AND GOVERNMENT

Christopher Columbus is said to have visited the islands in 1493 and claimed them for Spain. The first British colony was established on St. Kitts in 1623. Nevis was settled from St. Kitts in 1628. France also briefly controlled the islands. In 1967, the islands of St. Kitts, Nevis, and Anguilla became an associated state within the West Indies Associated States, with internal self-government. St. Kitts and Nevis negotiated for full independence in 1979. The British monarch, represented by a governor-general, is head of state. A prime minister chosen by the majority party in parliament is head of government.

HOWARD A. FERGUS
University of West Indies (Montserrat)

331

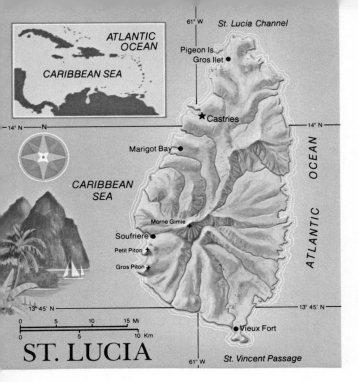

ST. LUCIA

SAINT LUCIA

St. Lucia, a small and rugged island in the Caribbean Sea, attained full independence from Britain in 1979. Its lush greenery, spectacular mountain scenery, pleasant climate, and white, sandy beaches have made it a popular tourist resort.

▶THE PEOPLE

Most of the people of St. Lucia are of black African descent. The official language is English, but many people speak a dialect based on French. The majority of the people are Roman Catholics. Primary education is free and compulsory, but the attendance law is not enforced. St. Lucia has a number of government-aided secondary schools and a branch of the University of the West Indies.

▶THE LAND

The green-clad mountains of St. Lucia rise abruptly from the sea. Because the land is mountainous, most of the people have settled on the western coast and the fertile river valleys. The highest point, volcanic Morne Gimie, is topped by twin cones. It is possible to drive a car to the rim of the volcano, which rises to 959 meters (3,145 feet).

The mountains are heavily forested, and some areas have never been explored.

St. Lucia has a pleasant tropical climate, with an average temperature of 26°C (79°F). There is abundant rainfall, particularly on the high mountain slopes. Most of the rain falls between May and August.

There is an excellent natural harbor at Castries, the nation's modern capital and chief port. Castries was rebuilt after 1948, when a fire destroyed much of the town. Pigeon Island, off the northern coast, has a lovely botanical garden and the ruins of an old fort.

▶THE ECONOMY

St. Lucia's rich volcanic soil supports a wide variety of tropical vegetation. Bananas are the chief commercial crop and most important export. Coconuts, cocoa, and various tropical food crops are also grown.

Fishing, handicrafts, and the making of furniture from trees that grow on the mountain slopes are traditional industries. Tourism has developed rapidly since St. Lucia's airport was modernized in 1975.

The government has launched an ambitious industrial development program to lessen the nation's dependence on agriculture. A large industrial free port, where foreign industries manufacture goods for export, is under construction. The harbor at Castries has been modernized, and a large oil refinery and transportation complex are being built nearby. New factories, especially around Vieux Fort in the south, manufacture plastics, clothing, industrial gases, and

---

FACTS AND FIGURES

SAINT LUCIA is the official name of the country.

CAPITAL: Castries.

LOCATION: Caribbean Sea. **Latitude**—13° 46' N to 14° 7' N. **Longitude**—60° 52' W to 61° 5' W.

AREA: 616 km² (238 sq mi).

POPULATION: 113,000 (estimate).

LANGUAGE: English (official), French dialect.

GOVERNMENT: Constitutional monarchy. **Head of state**—British monarch, represented by governor-general. **Head of government**—prime minister. **International co-operation**—United Nations, Commonwealth of Nations, Organization of American States (OAS).

ECONOMY: Agricultural products—bananas, coconuts, cocoa, other tropical food crops. **Industries and products**—copra, construction, tourism, oil refining, transshipment of goods, plastics, clothing, industrial gases, beer, fishing. **Chief exports**—bananas, copra, cocoa, beans, coconut oil, industrial products. **Chief imports**—textiles, machinery, vehicles, metal goods.

Monetary unit—East Caribbean dollar.

The green-clad mountains of St. Lucia rise abruptly from the sea.

beer. The sulfur springs at Soufrière, long a tourist attraction, may be harnessed as a source of geothermal energy.

▶HISTORY AND GOVERNMENT

St. Lucia was first settled by Carib Indians. It is thought that Christopher Columbus visited the island in 1502. But its inhabitants resisted early European attempts to establish settlements on the island. French settlers signed a treaty with the Carib Indians in 1660, and the island was claimed by both the British and the French before finally passing to British control in 1803. St. Lucia was part of the British Windward Islands colony until that colony was dissolved in 1959. The islanders were granted increasing control over local affairs after 1924. In 1967, St. Lucia became an associated state within the West Indies Associated States. It had complete internal self-government, but Britain retained responsibility for its defense and foreign affairs.

St. Lucia was granted independence in February, 1979. But there was some objection to the fact that the islanders were never permitted to vote on whether they wished to become independent of Britain. St. Lucia's first free elections as an independent nation were held in July, 1979. John G. M. Compton, who had been the prime minister at independence and had led the independence effort, was defeated. Allan Louisy, the head of the St. Lucia Labour Party, became the new prime minister. Louisy advocated limiting foreign investment and establishing stronger ties with the nonaligned nations.

According to its constitution, St. Lucia is a constitutional monarchy within the Commonwealth of Nations. The British monarch, represented by a governor-general, is head of state. A prime minister, who is assisted by a cabinet, serves as head of government. The members of the legislature, the House of Assembly, are elected.

In May, 1979, a meeting was held on St. Lucia to discuss the creation of a regional grouping of eastern Caribbean nations within the Caribbean Community (CARICOM). The new organization would promote co-operation and economic development in the area. There were also plans to develop a network of common services—such as diplomatic representation, police training, and a coast guard—with the neighboring countries of Barbados, Antigua and Barbuda, St. Vincent and the Grenadines, and St. Kitts–Nevis.

333

KIRIBATI

Kiribati, long known as the Gilbert Islands, is an island nation in the southwestern Pacific Ocean. Both the equator and the International Date Line run through the islands. They gained their independence from Britain in 1979.

▶THE PEOPLE

The people of Kiribati are mostly Micronesians, but a few are of Polynesian, mixed Micronesian and Polynesian, and European ancestry. Most of the people live on the island of Tarawa, which is the site of the capital of the same name. A distinct ethnic group known as the Banabans once lived on Ocean Island (Banaba). The Banabans were resettled in 1945 on the fertile island of Rabi, in the Fiji group, because phosphate mining had made their home island uninhabitable.

Most of the people are Christians, divided about equally between Roman Catholics and Protestants. They speak English and a local Micronesian language. Primary education is free for all children between the ages of 6 and 15. Most schools were once run by missionaries, but the schools have been gradually taken over by the government. The government maintains a teacher-training college and a marine training school. There is a branch of the University of the Pacific at Bikenibeu, on the island of Tarawa. Many students receive higher education at universities in Fiji, New Zealand, Australia, and Britain on government scholarships.

Most of the people live in small villages built around a community meeting house. Several generations of a family normally live together, and people usually own the land on which they live. Houses on the more urbanized island of Tarawa are often built of concrete blocks, with aluminum roofs.

▶THE LAND

The islands that make up the nation of Kiribati are atolls (coral islands made up of a reef surrounding a lagoon). There are three groups of islands—the 17 Gilbert Islands, the 8 Line Islands, and the 8 Phoenix Islands. The country also includes phosphate-rich Ocean Island, which was incorporated into Kiribati against the wishes of its people. Christmas Island, in the Line Islands, is thought to be the largest atoll in the world.

The climate is pleasant, with an average annual temperature of about 27°C (80°F). Rainfall usually comes in brief, violent showers and varies widely from island to island. This means that some islands suffer periods of drought, even though the average rainfall varies from about 1,000 millimeters (40 inches) near the equator to about 3,000 millimeters (120 inches) in the extreme north and south.

▶THE ECONOMY

Most of the people of Kiribati catch fish or grow food for their own needs. The chief crops are coconuts, breadfruit, bananas, and papaws. Pigs and poultry are raised. Copra (dried coconut meat) is the only agricultural export.

The government is encouraging the growth of commercial fishing. Kingfish, snapper, and tuna are among the many varieties of fish that are plentiful in the waters around the islands. Brine shrimp are raised commercially on Christmas Island. Small local industries include the making of food-

---

FACTS AND FIGURES

KIRIBATI is the offical name of the country.

CAPITAL: Tarawa.

LOCATION: Southwest Pacific Ocean. **Latitude**—11° 26′ S to 4° 40′ N. **Longitude**—177° E to 175° W.

AREA: 684 km² (264 sq mi).

POPULATION: 56,000 (estimate).

LANGUAGE: English, Samoan, local languages.

GOVERNMENT: Republic. **Head of state and government**—president. **International co-operation**—United Nations, Commonwealth of Nations.

ECONOMY: Agricultural products—coconuts, breadfruit, bananas, papaws. **Industries and products**—fishing, shrimp raising, copra, local industries. **Chief minerals**—phosphate rock. **Chief exports**—copra, phosphate rock. **Chief imports**—foodstuffs, consumer goods. **Monetary unit**—Kiribati dollar.

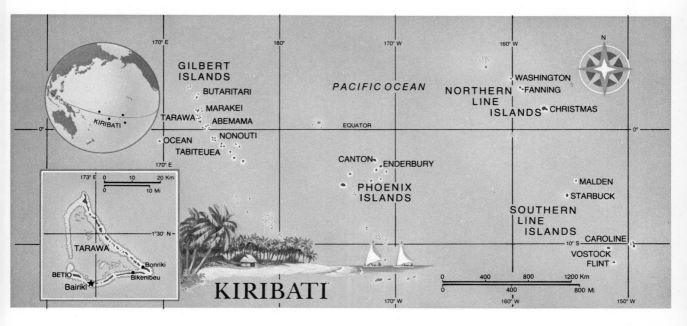
KIRIBATI

stuffs and beverages, construction, furniture making, electrical and automobile repair, and boatbuilding.

Phosphate rock has been mined for export on Ocean Island for nearly 75 years, but the deposits are almost exhausted. The Banabans of Ocean Island have received some compensation from the British Phosphate Commission, which runs the mining operation. But they have requested additional money to make their home island livable again once mining has ceased.

▶ HISTORY AND GOVERNMENT

Kiribati is believed to have been settled from Samoa in the 13th century. The first Europeans to sight the islands were Spanish explorers in the 16th and early 17th centuries. The islands were later seen by British and American navigators. The first European settlers were deserters from whaling ships who arrived in the mid-19th century. They were followed by Christian missionaries from Hawaii in 1857. A flourishing trade in coconut oil and copra was soon established.

The islanders were threatened with extinction because of slave raids, and the British extended their jurisdiction over the Pacific islands, including present-day Kiribati, in 1877. In that year the Office of the British High Commissioner for the Western Pacific was created to administer the islands. Britain formally annexed the various islands of Kiribati over a period of years. The Gilbert and Ellice Islands Colony was created in 1916. Several of the islands were occupied by the Japanese during World War II and were the scene of fierce fighting.

During the 1970's the islanders were given increasing control over their own affairs. The Ellice Islands were separated from the Gilberts in 1974 at their request and were renamed Tuvalu. The remainder of the former Gilbert and Ellice Islands Colony became known as the Gilbert Islands. It became the fully independent nation of Kiribati in 1979. Because the Banabans of Ocean Island had been living in Fiji for many years, they asked permission to become citizens of Fiji. But the British Government refused to grant their request for separation from Kiribati.

Kiribati is a republic. A president serves as head of state and government. There is an elected parliament. Elected island councils administer local affairs. Kiribati's first president, 29-year-old Ieremia Tabai, became one of the world's youngest heads of state.

335

SAINT VINCENT AND THE GRENADINES

St. Vincent and the Grenadines became an independent nation in 1979. It includes St. Vincent, one of the Windward Islands in the Lesser Antilles, and the northernmost islands of the Grenadine chain. Shortly before independence, Mount Soufrière, a long-inactive volcano on St. Vincent, erupted. People living on the slopes of the volcano were evacuated, and independence was briefly postponed.

▶ **THE PEOPLE**

Most of the people of St. Vincent and the Grenadines are of black African or mixed African and Carib Indian descent. There are also people whose ancestors came from Portugal and India. English is the official language, and most of the people are members of the Church of England. The government supports primary and secondary schools and a technical school.

▶ **THE LAND**

The main island, St. Vincent, is rugged and heavily forested. Mount Soufrière, the highest point, rises to 1,234 meters (4,048 feet). Only about one third of the island, chiefly along the coast, is suitable for farming. The temperature is pleasant, and there is abundant rainfall.

▶ **THE ECONOMY**

Agriculture is the chief economic activity. Many people grow food for their own use

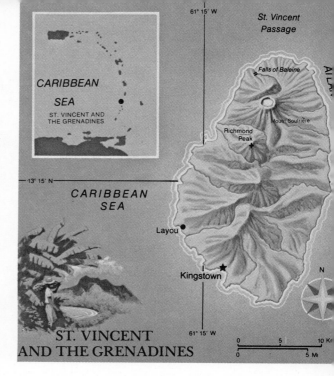

ST. VINCENT AND THE GRENADINES

on small farms. There are also many large plantations where crops are grown for export. St. Vincent is the world's leading producer of arrowroot. The roots of this plant yield a starch used chiefly in baby food. Bananas are the main export. The chief industries are tourism, fishing, and the making of copra, sugar, and rum.

▶ **HISTORY AND GOVERNMENT**

St. Vincent was originally settled by Arawak Indians, who were destroyed by warlike Carib Indians from South America. It is believed that Christopher Columbus sighted the island on Saint Vincent's Day in 1498. Britain and France fought for control of the island, but its Carib inhabitants fiercely resisted colonization. British rule was recognized in 1763. St. Vincent was seized by the French in 1779 and restored to Britain in 1783. It became part of the British colony of the Windward Islands. In 1969 it became a self-governing state within the West Indies Associated States. Britain remained responsible for its defense and foreign affairs.

St. Vincent and the Grenadines became an independent member of the Commonwealth of Nations in late 1979. The head of state is the British monarch, represented by a governor-general. A prime minister serves as head of government.

FACTS AND FIGURES

SAINT VINCENT AND THE GRENADINES is the official name of the country.

CAPITAL: Kingstown.

LOCATION: Caribbean Sea. **Latitude**—13° 7′ N to 13° 23′ N. **Longitude**—61° 7′ W to 61° 17′ W.

AREA: 388 km² (150 sq mi).

POPULATION: 100,000 (estimate).

LANGUAGE: English, French dialect.

GOVERNMENT: Constitutional monarchy. **Head of state**—British monarch, represented by governor-general. **Head of government**—prime minister. **International co-operation**—United Nations, Commonwealth of Nations, Organization of American States (OAS).

ECONOMY: Agricultural products—bananas, arrowroot, carrots, coconut palms, sweet potatoes, nutmeg, mace, groundnuts, cassava. **Industries and products**—fishing, tourism, processing of agricultural products. **Chief exports**—bananas, arrowroot flour, carrots, sweet potatoes, spices. **Chief imports**—manufactured goods. **Monetary unit**—East Caribbean dollar.

DOMINICA

The eastern Caribbean island of Dominica is one of the smallest nations in the Americas. It became independent in 1978, after more than 100 years of British rule.

▶ **THE PEOPLE AND THE ECONOMY**

The people of Dominica are mostly of black African or mixed African and European descent. There is a Carib Indian reservation on the island. English is the official language, but a French dialect is widely spoken. Most of the people are Roman Catholics. Education is free for all children between the ages of 5 and 15. There is a branch of the University of the West Indies at Roseau, the capital.

Most people live on small farms and grow food for their own use. Bananas, citrus fruits, coconuts, cocoa, and spices are grown commercially. The processing of agricultural products and fishing are the major industries. Pumice is mined for use in abrasive cleaners and building materials. Straw handicrafts, alcoholic beverages, and soap are manufactured, and construction is also important. The government is encouraging livestock raising and tourism.

▶ **THE LAND**

Dominica is one of the Windward Islands of the Lesser Antilles. Dense tropical for-

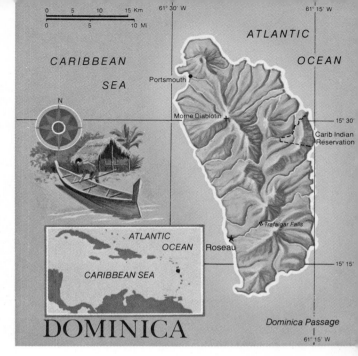

ests cover much of the mountainous interior. Unlike most Caribbean islands, Dominica has many shallow rivers that provide the country with drinking water and hydroelectric power. The climate is pleasant from December to March. In July the temperature rises to about 32°C (90°F). As much as 6,400 millimeters (250 inches) of rain fall each year in the mountains.

▶ **HISTORY AND GOVERNMENT**

Christopher Columbus sighted Dominica in 1493. But because the Carib Indians on the islands resisted European settlement, it was not until the mid-1700's that the French colonized the coast. Britain took the island in 1759. It was recaptured by France in 1778 and returned to Britain in 1783. Dominica attained full internal self-government in 1967 as one of the West Indies Associated States. Independence was granted in late 1978.

Dominica's first year of independence was a troubled one. The first prime minister, Patrick John, was replaced after a general strike halted all public services. And the island was devastated by a hurricane in 1979.

Under Dominica's constitution, the president serves as head of state, and the prime minister is the head of government. Most members of the legislature, the House of Assembly, are popularly elected.

FACTS AND FIGURES

COMMONWEALTH OF DOMINICA is the official name of the country.

CAPITAL: Roseau.

LOCATION: Caribbean Sea. **Latitude**—15° 11′ N to 15° 38′ N. **Longitude**—61° 15′ W to 61° 29′ W.

AREA: 751 km² (290 sq mi).

POPULATION: 81,000 (estimate).

LANGUAGE: English (official), French dialect.

GOVERNMENT: Republic. **Head of state**—president. **Head of government**—prime minister. **International co-operation**—United Nations, Organization of American States (OAS), Commonwealth of Nations.

ECONOMY: Agricultural products—bananas, citrus fruits, coconuts, cocoa, vegetables, spices. **Industries and products**—fishing, copra, food processing, clothing, soap, straw handicrafts, alcoholic beverages, construction, livestock, tourism. **Chief minerals**—pumice. **Chief exports**—bananas, citrus fruits and juices, cocoa, coconut oil, soap, spices. **Monetary unit**—East Caribbean dollar, franc, pound sterling.

AUSTRALIAN ABORIGINES

The Australian aborigines are the native people of Australia—its earliest known inhabitants. For thousands of years they roamed all parts of the vast continent, hunting and gathering food. Today most aborigines live in cities and towns. Only a few live as their ancestors did in prehistoric times.

The term "aborigine" comes from Latin words that mean "from the beginning." It can be applied to the first people of any region. The Australian aborigines form an ethnic group called Australoid. Most of them have brown skin and eyes and wavy, dark hair.

There are many ideas about how, when, and from where the aborigines traveled to Australia. It seems most likely that they first lived in India and the Malay Peninsula, perhaps more than 30,000 years ago. They may have traveled to Australia by raft or dugout canoe.

▶TRADITIONAL WAY OF LIFE

Over centuries, the aborigines spread out across Australia. Eventually each tribe— actually an extended family—claimed its own territory. Within each territory was a watering place that was very important to the tribe for two reasons. Water is scarce in Australia, and the aborigines believed that the spirits of their ancestors remained near the watering place where the tribe had first settled.

The aborigines were nomads—they moved from place to place within their territory to hunt, fish, and gather food. Their journeys, called walkabouts, gave them detailed knowledge of their territory and every kind of animal and plant in it.

Each tribe was made up of several clans. Members of these clans lived in family groups of 30 to 40 people. Each clan had a totem or emblem—perhaps an animal, a plant, or a fish. It served as a reminder of the clan's common ancestry and was painted on shields and weapons. And the totem animal or plant was honored as a member of the clan. The aborigines believed that all things—people, animals, plants, and even rocks—were important parts of nature and of the spirit world.

A tree-bark painting by a present-day aborigine artist.

The aborigines have left a rich heritage of cave paintings and rock carvings. And they were one of the few early peoples to make use of the principle of the lever. They used it in the design of the woomera, a spear-thrower. They also used the returning boomerang, which was made from a curved piece of wood. When thrown properly, the boomerang returned in a perfect arc. Different boomerangs were designed for fighting, hunting, and other uses.

By adapting to Australia's often harsh conditions, the aborigines survived for thousands of years. In 1788, when the first European settlers arrived, there may have been as many as 300,000 of these native people.

▶ABORIGINES IN MODERN AUSTRALIA

As the new settlers spread out, many aborigines were forced to change their way of life. In the 19th century, many were killed by settlers or disease. Others were driven into outlying areas or became workers on cattle and sheep ranches.

Today there are fewer than half as many aborigines as there were when Europeans first arrived, and fewer than half of these are considered pure-blooded. Since the 1940's, the Australian Government has worked to improve opportunities for the aborigines. They now have the same rights—and many of them, the same way of life—as other Australians. But often their incomes are lower. Several aborigine groups are trying to preserve some form of the old, nomadic way of life.

CAROL PERKINS
Author, *The Sound of Boomerangs*

338

AUTOMOBILE MODELS

How would you like to have a fleet of automobiles—everything from luxury cars and racing cars to trucks and vans, from motorcycles and buses to vehicles with four-wheel drive? You might even have automobiles that represent important developments in automobile history. Such a fleet is possible—in miniature—for those who build and collect automobile models.

▶ **A HOBBY WITH A HISTORY**

Toy cars became a hobby a few years after the first cast-metal models were produced in the early 1900's. Some of these toys were very realistic, and people wanted to collect them. The first kits to build model cars did not appear until the 1930's, and they were merely blocks of wood with wheels. Plastic model-car kits appeared after World War II. During the 1950's and 1960's, automobile dealers offered assembled plastic models of new full-size cars. Because these models are rare, they have become valuable and are considered collector's items.

The first model automobiles with internal-combustion engines were built from metal kits in the 1930's. In such models, fuel is burned inside the engines to produce power. These cars were guided by rollers that followed elevated rails on a wood or concrete racetrack. A few cars were guided in a circle with control lines like those used for some model airplanes.

Model racing cars with electric motors did not become widely available until the 1950's. The first of these racers were guided by rails. But the system of using a slot, or narrow opening in the track, to guide the car became universal by 1960. The slotless system, in which cars are guided by a curb or wall, appeared in the early 1970's.

Radio control was developed for use in model cars with fuel-burning engines by 1965. The combination of rechargeable batteries, electric motors, and radio controls was not perfected until about 1975.

▶ **TYPES OF MODELS**

More models of automobiles are sold than any other single type of hobby miniature. There are models of every imaginable type of full-size vehicle. Most of these are available as metal or plastic ready-built models or as plastic kits to be put together at home. There are also hundreds of different powered racing models that duplicate the action as well as the appearance of full-size automobiles.

Hobbyists refer to the size of a model, when compared to the size of the real vehicle, as its scale. The scale is expressed as a proportion (such as 1:43) or as a fraction (such as 1/43) of the size of the real vehicle. The larger the fraction, the larger the model. A 1/43 scale model of a Chevrolet Corvette is about the size of a credit card; a 1/8 scale model of the same car is about the size of a briefcase. The smallest size, 1/87 scale, is known as HO scale.

A 1/25 scale model of a classic car, the Stutz Bearcat.

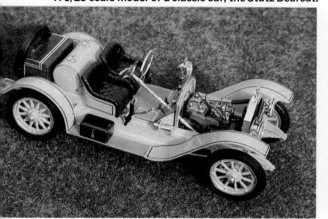

This 1/16 scale 1957 Chevrolet has working doors.

339

Electric slot racers can reach scale speeds of over 640 kilometers (400 miles) an hour.

Collector's Cars

Unpowered, ready-built model cars are by far the most popular hobby models. These vehicles can range from postage-stamp-size racing cars, molded in plastic and selling for about $1, to desk-size all-metal models selling for about $3,000. The most popular collector's cars are metal models with plastic detail pieces, in 1/43 scale.

Most plastic model kits must be glued together and painted. But there are kits available with simple snap-together construction. Both types of kits include full interior, engine, and chassis details, such as windshield wipers, chrome trim, and hoods and doors that open and close. Sometimes model builders will modify (change) parts from other kits to fit the car they are building.

Racing Cars

The two main types of model racing cars are tabletop racers, which run on special tracks, and radio-controlled models, which are usually raced outdoors.

Tabletop Racers. The racing of slot and slotless model cars requires almost as much "driving" skill as racing full-size automobiles. Slot cars must stay in a narrow opening, or slot, to get the electric power needed to race. The cars must be drifted or skidded through the turns without going too fast, or they might spin out and leave their slots.

Slot cars are driven by an electric motor that turns gears to drive the rear axle. A transformer is needed to convert household current to the 12-volt direct current needed for the motor. Metal strips on each side of the slot are rubbed by metal pickup strips, called shoes, on the bottom of the slot car. This carries the electric power from the track to the motor. Hand-held controllers are used to change the speed of the cars.

Slot car tracks range from simple ovals to figure eights. Accessories, such as a lap counter and a grandstand, may be added to the set.

Slotless cars are also powered by direct current. The cars have metal pickup shoes

340

similar to the ones on the slot cars. Imbedded in each lane of a slotless car track are three metal strips. One strip is shared by two cars and serves as a ground, to prevent an electrical shock. The remaining two strips provide power to the cars. This allows independent control of the two cars, even though both may be in the same lane. Cars are able to change lanes by moving from one set of strips to another.

Slotless cars must be steered in order to change lanes. Hand-held controllers, similar to the ones used for slot cars, are used. On each side of the track is a molded plastic fence. The cars rub against this fence and are guided by it around the turns. Because slotless cars can change lanes, more accessories are available. Detours and pit stops can be added to the track.

Radio-Controlled Racing. In radio-controlled racing, a hand-held transmitter sends radio signals to a receiver in the car. These signals make the car speed up, slow down, turn right or left, stop, or go into reverse.

Most radio-controlled cars are powered by battery-operated electric motors. Bat-

Slotless electric tabletop racing cars are guided by the "curbs" around the insides and outsides of the turns.

teries that can be recharged are available, so the cars can be raced many times on one set of batteries. Some cars may have internal-combustion engines for power. The most popular size for radio-controlled models is 1/12 scale. The large cars, known as hobby cars, are 1/8 scale and can exceed speeds of 50 kilometers (30 miles) an hour.

More expensive radio-controlled cars have transmitters and receivers that use different radio frequencies. This allows up to 14 cars to be raced at one time. In the United States, operators of these larger transmitters must obtain permits from the Federal Communications Commission. The transmitters for many of the smaller cars, known as toy cars, are not powerful enough to require a permit. The hobby racing cars have controls that respond instantly to any movement of the levers on the transmitter. With practice, you can duplicate all the maneuvers of a real racing car.

Both the electric- and gasoline-powered radio-controlled cars can be raced out-of-doors. Paved parking lots and school yards are ideal. In many cities, there are also special rental tracks for these cars. Radio-controlled cars with electric motors can be raced indoors, but they need an area that is at least the size of a tennis court. Radio-controlled dune buggies and other off-road vehicles are raced in the dirt.

ROBERT SCHLEICHER
Author, *Model Car Racing:
Tabletop & Radio Control*

A 1/12 scale electric-powered radio-controlled racer.

341

PALESTINE

Palestine, the area at the southeastern corner of the Mediterranean Sea, has played a far more important role in history than its small size would suggest. It is called the Holy Land because it is important to three great religions—Judaism, Christianity, and Islam. Located near where Asia and Africa join, it has been the scene of many migrations and invasions. Today it is the object of conflict between Arabs and Israelis.

There is now no country called Palestine. The word "Palestine" comes from "Philistine," the name of one of the early peoples who lived there. The Romans used "Palestina" as the name of one of their provinces in the area. This name passed into English as "Palestine." It came to be used for the geographical area from Sinai on the south to the mountains of Lebanon on the north and from the Mediterranean Sea on the west to the desert of the Arabian Peninsula on the east. Since 1948, the area has been divided between Israel and Jordan.

▶ EARLY HISTORY

People have lived in Palestine since prehistoric times. But it has been important in world history only since about 2000 B.C. Between then and the 20th century, its history can be divided into three broad periods.

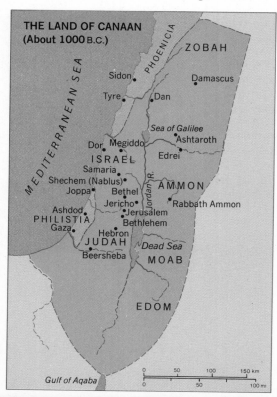

THE LAND OF CANAAN (About 1000 B.C.)

The Hebrews and Judaism

Shortly after 2000 B.C. the Hebrews, a migrating people from Mesopotamia, began to enter the area of Canaan, as Palestine was then called. Some of the Hebrews later traveled farther west to Egypt. After several centuries of bondage there, they returned to Canaan.

After 1200 B.C. the Hebrews conquered most of the area, defeating the Philistines and other groups. The twelve Hebrew tribes then united to form the kingdom of Israel. About 1000 B.C. their great king David made the city of Jerusalem the capital of the kingdom. For nearly 1,000 years, the Hebrews were the most important group in Palestine. Their history was troubled—first by division into the rival kingdoms of Israel and Judah. (The name "Jew," which was originally applied to a Hebrew of Judah, later was used to refer to any Hebrew.) After 600 B.C. they were ruled by the Assyrians, who forced many of them into exile in Babylonia. Later, the Persians ruled the area. They were followed by Greeks, who conquered the Persians under Alexander the Great. After Alexander's death, some of his followers founded the Seleucid dynasty in Mesopotamia. Palestine fell under their rule.

In 167 B.C. the Jews, under leaders called Maccabees, revolted against the Seleucids. They established a second kingdom of Judah, which lasted to about 60 B.C.

But long before, the Hebrews had developed Judaism, the first lasting monotheistic religion. (A monotheistic religion recognizes only one god.) Judaism gave a central place to Palestine, which the Jews called Israel. It was believed to be a land promised to the Jews by God in the past and a land to which they would return in the future.

Rome and Christianity

From 63 B.C. to about A.D. 630, Palestine was part of the Roman Empire and the Byzantine Empire. During the 1st century A.D. the Jews revolted against Roman rule, and most of them were driven from the land as a result of their rebellion.

The most important development in this

Arabs watch as Jews pray at the Wailing Wall in Jerusalem, a city held sacred by Christians, Jews, and Muslims. The present conflict over Palestine involves issues of land and culture that are deeply rooted in history.

period in Palestine was the birth of another major religion, Christianity. For several centuries after the expulsion of the Jews, most of the people of Palestine were Christians. Because Palestine was the land where Jesus Christ lived and died, it is a land holy to Christians throughout the world.

The Arabs and Islam

The third period in the early history of Palestine lasted from about A.D. 630 to the early 20th century. Shortly after 630, Palestine was conquered by the Arabs, a people from the Arabian Peninsula who had recently been united by the new religion of Islam. There continued to be Jewish and Christian minorities. But from then until the 20th century, most of the people of Palestine were Arab and Muslim. (Followers of Islam are called Muslims.)

Throughout this period, Palestine was usually part of some Muslim state. The main exception to this was the period of the 1100's, when the area was ruled by Christian Crusaders from Europe. After 1500, Palestine became part of the Ottoman Empire.

Palestine is also important to Muslims. They believe that Mohammed, the founder of Islam, made a miraculous journey to heaven from the city of Jerusalem. Thus Palestine is called the Holy Land by three religions, although for different reasons.

▶ JEWISH AND ARAB NATIONALISM

In the late 19th and early 20th centuries, two nationalist movements—both centered on Palestine—began to develop. The first was modern Jewish nationalism, or Zionism. (The term comes from the name "Zion," which was originally given to a hill in Jerusalem but was later used loosely to refer to the ancient home of the Jewish people.) The Zionists wanted to rebuild a Jewish nation in Palestine. From the 1880's on, large numbers of Jews from Europe moved to Palestine in the hope of doing this.

By the early 20th century, a movement of Arab nationalism was developing. Many of the Arabs of western Asia wanted to be free from Ottoman rule. This movement was not focused specifically on Palestine, as Zionism was. But its followers did consider Palestine and its Arabic-speaking population to be part of the Arab community. Thus the stage was set for the clash of Jews and Arabs over Palestine.

▶ THE BRITISH MANDATE

During World War I, the Ottoman Empire sided with Germany and was defeated by the Allies. Most of its territories were divided. From the end of World War I until after World War II, the British controlled Palestine. Britain's rule was called a mandate because the British governed under a charter, or mandate, from the League of

Nations. This charter placed certain obligations on the British. The most prominent was to promote the development of a Jewish "national home" in Palestine.

The British mandate included all of what is now Israel and Jordan. The obligation to promote a Jewish national home applied only to the area west of the Jordan River. East of the river, the Arab state of Transjordan, which was later called Jordan, was established.

There were two main developments in the 30 years of British rule. The first was the emergence of a Jewish national home, through Jewish immigration. This was caused in particular by the persecution of Jews in Europe, which reached horrible proportions under the Nazis during World War II. In 1922 the population of Palestine west of the Jordan River was estimated at about 89,000 Jews and 663,000 Arabs. By 1946 there were over 600,000 Jews and 1,300,000 Arabs. The second feature of British rule was the failure of the British to bring about an agreement between Jewish nationalists and Arab nationalists.

▶PARTITION

By 1947, the British were exhausted by World War II and frustrated by their inability to harmonize Arab and Jewish nationalism. They turned the issue of Palestine over to the newly formed United Nations. In November, 1947, the United Nations recommended the partition of Palestine west of the Jordan River into separate Jewish and Arab states.

The Jews of Palestine and Zionists elsewhere generally accepted this decision. The Arabs of Palestine and Arab nationalists generally rejected it. Thus, the first modern war over Palestine occurred. The new Jewish state of Israel was declared in May, 1948. War broke out immediately between Jews and Arabs. By 1949, Israel had been successful in preserving itself. As a result of the conflict, it obtained most of Palestine west of the Jordan river. The portion known as the West Bank fell to Jordan, and Egypt occupied the Gaza Strip along the coast.

▶THE PALESTINIAN PROBLEM

Palestine has been one of the main causes of continuing tension and hostility between Israel and the Arab countries since 1948. Until 1979 no Arab country had recognized Israel. There were Arab-Israeli wars in 1956, 1967, and 1973. In the 1967 war, Israel occupied the West Bank and the Gaza Strip, bringing all of Britain's former mandate west of the Jordan River under its control. Only in 1979 did Egypt and Israel conclude a peace treaty. Most of the other Arab countries opposed this treaty.

But peace between Israel and the Arab countries would not necessarily solve the problems of modern Palestine. This is because the Arab-Israeli war of 1948 created several groups of Palestinian Arabs. About 10 percent of the Palestinian Arabs stayed in their homes in what became Israel. About 40 percent stayed in their homes in the West Bank and the Gaza Strip. But about 50 percent of the Arabs of Palestine fled their homes in the course of the fighting. Most of them became refugees in neighboring Arab countries. For a variety of reasons, most of these refugees and their descendants neither returned to their homes nor were absorbed in other countries. Many of them continued to live in refugee camps.

By 1980, there were roughly 4,000,000 Palestinian Arabs. Of these, 500,000 lived

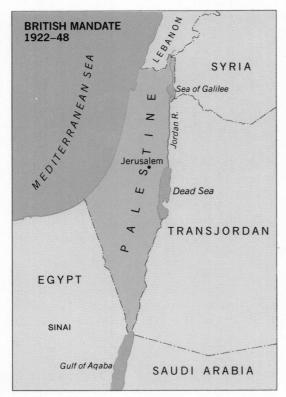

BRITISH MANDATE 1922–48

344

in Israel. (With further Jewish immigration, Israel's population had meanwhile grown to more than 3,000,000.) The rest of the Palestinian Arabs were divided approximately as follows: 1,150,000 in the Gaza Strip and the West Bank; 1,150,000 in Jordan; 400,000 in Lebanon; and 800,000 scattered in other Arab countries, Europe, and the Americas.

The "Palestinian problem" is the question of what will happen to these groups of Palestinian Arabs. For all or most of them, should there be a Palestinian Arab homeland? If so, where? Should the refugees return to their former homes, or should they be resettled elsewhere?

These questions have caused a great deal of strife since 1948. For most of the 1950's and 1960's, the Palestinian Arabs themselves had little to say about these issues. Governments of Arab countries took the lead in dealing with the problem. But since the mid-1960's, several Palestinian Arab movements have emerged. The most important of these is the Palestine Liberation Organization (PLO).

The different Palestinian Arab groups have had different aims. But most of them have shared at least the goal of replacing Israel with a predominantly Arab state. Most Israelis have opposed the creation of a Pal-estinian Arab state, fearing that it would mean the elimination of Israel. Attempts by other parties to get the Palestinian Arab movements and the Israelis to agree to accept two states—Israel and a Palestinian Arab state—have been unsuccessful.

The 1979 treaty between Israel and Egypt discussed, in general terms, the establishment of a Palestinian homeland in the Gaza Strip and the West Bank. But disagreement continued over how such a homeland should be set up and governed, and the Palestinian Arab groups did not approve the treaty.

In the effort to attain their goals, the Palestinian Arab movements have committed acts of violence against Israelis and others around the world. Israel has responded with acts of violence against the Palestinian Arab movements and their supporters. From time to time, the Palestinian Arab movements have also clashed with Arab governments that have tried to restrict their activities.

What will happen in the future is unknown. Many observers think that peace will not come to the Middle East until the Palestinian problem is solved—and its solution may take a long time.

JAMES JANKOWSKI
University of Colorado

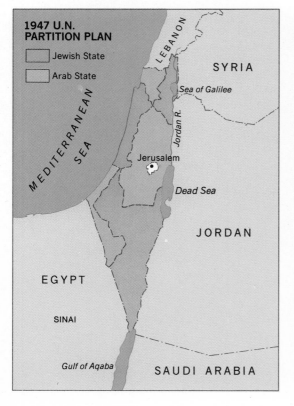

345

Africans believe that the spoken word is more powerful than the written word.

AFRICAN LITERATURE

An African philosopher once said, "Whenever an old man dies, it is as though a library had been burned to the ground." The philosopher said this because for centuries, the traditional literature of Africa was not written down. It was performed, and it was handed down from parent to child by word of mouth.

This article concerns the literature of black Africa (the part of the continent south of the Sahara) in its traditional and modern forms. The African nations that border the Mediterranean Sea belong to a different cultural tradition. Their literature and the literature of Europeans who settled in Africa will not be discussed here.

▶THE ORAL TRADITION

Literature, as we think of it, is written. But the traditional forms of African literature—stories, poems, and proverbs—are spoken and chanted. Something basic in the African approach to life and art resists the very notion of written records.

Africans believe that the spoken word is much more powerful than the written word. The spoken word is also an art and a celebration of life, to be shared by all who live in the community. Like life, this art constantly changes. When a story is repeated, it will be different. The storyteller's costume will have changed, and new verses will have been added to the song. And the audience, joining in singing and clapping, will be different, too. Each listener will be older and wiser than the last time.

Art in Africa is never just for fun. It has a purpose. Stories and poems are used to teach the duties and beliefs of the community. This knowledge is taught by the older people. Some of the truths that people have always lived by are dramatized in spoken performances, in masquerades, and in rituals. The members of the audience understand according to their ages. A story may mean one thing to a grandmother who tells it in the cool of the evening. It may mean another to the children eagerly listening. Everyone laughs, and everyone learns something appropriate.

Small children are encouraged to sharpen their wits by exchanging riddles such as "Going, they talk a lot; coming back, they keep silent." (Answer: water gourds. Empty gourds rattle together—"talk"—on the way to be filled. Full gourds do not rattle.) As the children grow older, they learn to tell stories well. They also flavor their everyday speech with proverbs, such as "Speed ends, distance continues." Beautiful and polite speech is required of adults. But not everyone goes on to become a famous storyteller. Those who do become storytellers must learn to play musical instruments—usually a guitar or harp—because music is an important part of this oral literature.

▶ORAL FORMS OF AFRICAN LITERATURE

There are many different kinds of traditional spoken literature in Africa. Trickster tales are very popular. These stories are about clever characters who outwit people and animals and humorously escape difficult situations. In western Sudan and in southern Africa, such stories are told about the hare. The spider, Anansi, is the mischievous, greedy hero of trickster tales in Ghana, Liberia, and Sierra Leone. In Nigeria and Cameroon, the tortoise is the cleverest animal. Sometimes, as in Benin (Dahomey) and Tanzania, the trickster is a human, or partly human, being. A god may also be a trickster. The Yoruba of Nigeria call this god Elegba.

Trickster stories were carried to the New World by Africans. The hare became Brer Rabbit. Anansi stories are still told in Jamaica, Surinam, and Belize (British Honduras). In the Carolinas and Georgia in the southern United States, Anansi became Aunt Nancy, a clever old woman.

Certain songs that are sung and stories that are told by young girls (like those about pale fox told among the Dogon of Mali) encourage young men to think of marriage. Tales of heroic ancestors, sung on the eve of battle, will inspire young men to brave deeds. Poems praising the gods and spirits are meant to persuade them to bring good fortune to the community.

In some parts of Africa south of the Sa-

hara, heroic or epic poetry still exists. (An epic is a long poem that tells the story of a legendary hero and often weaves the ideals and traditions of a people into the story.) The singing or chanting of these long poems may take hours or even several days. Such poetry requires an excellent memory. It also requires the ability to improvise (to make up as you go along). These things are beyond most people's skill. Therefore, the people who recite African epics are professional singers and storytellers.

Often these professionals are members of a special family or social group. In Mali, they are known as *djeli;* in eastern Zaïre, they are called *karisi.* In Cameroon and in Gabon, the bards, or heroic singers, bear the same name as the instrument they play and the type of tale they recite—*mvet.*

In return for an exhausting performance, the grateful community gives these professional bards food, money, and praise. But the performers must be good. African audiences expect the best and are critical. Many singers have to please an invisible as well as a visible audience. In Nigeria the professional Bini storyteller sings special songs for the witches and spirits of the night, who dance to the music and are thought to be angry if the songs end before they have finished their dances.

Sundiata is the national epic of the Malinke people of Mali. It honors the founder of the Mali empire, who was unable to walk until he was 7 years old but grew up to be a remarkable hunter, warrior, and magician. *Lianja* tells the fabulous story of the epic hero of the Mongo people of Zaïre. Liyongo, the spear lord, gives his name to an epic sung in the languages of eastern and central Africa. These are only three of the many epics that represent African imaginations at their greatest power.

Today some of these heroic poems have been written down. Times have changed in Africa, and there is a danger that young people who have talent for the profession will not choose to become bards. Several versions of *Sundiata* have been translated into English, as have stories of the deeds of Chaka, the Zulu warrior chief, and parts of *Lianja.* To the ruling class of Ethiopia, the written word was always more important than the spoken word. In Ethiopia the epic story of Solomon and Sheba, called *The Glory of Kings,* has been read for many centuries.

▶ WRITTEN FORMS OF AFRICAN LITERATURE

With the coming of European missionaries in the 18th and 19th centuries, African languages were written down. European schools were started in which Africans learned to read and write not only their own languages but also European languages. This learning produced a new literature—short stories, poems, and novels that were never meant to be recited and plays that were meant to be performed on a stage rather than in a village square.

Some of these literary forms, new to Africans, have been explored by African writers in their own languages. But those who write in English and French can hope for more readers. For this reason most recent African literature has been written in these languages. African writing in French developed in the regions once occupied by the French. African literature in English comes from countries in eastern, western, and southern Africa, where for a time English-speaking people ruled.

Because African societies are quite different from one another, some African writers have asked themselves this question: Is it possible to speak of the "African" qualities of literature? In other words, can literature express ideas that truly reflect all of black Africa? Those who have answered "yes" are known as the negritude poets and novelists. Most of them write in French.

The Spirit of Negritude

It was a West Indian from the island of Martinique, Aimé Césaire, who first used the word "negritude." Cesaire had been influenced by the American literary move-

---

Traditional and Modern African Literature

Benin (Dahomey)
Dahomean Narrative: A Cross-Cultural Analysis by Melville J. Herskovits and Frances S. Herskovits.

Cameroon
Houseboy by Ferdinand Oyono.
Old Man and the Medal by Ferdinand Oyono.

Ethiopia
Fire on the Mountain and Other Ethiopian Stories by Harold Courlander and Wolf Leslau.
Shinega's Village by Sahle Sellassie; translated by Wolf Leslau.

Ghana
The Adventures of Spider by Joyce Cooper Arkhurst.
Guardians of the Sacred Word, ed. by Kofi Awoonor.
More Adventures of Spider by Joyce Cooper.
Vulture-Vulture- by Efua T. Sutherland.

Guinea
The Dark Child by Camara Laye.

Kenya
The River Between by James Ngugi.
Weep Not Child by James Ngugi.

Mali
Sundiata: An Epic of Old Mali by D. T. Niane.

Nigeria
Arrow of God by Chinua Achebe.
The Calabash of Wisdom and Other Igbo Stories by Romanus Egudu.
Lion and the Jewel by Wole Soyinka.
My Life in the Bush of Ghosts by Amos Tutuola.
The Palm-Wine Drinkard by Amos Tutuola.

Poetic Heritage: Igbo Traditional Verse by Romanus Egudu and Donatus Nwoga.
Sweet Words: Storytelling Events in Benin by Dan Ben-Amos.
Things Fall Apart by Chinua Achebe.
Yoruba Poetry by H.U. Beier.
Yoruba Proverbs by Bernth Lindfors and Oyekan Owomoyela.

Senegal
Selected Poems by Léopold S. C. Senghor.
Tales of Amadou Koumba by Birago Diop.

South Africa
Chaka: An Historical Romance by Thomas Mofolo; translated by F. H. Dutton.
Down Second Avenue: Growing up in a South African Ghetto by Ezekiel Mphahlele.
Lion on the Path and Other African Stories by Hugh Tracey.
Zulu Poems by Mazisi Kunene.

Zaïre
The Mwindo Epic from the Banyanga by Daniel Biebuyck and Kahombo C. Mateene.
Myths and Legends of the Congo by Jan Knappert.

Anthologies
African Assertion: A Critical Anthology of African Literature, ed. by Austin J. Shelton, Jr.
African Myths and Tales, ed. by Susan Feldman.
Leaf and Bone: African Praise Poems, ed. by Judith Gleason.
Poems of Black Africa, ed. by Wole Soyinka.
Yes and No: The Intimate Folklore of Africa by Alta Jablow.

ment of the 1920's known as the Harlem Renaissance. His greatest poem, *Return to My Native Land,* was published in 1939. In this poem, he defined negritude as a celebration of blackness. The title of the poem points to a desire for a non-European way of life in the place where he grew up.

Césaire's friend Léopold Sédar Senghor became the president of Senegal and the most important writer of his generation. Senghor defined negritude as the cultural heritage, the values, and the spirit of black African civilization. In his poems, Senghor longs to be a child again, looking up into the peaceful face of his mother.

To the negritude writers, education in Paris—or even in French-language schools in Africa—meant that a person was changed by the European world and was not as African as before. Such a person would be less able to understand African problems. The works of Tchicaya U Tam'si, a poet from the Congo (Brazzaville), reflect the desire to return to an understanding of his own suffering and the suffering of his people.

Césaire wrote of return to his native land; Senghor, of the return to cultural heritage; and Tchicaya, of return to understanding. But in a novel called *The Dark Child,* by Camara Laye of Guinea, the going-back aspect of negritude is most simply and beautifully expressed. From this novel the reader may learn how it feels to grow up in an African village. And one may learn how it feels to say good-bye, perhaps forever, to the land of one's ancestors.

Another feeling expressed by negritude authors is anger. It is an anger that attacks the white world for inhumanity—for racism, for concern with wealth and material things, and for pretending one thing but being another. This anger may be seen in the novels of Ferdinand Oyono from Cameroon, especially in *Houseboy,* the story of an African servant in a white household.

Other Attitudes

Wole Soyinka, a Nigerian playwright, has a different view. To him, for a black person to insist on negritude is as silly as for a tiger to insist on "tigritude." Soyinka wrote *A Dance of the Forests* for the celebration of Nigerian independence in 1960. This play is

a fantasy in which traditional gods and spirits call up a small group of ancestors to accuse them of participating in the European slave trade. "Do not romanticize old Africa," the play is saying.

This no-nonsense attitude is shared by Ezekiel Mphahlele, an exiled South African writer, and by most Africans writing in English. To them, Senghor's homesickness has seemed self-indulgent, and his idea of traditional African life unrealistic.

The Nigerian novelist Chinua Achebe has recorded the strife within the traditional African community. He says it is useless to deny social change—the problem is how to meet it. His novels ask whether modern Nigerian leaders can develop the strength of character of certain old chiefs and priests who resisted European ways. *Things Fall Apart* (1958) and *Arrow of God* (1964) both deal with such heroic old men in a time of social change.

▶**AFRICAN LITERATURE AS WORLD LITERATURE**

The question remains—is it possible to speak of the African qualities of this literature? The pain of feeling separated from one's own people has been expressed by writers in many parts of the world, as well as by African writers. And Soyinka's humor and richness of language are sometimes like Shakespeare's. Thus, African writing is a part of world literature.

On the other hand, African literature, traditional or modern, is about a place many people have never visited, even in imagination. It is a place worth getting to know. The sights and sounds are unique. The rain beats heavily on tin roofs and thatched roofs. When the rain stops, a small bird begins to sing in a mango tree. Then people come out, talking. On their way they meet others and stop for a while to talk some more. The conversation may be in any one of the more than 800 languages spoken on the continent, but it is undeniably African. In the spoken word may be found what some African writers have called the genius of black civilization. And in the spoken word there is magic. The spoken word is the source of all African literature.

JUDITH GLEASON
Author, *Orisha: The Gods of Yorubaland*

349

GEORGIA O'KEEFFE (1887–)

Bones bleached white by the desert sun, flowers, rolling hills, rocks, trees, and the sky itself are frequent subjects of paintings by Georgia O'Keeffe, one of the most original artists in the United States. Her works portray nature simply but dramatically, with precise lines and glowing colors.

Georgia O'Keeffe was born on a farm in Sun Prairie, Wisconsin, on November 15, 1887. At the age of 16, she went to study art in Chicago. She later continued her studies in New York City. In 1912 she accepted a position as an art teacher at a small college in Texas.

Some of her drawings were exhibited in New York City in 1916, at the gallery of Alfred Stieglitz, the photographer. They were well received. In 1918, O'Keeffe moved to New York to paint. She became friendly with a group of artists who gathered at Stieglitz' gallery, and in 1924 she married Stieglitz and joined him in running the gallery. Some of her most famous works date from this period. In flower studies such as *Black Iris,* she would enlarge a flower and paint it in its simplest form by eliminating detail. During those years, she also painted many views of the New York City skyline.

Following the death of Stieglitz in 1946, O'Keeffe moved to New Mexico. She settled down in an adobe house near Abiquiu, on the edge of the desert. The wild juniper and aspen trees around her house and the stark hills of the desert became inspirations for her paintings, as did animal bones found on walks through the desert.

In all her works, O'Keeffe combines simplicity with great strength. She is known as an artist who draws inspiration from nature and develops it into an artistic expression wholly her own. You can see her paintings in many important museums.

PATRICK STEWART
Williams College

Yellow Hickory Leaves With Daisy, by Georgia O'Keeffe, who uses flowers and other aspects of nature as subjects for her paintings.

350

INTERNATIONAL STATISTICAL SUPPLEMENT

(as of January 1, 1980)

Independent Nations of the World

The Congress of the United States

  Senate

  House of Representatives

United States Cabinet

United States Supreme Court

Governors of the United States

Prime Ministers of the Provinces of Canada

INDEPENDENT NATIONS OF THE WORLD

NATION	CAPITAL	AREA (in sq mi)	POPULATION (estimate)	GOVERNMENT
Afghanistan	Kabul	250,000	15,100,000	Babrak Karmal—president
Albania	Tirana	11,100	2,600,000	Enver Hoxha—communist party secretary Mehmet Shehu—premier
Algeria	Algiers	919,593	18,500,000	Benjedid Chadli—president
Angola	Luanda	481,351	6,800,000	José Eduardo dos Santos—president
Argentina	Buenos Aires	1,068,297	26,500,000	Jorge Rafael Videla—president
Australia	Canberra	2,967,895	14,400,000	Malcolm Fraser—prime minister
Austria	Vienna	32,374	7,500,000	Rudolf Kirchschläger—president Bruno Kreisky—chancellor
Bahamas	Nassau	5,380	230,000	Lynden O. Pindling—prime minister
Bahrain	Manama	240	350,000	Isa ibn Sulman al-Khalifa—head of government
Bangladesh	Dacca	55,598	85,000,000	Ziaur Rahman—president
Barbados	Bridgetown	168	250,000	J. M. G. Adams—prime minister
Belgium	Brussels	11,781	9,900,000	Baudouin I—king Wilfried Martens—premier
Benin (Dahomey)	Porto-Novo	43,483	3,400,000	Mathieu Kerekou—president
Bhutan	Thimbu	18,147	1,200,000	Jigme Singye Wangchuk—king
Bolivia	La Paz Sucre	424,163	5,100,000	Lydia Gueiler Tejada—interim prime minister
Botswana	Gaborone	231,804	730,000	Sir Seretse Khama—president
Brazil	Brasília	3,286,478	116,000,000	João Figueiredo—president
Bulgaria	Sofia	42,823	8,800,000	Todor Zhivkov—communist party secretary Stanko Todorov—premier
Burma	Rangoon	261,217	31,200,000	U Ne Win—president U Maung Maung Kha—prime minister
Burundi	Bujumbura	10,747	4,300,000	Jean-Baptiste Bagaza—president
Cambodia (Kampuchea)	Pnompenh	69,898	5,000,000	Heng Samrin—president
Cameroon	Yaoundé	183,569	8,100,000	Ahmadou Ahidjo—president
Canada	Ottawa	3,851,809	23,600,000	Joe Clark—prime minister
Cape Verde	Praia	1,557	310,000	Aristides Pereira—president
Central African Republic	Bangui	240,535	2,100,000	David Dacko—president
Chad	N'Djemena	495,754	4,300,000	Goukouni Oueddei—president

NATION	CAPITAL	AREA (in sq mi)	POPULATION (estimate)	GOVERNMENT
Chile	Santiago	292,257	10,900,000	Augusto Pinochet Ugarte—president
China	Peking	3,705,390	975,000,000	Hua Kuo-feng—communist party chairman and premier
Colombia	Bogotá	439,736	25,600,000	Julio César Turbay Ayala—president
Comoros	Moroni	838	370,000	Ahmed Abdallah—president
Congo	Brazzaville	132,047	1,500,000	Denis Sassou-Nguessou—president
Costa Rica	San José	19,575	2,100,000	Rodrigo Carazo Odio—president
Cuba	Havana	44,218	9,700,000	Fidel Castro—president
Cyprus	Nicosia	3,572	620,000	Spyros Kyprianou—president
Czechoslovakia	Prague	49,370	15,200,000	Gustáv Husák—communist party secretary and president Lubomir Strougal—premier
Denmark	Copenhagen	16,629	5,100,000	Margrethe II—queen Anker Jorgensen—premier
Djibouti	Djibouti	8,494	110,000	Hassan Gouled—president
Dominica	Roseau	290	81,000	Oliver Seraphine—prime minister
Dominican Republic	Santo Domingo	18,816	5,100,000	Antonio Guzmán—president
Ecuador	Quito	109,483	7,800,000	Jaime Roldós Aguilera—president
Egypt	Cairo	386,660	40,000,000	Anwar el-Sadat—president Mustafa Khalil—premier
El Salvador	San Salvador	8,124	4,400,000	Ruben Zamora—head of junta
Equatorial Guinea	Malabo	10,831	350,000	Teodoro Obiang Nguema—president
Ethiopia	Addis Ababa	471,777	29,700,000	Mengistu Haile Mariam—head of state
Fiji	Suva	7,055	600,000	Ratu Sir Kamisese Mara—prime minister
Finland	Helsinki	130,120	4,800,000	Urho K. Kekkonen—president Mauno Koivisto—premier
France	Paris	211,207	53,300,000	Valéry Giscard d'Estaing—president Raymond Barre—premier
Gabon	Libreville	103,346	540,000	Albert B. Bongo—president
Gambia	Banjul	4,361	570,000	Sir Dauda K. Jawara—president
Germany (East)	East Berlin	41,768	16,800,000	Erich Honecker—communist party secretary Willi Stoph—premier
Germany (West)	Bonn	95,976	61,400,000	Karl Carstens—president Helmut Schmidt—chancellor
Ghana	Accra	92,099	11,000,000	Hilla Limann—president
Greece	Athens	50,944	9,400,000	Constantine Tsatsos—president Constantine Caramanlis—premier
Grenada	St. George's	133	100,000	Maurice Bishop—prime minister

NATION	CAPITAL	AREA (in sq mi)	POPULATION (estimate)	GOVERNMENT
Guatemala	Guatemala City	42,042	6,600,000	Romeo Lucas García—president
Guinea	Conakry	94,926	4,800,000	Sékou Touré—president
Guinea-Bissau	Bissau	13,948	550,000	Luiz de Almeida Cabral—president
Guyana	Georgetown	83,000	820,000	Arthur Chung—president Forbes Burnham—prime minister
Haiti	Port-au-Prince	10,714	4,800,000	Jean-Claude Duvalier—president
Honduras	Tegucigalpa	43,277	3,400,000	Policarpo Paz García—head of state
Hungary	Budapest	35,919	10,700,000	János Kádár—communist party secretary György Lazar—premier
Iceland	Reykjavik	39,768	220,000	Kristján Eldjárn—president Benedikt Gröndal— interim prime minister
India	New Delhi	1,269,340	640,000,000	Neelam Sanjiva Reddy—president Charan Singh—interim prime minister
Indonesia	Jakarta	735,269	145,000,000	Suharto—president
Iran	Teheran	636,294	34,200,000	Ruhollah Khomeini—head of state
Iraq	Baghdad	167,925	12,300,000	Saddam Hussein—president
Ireland	Dublin	27,136	3,200,000	Patrick Hillery—president Charles J. Haughey—prime minister
Israel	Jerusalem	8,019	3,700,000	Yitzhak Navon—president Menahem Begin—prime minister
Italy	Rome	116,303	56,800,000	Alessandro Pertini—president Francesco Cossiga—premier
Ivory Coast	Abidjan	124,503	7,600,000	Félix Houphouët-Boigny—president
Jamaica	Kingston	4,244	2,100,000	Michael N. Manley—prime minister
Japan	Tokyo	143,737	115,000,000	Hirohito—emperor Masayoshi Ohira—premier
Jordan	Amman	37,738	3,000,000	Hussein I—king Sharif Abdul Hamid Sharaf—premier
Kenya	Nairobi	224,959	15,000,000	Daniel Arap Moi—president
Kiribati	Tarawa	264	56,000	Ieremia Tabai—president
Korea (North)	Pyongyang	46,540	17,000,000	Kim Il Sung—president Li Jong-ok—premier
Korea (South)	Seoul	38,025	37,000,000	Choi Kyu Hah—president Shin Hyon Hwack—premier
Kuwait	Kuwait	6,880	1,200,000	Jaber al-Ahmed al-Sabah—head of state
Laos	Vientiane	91,429	3,500,000	Souphanouvong—president Kaysone Phomvihan—premier
Lebanon	Beirut	4,015	3,000,000	Elias Sarkis—president Selim al-Hoss—premier

NATION	CAPITAL	AREA (in sq mi)	POPULATION (estimate)	GOVERNMENT
Lesotho	Maseru	11,720	1,300,000	Moshoeshoe II—king Leabua Jonathan—prime minister
Liberia	Monrovia	43,000	1,700,000	William R. Tolbert—president
Libya	Tripoli	679,360	2,700,000	Muammar el-Qaddafi—president
Liechtenstein	Vaduz	61	25,000	Francis Joseph II—prince
Luxembourg	Luxembourg	999	360,000	Jean—grand duke Pierre Werner—premier
Madagascar	Antananarivo	226,657	8,300,000	Didier Ratsiraka—president
Malawi	Lilongwe	45,747	5,700,000	H. Kamuzu Banda—president
Malaysia	Kuala Lumpur	127,316	13,000,000	Sultan Ahmad Shah—paramount ruler Hussein Onn—prime minister
Maldives	Male	115	140,000	Maumoon Abdul Gayoom—president
Mali	Bamako	478,765	6,300,000	Moussa Traoré—president
Malta	Valletta	122	340,000	Sir Anthony Mamo—president Dom Mintoff—prime minister
Mauritania	Nouakchott	397,954	1,500,000	Mohammed Mahmoud Ould Luly—president
Mauritius	Port Louis	790	920,000	Sir Seewoosagur Ramgoolam—prime minister
Mexico	Mexico City	761,602	67,000,000	José López Portillo—president
Monaco	Monaco-Ville	0.6	25,000	Rainier III—prince
Mongolia	Ulan Bator	604,248	1,600,000	Yumzhagiyn Tsedenbal—communist party secretary
Morocco	Rabat	172,413	19,000,000	Hassan II—king Maati Bouabid—premier
Mozambique	Maputo	309,494	10,000,000	Samora Machel—president
Nauru	—	8	8,000	Hammer DeRoburt—president
Nepal	Katmandu	54,362	13,400,000	Birendra Bir Bikram Shah Deva—king Kirtinidhi Bista—prime minister
Netherlands	Amsterdam	15,770	14,000,000	Juliana—queen Andreas A. M. van Agt—premier
New Zealand	Wellington	103,736	3,100,000	Robert D. Muldoon—prime minister
Nicaragua	Managua	50,193	2,400,000	Sergio Ramírez Mercado—head of junta
Niger	Niamey	489,190	5,000,000	Seyni Kountche—head of government
Nigeria	Lagos	356,668	72,000,000	Shehu Shagari—president
Norway	Oslo	125,181	4,100,000	Olav V—king Odvar Nordli—prime minister
Oman	Muscat	82,030	820,000	Qabus ibn Said—sultan

NATION	CAPITAL	AREA (in sq mi)	POPULATION (estimate)	GOVERNMENT
Pakistan	Islamabad	310,403	77,000,000	Mohammed Zia ul-Haq—president
Panama	Panama City	29,761	1,800,000	Aristides Royo—president
Papua New Guinea	Port Moresby	178,260	3,000,000	Michael Somare—prime minister
Paraguay	Asunción	157,047	2,900,000	Alfredo Stroessner—president
Peru	Lima	496,223	16,800,000	Francisco Morales Bermúdez—president
Philippines	Manila	115,830	46,400,000	Ferdinand E. Marcos—president
Poland	Warsaw	120,724	35,100,000	Edward Gierek—communist party secretary Piotr Jaroszewicz—premier
Portugal	Lisbon	35,553	9,800,000	António Ramalho Eanes—president Francisco Sá Carneiro—premier
Qatar	Doha	4,247	200,000	Khalifa ibn Hamad al-Thani—head of government
Rumania	Bucharest	91,700	21,900,000	Nicolae Ceauşescu—communist party secretary Ilie Verdet—premier
Rwanda	Kigali	10,169	4,500,000	Juvénal Habyalimana—president
St. Lucia	Castries	238	113,000	Allan Louisy—prime minister
St. Vincent and the Grenadines	Kingstown	150	100,000	Milton Cato—prime minister
São Tomé and Príncipe	São Tomé	372	83,000	Manuel Pinto da Costa—president
Saudi Arabia	Riyadh	829,997	7,900,000	Khalid ibn Abdul-Aziz—king
Senegal	Dakar	75,750	5,400,000	Léopold Senghor—president
Seychelles	Victoria	107	62,000	France Albert René—president
Sierre Leone	Freetown	27,700	3,300,000	Siaka P. Stevens—president
Singapore	Singapore	224	2,300,000	Benjamin H. Sheares—president Lee Kuan Yew—prime minister
Solomon Islands	Honiara	10,983	200,000	Peter Kenilorea—prime minister
Somalia	Mogadishu	246,200	3,400,000	Mohammed Siad Barre—head of government
South Africa	Pretoria Cape Town	471,444	27,700,000	Marais Viljoen—president Pieter W. Botha—prime minister
Spain	Madrid	194,897	37,100,000	Juan Carlos I—king Adolfo Suárez González—premier
Sri Lanka (Ceylon)	Colombo	25,332	14,300,000	Junius R. Jayewardene—president Ranasinghe Premadasa—prime minister
Sudan	Khartoum	967,497	17,400,000	Gaafar al-Numeiry—president
Surinam	Paramaribo	63,037	400,000	Henck A. E. Arron—prime minister
Swaziland	Mbabane	6,704	500,000	Sobhuza II—king

NATION	CAPITAL	AREA (in sq mi)	POPULATION (estimate)	GOVERNMENT
Sweden	Stockholm	173,731	8,300,000	Carl XVI Gustaf—king Thorbjörn Fälldin—prime minister
Switzerland	Bern	15,941	6,300,000	Georges-André Chevallaz—president
Syria	Damascus	71,498	8,000,000	Hafez al-Assad—president Mohammed Ali al-Halabi—premier
Taiwan	Taipei	13,885	16,800,000	Chiang Ching-kuo—president Sun Yun-suan—premier
Tanzania	Dar es Salaam	364,898	16,600,000	Julius K. Nyerere—president
Thailand	Bangkok	198,456	45,100,000	Bhumibol Adulyadej—king Kriangsak Chamanand—premier
Togo	Lomé	21,622	2,400,000	Gnassingbe Eyadema—president
Tonga	Nuku'alofa	270	93,000	Taufa'ahau Tupou IV—king Prince Tu'ipelehake—prime minister
Trinidad & Tobago	Port of Spain	1,980	1,100,000	Sir Ellis Clarke—president Eric Williams—prime minister
Tunisia	Tunis	63,170	6,100,000	Habib Bourguiba—president
Turkey	Ankara	301,381	43,200,000	Fahri Korutürk—president Suleyman Demirel—prime minister
Tuvalu	Funafuti	10	8,000	Toalipi Lauti—prime minister
Uganda	Kampala	91,134	12,800,000	Godfrey Binaisa—president
U.S.S.R.	Moscow	8,649,512	262,000,000	Leonid I. Brezhnev—communist party secretary and president Aleksei N. Kosygin—premier
United Arab Emirates	Abu Dhabi	32,278	711,000	Zayd ibn Sultan—president
United Kingdom	London	94,226	55,800,000	Elizabeth II—queen Margaret Thatcher—prime minister
United States	Washington, D.C.	3,618,467	220,000,000	James Earl Carter, Jr.—president Walter F. Mondale—vice-president
Upper Volta	Ouagadougou	105,869	6,600,000	Sangoulé Lamizana—president
Uruguay	Montevideo	68,037	2,900,000	Aparicio Méndez—president
Venezuela	Caracas	352,143	13,100,000	Luis Herrera Campíns—president
Vietnam	Hanoi	127,202	50,000,000	Le Duan—communist party secretary Ton Duc Thang—president Pham Van Dong—premier
Western Samoa	Apia	1,097	150,000	Malietoa Tanumafili II—head of state
Yemen (Aden)	Madinat al-Shaab	128,559	1,900,000	Abdul Fatah Ismail—president
Yemen (Sana)	Sana	75,290	5,600,000	Ali Abdullah Saleh—president
Yugoslavia	Belgrade	98,766	22,100,000	Josip Broz Tito—president Veselin Djuranovic—premier
Zaïre	Kinshasa	905,565	27,700,000	Mobutu Sese Seko—president
Zambia	Lusaka	290,585	5,500,000	Kenneth D. Kaunda—president

THE CONGRESS OF THE UNITED STATES

(As of January 1, 1980)

UNITED STATES SENATE

Alabama
Donald W. Stewart (D)
Howell T. Heflin (D)

Alaska
Ted Stevens (R)
Mike Gravel (D)

Arizona
Barry Goldwater (R)
Dennis DeConcini (D)

Arkansas
Dale Bumpers (D)
David H. Pryor (D)

California
Alan Cranston (D)
S. I. Hayakawa (R)

Colorado
Gary W. Hart (D)
William L. Armstrong (R)

Connecticut
Abraham A. Ribicoff (D)
Lowell P. Weicker, Jr. (R)

Delaware
William V. Roth, Jr. (R)
Joseph R. Biden, Jr. (D)

Florida
Lawton Chiles (D)
Richard Stone (D)

Georgia
Herman E. Talmadge (D)
Sam Nunn (D)

Hawaii
Daniel K. Inouye (D)
Spark M. Matsunaga (D)

Idaho
Frank Church (D)
James A. McClure (R)

Illinois
Charles H. Percy (R)
Adlai E. Stevenson (D)

Indiana
Birch Bayh (D)
Richard G. Lugar (R)

Iowa
John C. Culver (D)
Roger W. Jepsen (R)

Kansas
Robert J. Dole (R)
Nancy Landon Kassebaum (R)

Kentucky
Walter Huddleston (D)
Wendell H. Ford (D)

Louisiana
Russell B. Long (D)
J. Bennett Johnston (D)

Maine
Edmund S. Muskie (D)
William S. Cohen (R)

Maryland
Charles M. Mathias, Jr. (R)
Paul S. Sarbanes (D)

Massachusetts
Edward M. Kennedy (D)
Paul E. Tsongas (D)

Michigan
Donald W. Riegle, Jr. (D)
Carl Levin (D)

Minnesota
David F. Durenberger (R)
Rudy Boschwitz (R)

Mississippi
John C. Stennis (D)
Thad Cochran (R)

Missouri
Thomas F. Eagleton (D)
John C. Danforth (R)

Montana
John Melcher (D)
Max Baucus (D)

Nebraska
Edward Zorinsky (D)
J. James Exon (D)

Nevada
Howard W. Cannon (D)
Paul Laxalt (R)

New Hampshire
John A. Durkin (D)
Gordon J. Humphrey (R)

New Jersey
Harrison A. Williams, Jr. (D)
Bill Bradley (D)

New Mexico
Pete V. Domenici (R)
Harrison H. Schmitt (R)

New York
Jacob K. Javits (R)
Daniel P. Moynihan (D)

North Carolina
Jesse Helms (R)
Robert B. Morgan (D)

North Dakota
Milton R. Young (R)
Quentin N. Burdick (D)

Ohio
John H. Glenn, Jr. (D)
Howard M. Metzenbaum (D)

Oklahoma
Henry L. Bellmon (R)
David L. Boren (D)

Oregon
Mark O. Hatfield (R)
Bob Packwood (R)

Pennsylvania
Richard S. Schweiker (R)
H. John Heinz III (R)

Rhode Island
Claiborne Pell (D)
John H. Chafee (R)

South Carolina
Strom Thurmond (R)
Ernest F. Hollings (D)

South Dakota
George McGovern (D)
Larry Pressler (R)

Tennessee
Howard H. Baker, Jr. (R)
James R. Sasser (D)

Texas
John G. Tower (R)
Lloyd M. Bentsen (D)

Utah
E. J. (Jake) Garn (R)
Orrin G. Hatch (R)

Vermont
Robert T. Stafford (R)
Patrick J. Leahy (D)

Virginia
Harry F. Byrd, Jr. (I)
John W. Warner (R)

Washington
Warren G. Magnuson (D)
Henry M. Jackson (D)

West Virginia
Jennings Randolph (D)
Robert C. Byrd (D)

Wisconsin
William Proxmire (D)
Gaylord Nelson (D)

Wyoming
Malcolm Wallop (R)
Alan K. Simpson (R)

(R) Republican
(D) Democrat
(I) Independent

358

UNITED STATES HOUSE OF REPRESENTATIVES

Alabama
1. J. Edwards (R)
2. W. L. Dickinson (R)
3. W. Nichols (D)
4. T. Bevil (D)
5. R. Flippo (D)
6. J. H. Buchanan, Jr. (R)
7. R. Shelby (D)

Alaska
D. Young (R)

Arizona
1. J. J. Rhodes (R)
2. M. K. Udall (D)
3. B. Stump (D)
4. E. Rudd (R)

Arkansas
1. W. V. Alexander, Jr. (D)
2. E. Bethune, Jr. (R)
3. J. P. Hammerschmidt (R)
4. B. Anthony, Jr. (D)

California
1. H. T. Johnson (D)
2. D. H. Clausen (R)
3. R. Matsui (D)
4. V. Fazio (D)
5. J. L. Burton (D)
6. P. Burton (D)
7. G. Miller (D)
8. R. V. Dellums (D)
9. F. H. Stark, Jr. (D)
10. D. Edwards (D)
11. W. H. Royer (R)*
12. P. N. McCloskey, Jr. (R)
13. N. Y. Mineta (D)
14. N. Shumway (R)
15. T. Coelho (D)
16. L. E. Panetta (D)
17. C. Pashayan (R)
18. W. Thomas (R)
19. R. J. Lagomarsino (R)
20. B. M. Goldwater, Jr. (R)
21. J. C. Corman (D)
22. C. J. Moorhead (R)
23. A. C. Beilenson (D)
24. H. A. Waxman (D)
25. E. R. Roybal (D)
26. J. H. Rousselot (R)
27. R. K. Dornan (R)
28. J. Dixon (D)
29. A. F. Hawkins (D)
30. G. E. Danielson (D)
31. C. H. Wilson (D)
32. G. M. Anderson (D)
33. W. Grisham (R)
34. D. Lungren (R)
35. J. Lloyd (D)
36. G. E. Brown, Jr. (D)
37. J. Lewis (R)
38. J. M. Patterson (D)
39. W. Dannemeyer (R)
40. R. E. Badham (R)
41. B. Wilson (R)
42. L. Van Deerlin (D)
43. C. W. Burgener (R)

Colorado
1. P. Schroeder (D)
2. T. E. Wirth (D)
3. R. Kogovsek (D)
4. J. P. Johnson (R)
5. K. Kramer (R)

Connecticut
1. W. R. Cotter (D)
2. C. J. Dodd (D)
3. R. N. Giaimo (D)
4. S. B. McKinney (R)
5. W. Ratchford (D)
6. T. Moffett (D)

Delaware
T. B. Evans, Jr. (R)

Florida
1. E. Hutto (D)
2. D. Fuqua (D)
3. C. E. Bennett (D)
4. W. V. Chappell, Jr. (D)
5. R. Kelly (R)
6. C. W. Young (R)
7. S. M. Gibbons (D)
8. A. P. Ireland (D)
9. B. Nelson (D)
10. L. A. Bafalis (R)
11. D. Mica (D)
12. E. Stack (D)
13. W. Lehman (D)
14. C. D. Pepper (D)
15. D. B. Fascell (D)

Georgia
1. R. B. Ginn (D)
2. M. D. Mathis (D)
3. J. Brinkley (D)
4. E. H. Levitas (D)
5. W. F. Fowler, Jr. (D)
6. N. Gingrich (R)
7. L. P. McDonald (D)
8. B. L. Evans (D)
9. E. L. Jenkins (D)
10. D. D. Barnard, Jr. (D)

Hawaii
1. C. Heftel (D)
2. D. K. Akaka (D)

Idaho
1. S. D. Symms (R)
2. G. V. Hansen (R)

Illinois
1. B. Stewart (D)
2. M. F. Murphy (D)
3. M. A. Russo (D)
4. E. J. Derwinski (R)
5. J. G. Fary (D)
6. H. J. Hyde (R)
7. C. Collins (D)
8. D. Rostenkowski (D)
9. S. R. Yates (D)

10. Vacancy
11. F. Annunzio (D)
12. P. M. Crane (R)
13. R. McClory (R)
14. J. N. Erlenborn (R)
15. T. J. Corcoran (R)
16. J. B. Anderson (R)
17. G. M. O'Brien (R)
18. R. H. Michel (R)
19. T. Railsback (R)
20. P. Findley (R)
21. E. R. Madigan (R)
22. D. Crane (R)
23. C. M. Price (D)
24. P. Simon (D)

Indiana
1. A. Benjamin, Jr. (D)
2. F. J. Fithian (D)
3. J. Brademas (D)
4. D. Quayle (R)
5. E. H. Hillis (R)
6. D. W. Evans (D)
7. J. T. Myers (R)
8. H. Deckard (R)
9. L. H. Hamilton (D)
10. P. R. Sharp (D)
11. A. Jacobs, Jr. (D)

Iowa
1. J. A. S. Leach (R)
2. T. Tauke (R)
3. C. E. Grassley (R)
4. N. Smith (D)
5. T. R. Harkin (D)
6. B. W. Bedell (D)

Kansas
1. K. G. Sebelius (R)
2. J. Jeffries (R)
3. L. Winn, Jr. (R)
4. D. Glickman (D)
5. R. Whittaker (R)

Kentucky
1. C. Hubbard, Jr. (D)
2. W. H. Natcher (D)
3. R. L. Mazzoli (D)
4. G. Snyder (R)
5. T. L. Carter (R)
6. L. Hopkins (R)
7. C. D. Perkins (D)

Louisiana
1. R. L. Livingston, Jr. (R)
2. C. C. Boggs (D)
3. D. C. Treen (R)**
4. C. Leach, Jr. (D)
5. J. Huckaby (D)
6. W. H. Moore (R)
7. J. B. Breaux (D)
8. G. W. Long (D)

Maine
1. D. F. Emery (R)
2. O. Snowe (R)

Maryland
1. R. E. Bauman (R)
2. C. D. Long (D)
3. B. A. Mikulski (D)
4. M. S. Holt (R)
5. G. N. Spellman (D)
6. B. Byron (D)
7. P. J. Mitchell (D)
8. M. Barnes (D)

Massachusetts
1. S. O. Conte (R)
2. E. P. Boland (D)
3. J. D. Early (D)
4. R. F. Drinan (D)
5. J. Shannon (D)
6. N. Mavroules (D)
7. E. J. Markey (D)
8. T. P. O'Neill, Jr. (D)
9. J. J. Moakley (D)
10. M. M. Heckler (R)
11. B. Donnelly (D)
12. G. E. Studds (D)

Michigan
1. J. Conyers, Jr. (D)
2. C. D. Pursell (R)
3. H. Wolpe (D)
4. D. A. Stockman (R)
5. H. S. Sawyer (R)
6. M. R. Carr (D)
7. D. E. Kildee (D)
8. B. Traxler (D)
9. G. A. Vander Jagt (R)
10. D. Albosta (D)
11. R. Davis (R)
12. D. E. Bonior (D)
13. C. C. Diggs, Jr. (D)
14. L. N. Nedzi (D)
15. W. D. Ford (D)
16. J. D. Dingell (D)
17. W. M. Brodhead (D)
18. J. J. Blanchard (D)
19. W. S. Broomfield (R)

Minnesota
1. A. Erdahl (R)
2. T. M. Hagedorn (R)
3. B. Frenzel (R)
4. B. F. Vento (D)
5. M. Sabo (D)
6. R. M. Nolan (D)
7. A. Stangeland (R)
8. J. L. Oberstar (D)

Mississippi
1. J. L. Whitten (D)
2. D. R. Bowen (D)
3. G. V. Montgomery (D)
4. J. Hinson (R)
5. T. Lott (R)

Missouri
1. W. L. Clay (D)
2. R. A. Young (D)
3. R. A. Gephardt (D)
4. I. Skelton (D)

5. R. Bolling (D)
6. E. T. Coleman (R)
7. G. Taylor (R)
8. R. H. Ichord (D)
9. H. L. Volkmer (D)
10. B. D. Burlison (D)

Montana
1. P. Williams (D)
2. R. Marlenee (R)

Nebraska
1. D. Bereuter (R)
2. J. J. Cavanaugh (D)
3. V. Smith (R)

Nevada
J. D. Santini (D)

New Hampshire
1. N. E. D'Amours (D)
2. J. C. Cleveland (R)

New Jersey
1. J. J. Florio (D)
2. W. J. Hughes (D)
3. J. J. Howard (D)
4. F. Thompson, Jr. (D)
5. M. Fenwick (R)
6. E. B. Forsythe (R)
7. A. Maguire (D)
8. R. A. Roe (D)
9. H. C. Hollenbeck (R)
10. P. W. Rodino, Jr. (D)
11. J. G. Minish (D)
12. M. J. Rinaldo (R)
13. J. Courter (R)
14. F. Guarini (D)
15. E. J. Patten (D)

New Mexico
1. M. Lujan, Jr. (R)
2. H. Runnels (D)

New York
1. W. Carney (R)
2. T. J. Downey (D)
3. J. A. Ambro (D)
4. N. F. Lent (R)
5. J. W. Wydler (R)
6. L. L. Wolff (D)
7. J. P. Addabbo (D)
8. B. S. Rosenthal (D)
9. G. Ferraro (D)
10. M. Biaggi (D)
11. J. H. Scheuer (D)
12. S. A. Chisholm (D)
13. S. J. Solarz (D)
14. F. W. Richmond (D)
15. L. C. Zeferetti (D)
16. E. Holtzman (D)
17. J. M. Murphy (D)
18. S. W. Green (R)
19. C. B. Rangel (D)
20. T. Weiss (D)
21. R. Garcia (D)
22. J. B. Bingham (D)
23. P. Peyser (D)
24. R. L. Ottinger (D)
25. H. Fish, Jr. (R)
26. B. A. Gilman (R)

27. M. F. McHugh (D)
28. S. S. Stratton (D)
29. G. Solomon (R)
30. R. C. McEwen (R)
31. D. J. Mitchell (R)
32. J. M. Hanley (D)
33. G. Lee (R)
34. F. Horton (R)
35. B. B. Conable, Jr. (R)
36. J. J. LaFalce (D)
37. H. J. Nowak (D)
38. J. Kemp (R)
39. S. N. Lundine (D)

North Carolina
1. W. B. Jones (D)
2. L. H. Fountain (D)
3. C. O. Whitley, Sr. (D)
4. I. F. Andrews (D)
5. S. L. Neal (D)
6. L. R. Preyer (D)
7. C. Rose (D)
8. W. G. Hefner (D)
9. J. G. Martin (R)
10. J. T. Broyhill (R)
11. L. Gudger (D)

North Dakota
M. Andrews (R)

Ohio
1. W. D. Gradison, Jr. (R)
2. T. A. Luken (D)
3. T. Hall (D)
4. T. Guyer (R)
5. D. L. Latta (R)
6. W. H. Harsha (R)
7. C. J. Brown (R)
8. T. N. Kindness (R)
9. T. L. Ashley (D)
10. C. E. Miller (R)
11. J. W. Stanton (R)
12. S. L. Devine (R)
13. D. J. Pease (D)
14. J. F. Seiberling (D)
15. C. P. Wylie (R)
16. R. Regula (R)
17. J. M. Ashbrook (R)
18. D. Applegate (D)
19. L. Williams (R)
20. M. R. Oakar (D)
21. L. Stokes (D)
22. C. A. Vanik (D)
23. R. M. Mottl (D)

Oklahoma
1. J. R. Jones (D)
2. M. Synar (D)
3. W. W. Watkins (D)
4. T. Steed (D)
5. M. Edwards (R)
6. G. English (D)

Oregon
1. L. AuCoin (D)
2. A. Ullman (D)
3. R. B. Duncan (D)
4. J. Weaver (D)

Pennsylvania
1. M. Myers (D)
2. W. Gray (D)

3. R. F. Lederer (D)
4. C. Dougherty (R)
5. R. T. Schulze (R)
6. G. Yatron (D)
7. R. W. Edgar·(D)
8. P. H. Kostmayer (D)
9. B. Shuster (R)
10. J. M. McDade (R)
11. D. J. Flood (D)
12. J. P. Murtha (D)
13. L. Coughlin (R)
14. W. S. Moorhead (D)
15. D. Ritter (R)
16. R. S. Walker (R)
17. A. E. Ertel (D)
18. D. Walgren (D)
19. W. F. Goodling (R)
20. J. M. Gaydos (D)
21. D. Bailey (D)
22. A. J. Murphy (D)
23. W. Clinger, Jr. (R)
24. M. L. Marks (R)
25. E. Atkinson (D)

Rhode Island
1. F. J. St. Germain (D)
2. E. P. Beard (D)

South Carolina
1. M. J. Davis (D)
2. F. D. Spence (R)
3. B. C. Derrick, Jr. (D)
4. C. Campbell, Jr. (R)
5. K. Holland (D)
6. J. W. Jenrette, Jr. (D)

South Dakota
1. T. A. Daschle (D)
2. J. Abdnor (R)

Tennessee
1. J. H. Quillen (R)
2. J. J. Duncan (R)
3. M. L. Bouquard (D)
4. A. Gore, Jr. (D)
5. W. H. Boner (D)
6. R. L. Beard, Jr. (R)
7. E. Jones (D)
8. H. Ford (D)

Texas
1. S. B. Hall, Jr. (D)
2. C. Wilson (D)
3. J. M. Collins (R)
4. R. Roberts (D)
5. J. A. Mattox (D)
6. P. Gramm (D)
7. B. Archer (R)
8. B. Eckhardt (D)
9. J. Brooks (D)
10. J. J. Pickle (D)
11. J. M. Leath (D)
12. J. C. Wright, Jr. (D)
13. J. E. Hightower (D)
14. J. Wyatt (D)
15. E. de la Garza (D)
16. R. C. White (D)
17. C. Stenholm (D)
18. M. Leland (D)
19. K. Hance (D)
20. H. B. Gonzalez (D)
21. T. Loeffler (R)
22. R. Paul (R)

23. A. Kazen, Jr. (D)
24. M. Frost (D)

Utah
1. G. McKay (D)
2. D. D. Marriott (R)

Vermont
J. M. Jeffords (R)

Virginia
1. P. S. Trible, Jr. (R)
2. G. W. Whitehurst (R)
3. D. E. Satterfield, III (D)
4. R. W. Daniel, Jr. (R)
5. D. Daniel (D)
6. M. C. Butler (R)
7. J. K. Robinson (R)
8. H. E. Harris, II (D)
9. W. C. Wampler (R)
10. J. L. Fisher (D)

Washington
1. J. M. Pritchard (R)
2. A. Swift (D)
3. D. L. Bonker (D)
4. M. McCormack (D)
5. T. S. Foley (D)
6. N. D. Dicks (D)
7. M. Lowry (D)

West Virginia
1. R. H. Mollohan (D)
2. H. O. Staggers (D)
3. J. Slack (D)
4. N. J. Rahall (D)

Wisconsin
1. L. Aspin (D)
2. R. W. Kastenmeier (D)
3. A. J. Baldus (D)
4. C. J. Zablocki (D)
5. H. S. Reuss (D)
6. T. E. Petri (R)*
7. D. R. Obey (D)
8. T. Roth (R)
9. F. J. Sensenbrenner, Jr. (R)

Wyoming
R. Cheney (R)

*elected in 1979
**to be inaugurated governor of
Louisiana in 1980

360

UNITED STATES CABINET

Secretary of Agriculture: Bob S. Bergland
Attorney General: Benjamin R. Civiletti
Secretary of Commerce: Philip M. Klutznick
Secretary of Defense: Harold Brown
Secretary of Education: Shirley Mount Hufstedler
Secretary of Energy: Charles W. Duncan, Jr.
Secretary of Health and Human Services:
  Patricia Roberts Harris
Secretary of Housing and Urban Development:
  Moon Landrieu
Secretary of the Interior: Cecil D. Andrus
Secretary of Labor: F. Ray Marshall
Secretary of State: Cyrus R. Vance
Secretary of Transportation: Neil E. Goldschmidt
Secretary of the Treasury: G. William Miller

UNITED STATES SUPREME COURT

Chief Justice: Warren E. Burger (1969)
Associate Justices:
  William J. Brennan, Jr. (1956)
  Potter Stewart (1958)
  Byron R. White (1962)
  Thurgood Marshall (1967)
  Harry A. Blackmun (1970)
  Lewis F. Powell, Jr. (1971)
  William H. Rehnquist (1971)
  John Paul Stevens (1975)

PRIME MINISTERS OF THE PROVINCES OF CANADA

British Columbia
William Bennett (Social Credit Party)

Alberta
Peter Loughheed (Conservative Party)

Saskatchewan
Allan Blakeney (New Democratic Party)

Manitoba
Sterling Lyon (Conservative Party)

Ontario
William Davis (Conservative Party)

Quebec
René Lévesque (Parti Quebécois)

New Brunswick
Richard Hatfield (Conservative Party)

Nova Scotia
John Buchanan (Conservative Party)

Prince Edward Island
J. Angus MacLean (Conservative Party)

Newfoundland
Brian Peckford (Conservative Party)

GOVERNORS OF THE UNITED STATES

Alabama	Forrest H. James, Jr. (D)	**Montana**	Thomas L. Judge (D)
Alaska	Jay S. Hammond (R)	**Nebraska**	Charles Thone (R)
Arizona	Bruce E. Babbitt (D)	**Nevada**	Robert List (R)
Arkansas	Bill Clinton (D)	**New Hampshire**	Hugh J. Gallen (D)
California	Edmund G. Brown, Jr. (D)	**New Jersey**	Brendan T. Byrne (D)
Colorado	Richard D. Lamm (D)	**New Mexico**	Bruce King (D)
Connecticut	Ella T. Grasso (D)	**New York**	Hugh L. Carey (D)
Delaware	Pierre S. du Pont IV (R)	**North Carolina**	James B. Hunt, Jr. (D)
Florida	Robert Graham (D)	**North Dakota**	Arthur A. Link (D)
Georgia	George Busbee (D)	**Ohio**	James A. Rhodes (R)
Hawaii	George R. Ariyoshi (D)	**Oklahoma**	George Nigh (D)
Idaho	John V. Evans (D)	**Oregon**	Victor Atiyeh (R)
Illinois	James R. Thompson (R)	**Pennsylvania**	Richard L. Thornburgh (R)
Indiana	Otis R. Bowen (R)	**Rhode Island**	J. Joseph Garrahy (D)
Iowa	Robert D. Ray (R)	**South Carolina**	Richard W. Riley (D)
Kansas	John Carlin (D)	**South Dakota**	William J. Janklow (R)
Kentucky	Julian M. Carroll (D)	**Tennessee**	Lamar Alexander (R)
Louisiana	David C. Treen (R)	**Texas**	William P. Clements (R)
Maine	Joseph R. Brennan (D)	**Utah**	Scott M. Matheson (D)
Maryland	Harry Hughes (D)	**Vermont**	Richard A. Snelling (R)
Massachusetts	Edward J. King (D)	**Virginia**	John N. Dalton (R)
Michigan	William G. Milliken (R)	**Washington**	Dixy Lee Ray (D)
Minnesota	Albert Quie (R)	**West Virginia**	John D. Rockefeller IV (D)
Mississippi	Cliff Finch (D)	**Wisconsin**	Lee S. Dreyfus (R)
Missouri	Joseph P. Teasdale (D)	**Wyoming**	Ed Herschler (D)

INDEX

A

362

B

G

H

S

T

U

V

W

ILLUSTRATION CREDITS AND ACKNOWLEDGMENTS

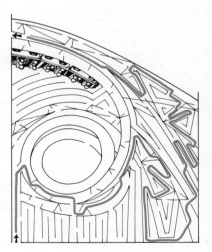

383

Put The World At Your Fingertips . . .
ORDER THIS EXQUISITELY DETAILED LENOX GLOBE!

The world's never looked better! Why? Because this Lenox Globe — the most popular raised-relief model made by Replogle — is as stunning to look at as the living planet it represents.

Handsomely crafted and easy-to-use, the Lenox is the latest word in the state of the mapmaker's art — an ingenious marriage of classic, antique styling with clean, modern readability.

The Lenox is a giant 12-inch globe, beautifully inscribed with eye-catching "cartouches" and colorful compass "roses" . . . solidly-mounted on an elegantly sturdy, 18-inch Fruitwood stand . . . and covered with three dimensional "mountain ranges" children love to touch!

Five pounds light, the Lenox comes complete with a 32-page **STORY OF THE GLOBE** — a richly-illustrated, full-color handbook you and your whole family will refer to over and over again.

TO ORDER, simply send us your name and address, along with a check or money order for $29.95* to:

Grolier Yearbook, Inc.
Lenox Globe
Sherman Turnpike
Danbury, Connecticut 06816

*Please note: New York and Connecticut residents must add state sales tax.

THE LENOX GLOBE . . . by Replogle. Make it yours *today*.

(This offer good through May, 1981.)